Live & Work in

Canada

Frances Lemon

crimson

While every effort has been made to ensure that the material in this book is as reliable, accurate and up to date as possible, facts, regulations and contact details change constantly, and some information is bound to alter within the lifetime of this edition. *Live & Work in Canada* is intended to provide general guidance only, and does not constitute professional lifestyle, career or legal advice. Readers are strongly advised to check specific details and credentials themselves.

Published by Crimson Publishing, 2009
www.crimsonpublishing.com
4501 Forbes Blvd., Suite 200, Lanham MD 20706
Westminster House, Kew Road, Richmond, Surrey TW9 2ND
Distributed in North America by National Book Network
www.nbnbooks.com
Distributed in the UK by Portfolio Books
www.portfoliobooks.com

Photographs © Frances Lemon and others, 2009 (see p. 1)

A catalogue record for this book is available from the British Library.

ISBN 978 1 85458 427 4

Printed and bound in Britain by Ashford Colour Press Ltd

Acknowledgements

Thanks for this book go to my parents, for the wisdom and the wine; to Ben, for his enduring patience and ability to talk me down from various ledges; and to the rest of my family, both the originals back home in Australia and the surrogates here in Canada, for their ongoing love and support. I also extend my gratitude to those who provided invaluable information to help me fill in the gaps: Christina, for her rapid-fire responses in spite of broken bones; Blair, for his on-the-ground reporting in Calgary; Peter, for his concise Vancouver analysis; and the Firefly crew – Steve, Kate, Jess, George and particularly Erin. Grateful thanks go to those who agreed to share their own 'live and work abroad' experiences with readers: Christina Chiam, Andrea Crengle, Gerald Garnett, Steven Maine and Dante Pizarro. To the photographers who generously permitted the use of their work – Ben Bruhmuller, Christina Chiam, Samantha Chrysanthou, Trent Collins, Judith Cordingley, Andrea Crengle, Tara Levesque, and Lianne Slavin – I remain indebted. Thanks also to all those people whose efforts went into creating the previous editions of this book; and, last but not least, to Lucy, Beth and Sally at Crimson, for their assistance and encouragement, and for making the somewhat disorienting experience of being an Australian writing a book about Canada for a British publisher a reality.

The publishers would like to thank Fawn Wilson White for her assistance with this publication.

OVERVIEW**OF**CANADA

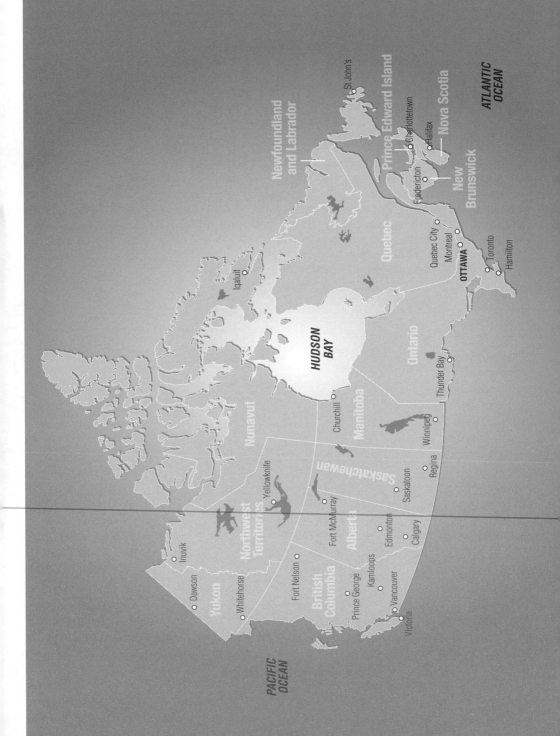

REGIONS OF CANADA

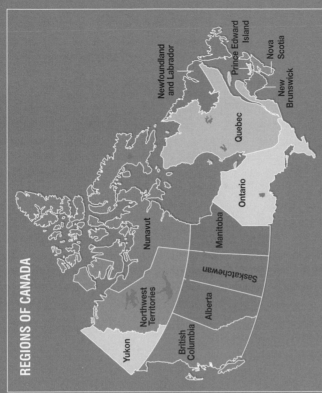

Yukon
Northwest Territories
Nunavut
British Columbia
Alberta
Saskatchewan
Manitoba
Ontario
Quebec
Newfoundland and Labrador
Prince Edward Island
Nova Scotia
New Brunswick

CANADA

UNITED STATES OF AMERICA

MEXICO

NORTH

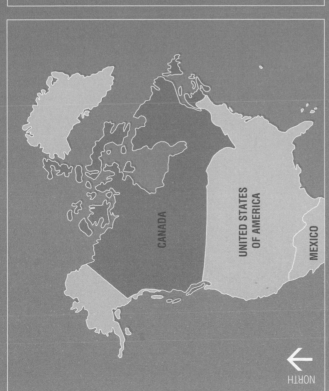

Preface

Fresh off the plane at Vancouver International Airport, I experienced the odd sensation of having my familiar landscape replaced with something new. Airports are all strange and transitory places, so it wasn't that. It was the fact that the *sound* of the world had changed. All around me was the medley and buzz of voices – but they were Canadian voices. The 'hello's and 'welcome to Canada's from these happy, smiling airport people were all expressed in Canadian tones (an accent I would become so used to that I sometimes wouldn't hear it at all, and would have to listen acutely to see whether it was coming from a fellow Australian). That was the beginning. There were various phases to follow: travelling from coast to coast; job-hunting; apartment finding; settling in; not wanting to speak in case one more person realised I wasn't Canadian; the occasional bout of homesickness. I remember when two months in Canada felt like an achievement – after all, it was the longest I'd ever been away from home. That was two years ago.

Moving to a new country is a big change. Even if it's a wanted, anticipated, longed-for change, it's still demanding and unsettling, often in unexpected ways. For most people it means saying goodbye to family members and friends; it means missing births, deaths, birthdays and marriages; it means accepting that life back 'home' will keep on happening without you. And it means finding your way in a new place, without the usual points of reference, the usual networks of colleagues and friends, or the usual systems in place to guide you. The aim of this book is to provide practical information, advice and resources to help you with the essential elements of moving to and living in Canada, and making this country – whether for a long time or just a good time – your home.

Live & Work in Canada is a new edition of the previous *Live & Work in the USA & Canada,* one of many titles in the *Live & Work* series. In 2009, for the first time, the USA and Canada will no longer be pinned together within the covers of a single book: each country has its own dedicated edition. This volume, with substantially revised, updated and expanded material, focuses exclusively on Canada. It continues to explain how to navigate Canada's complex and lengthy immigration processes, get assistance with having your foreign qualifications recognised, search for and find a job, look for a home, manage your finances and understand the education system. Detailed information covers all aspects of working life, from finding a job to retiring: comprehensive job search options; a directory of major employers; overviews by occupation, industry and region; and advice on starting a business. A brand-new regional guide offers a taste of Canada's 10 provinces and three territories, while city and neighbourhood guides dig a little further into some of the possible places to live. Daily life, socialising, workplace culture, sports and fitness, entertainment and the arts are all included, and a helpful backgrounder on Canadian history, geography, politics, economy and religion provides a rounded picture of the Canada of today.

With a stunning new full-colour design, useful tips and facts, maps, loads of contact details, personal quotes from people who've lived and worked in Canada themselves, and almost 100 beautiful 'real-life' photos, *Live & Work in Canada* is designed to help you make the move successfully. I hope it succeeds.

Frances Lemon
November 2008

Contents

Telephone numbers

Canadian phone numbers have 10-digits including a three-digit area code. Numbers in this edition are written as they would be dialled from within their local calling area. To call long-distance anywhere within Canada, dial 1 before the 10-digit number. (To call the USA from Canada you also add 1.) To call a Canadian number from outside Canada or the USA, dial the international access code, plus 1, plus the 10-digit number. Toll-free numbers (which may apply within a limited area or single province only, or Canada-wide) normally begin with 800, 888, 877 or 866 and are always preceded by 1. For this reason, they appear in this book with the 1 included. Phone numbers in Chapter 2, *Before you go*, appear differently: Canadian numbers are written as dialled from outside the country; numbers from other countries (such as the UK or Germany) are written as dialled from within that country.

Exchange rates

Throughout the book, Canadian dollars have been used. Where US dollars are used, they are written as US$. The table below gives an indication of the exchange rates for other countries (at time of press):

Canadian dollar $	US dollar US$	British pound £	Australian dollar A$	New Zealand dollar NZ$	Euro €
$1	US$0.78	£0.53	A$1.21	NZ$1.47	€0.61
$10	US$7.80	£5.30	A$12.1	NZ$15	€6.14
$20	US$15.6	£10.70	A$24	NZ$29	€12
$50	US$39	£26	A$60	NZ$73	€30
$100	US$78	£53	A$121	NZ$147	€61
$1,000	US$783	£5.30	A$1,214	NZ$1,473	€614

PHOTOGRAPHY CREDITS

All photographs © Frances Lemon, with the following exceptions:
Pages 185, 220–221, 226, 261 © Ben Bruhmuller
Page 121 © Christina Chiam
Page 342 © Samantha Chrysanthou
Pages 247, 273, 354 © Trent Collins
Page 291 © Judith Cordingley
Page 119 © Andrea Crengle
Page 81 © Tara Levesque
Pages 217, 284, 296–297, 310, 316–317, 322, 336 © Lianne Slavin
Page 87 © iStock

Why Live & Work in Canada?

■ ABOUT CANADA

CANADA FACTS	
Population:	33.3 million
Area:	9,984,670 sq km
Highest elevation:	Mount Logan, Yukon, 5959m
Currency:	Canadian Dollar (C$)
Provinces:	Newfoundland and Labrador, Nova Scotia, Prince Edward Island, New Brunswick, Quebec, Ontario, Manitoba, Saskatchewan, Alberta, British Columbia
Territories:	Yukon, Northwest Territories, Nunavut
Main ethnic origins:	Canadian (reported as sole or mixed origin by 32% of Canadians), English (21% reported), French (16%), Scottish (15%), Irish (14%), German (10%), Aboriginal (5%), Italian (5%), Chinese (4%), Ukrainian (4%), Polish (3%), Dutch (3%), Scandinavian (3%), Caribbean (2%), Latin, Central and South American (1%)
Official languages:	English and French
Languages (mother tongue):	English 57.8%, French 22.1%, allophone 20.1% (including Chinese, Italian, German and Aboriginal languages)
Government:	Federal parliamentary democracy and constitutional monarchy
National holiday:	Canada Day, 1 July
National anthem:	O Canada

A cliché it may be, but Canada – from its craggy mountain peaks, to its endless prairie stretches and its busy and vibrant cities – is a land of contrasts. The second-largest country in the world, Canada covers an area of almost 10 million sq km. It is so large, in fact, that its 10 provinces and three territories cross six international time zones, with Newfoundland (on the far east) four and a half hours ahead of the west coast. Yet it is home to only one-tenth of the number of people living in the USA – its globally significant but physically smaller southern neighbour – and supports just 0.5% of the world's population. Its vastness, its geographical diversity and its extreme climatic variations make it an intriguing place to live. Winters are cold and snowy, in some places plunging below −30°C or even −40°C on a semi-regular basis (though Toronto and the west coast are not hit so hard). But spring is glorious, fall is stunningly beautiful, and summers in many parts are hot, sunny, and long enough to well and truly forget the winter chill.

Pinpointing the Canadian national identity is not a straightforward task. The power and proximity of the USA, and the strong trading relationship cultivated between the two countries, is an undeniable influence. Over three-quarters of Canada's exports go to the USA, and the USA supplies around 65% of Canada's imports. American television, music and movies are staples of Canada's entertainment diet, and many US films are shot and produced on Canadian soil. Offsetting this is Canada's urge to differentiate itself from the States. As former Prime Minister Pierre Elliott Trudeau put it, 'We're different people from you and we're different people because of you.'

Canadians are quick to clarify their non-US status if confusion arises and, as tourists or backpackers, often label their luggage with flags or maple leaves to avoid being mistaken for Americans. (Interestingly, particularly since the September 11 attacks of 2001, some US travellers have been known to do the same.)

Yet such a disparate collection of people, with such differing histories and cultures, can't be defined merely by what they're not – nor by the beaver, moose or deep white snow of simple stereotype. Canadians have a reputation for their friendly and welcoming nature, low-key approach and often self-deprecating humour. They've made a hefty creative contribution to the world (sometimes attributed to the enforced introspection of long winters), with renowned artists, writers, actors, filmmakers, satirists, comedians and musicians filtering into the States and much, much further afield. An integral part of the country's cultural history is tied to its Aboriginal people: the Inuit, who live in the northern regions; the Métis, who descend primarily from early French traders; and the First Nations peoples, as the majority of Canada's native people are formally and collectively known. The country's treatment of its indigenous people has been deeply flawed – a common story among colonised nations – and remains problematic today. Land-claim settlements (including the creation of Nunavut) and a greater understanding of Aboriginal traditions and cultures have gone some small way towards healing the rift. The long-standing cohabitation and conflict between Canada's French and English speakers is also core to its identity, and the basis of the dual official language policy.

> I grew up with stories about Canada from my uncle, who had to move here to work on a Nova Scotia potato farm at 16. My grandparents had stories from when they lived here in the 1930s.
> **Gerald Garnett**

A Canadian icon: the red-tinged maple leaf of fall

The Petite chapelle (little chapel) de Tadoussac, built in 1747, overlooks sparkling Tadoussac Bay, Quebec

Today, Canadians come from all walks of life and from every part of the world. They speak over 200 languages and represent a myriad of cultures, religions and philosophies. While some have been in the country for generations, others – in increasing numbers – are just starting out. Whether they make the journey to see the sights, to begin a new life or to follow a dream (or build a new one), all come to be a part of Canada – its beauty, its freedom and its promise of opportunity.

■ REASONS TO LIVE IN CANADA

World-class liveability

For more than a decade, the United Nations' annual Human Development Report has listed Canada among the best places to live in the world. Most Canadians – including hundreds of thousands of immigrants – reached the same conclusion long ago. In the 2007–2008 report, the Human Development Index (HDI) ranked Canada fourth among the 177 countries included, behind only Iceland, Norway and Australia. The HDI measures the human development achievements of a country based on a number of factors: life expectancy (or the opportunity for a long and healthy life), income or standard of living, and attainment of education. Canada's advantages in each of these areas are clear: with an average life expectancy of 80.3 years, a gross enrollment ratio (combining primary, secondary and tertiary studies) of 99.2%, and a median income for full-time workers of over $41,400, it's no surprise this country continues to be a prime immigration destination. In the 1980s, an average of 125,000 new permanent residents were admitted each year. This average rose to over 220,000 per year in the 1990s, and since the year 2000, numbers have peaked at over 260,000. Added to this is a sizeable influx of temporary residents approximately 250,000 annually in recent years, of which around 100,000 are foreign workers.

The great outdoors

With dramatic mountain ranges, national parks covering 224,466 sq km of the country and an estimated 32,000 lakes across 13 provinces and territories, Canada is an adventure playground for outdoor enthusiasts. Its distinct seasons make a range of activities possible: skiing, snowboarding and snowmobiling in winter; kayaking and camping in spring and summer; hiking through the changing colours in the fall. Experiencing the natural world is an important part of life for most Canadians – even if this is just a weekend escape to a campground, lakeside holiday home or the ski slopes. An active lifestyle is promoted for both adults and children, with popular sports including hockey, soccer, baseball, football and basketball. (The official national summer sport is lacrosse, though this is not so widely played.) Recreation and sporting associations abound – see p. 308 for more.

O Canada! The Mistaya River rushes through Banff National Park, Alberta

Canada was next on my list of English-speaking countries with working-holiday opportunities. Its reputation for breathtaking landscapes, wild winters and cultural diversity was a further incentive.

Christina Chiam

A culture of diversity

According to the 2006 census, over six million foreign-born people – almost 20% of the total population – now live in Canada. (Only Australia has a higher percentage of residents born outside the country.) The largest proportion in 75 years, they account for two-thirds of the country's population growth since the 2001 census. Back in 1962, the government introduced new immigration laws to eliminate discrimination based on race, national origin or religion. The previous laws had traditionally favoured British and American applicants. Based on 2007 figures, the top three source countries for immigrants are China, India and the Philippines. The USA and Pakistan are next on the list, followed by the UK, Iran, and Korea. France and Columbia round out the top 10 (though similar numbers of people also emigrate from Sri Lanka and Romania). The history of high immigration from Europe, and from Britain in particular, has had a lasting effect on Canada's cultural make-up: in the recent census, almost 580,000 people recorded the UK as their place of birth, compared with around 465,000 for China and 445,000 for India. However, the shifts that have occurred over the last few decades – due partly to changes in Canada's immigration system and partly to world events – have seen substantial increases in immigration from Asian countries. Close to 60% of all immigrants coming to Canada in the last few years were born in Asia (including the Middle East). The number of US citizens moving to Canada is also growing: while they are not exempt from the immigration process, the North American Free Trade Agreement (NAFTA) has made it easier to move across the border temporarily (and sometimes long-term) to work in Canada. With temporary foreign workers from places as diverse as Mexico, Australia, Germany, Japan and Jamaica, and an immigrant population drawn from more than 200 countries, Canada offers an incredibly – and increasingly – multiethnic culture.

Future opportunities

Immigration policy changes frequently, and the latest developments are intended to be more responsive to the country's economic and social objectives. The Minister of Citizenship and Immigration recently described immigration as 'vital to Canada's cultural diversity and economic prosperity'. It is key to economic and labour-force growth, and will become increasingly important in addressing labour shortages. With shortages already being felt across certain regions, occupations and industry sectors, the need to recruit skilled workers – whether temporary or permanent – is well recognised. In the coming years, the government hopes to attract between 240,000 and 265,000 new immigrants annually. For 2008, 58% of places were allocated to skilled workers, business owners or investors, live-in caregivers, and people admitted through the Provincial Nominee Program or the newly created Canadian Experience Class (an initiative aimed at retaining temporary residents with sufficient Canadian education or work experience). The proportion of family reunification immigrants – spouses or partners, children, parents and grandparents – was around 28%, with refugees making up just over 10% of newcomers. The main downside for workers is that the Federal Skilled Worker category has lost at least 20,000 places. However, the Canadian Experience Class has partially offset this reduction, with up to 12,000 admissions projected. Numbers have also increased for business applicants and live-in caregivers, and, substantially, for provincial nominees. As many as 150,000 foreign workers and 60,000 foreign students were offered temporary residence opportunities.

A complementary streetscape catches the evening sun in Saint John, New Brunswick

Safety and security

Canada has a strong tradition as a peacekeeping rather than a war-making nation, one that plays a mediating role in international conflict. The actions of another former Prime Minister, Lester B. Pearson, cemented this view: his involved work with the UN and contribution to the organisation's first peacekeeping force earned him the Nobel Peace Prize in 1957. The need for additional recruits and funding has been felt by the Canadian Forces in recent years, and opinion about Canadian troops serving on certain missions, such as that in Afghanistan, has been political and divided. However, Canadian personnel continue to be actively involved in both UN and non-UN peace operations. This attitude of non-confrontation seems to be present within Canadian society as well. Though crime and violence is still a fact of life – particularly in certain areas of the bigger cities – Canada is largely a safe place to live, and according to Statistics Canada, crime is officially at a 30-year low. Gun control is strictly enforced: there are an estimated one million handguns in Canada, while the USA has over 76 million. The small number of handguns that do make it into circulation tend to be brought illegally across the border from the south.

I remember sitting on the steps of my primary (grade) school asking a new Canadian student what it was like there, and imagining it to be this hot, red and dusty place for some reason (much like Mars!).
Andrea Crengle

PROS AND CONS OF LIVING IN CANADA

Pros
- High standard of living
- Sound economic position in comparison with other countries
- Friendly and sociable people
- Ethnically diverse society
- Excellent education opportunities
- Varied and beautiful landscape
- Sports and outdoor pursuits
- Opportunities for foreign workers
- Relatively low crime rate
- Peacekeeping mentality
- Public health system and social services

Cons
- Immigration process can be long and difficult
- Cold winters in much of the country
- Vast distances between cities and regions
- High taxes

Water surges over the Horseshoe Falls – part of the must-see natural phenomenon Niagara Falls in southern Ontario

Gerald Garnett – Kaslo, British Columbia

Born in England in 1949, Gerald Garnett has lived in Canada for over 30 years. At the age of 12 he moved with his family to Australia, where his father had been appointed headmaster of a prestigious private boarding school. After completing school and a bachelor's degree he returned to England to take his MA and pick up the threads of his previous life, but found it was a life he no longer identified with. Unenthusiastic about going directly back to Australia, where he would be liable for the Vietnam draft, he returned via Vancouver Island, where his aunt and cousins lived, and where he got his first taste of Canada. He and his wife Mary now live in Kaslo, BC.

Why did you decide to move to Canada?

On that first visit I fell in love with a person and a place. My aunt worked in the Saanich library, and my future wife Mary was one of her assistants. It was September and a time of Indian-summer weather. I left the gloom of England behind and bicycled and camped around the Gulf Islands. There can be few more beautiful places on earth and I was ecstatically happy. In my saddlebag I carried a history of early pioneer life on Saltspring Island, Saturna, Mayne, and North and South Pender, and I used it to talk to the locals. They were incredibly kind and hospitable. It cost me $0.50 to wheel my bike onto the ferries between islands and I would enjoy the cafeteria and the hot water provided. It was a time of great upheaval and I met a lot of draft dodgers and back-to-the-landers. My temporary visitor's visa expired and I reluctantly boarded a plane for Melbourne and a two-year internment in the Australian army. But I knew I was going to come back.

How were you able to immigrate?

After serving in the Australian Medical Corps the army paid for my teaching diploma. Mary came over to join me in Australia and our son Jody was born in 1973. My wife's parents, who had retired to Algonquin Park in Ontario, agreed to sponsor us to immigrate to Canada, because Mary still retained American citizenship from growing up in Minneapolis. We needed to get a sufficient number of points to do with age and educational training, etc. There were a number of forms and an interview, and we were accepted as landed immigrants. As soon as I could I became a Canadian citizen, and my Australian citizenship was eliminated. We had burnt our boats; there was no returning.

Was it difficult, arriving in the middle of winter?

We landed at JFK airport near New York City and crossed into Canada by land on Christmas Eve, 1975. It was intensely cold, with deep snow, yet the houses were so warm that inside you went around in a shirt. We drove north to Mary's parents' house near Barry's Bay. I was quite scared, as we had gambled everything, jumping into the dark with a three-year-old child and no jobs in a new country.

I tried to make a good impression on my in-laws. Both came from Scandinavian stock and were second-generation Americans. They were strong Southern Baptists and their fundamentalism was a little bemusing. I did not know that it meant they were teetotallers. I bought a bottle of red wine to celebrate our arrival, which I then spilt on their brand-new white shag carpet. To make amends, when they were at church next day, I decided to surprise them by lighting a fire in their living room. Unfortunately, I had never encountered a damper before, a little flap that seals off the chimney when it's not in use. They arrived back from morning service, with, no doubt, charity brimming in their hearts, to find their house full of smoke. Vivian, my new mother-in-law, was very house proud I discovered. I decided my best approach was to keep out of the way outdoors, and learnt to cross-country ski. There was a maze of old logging roads all around, twisting around small frozen lakes with lumps in the middle that were beaver houses. It was so intensely cold that my red beard would freeze from my breath – so that's what −30°F (−34.5°C) feels like.

How did you go about finding work?

My wife is very organised, confident, and determined and I needed to borrow some of those qualities to be so brazen at getting interviews, following up with phone calls, and knocking at doors. I am naturally quite reserved and shy, but desperation made me push the limits. All I can say is that we had an extraordinary amount of luck. When Mary graduated, we sent out 30 resumes and went to 15 interviews. We very nearly ended up teaching at Quesnel or Masset, but in the end were offered two jobs in Kaslo in the Kootenays. We have just retired after teaching there for nearly 30 years. In the early days it was tremendously challenging. I had to teach Grade 10 Business and was barely a chapter ahead of my students the whole year. It was useful though. The pupils were not interested, but I, at 28, needed to know about mortgages, insurance, and tax returns. Then I had lots of Grade 8 classes of English, Guidance, Physical Education. I had never taught any of these before and had never been in the public school system at all.

I often lost the discipline battles in those early years and would reach the end of the day like a punch-drunk boxer just hanging on to the end of the round. But I had chosen this. It fitted in with my left-wing ideals. I could not throw in the towel. When I retired a couple of years ago, I was teaching the children of those earlier students and had learnt to handle them a bit more like an experienced bee-keeper. No bee veil, no smoker, a quiet voice, but underneath a hardened will and a discipline plan. I learned to really admire and respect my co-workers, especially the early primary school teachers, who are the most important people in the system in my opinion.

You have a beautiful home. How did you end up there?

We had to start off in Victoria, British Columbia, where my wife had one year to complete her degree or the time limit on completion would expire. After that we planned to apply for work everywhere, but we were going to be near the mountains and ocean of BC if I could possibly make it happen.

Unknown to us, our first landlord was a major marijuana grower for the Saanich Peninsula and our second landlord, we discovered later, was an armed bank-robber.

My cousin's first husband was looking after a house for the owner, who lived in Kitimat. He offered to rent us the unfinished basement cheaply while I looked for a job. He seemed to be able to have a car and a motorbike, but no visible means of support. It was only later that we discovered he was growing marijuana in a shed at the bottom of the property. Eventually the real owner retired from his work at Kitimat, but let us stay on in the basement until we found a duplex in Victoria. When we returned for a visit two years later we found the owner was in prison. He had been reluctant to dip into his savings, so over the course of a year had committed 11 armed bank robberies on the mainland, returning by ferry. Our next landlord was a Scottish shipyard worker who lived through the thin walls of our duplex; we used to hear his drunken raving on Friday nights.

At Kaslo we were able to rent and later buy a cottage about 10km south of town. The original pioneer, a remittance man from England called Mr Dredge, had lived in a sod-roofed shack on a lower bench of land. He married a cultured music teacher at a very late age. She inherited a little money and ordered this 'English Cottage' from the Montgomery Ward catalogue, and it was shipped to the site on the S.S. *Moyie* paddle wheeler because there were no roads. It sits in the middle of eight acres with springs and a little creek. There are rock bluffs and some old-growth cedar, Douglas fir, and larch. We look across Kootenay Lake at the Matterhorn peak of Mt Loki at 9,070 ft. If I dream of 'home' now, this is where my mind will wander.

What about family and school life?

In this remote environment there are only enough students for one class. Those students, for better or worse, are your peer group for your entire school career. When our son was in Grade 9 we sent him back to Australia for a year to get a wider perspective, and that proved to be a very good move. In those desperate early years of learning to be a classroom teacher, we also had many problems having more children. We adopted a six-month-old baby girl from Korea, and in our hearts she is our daughter. Despite being about the only Asian-looking child in Kaslo, she experienced no racism from students or residents. Sometimes I think that when the children were older it would have been better to be in a larger centre, to experience a wider variety of role models and activities.

What's the culture of a smaller community like Kaslo?

Working at the school, we were in one of the hubs of the community and got to know all the children and families of the district. There is a constant need for volunteers in all the clubs and societies; we have to limit ourselves or we can be sucked into a whirlpool of commitments. My wife is linked with a lot of horse riders, artists, a book and gossip club, and a gym. I work with an outdoor recreation club and do yoga. It takes a long time shopping on Kaslo's only business street. It's a chilling experience to go shopping in a bigger centre like Vancouver, where no one meets your gaze or says hello. The downside is that there is little privacy, but it means if anyone has a disaster there is food brought to the door and hugs in the street.

How do you find Canadian bureaucracy, and the cost of living?

I think it's a model of efficiency and politeness compared to others I have experienced. Of course English is my first language, and I am not intimidated. I love the way Canadian officials say 'You're welcome.'

The standard and cost of living seems to me to be slightly better than in Australia or England. Mind you, houses have to be built more robustly to withstand the climate. Meat is more expensive than in Oz, but there are the huge box stores of Wal-Mart, Roma, etc. (though maybe they are worldwide now).

How have you found the climate? Was it hard to get used to the winters?

I think the European in me loves the definite division into four seasons. There is something so exhilarating about the return of the swallows and the flowering crocuses in the spring. I love all this water. There's over 3m of snow each year at our ski cabin. It's just magical touring around at 6,000ft in the depths of winter. In the summer in the Kootenays a hot day is 80°F (26.5°C), with none of that open-oven-door wind of Australia, or hot nights sweating under a sheet.

Yet the first winter our water pipes froze on Christmas morning. We had to run a black plastic hose from the creek through the snow and leave it running 24 hours a day for the next three months. If it froze, we would drag it inside and wind it around our kitchen, living room and dining room until it coughed up buckets of little ice pellets. There were new driving skills to learn on our twisting, icy mountain roads: do everything in slow motion, especially braking. If you make any abrupt move, it's possible to be caught in a relentless skid.

What do you love about Canada?

I love most everything about Canada and would like to keep it a selfish secret. I especially love the feeling that it has only just emerged from the ice, so all the landscape has a new-minted quality. It doesn't have that soiled and smeared-by-human-footprints feel of Europe, where present life seems a ragged fringe of new growth on all that previous history. It doesn't have that bone-weariness in the old weathered soils of Australia, which have baked relentlessly in the sun for eternity. I love the flavour that the French-Canadians bring to this impossible country, although I hope it does not decay into ugly tribal nationalism. Only distance prevents us from seeing what a disparate bunch of people are supposed to be one culture. Just what are the Texas swagger of Alberta, the French musicians of the Gaspé, and the Newfoundlanders on their rock doing in one country? In BC I think it's a wonderful experiment in multi-nationalism, which the world itself has to undertake peacefully. I just wish the mixing and racial intermarriage would happen a little quicker. (Is there a 'fast-forward button' I can press?)

What do you like least?

I wish Canada had more of that American Midwestern openness and acceptance. Did those first British Loyalists bring some of the stodgy chilliness of England with them? Yet what I like least is seeing the culture threatened by the Hollywood glitz, the consumer materialism, the Republican neo-conservative ignorance and arrogance from our elephant neighbour to the south.

Is Canada what you expected?

I grew up with stories about Canada from my uncle, who had to move here to work on a Nova Scotia potato farm at 16. My grandparents had stories from when they lived here in the 1930s. Canada is everything I expected. The surprise is just how beautiful and special it is beyond my childhood imagination. The hardest thing was the anxiety about the huge gamble of moving with little money, a family, and no job. A leap in the dark.

Do you have any regrets about moving here?

Living in Canada solved many problems for me. I can get nostalgic about Australia when I smell smoke from a eucalyptus campfire, but Canada seems a gentler, kindlier country, and the long winters seem to lead to a deeper interior life. In Canada I could take full responsibility for a life I chose, free from any inherited baggage.

I would like to see more of my family. My mother is 81. I miss the family reunions with my four brothers and sisters and their 11 children. It is so far to travel, and expensive, and a flight emits so much guilty carbon. Australia has become a more attractive place though, now that Kevin Rudd is Prime Minister.

Would you encourage others to come to Canada to live and work?

There's a children's game called 'Sardines', where you go and hide, and everyone else has to find you. Gradually your hiding place becomes more and more squashed as you are discovered and people press in beside you. I feel that I have found the most beautiful hiding spot in the whole world. When asked to give advice to other people thinking of coming to live and work in Canada, I am tempted to say that I heard Chile was nice, or perhaps New Zealand or Tasmania.

Andrea Crengle – Calgary, Alberta

Like many young travellers, Andrea Crengle and her husband Stefan came to Canada looking for new experiences, new adventures, and a change of pace. Armed with 12-month working holiday permits they made the trip over in early 2006, leaving the warmth of the New Zealand summer for the mid-winter chill of Alberta.

Why did you decide to come to Canada?

My husband and I were leading fairly typical 'routine' lives. Not that there was (or is) anything wrong with that, but it became apparent to us that we both wanted more out of our life journey. We had both completed schooling with higher education, and had been in the workforce full time for around 10 years. I was working as a sales manager for an Australasian hotel chain, while Stefan was working as a supply chain manager for a forestry company. Forestry was all Stefan had known and is a volatile market, and I had been in the hotel industry for around seven years, so it was time for a change. I had also lost both of my parents by the time I was 29 years old, and this had made us both realise just how short life can be and that we should make the most of it.

For both of us, Canada was a place we had individually wanted to visit, long before we met. I remember sitting on the steps of my primary (grade) school asking a new Canadian student what it was like there, and imagining it to be this hot, red and dusty place for some reason (much like Mars!).

Was the immigration process complicated?

We came to Canada on a working holiday permit, which entitled us to work for a total of one year from the time we first entered the country (so if we were to leave and visit another country in that time, it would detract from the length of time we could work in Canada). We also had to enter Canada and validate the visa within one year of it being issued. Coming from New Zealand, we found the immigration process to be smooth and relatively simple. There were several forms to complete and documents to provide in support of our application, and once lodged, it was simply a waiting game to see if we had been lucky enough to secure places in the limited quota for that year. The type of visa we were applying for made the process easier as well. Had we been applying for either a permanent visa or a full work visa, a lot more would have been required of us.

What were your main impressions of Canada?

Beautiful. Spatial. Extreme. Welcoming. Canada is such an amazing place, offering so much diversity and so many new experiences. We had heard many times how similar Canada and New Zealand were and to some extent they are – only Canada is *extreme*. The climate goes from one extreme to the other; the landscape is so extreme; the scenery is stunning; the cultures within the one country are many and varied. We found Canadians to be very friendly and welcoming. I guess the fact that it is also a largely European country played a big part in there not being any real culture shock for us – it was very interesting to learn of the First Nations people and their history, and to realise that their past and ongoing issues are very similar to those of the New Zealand indigenous people, the Maori.

The cost of living is relatively similar to that in New Zealand, although a few things stand out, such as the price of gas being far cheaper, and the lack of availability of yummy whole-grain breads.

How did you decide what area to live and work in?

For us, the main deciding factor was simply that a very good friend of my husband's from New Zealand has been living in Calgary for many years now, with his wonderful Canadian partner. So Calgary was always to be our starting point and we would 'go from there'. However, having arrived and seeing how close to the Rocky Mountains Calgary is, we decided to stay put. Weekends were filled with short trips to the Rockies for hiking and car trips to the many nearby regions.

How did you go about looking for work?

We both used the newspaper and internet for work searches. As we were only after semi-casual employment (as in little responsibility, nine-to-five type jobs, not in our usual profession) we had more options open to us than if we were looking for corporate employment. Our only stipulation was that we didn't work evenings and weekends so that we were free to explore the country and experience it to the max. I secured a receptionist job at a spa within three days of looking for work, and Stefan gained employment with a pellet-making company within a few weeks.

What about finding a place to live?

After staying with our friends for the first four weeks, and both being in employment, we decided to venture out and find our own place. Renting was the only option for us as we knew we would be moving on sooner rather than later. The internet again was the way we found our condo, and renting it was relatively simple, with our Canadian-based friends and new employers being referees for us. I think we were lucky in that our new landlord was not from Canada either and so understood our position. So we moved into our one-bedroom condo, which was a new experience for us as apartment living is not that typical in New Zealand. We loved it – although cannot see wanting to do it as a longer-term lifestyle.

Were people friendly?

The people are fantastic – we found almost all to be very welcoming and interested in learning about our own culture and country. Through our New Zealand friends and new work colleagues we met their Canadian friends, who welcomed us with open arms and wanted to help us get involved in Canadian life. I remember putting up notices at my work, with little facts such as 'Kiwis are actually named after a bird, not a fruit!'

How was the process of getting set up with a bank account, driver's licence, and so on?

The first thing we had to do was get a Social Insurance Number, followed by a bank account and then a driver's licence. All processes were smooth and not particularly difficult just because we were not Canadian residents. The most difficult process was probably obtaining the driver's licence, as my husband (I didn't apply) had to learn all the new (and very different from New Zealand) road rules, plus sit a practical test – the first of which he failed due to the car breaking down! We made good use of our short AAA emergency membership.

Was it hard to get used to the winter in Calgary?

Having arrived in mid February to −14°C (7°F) it sure was cold. But a different cold from what we are used to. New Zealand is very wet during wintertime, and so the cold is icy and goes right to your bones. We found the Canadian winter to be very much a dry cold and this is much easier to handle. You simply put lots of layers on to go outside and then peel them off when inside – there are no wet and damp clothes to worry about. Acclimatising was a fun part of the process, and enjoyable – although it was surprising to suffer from nose bleeds due to the dryness of the air, and electric shocks – again due to the dryness. And, for the first time ever, we were living with snow all around us (this doesn't happen where we live in New Zealand), which was a novelty in itself. Then when summer rolled around, we had no idea how hot it could be in Canada – you typically don't think of Canada as being a hot country.

What did you like most about Canada?

Everything! Canada filled so many of our expectations and more.

Was there anything you didn't like?

The fact that in the 'off-season', almost everything shuts down. We bought a car and travelled east to west basically across the whole country, and at times it was hard to find accommodation and activities as they were closed for the season.

Do you see yourself living in Canada again?

Staying was an option we would have loved to explore had we been able to wangle the visas. We ended up having to leave Canada because our temporary visa was expiring, and after extensive investigation it was our only option. There was lots of conflicting advice about possible visas, so while in Calgary we paid to see an independent immigration consultant who gave us the facts and outlined our options. The only way we could have stayed would have been if we were wanting to apply for permanent residence, or for full work visas, which would mean finding 'serious' employment, getting an offer of employment, and that potential employer then providing evidence as to why a Canadian couldn't do that job.

We had no regrets about leaving New Zealand to come to Canada, though we knew it was not permanent and so likely had a different frame of mind. We would love to return and do another stint (a couple of years perhaps), as there is still so much to explore and experience, and we have such great memories.

What's your advice to others thinking of coming to Canada, either temporarily or permanently?

Go for it! There is nothing too scary, nothing too hard, and nothing to lose. Give it a try and see for yourself – if it doesn't work out, at least you know and won't spend the rest of your life wondering 'what if?'. Canada is a great place to do this, as there is no major culture shock in terms of the climate or language or living conditions. Besides, who doesn't want to see a wild bear in its native woods (even if from the safety of their car), or spend their evenings looking for beavers!

Dante Pizarro – Montreal, Quebec

Dante Pizarro moved to Montreal from Chile in 1996. He and his wife had divorced two years before, and he was living with his parents while renting out his house. He and his brother Marco became interested in visiting Canada after a visit in 1995 from their aunt, who had been living in Toronto for 15 years. In 1996, Dante lost his job as a financial collector for a hospital. Unable to find a similar position elsewhere, and feeling it was economically and emotionally time for a change, he began to think about leaving Chile and immigrating to Canada.

How were you able to come to Canada?

In 1996, Canada opened the borders for Chileans, so my brother decided it was time to come. He came first, in April 1996, and I came one month later. We decided to come as political refugees. As political refugees we were accepted into the country until our case was reviewed. Meanwhile, we started looking for jobs. After 18 months we received a response from the immigration department saying that we were not accepted. My brother left, but I decided to stay without papers. I had already met Eileen, who later became the mother of my son Kevin. We got married, and then I became a permanent resident. I had to fill out a lot of forms to apply for permanent resident status, and I also had to leave the country in order to apply from the Canadian Embassy in Chile. The process took eight months.

How did you decide where to live?

My brother Marco came to Montreal first. I don't know exactly why he wanted to come here, but I decided to follow him. I think I also chose to come to Quebec because it was easier to immigrate here.

During my flight from Chile I met other Chileans who were coming to Montreal to work and they offered me a place to stay, as they had some Chilean friends living in Montreal. I stayed with them a few days, but I was looking for my brother, because he didn't know I was here. I finally found him and we rented an apartment. I wasn't used to renting an apartment, because all my life in Chile I had lived in a house with a yard and trees.

What were your first impressions of Montreal?

There are so many different cultures and people from different countries; this was something I wasn't used to. Some areas of Montreal I liked very much – there are some very beautiful neighbourhoods. I also liked the parks – there are so many of them and they are all very clean and well kept. There are many shopping centres too, all very clean, even the washrooms. The public transit system is very good, with schedules posted in the bus stops. The buses are comfortable, and the drivers are very polite. In general, people here are very polite. In Montreal I saw snow for the first time, and it was a great experience.

What's been your experience of working in Canada?

I didn't know anyone in this city apart from my brother, so it wasn't easy to find work to begin with. Marco knew some people from his church. One of them gave him some ideas about where he could find work, so afterwards Marco introduced me to some people who gave me information about work. It's pretty hard to get work if you don't speak the official languages, in this case English or French, so the best way is through contact with people in your community. When I became more familiar with the city I started looking for myself, checking ads in the paper and showing up with my resume. The first job I got was in a clothing factory, doing simple work like packaging the clothes. The pay was really bad because it paid by piecework: $0.05 for wrapping each item in plastic, $0.10 for cutting and putting on a sticker, etc. It didn't end up being a high hourly wage. I left this job and started working in a pizzeria, making pizzas, cleaning, and sometimes washing the dishes. It was also hard work and low pay. They didn't even pay minimum wage, and we had to pay for any food we ate in the restaurant. Finally, I found a good job with a good company that has many benefits.

There are many different types of jobs out there, some much better than others, and some employers do try to take advantage when they see you are an immigrant.

When I first arrived I had to open a bank account, and it was very easy to get a chequing account. In my country, for example, it is really difficult to open a chequing account, because the bank will ask you for references, and you must have a good job with a good salary.

What about culture, family and friends?

Canada is a multicultural country with people from many different countries, different cultures and different races. The mix of cultures enriches the country and we can learn a lot from it. Canada needs immigrants – this is a huge country with a little population. I have found the Canadian people to be very nice, educated, tolerant, and sociable. Many of them are interested in learning about other people's origins and cultures. It's a good place to raise a family. The government takes care of families with kids through benefits, and provides school for everybody. The only problem is that the kids must get used to the long winters. It is a peaceful country, and people here have so many rights. But because Quebec promotes its own language – French – the education system in Quebec makes it difficult for immigrants who want their children educated in English.

Most of the people I meet in Canada are from my workplace, co-workers. I spend a lot of time at work so I know many of my co-workers who are immigrants like me. I also meet people through religious centres and community organisations.

How does the standard and cost of living compare with that in Chile?

I had a better type of work in my country, in that there I could work in an office or in sales, but here I must do blue-collar work. The salary here is much better than in my country, though. The cost of living is not too much different to that in Chile. At the supermarket, the cost of buying groceries is about the same. The only thing that is better in my country is that it's much easier to buy a house or apartment.

The government helps people with a low or middle income by giving them some money for a down payment.

How have you found the weather, and the winters?

I was very worried about the winter when I first arrived in May. However, in May the temperature is very similar to the weather in Chile. But when the summer came, it was so warm and humid that it was difficult without air conditioning. I found June and July really hard. August, September, and October were not bad. November through to February was the most difficult. Although the snow is beautiful, it's very complicated to walk in it. Montreal has very extreme temperatures: summer is too short, hot and humid, and winter is too long and very cold. I have lived 12 years in Montreal now, but I still find the winters so hard. I can't get used to snow five months a year, and it gets dark early. I really miss my country in the wintertime.

What do you like most, and least, about Canada?

The thing I like best is that there are lots of jobs. If you lose your job you can usually find another one, and the pay isn't too bad compared with Chile. It is a peaceful country and it has so many lakes – water will be a very important resource in the future. There isn't a lot of crime. Canadians are very nice, polite, educated people.

What I like least, of course, are the winters, which are too long and cold. It's difficult to buy a house, and apartments are expensive. I also don't like the fact that there are so many homeless people, and that young people ask for money on the street when there are so many jobs available.

What's been surprising or difficult about the move?

Canada was what I expected in terms of getting a job, living decently, and saving some money. I thought Montreal would be bigger, and that there would be high-rise buildings everywhere, but mostly they are just downtown. I was also surprised by the number of people with mental illnesses out in the community. The hardest thing about leaving my country has been missing my family and friends, the weather, the food, and the ocean (I was used to seeing the sea).

Any regrets, or advice for others?

I don't have any regrets about leaving my country and coming here. I feel very comfortable here. I'd like to stay, but I don't know for how long. My parents are old, though, and I would like to visit my country more often.

If you want to immigrate to Canada you should think about it carefully. You win in some ways, but lose in others. The best way in life is to have our own experiences, and for me it has been a positive experience.

Christina Chiam – Toronto, Ontario

Christina Chiam worked for many years at the University of Melbourne in Australia before making a career change to arts management. After completing a graduate diploma in her new field (while concurrently volunteering and contracting her way around Melbourne's festival circuit) she took up a contract position with the Melbourne International Film Festival. In mid-2007 the lure of overseas travel, living in a new country, and potentially working at international arts festivals brought her to Toronto.

What made you choose Canada?

I had been leading a very hectic life, and after two intense years of studying and working I needed a change of scenery. My role with the Melbourne International Film Festival provided me with valuable work experience in the arts and gave me an insight into the world of festivals, so I decided to pursue this type of work overseas.

Having already spent 18 months in London on a working holiday visa during my early 20s, Canada was next on my list of English-speaking countries with working-holiday opportunities. Its reputation for breathtaking landscapes, wild winters, and cultural diversity was a further incentive. Another factor was the chance of working at the Toronto International Film Festival (TIFF). The mix of beautiful scenery and potential for career progress was motivation enough to make Canada my overseas destination.

What type of visa or permit were you granted?

Initially, I moved to Canada on a one-year working holiday permit, which allows you to work in most sectors without additional approval – this made it straightforward for me to find employment in the arts. The Australian and Canadian governments have since changed the terms of the visa, which allowed me to apply for a second permit for another two years. The immigration process was very straightforward. I had to submit an online application form and send the Canadian Consulate a processing fee and passport photos. They say the process can take up to six to eight weeks but I received both my permits within a month of applying.

Because I'm on a working holiday permit I'm not considered a temporary resident, so I'm ineligible for government benefits such as health cover. As yet, I don't intend to change my status to anything more permanent, but from what I've heard, the process for obtaining permanent residence is quite expensive and involved.

What were your first impressions of Toronto?

I was struck by the similarities between Toronto and my hometown of Melbourne, Australia. Toronto's downtown streets form a grid, as do Melbourne's, so I could easily navigate my way around. The similarities extend to the different cultural pockets of the city. Like Melbourne, Toronto has little communities dotted around the city that celebrate particular ethnicities and cultures, such as Chinatown, Little Italy, and the Danforth with its strong Greek influences.

I arrived at the beginning of summer so a strong first impression was the high level of humidity. My hair had never seen anything like it! I was also made aware very early on of the important tipping culture in Canada. Unlike in Australia, Canadians are expected to tip their service staff roughly 15% on top of the bill. When combined with the various government taxes that are also added, serious mathematical skills are required to tally your bill!

Did you have to make any cultural adjustments?

Moving to any new country requires an adjustment period, but given Canada and Australia's close ties and cultural similarities, this wasn't overwhelming. There are no language barriers, except for the occasional confused look when slang terms are bandied about! Their currency is straightforward, their obsession with sport entertainingly familiar, and their pop-culture references – while heavy on the North-American side – are easily translatable for Australians.

How did you decide where to live?

My goal was to work for Canada's major film festival, so the decision of where to live was dictated by that. When my first contract finished I looked for work outside Toronto, but by that stage I'd been living in the city for three to four months and had begun establishing friendships, and I'd grown accustomed to the city. The thought of moving and starting all over again was not so appealing. Thankfully I secured a permanent job in Toronto so the decision to stay paid off.

What's been your experience of working in Canada?

My motivation for moving to Canada was work based so I did a lot of research before I moved, and more when I arrived. Through contacts in Canada I learnt about relevant job websites for employment in the arts, and these became my main source for job vacancies.

Being a 'foreigner' within a small arts community did make it difficult to find work initially. I didn't have the necessary contacts or 'foot in the door', and was applying for jobs without any Canadian experience. I was focused on one particular organisation but also applied for other positions that interested me. It took a small-world coincidence to get my application noticed, and thankfully an interview and job offer soon followed.

My experience at TIFF has shown me that the work environment in Canadian not-for-profit arts organisations is similar to that in Australia. Both countries face the same issues of limited and competitive government funding, the need for private and corporate support to enable organisations to sustain themselves, and a passionate but under-resourced workforce. So while the end product may vary, the work environment and challenges remain the same.

How did you find a place to live?

Craigslist.com is an excellent website for shared housing, rentals, and sublets, and has become my main resource for house hunting. Having so few belongings lessens the challenge of moving but also limits the types of places I can look for. Given the temporary nature of my stay, I'm only interested in renting and don't want to invest in large pieces of furniture, so I've been living in shared accommodation.

I was accustomed to share-house living in Australia but generally with friends, so I've had to adapt to living with strangers, and accept the pitfalls (and joys) that come with it!

What about the social and cultural aspects of living in Canada?

My social transition was helped by the fact that a good friend from Melbourne also lives in Toronto. She and her Canadian boyfriend gave me a roof over my head and introduced me to the social nuances and trends of Canadian culture. I've found the social scene to be fairly similar to what I'm used to – music gigs, dining out, socialising at bars or at people's homes. Canadians have a more pronounced love of everything outdoors – be it summer or winter, they'll find an excuse to get out of the city and into natural surrounds.

My experience with Canadians has been overwhelmingly positive. I find them friendly, easygoing, self-deprecating, and warm. I've been fortunate to work with young, like-minded people who are welcoming and thoughtful. I've met most of my friends through work, and some through mutual friends in Australia. I also met fellow travellers on a trip through Nova Scotia – given our similar experience living and working in a foreign country, we bonded quickly and easily.

Is it easy to open a bank account or get a driver's licence?

My bank account was simple to set up, but credit cards aren't easily issued to those on working holiday permits. Depending on the bank, a security deposit may be required for approval, and in most cases the credit limit is low. A key difference I've noticed here is that Canadians still use cheques, which have pretty much been out of commission in Australia for some time! Coming from a culture where money transfers from one account or person to another are done over the internet, it's strange to revert to paper-based banking. This also makes transfers more time consuming and the reliance on bank tellers more pronounced.

While I have an international driver's licence, a separate Canadian licence is required. I decided to buy a bike instead, as the streets are fairly well equipped for cyclists. Biking also saves me money I would have spent on public transport.

How does the standard and cost of living compare with that in Australia?

The cost of living in Toronto is slightly higher than in Melbourne. Public transport is more expensive as it's charged on a per-use basis, rather than a time limit. The cost of consumables and services seems fairly similar initially, but taxes are added at the time of purchase rather than included on the price tag, plus a service tip has to be added for restaurants, hairdressers, and taxis. This slight increase in my living expenses, combined with a low arts salary, has made for a difficult juggling act financially.

How have you found the Canadian climate?

Canadians love to talk about the weather. And no wonder, because in both summer and winter, you'll find something to talk about – extreme cold and snowstorms in winter, followed by extreme heat and humidity in summer. The summer was bearable, with only a short burst of extreme heat. I find the humidity more difficult to handle.

I'm proud to say that I have just survived my first Canadian winter! This is particularly satisfying as it was one of the longest and 'hardest', by Canadian standards. While temperatures didn't drop as low as in some years, there was a near record-breaking amount of snow. Having never experienced snow before – not even on a ski hill – I was determined to make the most of it. I went ice skating, tobogganing, and happily tracked my way through slush and snow on my way to work. The novelty wore off after about four relentless months. People's moods change and the desire to see sunlight increases. I would live through another winter, but will be better prepared for the long, hard slog.

What do you like most about Canada?

I love the opportunities that Canada has afforded me. I'm gaining valuable experience within my chosen field. I'm travelling to different parts of the world. I'm meeting talented individuals and gaining a better understanding of various forms of art. I like that Canada, and in particular Toronto, challenges me by the mere fact that it's not my home; there is no safety net. But at the same time, it makes me feel at home through its familiar setting and cultural norms. I love the laid-back nature of Canadians, their love of the outdoors, and their quirky sayings, eh?

What do you like least?

I find that some everyday needs are not as well serviced in Canada as they are in Australia. For example, cell-phone users are charged to *receive* calls. Cell-phone coverage is province specific, so if you travel outside of Ontario, you're charged a long-distance rate. I've also found the transport system frustrating. In Toronto, it's expensive without being extensive – only three subway lines for over five million people! Air travel and train travel across long distances is also expensive.

Is Canada what you expected?

Canada has met most of my expectations, namely the beautiful landscape, friendly population and similar cultural aspirations to Australia. The biggest surprises have been Toronto's seemingly archaic transport and cell-phone services, along with its thriving arts scene at both international and local levels. The hardest aspect of moving here would apply regardless of where I lived – being away from family and friends. The long distance between Canada and Australia exacerbates this.

Do you think you'll stay?

I don't have a timeframe in mind for my stay. I'll continue living here as long as I'm enjoying myself, finding career satisfaction, and exploring the country and its communities further. I don't have any regrets about leaving Australia, other than missing my little nieces and nephews grow up. But this isn't forever – and they'll get their fair share of maple-emblazoned memorabilia to show for it!

Any advice for others, on preparing for the move?

For other young professionals thinking of coming to Canada, I would suggest thoroughly researching your chosen field – the main players, recruitment cycles, and so on – especially in the city where you plan to live. Try to establish contacts before arriving, be prepared to befriend strangers and ask their advice, and don't be perturbed by the knock-backs. Canada and Canadians are worth getting to know.

Steven Maine – Bedford, Nova Scotia

Originally from the UK, Steven Maine was living in France and working for a large multinational company when he was approached at a conference – and ultimately recruited – by a Canadian company based in Dartmouth, near Halifax, Nova Scotia. He and his wife, two daughters and son packed up and made the move to Bedford in 2005.

What was the immigration process like?

It was relatively easy for us. We said we would only come to Canada if permanent resident status was given. I'd worked on a work permit before, when we spent three years in Namibia, and wouldn't do it again – it's too stressful. We went through the Provincial Nominee Program for permanent residence. I think it was probably because we applied from France that it was so quick, but it only took eight months for us to get permanent residence.

You've lived in various parts of the world. How did you prepare for the move to Canada?

The company in Canada flew me and my wife across twice, to look around and for the Provincial Nominee Program interview. We had never been to Canada before. We spent about five days here during each trip. We did lots of homework and checked up on things, but nothing prepared us for how life was when we first arrived.

Did it take long to adjust?

We've lived in a number of other countries before – the Netherlands, South Africa, Israel, Namibia and France – including some where English was not the first language, but I have to say this was the hardest move we'd ever made. Maybe it was because we were older, I don't know. We did have a big culture shock. We found Nova Scotia very isolated, although it's a relatively short flight back to the UK or Europe. The culture here, though, is almost like an island mentality, cut off from the mainland. People are very friendly, but in Bedford (Halifax), where we live, they are very wary of strangers, and you are often referred to as 'coming from away' – even if you are from another part of Canada!

How did you go about finding a place to live?

We didn't get much of a choice on where in Canada to live – because of the work the company does, it's based in Nova Scotia. The company was very good and provided furnished rental accommodation for the first three months we were here. This meant we had time to look around for a house to buy – essential, as we had brought our pets with us, and many rentals won't consider tenants with animals. One thing we didn't realise is that there aren't many houses for sale around September to November, when we were looking, so we had only a handful to choose from in our price range that had the number of bedrooms we needed, etc. Another thing we found hard to get to used to is how close the houses are to each other in the towns in this area – very little garden, all built on top of each other, with little privacy. Many also have restrictions so you can't put up fences or hang washing on a line to dry.

We managed to get a mortgage with RBC easily, mainly because we asked for less than we qualified for, put down a decent deposit, and had permanent residence. We also used the branch that my company banks with. The estate agents here, realtors, normally work for either the buyer or the seller, so if you are buying, make sure you get a realtor working for you.

What's the working environment like?

For me, getting this job was easy as the company wanted me to work for them. If I left though, I think it would be very difficult for me to find another job in Canada. I'm in a senior position here – vice president in charge of research at the company. I also do guest lectures at a local college and have been given adjunct professor status by them. From my experience, I think the working environment is generally quite hard, and I have tried hard to make things better for the people who work for me. The lack of holidays and the long working hours are very stressful. Most people only get two or three weeks' annual leave, and Nova Scotia has the fewest public holidays in Canada.

My wife trained as a registered nurse in the UK and has 30 years' experience, but she found her qualifications were not accepted here, and that she would have to sit an examination before being allowed to work. It seems very strange that even if a nurse has qualified in another part of Canada, he or she still has to sit the local exam before being allowed to work here – especially as there is such a shortage of nurses and other medical professionals in the province. I am sure this is a form of protectionism in the unions.

How did your children adapt to life in Canada?

Our youngest was 16 when we arrived. We were lucky that we could afford for him to go to the Halifax Grammar School. We felt this was important as they sit the International Baccalaureate exam, instead of the Canadian leaving exams. He had already been studying for the French Baccalaureate when we were living in France, so the move wasn't too disruptive for him. He found the other children very friendly and helpful, and although he has now finished school and is at university, he still keeps in touch with many of his school friends. The girls weren't so lucky. Our eldest had already completed her first year of university in France, and despite the fact she was fully bilingual, one university here wouldn't accept sufficient credits for that year, and wanted her to start again in first year. After a lot of communication and intervention, she was finally allowed into second year at another university, but it was very stressful for her and she has never really settled here. She is just finishing her master's degree and is now looking for opportunities overseas. I do think though that if you have young children, Canada wouldn't be a bad place to raise them, although some people we know here are very critical of the education system in Nova Scotia.

What's the social life like?

This is one of the things we found hardest to adapt to. We were used to mixing and having a fairly hectic social life. People are friendly on the surface, but seem reluctant to go further until they've known you for a long time. My wife, especially as she wasn't working, found this very difficult. We lived in the house for a year before our neighbours finally really spoke to us. Really the only people we know here are from my work, and members of the British Expats forum who have also moved to Nova Scotia. I honestly do think it is different in other parts of the province though, especially once you move away from the Halifax area.

What about the bureaucratic things, credit cards and driver's licenses?

Again, we were incredibly lucky in that my company helped with many things, especially with an introduction to the bank (RBC). Even so, getting store cards was hard. We knew we'd finally made it when we were given a Sears card! However, now we've been here just over two years, we've had lots of phone calls and mail telling us we've qualified for all sorts of credit facilities – none of which we now want. We also had to apply for Nova Scotia driver's licenses, sitting a written exam first and then taking a physical test. A bit nerve-wracking after years of picking up bad habits. To be honest though, it really wasn't that bad, and we all passed first time.

How does the standard and cost of living compare with that in France?

When we moved here, we were really surprised by the level of taxation in Nova Scotia (especially when you compare it to other provinces), to the extent that financially we're not really that much better off here, especially as my wife isn't working as a registered nurse. Compared to house prices back in Europe, houses in this region probably still give more value for money (even if they are built of wood with plastic siding as opposed to stone or bricks and mortar) – even more so when you move away from the city. House tax is high though (we now pay about $3,200 a year – I'm not sure I get value for money!). We found food prices generally pretty high here as well, and the standard of food is not as good – especially the fresh fruit and vegetables, mainly because much of it has to travel quite a distance before it gets here.

Healthcare is also not as good here as in France: many of the facilities are old and out of date; it's difficult to find a GP who will take new patients in the area around Bedford; and the waiting list at the hospital is so long for certain procedures that patients are being told they can be treated in places like Toronto as long as they can pay to get there. We didn't realise there's no private healthcare system here, so you just have to wait until you can get an appointment. Also, oil to heat the house is very expensive now – we pay around $250 a month all year for this. I would say that you probably have a better standard of living in France compared to Nova Scotia, depending on what you are looking for. It also doesn't help that the annual leave is so short, and you have to travel such long distances to get anywhere else.

How have you found the climate in Nova Scotia?

Winter is not too bad here, but we don't get as much snow as other parts of Canada and it doesn't get so cold – down to around –25°C at the coldest from December to

March. Many places close down, though, and there's not that much to do. Because there's less snow, even winter sports are limited. Spring is worse – it's damp and can be very foggy.

Is Canada what you expected?

No, it's not as we expected. We've moved internationally several times, so thought we'd asked all the right questions and done our homework. The lack of facilities here in Nova Scotia was a surprise. A hard part of the move was being so far from friends and family. Although the flight from the UK is not that long, the price is pretty high, especially as so few airlines fly to Nova Scotia direct. In winter it's mainly Air Canada, so they can dictate prices.

Favourite (and least favourite) things?

Favourite: incredible countryside, very scenic. Least favourite: the sense of isolation, of feeling cut off from the rest of the world.

What advice would you give to others contemplating the move?

If you're coming from Europe, don't think it's going to be anything like life is there. The way people look at things here is completely different. If you drive 30km a day to work there, don't think you can do the same here, especially in winter. Make sure you get everything in writing to ensure job security. Look for quicker ways of getting permanent residence such as Provincial Nominee Programs. Accept that work experience and qualifications gained outside Canada probably won't be accepted here. Likewise, you will start from the beginning for things like credit ratings and insurance, as previous history outside Canada generally won't be accepted. If possible, try to rent a house when you first get here, so you can get a feel for the area, especially if you have young children at school. Accept that it's expensive to travel within the country, as well as outside it. What happens in one province will probably not be the same in another, so if you do move from one area to another, be prepared for these differences.

Rex Baldwin – Saint John, New Brunswick

Rex Baldwin had no plans to leave the UK before he went on holiday with an old school friend to Vancouver, British Columbia. Within five weeks he had quit his well-paid job with Citibank and relocated to Vancouver. Ten years on, he has no regrets and has recently moved to Saint John, New Brunswick.

What made you decide to move to Canada?

The scenery and the quality of life far compensated for the significant reduction in salary. I moved to Saint John, New Brunswick for a job opportunity in February of 2008. Now that I'm here, I don't have any plans to return to Vancouver or the UK!

How were you able to immigrate?

Immigration back in 2000 was different to how it is now. If you could secure a job, the company would get you a work permit. Once I had my work permit I could apply for landed immigrant status, which took about 18 months.

I then applied for citizenship, which took several years. As my job required a lot of travel across the border, it took me over five years to gain citizenship. I decided to pursue citizenship to benefit my two daughters who live with my ex-wife in the Netherlands. I wanted to give my daughters the opportunity of coming to Canada and being able to live, study or work here with relative ease.

Did you have any trouble finding work?

My wife and I were recruited by the same company but decided quickly that working for the same company was not conducive to a balanced lifestyle. So I managed to find another senior role in town within a week.

There is a definite need for skilled people in this city. Because salary levels are lower than in Western Canada, many people move away, but then return later for a better quality of life. There is however, a core group of talented people here who choose to stay because of the quality of life.

How did you choose where to live?

When we first moved to Saint John we were in Chipman Hill Suites (high-end furnished apartments), which was an awesome place to move to knowing nothing about the city. They aren't cheap, but their central location allowed us to explore the area.

After considering buying a home, we opted for renting a nice, central apartment in Uptown Saint John. Many apartments have everything included and when you calculate the cost of heating, air conditioning, etc, rent may appear to be a little more expensive Uptown, but realistically it's good value for what you get.

What's life like in a smaller city like Saint John?

All sports facilities are really close to our home, and anything else we need is within a five-minute walk or 10-minute drive. The quality of life is better than when we lived in Vancouver. While we don't have all of the amenities you might get in a huge city, we do have access to all of the essentials.

When we start a family at some stage, we will probably move into a house with a garden, and with such affordable real estate here it won't be a stretch for us. For now though, we're going to stay where we are and enjoy the urban life.

The culture is extremely friendly. More people are interested in what's in it for the community rather than themselves. In terms of local community you get out what you put in. My wife and I have only lived here for six months, and are already involved in several events and initiatives.

Saint John is an old industrial town that is making the transition to a more cosmopolitan place to live.

How do you find Canadian bureaucracy, and the cost of living?

I wouldn't say that Canadian bureaucracy is any worse or any better than that in, say Germany or Singapore, which have a lot more rules and regulations. When you relocate to a country you have to accept their ways – after all you chose to live there. There is always a certain amount of paperwork.

One detail that I find highly frustrating is that you have to pay for a new driving licence or motorbike licence every five years, even though I have a UK one that is valid until I am 65.

What's been your experience of the Canadian climate – particularly the winter?

Winter was not bad. I've stayed in Edmonton, Alberta in –47°C winter, and so –20°C here is not bad. Buildings are well heated so you do not really notice unless you're out and about. When I moved to Saint John my wife and I arrived at the beginning of February. The trip from Vancouver should have taken eight hours, but instead took us 24 hours! There were storms along the way, and the bad weather continued on the East Coast. The drive to Saint John that should have taken just over an hour was a nerve-wracking three-hour ordeal in the blizzard.

What do you like best about Canada?

There are many things. It's such a big country and every province is different. The people are friendly and the scenery so diverse and spectacular. The history is also diverse, depending on which part of Canada you live in. I prefer it considerably to the USA, where I have worked extensively. The social network and health system in Canada is far better than that of the USA.

Is Canada what you expected?

I didn't know what to expect really, as I first came to Canada on vacation. I approach everything with an open mind and tend to look at the positives. I have not regretted giving up a serious, well-paid career for living here. The quality of life is better than most anywhere else I have lived.

Frédéric Michel – Montreal, Quebec

Before his move to Quebec, his wife's home province, Frédéric Michel was working as a methods engineer at Delphi, an American company that manufactures automobile components. Once in Canada he began an MBA programme in the Telfer School of Management at the University of Ottawa. He is now 35 years old, and lives and works in Montreal.

Why did you decide to move to Canada?

I wanted to broaden my area of competencies, particularly in strategy and finance, so I decided to quit my job in Luxembourg and enter the MBA programme I had dreamed for a long time of studying in North America. I chose Canada and more specifically Quebec, where I could both speak my mother tongue and improve my knowledge of English.

How difficult was the immigration process?

The whole thing was not really difficult, but it was long. There was a lot of paperwork. The process began in September 2000 and I received my permanent resident status in December 2001. We settled in Quebec in the summer of 2002.

How did you go about finding work?

While studying in Ottawa, I became involved in the MBA Students Association as alumni and networking director. I took part in several other initiatives including fundraising for the MBA Games, creation of a career centre at the School of Management and organisation of the Montreal Executive Forum. As a result of my involvement and my new social and professional network, I had little difficulty finding a job. After completing the MBA, I knew that I wanted to work in Montreal and specifically at Bombardier, a well-known manufacturing company. Advised and supported by my mentor, I was able to join the corporate audit and risk assessment department of Bombardier in 2004.

How did you find a home? Are you renting or have you bought somewhere?

Obviously when we moved to Canada, we didn't buy right away. First of all, we were in transition in Ottawa during my studies and we did not know where life would lead us. When we arrived in Montreal, we wanted to discover different neighbourhoods before buying property. It was 2006 when we decided to buy an apartment in the Plateau Mont-Royal area. We chose this lively neighborhood where everything can be done on foot since we do not have a car.

How did your family settle in?

My wife is a Quebecer, so she was settling in familiar territory. My two daughters were both born in Montreal, so Quebec is the only reality that they know. They both attend a day-care centre in the neighbourhood, and like all Quebecers, we had to wait two years before the oldest could find a place in a subsidised centre de la petite enfance (CPE).

How do you find Canadian bureaucracy, and the cost of living?

I find that the telephone systems with robotic voices are horrible. Sometimes the bureaucracy is very heavy and I quickly become annoyed by this robot that cannot answer me. The cost of living in Montreal is a reasonable compared to Toronto or Vancouver. However, I think that Montreal offers a quality of life that is priceless. Everything is accessible: we have a beach in summer, hills for sledding in winter, public pools. On weekends, we can leave the city quickly or else stay to enjoy the museums, exhibitions or festivals.

Has the climate been a challenge for you?

I adore the winter, I adore the rain, I adore the sun, I am not difficult! I am the type who takes life as it comes. At any rate, we can't do anything to change the climate. If a person doesn't like winter, the cold and the snow, he or she should not choose to live in Quebec. I am astonished to hear people complain about the cold as if they had not asked about the climate. I think that when you are aware that winter lasts five months, you must ask yourself if this is right for you. I participate in several winter sports: if there is lots of snow, I will go sledding. When the weather is milder, I go skating. It's up to us to adapt to the climate and not the other way around. Dressed in warm clothing, I can face the icy wind and take advantage of a blue sky.

What aspects of Quebec do you like most?

I believe that the pace of life in Quebec suits me. We work hard, but we can also enjoy family and life, values that are dear to me. The seasons are very distinct and that pleases me. The creativity of Quebec artists impresses me. The ease with which I can communicate with people in high places leads me to believe that everyone has value and that being president does not mean that you don't speak with your workers. Of course, there is a hierarchy, but it does not take a tyrannical form.

What do you like least?

The recognition of credentials. I had eight years of experience as an engineer. The Ordre des Ingénieurs du Québec recognised only one year. I find that there is a gap to fill to facilitate the recognition of competencies acquired elsewhere in the world.

Is Canada what you expected?

Yes and even more. I did not think I could feel at home anywhere other than in my native country. Quebec is a land of opportunity if you are determined. Everything is possible if you apply yourself to it.

Do you have any regrets about moving here?

No regrets, only projects!

Before You Go

Assistance from immigration specialists

A new life abroad is a dream shared by many but achieved by few. A lot of people fail to achieve this dream simply because they either don't know where to start, or they struggle with the legal systems in place and give up. Many rush head-on into the process, without understanding the steps that must be taken, and therefore are stumped by the unique difficulties and uncertainties associated with such an important decision.

To describe Canada's immigration legislation as 'complex' is a huge understatement. The process of obtaining any form of visa or work permit is fraught with problems and the documentation can be daunting. It is not commonly understood, for example, that there are numerous categories of visas or permits providing legal entrance and residence, all of which are dependent on an applicant's individual circumstances.

As a worldwide relocation specialist, A NEW LIFE ABROAD has helped people from all walks of life achieve their aim of a new lifestyle in a different country. They explain the intricacies of the immigration process and how it's often best to seek expert help:

TOP MIGRATION TIPS AND ADVICE

1. Decide where you want your family to settle. Canada is an excellent all-round choice for quality of life, and also has good employment, business, social and financial opportunities.
2. Consider which visa route will give you and your family the best chance of qualifying. Also think of the need for visa and permit applications for partners and children as they may need a different category of visa or permit.
3. Ensure you time your application well, as this can be crucial. Like many countries, Canada imposes quotas to regulate and vary the number and quality of immigrants via a fairly intricate points system.
4. Overcoming officialdom is a requisite for success. You should be prepared for a time-consuming process with complex forms to complete accurately. Even some of the most carefully prepared visa applications can be rejected for seemingly the slightest of reasons. Embassy officials are under no obligation to give you in-depth explanation as to why an application has been rejected, so you could easily find yourself turned down without understanding why, and unable to rectify the situation.
5. Domestic and personal matters are often considered last. However one of your first actions should be to carefully research, then think through, all the ramifications of permanently moving to Canada. Issues like finance, education, children, possessions, pets and willingness to tackle the French language need consideration. You may need advice on 'partner career issues' that are increasingly proving a barrier to successful migrations.
6. When considering employment, a firm job offer will greatly help the success of your application. However you may need a 'credentials

Provided by expert contributor

evaluation', to ensure that your UK qualifications will be recognised by local employers. Depending on your occupation, you may also need to be licensed or accredited by a professional or trade body before being permitted to take up your employment.

7. You'll need to carefully research information on the current employment market in various regions of Canada to establish where your specific skills and experience are currently in demand. This is no easy task from thousands of miles away but the internet can help. As a short cut, contact immigration specialists for professional advice.

WHAT IMMIGRATION SPECIALISTS CAN OFFER

Due to Canada's complex visa application system, many people choose to apply through an immigration specialist. This can have multiple benefits, and can ensure your application is as accurate as possible.

Firstly, they know immigration legislation back to front. Not just as it relates to employment, but as it relates to all the categories of migration permitted by the Canadian government – many of which are not public knowledge. They are therefore able to recommend a route which you had not contemplated – or even thought possible!

Visa specialists have a vast wealth of expertise in the preparation of visa applications, allowing them to present the facts about you in the most favourable manner. This can make the difference between your application being rejected and obtaining approval within your desired timescale.

And if the success of your application rests on an offer of employment, they can liaise with your future employer so that your job offer meets with every requirement of your visa. If you need to comply with any other regulations – such as the need for licensing or accreditation by a professional or trade body – they can prepare all the necessary paperwork on your behalf. They are uniquely qualified to evaluate the options available to you personally – and to provide you with means of exploiting them.

In most cases, you will need a visa or work permit before you can live in your new country. But immigration legislation can be baffling and without understanding the system your chances of success are reduced. Your consultant, backed up by an in-house legal team, will play a vital role from the outset in identifying the basis on which you, personally, are most likely to qualify.

A NEW LIFE ABROAD specialises in helping private individuals (not companies or large organisations) relocate to a different country. In the face of complex immigration legislation, they ensure you don't have to get involved in any of the paperwork and bureaucracy that is involved in the visa application process. Go to their website, www.anewlifeabroad.co.uk or call 0800 63 44 991 for more information on how they can make your move a lot easier.

Provided by expert contributor

A New Life Abroad!

Many people long to live abroad, but do not know where to start...

Help is at hand!

As a worldwide relocation specialist, we have assisted people from all walks of life to achieve their aim of a new lifestyle in a different country. It is likely we can do the same for you.

We will help to secure that vital visa and provide other forms of practical assistance.

Why delay a dream?

Call our **24 hour helpline** with any queries or request a **FREE** information pack.

FREEPHONE: 0800 63 44 991

You may also visit our website: www.anewlifeabroad.co.uk

100, Pall Mall, London, SW1Y 5NQ

■ VISAS, WORK PERMITS, AND CITIZENSHIP

Canadian immigration policy

Canada has several categories of immigrants, which correspond to the economic, social, and humanitarian aims of its immigration programme. The policy is designed to:

- ■ attract qualified workers or investors who can strengthen the Canadian workforce or economy
- ■ reunite families, where at least one member is already resident in Canada
- ■ help those seeking refuge from persecution in their own country.

The 2008 government targets called for a maximum of 71,000 Family Class immigrants, and between 139,000 and 154,000 immigrants in the economic classes, which include federal skilled workers, Quebec-selected skilled workers, both federal and Quebec business immigrants, live-in caregivers, provincial or territorial nominees, and the Canadian Experience Class. (Family members accompanying economic immigrants make up a proportion of these figures.) Citizenship and Immigration Canada (CIC) also admits temporary workers, working holiday programme participants and foreign students. The information in this section is designed to help you determine whether you qualify for consideration under Canadian immigration law.

 Download copies of CIC's Overseas Processing guides for each immigration category at www.cic.gc.ca (select *Publications*, then see under *Operational Manuals*). These guides are written to help CIC officers process applications, and are packed with useful information on eligibility, requirements and assessment.

Securing Canada's future

Citizens of the EU who've become accustomed to flexible borders, or those familiar with Australia and New Zealand's relatively rapid visa processing, may find Canada's immigration procedures a bit laborious. Canada currently accepts between 240,000

ENTRY REQUIREMENTS: MAKE IT QUICK

For a convenient, super-fast way to check what entry requirements are likely to apply to you, visit the Going to Canada website at www.goingtocanada.gc.ca. The Entry Requirements Tool, accessible from the home page, allows you to select your entry intentions (such as immigrating or working temporarily) and your country of citizenship, and provides instant information on what requirements you need to meet and what processes to follow. You can also email inquiries to Questions-goingtocanada@cic.gc.ca.

and 265,000 immigrants a year, including around 30,000 refugees and protected people. The government's goal is to achieve an immigration rate equal to 1% of the Canadian population. While the nation clearly wants to attract immigrants (and needs to do so to support its economy) the question of 'which' immigrants has gained force. The terrorist attacks of September 11, 2001 heightened concerns about Canada's border security, its refugee policy and, to a lesser degree, its immigration policy.

Extensive security checks are now standard for all potential immigrants to Canada. With border 'protection' between Canada and the USA shifting from a trade issue to one of security, the two countries have taken steps to harmonise their policies on visas and border defence. Many people believe a common immigration policy is inevitable, and the Security and Prosperity Partnership of North America (SPP) – a 'non-binding partnership' between Canada, the USA, and Mexico established in 2005 to address common issues – is seen by some as a step in that direction. Key figures south of the border (including the US Ambassador to Canada) have certainly argued for a synchronised policy on immigration, but Canadian practices, processes, and immigration requirements remain distinct from those of the USA. Since June 2002, all new Canadian permanent residents are issued with a proof-of-status Permanent Resident Card. This card is mandatory for re-entry for any permanent resident travelling outside of Canada, who returns on a commercial carrier such as an aeroplane, bus, train or ferry. (It will also help you clear US customs.)

TIP

■ Since June 2002, all new permanent residents are issued with a proof-of-status Permanent Resident Card. This card is mandatory for re-entry for permanent residents travelling outside of Canada.

Policy changes

Even before September 11, Canada's immigration policy was changing to reflect concerns about cost and integration. Back in 1996, 41% of immigrants arriving in

Canadiana flutters among the city buildings in Toronto, Ontario

Canada spoke neither English nor French – the cost to taxpayers of subsidising language training the following year was $102m. Concerns were also raised about the perceived failure of non-English or non-French speakers to adjust to Canadian society and find work because of language difficulties, and the potential strain on the welfare system. In 2002, significant policy changes were brought in with the new Immigration and Refugee Protection Act (IRPA). Basic language skills in English or French are now considered desirable in the principal applicant, and requirements for post-secondary education and work experience have increased. Common-law and conjugal unions (both opposite sex and same sex) are recognised as spousal relationships and are subject to the same rights and privileges. The most recent changes include the introduction of the Canadian Experience Class (discussed on p. 50), and modifications to the regulations that govern application processing. These modifications, approved on 18 June 2008, currently affect people applying as federal skilled workers, and only pertain to applications received on or after 27 February 2008. They allow

CIC, under instruction from the department minister, to determine the eligibility of applications for processing based on a more restrictive set of criteria, which focus on the applicant's potential to meet Canada's labour-market needs. Those applications deemed eligible for processing are still subject to existing immigration criteria, including assessment under the point system. Applications that don't meet the revised criteria for eligibility are returned with a full refund to the applicant. The changes are intended to reduce lengthy processing times (particularly in the skilled worker category) and erode some of the multi-year backlog that has begun to hamper Canada's reputation as a preferred immigration destination. The new regulations have also raised considerable questions. The immigration minister now has the ability – and the flexibility – to issue instructions that respond to Canada's changing immigration needs. However, critics have expressed concern that giving the minister this 'power' risks exposing the system to bias and discrimination. For details of the changes, go to www.cic.gc.ca and follow the *About Us* and *Laws and Policies* links. Ongoing changes to immigration policy are inevitable, so check the CIC website regularly for the most up-to-date information. Additional details on the new regulations can be found under *Skilled workers* on p. 47.

 The website for Citizenship and Immigration Canada (CIC) is www.cic.gc.ca, or you can phone the CIC Call Centre from within Canada on 1 888 242 2100. To speak with an agent, select your preferred language, then either dial 0 or just stay on the line. If you're outside Canada, contact the Canadian embassy, consulate or high commission in your region.

FACT

▌ The most recent changes include the introduction of the Canadian Experience Class, and modifications to the regulations that govern application processing for skilled workers.

Family class

If you're lucky enough to have a close relative already in Canada it can help your immigration chances. The Canadian system has traditionally been weighted in

WHERE TO APPLY?

In most cases, you have to be outside Canada to begin immigration procedures. You can generally only apply for permanent residence from within the country if you have status as a protected person or refugee, have grounds for humanitarian or compassionate consideration, are a live-in caregiver, hold a temporary resident permit (not a temporary resident visa), or are a spouse, common-law or conjugal partner of a Canadian or permanent resident (or the dependent child of one or both). Prospective skilled workers who've already legally resided in Canada for at least a year can also apply in Canada. If you come to visit relatives in Canada and decide you want stay, however you need to return home to begin the application process. People who overstay their visas or who are in Canada illegally risk deportation, which doesn't help their immigration cause later on.

favour of Family Class immigrants; a little over a decade ago, most applications were approved almost automatically. Barring medical or security problems, and provided that your sponsor pledged to support you, your application was likely to be approved. Today, policies are much the same, but tighter quotas – a result of the shift in immigration priorities from family reunification to economic development – have reduced the chance of success, and waiting times can be long. A Canadian citizen or permanent resident aged 18 or over can sponsor one or more members of his or her immediate family. This includes a spouse (opposite sex or same sex, provided the marriage is legally recognised in Canada, as well as in the country where it took place if this was not Canada) or a common-law or conjugal partner (opposite sex or same sex), parents, grandparents, dependent children under 22 (as well as substantially dependent children over 22 under certain conditions), and orphaned relatives under 18. The Conjugal Partner category only applies in exceptional circumstances, and was introduced in 2002 for people prevented from living together or marrying – usually because of an immigration barrier – who would otherwise qualify as spouses or common-law partners. The 'fiancé' category no longer exists. Someone with no relatives in the above categories, and no other family in Canada, may apply to sponsor one relative outside their immediate family.

My wife's parents, who had retired to Algonquin Park in Ontario, agreed to sponsor us to immigrate to Canada.

Gerald Garnett

The length of time it takes to grant landed-immigrant status to Family Class applicants can be frustrating. Processing times vary depending on the specific family category and visa office, and can take anywhere from four months to over five years. (Applications for partners and dependent children are processed most quickly; those for parents and grandparents take the longest.) While it may be possible to reside in Canada during part or all of that time, you won't have ongoing legal status without a temporary resident document of some kind, and you won't be permitted to work unless you obtain a work permit. If you're intending to come to Canada before being granted permanent residence, be aware that your career might have to be put on hold for a while. Private health insurance can be a costly necessity as well, as you won't be eligible for provincial health cover until – at the very earliest – CIC confirms that you've met the medical requirements for residency. (See p. 175 for information on the healthcare system.)

How to apply

There are two different application processes for Family Class immigration – one for a spouse, common-law or conjugal partner and for dependent children, and one for all other family members. The main difference is that in the first category, the sponsoring relative and potential immigrant submit a joint application (rather than sending them in separately) and the potential immigrant must undergo his or her medical examination before applying, rather than having the option of waiting until the application has been provisionally approved. If you have a relative who's willing to sponsor your application, he or she needs to obtain the relevant forms and instructions from a Canadian visa office. These can also be downloaded from the CIC website, or mailed on request by phoning the CIC Call Centre. (If outside Canada, contact the Canadian embassy, High Commission or consulate in your region.) Note that there are different forms for partners and dependent children depending on whether they reside in or outside Canada, so make sure you use the correct ones. Fees are $75 for the sponsorship application and $475 for the principal applicant ($75 if he or she is under 22 and is not married or in a common-law or conjugal relationship), plus an additional $550 for each accompanying family member who is 22 or older, *or* married or in a common-law relationship ($150 for those who are under 22 and not in such a relationship). These fees are non-refundable once processing of the permanent residence application has begun, and won't be returned to you if your application is unsuccesful. In most cases, unless you are being sponsored as a dependent child or orphaned relative, or are a protected person, an additional Right of Permanent Residence Fee (RPRF) of $490 (which *is* refundable) has to be paid before permanent resident status is granted. Sponsors and certain applicants may be eligible for a loan to help cover the cost of the RPRF, though there is no loan option for the actual application fees. Other loans exist to help some new immigrants travel to and settle in Canada. Contact CIC or your home country's Canadian visa office for details.

Your sponsor is required to provide proof of age, Canadian citizenship or permanent residence, proof of your relationship (and that this is eligible under the Family Class), and proof of income (though this is not required if sponsoring a spouse or common-law partner, or dependent children). In 2000, steps were taken to tighten sponsorship requirements, due to concerns that immigrants unable to financially support themselves – especially those sponsoring many family members – were putting additional strain on the welfare system. Historically, about one in seven sponsorships break down, resulting in a welfare bill of over $700m for the Canadian government. Higher requisite income levels and official sponsorship agreements are designed to rectify this problem. Social assistance is not available to sponsored relatives, and your sponsor must sign an official 'undertaking' assuming financial responsibility for you and your dependants for up to 10 years (three years for a spouse or spousal equivalent, or for dependent children aged 22 or over at the time permanent residence is granted). There is no limit to the number of relatives an individual may sponsor; however, the sponsor's income must be sufficient to support all those he or she brings to Canada. The regularly updated Low-Income Cut-off (LICO) table gives the minimum income levels – a copy is included as part of the application kit, or you can contact CIC for the most up-to-date figures. The bar is set quite low. For example, to sponsor two relatives, a minimum annual income of around $26,500 is required. In practice, the Canadian government won't leave you to starve if your sponsor proves unable to support you – though they may demand that he or she repay any social assistance payments you receive. (If you find employment in Canada you will be eligible for Employment Insurance and the Canada Pension Plan, see p. 194.) At the application stage, though, it's important to show that prospective immigrants won't be a burden on the social security system.

Sponsorship applications for partners or dependent children are usually accepted or rejected within 30 to 40 days, but those for parents, grandparents or other relatives take close to two years. Once the sponsorship application has been accepted, processing of permanent residence applications for partners or dependent children begins automatically. For other family members, the permanent residence application forms are sent to the sponsor, who forwards them to the prospective immigrant. The prospective immigrant completes the application and returns it to the designated visa office for his or her country. The visa office contacts all applicants to let them know whether additional documents or an interview are required. Criminal, background, and medical checks are then carried out – if you haven't previously undergone the medical examination, this is done now. All examinations have to be

see p. 194

FACT

There are two different application processes for Family Class immigration – one for a spouse, common-law or conjugal partners and for dependent children, and one for all other family members.

TIP

There are different forms for partners and dependent children depending on whether they reside in or outside Canada, so make sure you use the correct ones.

FACT

Applications for permission to sponsor partners or dependent children are usually accepted or rejected within 30 to 40 days, but those for parents, grandparents or other relatives take close to two years.

performed by a CIC-approved doctor (though you'll be responsible for the fee), and the results are valid for 12 months. Medical clearances can be an obstacle for Family Class immigrants. A major medical condition could result in your application being refused, if it's considered a danger to others or is likely to place a significant burden on the health or social system. People with a criminal record will also encounter difficulties, as they may be considered a risk to Canadian society or security.

 A list of designated medical practitioners for specific countries and cities is available on the CIC website (www.cic.gc.ca). See the links on the home page under *I Need To...*

Processing times for permanent resident visas vary considerably between (and even within) countries, so visit the CIC website for current estimates. If your visa is granted you'll have a limited time in which to move to Canada. This may be based on the expiry date of your immigration medical examination, or that of your passport, but is always at the discretion of the immigration department. As a permanent resident you can work and study, and will have most of the same rights as a Canadian citizen.

Applying as an independent immigrant

Categories and fees

People not eligible as Family Class immigrants need to apply independently under one of the economic immigration categories. These consist of the Federal Skilled Worker Class, for skilled workers or professionals, the Canadian Experience Class, for those with skilled work experience in Canada, and the Business Immigration Program, which includes entrepreneurs, investors, and the self-employed. The Provincial Nominee Program is also part of the economic class, and Quebec has additional economic immigration categories. Skilled workers and their spouses are charged $550 each to apply for permanent residence; there is an additional $150 fee each for any dependants they wish to bring who are under 22 ($550 for those aged 22 or over). Canadian Experience Class applicants and provincial nominees are subject to the same application fees as skilled workers. Fees for entrepreneurs, investors and self-employed immigrants are also the same, except that the principal applicant pays $1050. The Right of Permanent Residence Fee (RPRF) of $490 per non-exempt applicant is also payable. Loans may be available to help cover some costs, as mentioned on p. 45.

The point system

Being approved as an independent, economic immigrant is by no means routine. It can be difficult to meet the eligibility requirements set out by CIC, and these also change from time to time. All independent applicants (with the exception of provincial nominees in some provinces) are assessed according to a point system. This is designed to determine your suitability for the Canadian labour market and the likelihood that you'll settle successfully into Canadian society. Quebec has its own immigration requirements and point system and is discussed under *Immigrating to Quebec*. Since 2003, the pass mark for skilled workers has been 67 points out of a possible 100, based on six selection factors. Business Class immigrants are assessed on slightly different criteria and must obtain 35 out of

It's important to have the correct application forms, as well as any other documents you might need

100 – see *Business immigration*, for details. Provincial nominees are assessed on criteria specific to each province or territory.

 Prospective skilled workers can take a self-assessment test on the CIC website at www.cic.gc.ca/english/immigrate/skilled/assess/index.asp to see whether they are likely to meet the points requirement.

Skilled workers

As discussed on p. 9, a number of important changes have recently been made to this immigration category. To be considered as a skilled worker, an applicant was previously required to score at least 67 points under the point system, and to have work experience in an occupation listed in Canada's National Occupational Classification (NOC), under either skill type 0, or skill level A or B. The new regulations, which affect applications received on or after 27 February 2008, are far more restrictive. Now, for your application to be considered eligible for processing, you must either have a permanent job offer from a Canadian employer, have already legally resided in Canada for one year as a foreign student or temporary foreign worker, or have work experience in one of a limited number of approved occupations (a list of these is available on the CIC website). Eligible applicants must also meet minimum requirements for skilled work experience. Assessment of eligible applications is then based on the point system. See the CIC website for complete details of the revised process. An eligibility tool is also provided to help you determine whether you meet the new criteria. If you decide to apply, you need

POINT SYSTEM SELECTION CRITERIA FOR SKILLED WORKERS

■ **Education** (maximum 25 points): Five points awarded for high school completion; 12–15 for a one-year diploma, trade certificate, apprenticeship or bachelor's degree; 20 for a two-year qualification, 22 for a three-year qualification or multiple bachelor's degrees; 25 for a master's degree or PhD.

■ **Ability in official languages** (maximum 24 points): Applicants highly proficient in speaking, listening, reading, and writing in one official language (either English or French) will receive 16 points, with two points awarded in each category for moderate abilities and one per category (to a maximum of two points only) for basic abilities. Fluency in the other official language is worth up to eight points.

■ **Experience** (maximum 21 points): 15 points for the first year of continuous, full-time experience in a given field; two points for every additional year to a maximum of 21. (If you have less than one year's experience you are ineligible.)

■ **Age** (maximum 10 points): 10 points if aged 21 to 49; two points deducted for each year under 21 or over 49.

■ **Arranged employment** (10 points): Awarded if you have a job offer cleared by Human Resources and Social Development Canada (HRSDC) (or designated as exempt from this requirement). Your potential employer must make this application on your behalf. (See *Getting an approved job offer*, p. 49.)

■ **Adaptability** (maximum 10 points): Points awarded for spouse or common-law partner's education level, previous work or study in Canada, family members in Canada, and arranged employment in Canada.

to ensure (and be able to prove to CIC) that you have enough money to support your family for a few months while you get established in Canada. The funds requirement for a single person is currently $10,601; a family of four needs $19,700. If you have arranged employment in Canada you're exempt from this requirement. Application processing times have typically been between 18 months and three years, though this should reduce as the new processing regulations take effect.

i Download skilled worker application forms and guides at www.cic.gc.ca. The comprehensive CIC *Foreign Worker Manual* can be downloaded at www.cic.gc.ca (select *Publications* then *Temporary Foreign Workers Guidelines*).

Getting an approved job offer

Suggested methods of finding a job in Canada are discussed in the *Working in Canada* chapter. Once you find a company or individual who wants to employ you, you can proceed in one of two ways: you can apply for a temporary work permit so you can work in Canada while your skilled worker application is being processed, or you can wait until you are granted permanent residence. Temporary work permits are normally processed much more quickly, so this is a preferable option for some. However, they usually require the employer to request and obtain a positive Labour Market Opinion (LMO), which is not always easy. (See *Temporary work permits* on p. 61 for more on this.) If you're intending to apply for both a temporary permit and permanent residence, your employer should indicate on the LMO application that your employment would be temporary with intent to become permanent. If the application is approved you can come to Canada and begin work. You can either submit your permanent residence application at the same time you apply for your temporary work permit, or you can apply once you get to Canada.

If you decide to wait until your skilled worker application is processed, your prospective employer needs to apply instead for an Arranged Employment Opinion (AEO). This must be approved by Human Resources and Social Development Canada (HRSDC) for your job offer to be eligible as arranged employment. If the AEO is positive, your prospective employer sends you a copy of this, and of the permanent job offer, to include with your application for permanent residence. Note that even if you have a positive LMO, you need to obtain an AEO if you want to claim arranged employment on your permanent residence application.

Gaining equal recognition for qualifications obtained outside of Canada can be difficult – see *Recognition of foreign qualifications* p. 241.

Occupations in demand

Since the implementation of the new immigration act (IRPA) in 2002, selection of immigrants was driven by general skills rather than specific occupation. The recent modifications to the system, however represent a return to occupation-influenced prioritising. Many provinces and territories have skills shortages in certain industries, or for particular occupations. A major purpose of the Provincial and Territorial Nominee Programs – which are targeted directly at prospective immigrants – is to help fill these gaps. If you have work experience in an area in which a province has shortages, you can increase your chances of finding employment by focusing your job search on that province. Once you have a job offer, you can apply for provincial nomination (see p. 54 for further details), which may improve your immigration chances.

HRSDC also identifies occupations that are 'under pressure', and publishes regional lists of these for Alberta, BC, Manitoba, Nova Scotia, Ontario, PEI, and Quebec, with the aim of helping employers to hire temporary foreign workers. If you plan to come

TIP

◼ If you have work experience in an area in which a province has shortages, you can increase your chances of finding employment by focusing your job search on that province.

to Canada on a temporary work permit and apply for permanent residence later (as discussed above), your prospective employer can check to see whether your occupation is on the relevant provincial list. The normal advertising and recruitment requirements that employers must meet are reduced for these occupations. There's also a pilot project in place to expedite LMO processing for Alberta and BC. Under this project, applications for designated occupations – primarily in tourism, trade, engineering, and hospitality – are processed in just five days.

 For regional lists of occupations under pressure, and details of the expedited LMO pilot project (employer oriented, but still relevant) go to www.hrsdc. gc.ca. Select *Topic* then *Foreign Workers*, and see the quick links at the bottom of the webpage.

Canadian Experience Class

This brand-new immigration category, implemented on 17 September 2008, is targeted specifically at skilled temporary foreign workers with sufficient Canadian experience, and international students with a recent Canadian post-secondary and subsequent work experience. These people represent a huge resource pool for the government: they've proven they can find employment in Canada; they've settled into Canadian society; and they're already in the country, in many cases helping to address labour shortages. This class recognises their value as potential immigrants and aims to capitalise on it. It's also a winning situation for the applicants – provided they have the requisite experience and meet all other criteria, it proposes a smoother and easier transition to permanent residence. It also means they don't have to leave the country to apply. There are two types of eligible candidates:

- Recent Foreign graduates from a Canadian post-secondary institution, with the equivalent of one year of full-time skilled work experience in Canada.
- Temporary foreign workers with the equivalent two years of full-time skilled work experience in Canada.

All applicants must have valid temporary status in Canada, and work experience must be in an occupation (or several occupations) listed under skill type 0 or skill level A or B in the National Occupational Classification (NOC). Full details can be found on the CIC website.

 The National Occupational Classification (NOC) can be accessed through Human Resources and Social Development Canada (HRSDC) at www.hrsdc. gc.ca./NOC–CNP.

Business immigration

The Business Immigration Program represents around 5% of total immigrants, and is divided into three categories: entrepreneurs, the self-employed, and investors. Many Provincial Nominee Programs also have categories for business people, so the actual proportion of business-related immigrants is somewhat higher than this. In addition to meeting the requirements for their specific category, business immigrants need to score at least 35 points out of 100 on a point system, based on five categories. Up to 25 points are awarded for education, 35 for business experience (20 for the first two years plus five for each additional year, to a maximum of 35 points), 10 for age, 24 for language proficiency and six for adaptability. Adaptability for entrepreneurs and investors is assessed on specific criteria to do with previous business involvement in Canada (the CIC website includes full details). To be eligible for these points, you need to contact the government of the province or territory you'll be living in, and obtain documentation from them confirming that you have met the criteria (see website address below). All prospective business immigrants have to undergo security and medical checks, and may have to attend an interview at a visa office. There are two application processes for business immigration: the regular process, and a simplified process, which is used by most applicants. The simplified process holds your place in the queue, but doesn't require you to submit any supporting documentation until later. Forms and guides are available from CIC.

 Provincial and territorial contacts for business immigrants are listed at www.cic.gc.ca/english/immigrate/business/investors/provinces.asp

Entrepreneurs

You can apply to immigrate as an entrepreneur if you have the capital and ability to establish, purchase, or make a substantial investment in a business that will create jobs for one or more Canadian citizens or residents (not including your family members). Applicants must have a legally obtained net worth of at least $300,000. You don't have to submit a formal business plan – in fact, the immigration department strongly discourages it. However, you need to show that you have business experience, which is defined as managing and having control of a percentage of equity in a business for at least two years (two one-year periods) out of the last five. CIC provides detailed definitions for what constitutes a percentage of equity at www.cic.gc.ca/english/immigrate/business/entrepreneurs/definitions. asp. Entrepreneurs and their dependants are admitted to Canada as permanent residents on the condition that the entrepreneur shows, within three years of residence, that he or she has met the requirements set by CIC for at least one year. These include controlling a minimum of one-third of the equity in a business of a defined size, playing an active and ongoing role in its management, and providing employment as outlined above. To immigrate as an entrepreneur you must sign a declaration committing to these conditions, and report regularly to a CIC immigration centre. Failure to comply with the conditions could result in your permanent resident status, and that of your family, being revoked.

Prospective immigrants in this category may also wish to consider applying through one of the Provincial Nominee Business Programs (see *Provincial Nominees*, p. 54), which can accelerate the immigration process. Regulations vary between provinces, and some Nominee Programs do require you to submit a business plan. If this is the case, it can be wise (though sometimes expensive) to get assistance from a lawyer with knowledge of Canadian business law.

Investors

Since 1986, wealthy immigrants have poured billions of dollars into Canada in exchange for permanent resident status. Most are from Asian countries, with the largest number coming from China, and over half settle in Vancouver. The investor

Immigrating to Saint John, New Brunswick, Canada

If you are planning to immigrate to Saint John, NB, there are a few different ways to apply. You will need to decide which immigration programme will work best for you and your family and then apply at a Canadian Visa Office outside of Canada.

Skilled workers and professionals

Check the education, experience and language skills you need on:

- www.gnb.ca/immigration
- www.cicic.ca
- www.cic.gc.ca/english/immigrate/skilled/index.asp

Skilled workers require a permanent, full-time job offer from an established New Brunswick employer. The job must meet provincial employment standards and offer comparable industry rates of pay. In most cases, the skills offered by the potential immigrant are not readily available in New Brunswick and employers must demonstrate that they have attempted to find these skills in the Canadian job market.

In Canada, approximately 20% of occupations are regulated to protect the health and safety of Canadians (eg nurses, engineers, teachers, and electricians). Licensing requirements often include education from a recognised school, Canadian work experience and completion of a technical exam.

Visit the Canadian Information Centre for International Credentials at www.cicic.ca for detailed information regarding employment in Canada for specific professions and trades.

Provincial nominees

To learn about settling in New Brunswick as a provincial nominee, go to:

- www.gnb.ca/iammigation
- www.cic.gc.ca/english/immigrate/provincial/index.asp

New Brunswick recognises that immigration is a source of skills, entrepreneurship, expertise, international links, and capital, which create additional employment and investment. Through the Provincial Nominee Program, New Brunswick actively seeks qualified immigrants who will fill labour market shortages, or create employment and business opportunities there.

To be considered for nomination by New Brunswick, applicants must have a guaranteed job offer in their intended occupation or an approved plan to do business in New Brunswick.

New Brunswick PNP job offer applicants

Applicants must be able settle permanently in New Brunswick, must score at least 50 points on a self-assessment and must have a New Brunswick job offer from an employer who:

- Has been unable to fill the position with a Canadian citizen or permanent resident
- Is offering full-time, permanent position
- Offers compensation consistent with regional wages and existing collective bargaining agreements.

New Brunswick PNP business applicants

To qualify, the applicant must be willing to establish a business in New Brunswick, must score at least 50 points on a self-assessment and must:

- Be willing to sign an agreement to settle permanently in New Brunswick
- Have previous management experience

Provided by expert contributor

Have sufficient funds to finance the planned business venture and to support their family for a period of up to two years

Participate in the business in an active managerial role

Speak English and/or French or take intensive language lessons prior to nomination.

One of the benefits of the PNP is that applicants are likely to see their application for immigration to Canada processed more quickly.

You may send your completed Provincial Nominee application package to:

Population Growth Secretariat
New Brunswick Provincial Nominee Program
PO Box 6000
Fredericton, New Brunswick
Canada E3B 5H1

TIP: Legal representation may help your application; please contact the Law Society of New Brunswick for referrals.

Law Society of New Brunswick
1133 Regent Street, Suite 206
Fredericton, New Brunswick
Canada E3B 3Z2
Telephone: 506 4588540
Fax: 506 4511421
Email: general@lawsociety-barreau.nb.ca

Further resource links to Saint John, New Brunswick:

www.saintjohnlifeonyourterms.ca
www.enterprisesj.com
www.saintjohn.ca
www.sjboardoftrade.com
www.gnb.ca

Provided by expert contributor

category is perhaps the most controversial aspect of Canada's immigration policy, viewed by many as a way for people to 'buy' their way into Canada without making a genuine contribution to the country or the economy. However, prospective immigrants must have sufficient business experience and meet all other selection criteria in order to be considered. They must also have a personal net worth of at least $800,000, and make an investment of $400,000. Investors could once choose their own projects or funds, but the system became riddled with kickback schemes and other criminal activity. Now, the $400,000 is submitted directly to CIC, preferably through an approved facilitator or financial organisation that is a member of the Canada Deposit Insurance Corporation (CDIC). Canadian provinces and territories use the money for economically based projects and job creation. CIC then returns the capital – with no interest – after about five years. The prime advantage of immigrating as an investor is that your permanent resident status is not contingent on any further business activity. You may also be able to use your investment as security against a loan; the facilitators approved by CIC can outline your options and arrange this.

Self-employed immigrants

This category has narrowed in recent years, and applicants now have to show evidence of either self-employment or participation at a world-class level in cultural activities or athletics, or experience in farm management. Authors, performing artists, musicians, athletes, and sporting instructors are among those who may qualify. You must intend to be self-employed in Canada, be able to create employment for yourself through your area of expertise, and demonstrate your ability either to make a 'significant contribution' to Canada's cultural or athletic life, or to buy and manage a farm. Like other business immigrants, you need two years of applicable experience within the last five, and must meet all other selection criteria. (If you're applying as a provincial nominee, the requirements are set by the province.) Proof of sufficient funds to initially support yourself and your family is also required – levels are the same as for skilled workers (see p. 47). As with entrepreneurs, no formal business plan is necessary (unless required for provincial nomination), but you do need to demonstrate that you can finance your intended business venture in Canada. You may also have to show that you've researched the Canadian labour market and that your endeavour can be a viable means of self-employment. Though self-employed immigrants are expected to make an economic contribution to the country, unlike entrepreneurs they don't have to meet any specific conditions once they become permanent residents.

Useful contacts for business immigrants

Canada Business: Joint federal–provincial/territorial government information service for businesses and entrepreneurs in Canada. Home page provides links to individual provincial and territorial websites (see bottom of home page): 1 888 576 4444; www.cbsc.org

Canada Deposit Insurance Corporation (CDIC): 1 800 461 2342; info@cdic.ca; www.cdic.ca

Canada International: enqserv@international.gc.ca; www.canadainternational.gc.ca

CIC Business Immigration: Nat-Business-Immigration@cic.gc.ca

CIC Business Immigrant Program (provincial and territorial partners): Contact details for business immigration information and services from each province and territory can be found at www.cic.gc.ca

Industry Canada: Provides valuable information on business development, investment, trade, and the Canadian marketplace. Regional offices are located across Canada: 1 613 954 5031 or 1 800 328 6189; info@ic.gc.ca; www.ic.gc.ca

Provincial nominees

The Provincial Nominee Program was established to encourage immigrants to work and settle in specific provinces or territories. Programmes are operated by the provincial or territorial governments, and are currently available in Alberta, Manitoba, Newfoundland and Labrador, Ontario (as a pilot programme only at this stage), Saskatchewan, BC, New Brunswick, Nova Scotia, PEI, and the Yukon. Each province's program is based on its particular needs, and has different requirements and regulations. Many provinces actively recruit workers in certain fields – often internationally. They may have opportunities for skilled workers, semi-skilled workers, entrepreneurs, investors, the self-employed, and other business immigrants. Some also offer a 'family members' category in which permanent residents already living and working in the province can sponsor other family members (usually not a spouse or partner, or children, parents or grandparents) to immigrate to that province to work. Provincial nominee programmes offer a number of advantages to prospective immigrants: they encourage employers to hire foreign workers; they identify areas in which people with certain skills or experience are needed; and they can considerably speed up the immigration process. The government target for provincial nominees was 20,000 in 2008 (around twice the number allocated for non-provincial business immigrants). Applicants first need to contact the province or territory they wish to work in, and meet any program requirements (which may include securing a job offer). If you are approved as a provincial nominee, you can then apply to CIC for permanent residence. Application forms and detailed information on applying for nomination can be obtained from the relevant province or territory website (see below). For permanent residence forms and guides, contact CIC.

Provincial Nominee Program contacts

Alberta: 1 780 427 6419 or 1 877 427 6419;
www.albertacanada.com/immigration/immigrate/ainp.html
British Columbia: 1 250 387 2190; PNPinfo@gems9.gov.bc.ca;
www.ecdev.gov.bc.ca
Manitoba: 1 204 945 2806; www.gov.mb.ca/labour/immigrate
New Brunswick: 1 506 453 3981; immigration@gnb.ca; www.gnb.ca/immigration
Newfoundland and Labrador: 1 709 729 6607; www.nlpnp.ca
Nova Scotia: 1 902 424 5230 or 1 877 292 9597; nsnp@gov.ns.ca;
www.novascotiaimmigration.com
Ontario: 1 416 327 0374 or 1 866 214 6820;
www.ontarioimmigration.ca
Prince Edward Island: 1 902 620 3628; peinominee@gov.pe.ca;
www.gov.pe.ca
Saskatchewan: 1 306 798 7467; www.immigration.gov.sk.ca/Contact;
www.immigration.gov.sk.ca
Yukon: 1 867 667 3014; bob.snyder@gov.yk.ca;
www.immigration.gov.yk.ca

Immigrating to Quebec

Through an agreement with the federal government (the Canada-Quebec Accord on Immigration), Quebec is entitled to a certain proportion of Canada's immigrants.

Around 45,000 are currently admitted to Quebec each year, from all categories. The Government of Quebec has its own immigration department, the Ministère de l'Immigration et des Communautés culturelles (MICC), and selects applicants who will contribute to the province's uniquely French cultural and social character. Only those applicants selected by the province are able to immigrate to Quebec, though CIC makes the actual decision on whether they will be admitted to Canada. Being able to speak and understand the language is considered essential to living, working, and communicating in Quebec – in most cases you must have at least a basic knowledge of French to be considered (though you may be able to circumvent this if your spouse or common-law partner has some French ability). Agreements are in place with French-language institutes in some countries to help potential immigrants with poor French abilities improve to an acceptable level. Immigrants are actively recruited from Europe, Africa, the Caribbean, South America, North America, Asia, and the Middle East. The Office québécois de la langue française provides

i Guides to French-language usage in Quebec can be downloaded at the Office québécois de la langue française webpage, www.olf.gouv.qc.ca/english/infoguides/index.html. For more on French essentials and classes, see the MICC webpage at www.immigration-quebec.gouv.qc.ca/en/french-language

invaluable information on French-language policy in Quebec, and on conventions and requirements relating to living and working in the province. A downloadable guide, *Questions and Answers about Quebec's Language Policy*, is particularly helpful.

Regulations for Family Class and business applicants are similar to those in the federal programme, though some variations and additional requirements apply. Business applicants need to be willing and able to conduct business in French: Quebec's language policy gives all employees the right to work in French, which means you must be able to communicate with them in French. (Businesses with over 50 employees also have to meet additional requirements.) In Quebec, the MICC refers to skilled workers as 'permanent workers'. Would-be applicants (and their spouse or common-law partner, if applicable) complete an online self-evaluation on the MICC's Immigration-Québec website to check their eligibility before submitting an official application. Training and education, work experience, age, language, ties to Quebec and financial self-sufficiency are important factors in qualifying for admission. (Though the provincial government makes language lessons available to those with little or no French knowledge, the self-evaluation is likely to reject you if you indicate such a low level of language ability – unless, as mentioned above, your spouse or common-law partner has French-language skills.) The Quebec government charges its own processing fees, which are in addition to

A pretty pathway in Mount Royal Park, Montreal, Quebec

those levied by CIC. For permanent workers, fees are $390 for the principal applicant and $150 for a spouse or partner and for each dependent child. Entrepreneurs and self-employed workers pay $950 for the principal applicant; investors pay $3,850. If you are approved by the province you receive a confirmation certificate, the Certificat de sélection du Québec (CSQ). You then apply for permanent residence through CIC, and the usual medical and security clearances are carried out. Prospective immigrants can find details of Immigration-Québec bureaus in different countries (including Canada) by visiting the ministry website.

 The Ministère de l'Immigration et des Communautés culturelles (MICC) website is www.immigration-quebec.gouv.qc.ca. You can also reach the MICC by phone on 1 514 864 9191 or 1 877 864 9191, or by email at Renseignements@micc.gouv.qc.ca

Immigration consultants, lawyers, and representatives

Many firms in Canada and around the world specialise in immigration law. They can provide advice, help you prepare a business proposal if one is required, and, if you wish, represent you in your dealings with CIC. You're not obliged to use a consultant, and applications handled by consultants don't receive preferential treatment – nor are they processed more quickly. If you appoint someone to be your actual immigration representative you must declare this in your application. The Canadian government recognises two types of immigration representatives: paid and unpaid. An unpaid representative is a person or organisation (relatives and friends included) who represents you without charging a fee. Since April 2004, paid representatives – those who collect money for their services – must be authorised. Authorisation is only available to members in good standing of a Canadian provincial or territorial law society, the Canadian Society of Immigration Consultants, or the Chambre des notaires du Québec. No company can guarantee that your application will be successful – you should be very wary of any company that makes such a claim. However, if business proposals are involved, time is an issue, or complications arise, immigration consultants and lawyers can be very helpful.

◼ Law societies

These regulatory organisations can help you find a lawyer or representative. If you are already using a paid representative, contact the relevant organisation to verify whether he or she is in good standing.

Canadian Society of Immigration Consultants: 1 416 572 2800 or 1 866 308 2742; information@csic-scci.ca; www.csic-scci.ca

Law Society of Alberta: 1 403 229 4700 or 1 800 661 9003; membership@lawsocietyalberta.com; www.lawsocietyalberta.com

Law Society of British Columbia: 1 604 669 2533 or 1 800 903 5300; memberinfo@lsbc.org; www.lawsociety.bc.ca

Law Society of Manitoba: 1 204 942 5571; admin@lawsociety.mb.ca; www.lawsociety.mb.ca

Law Society of New Brunswick: 1 506 458 8540; general@lawsociety-barreau.nb.ca; www.lawsociety-barreau.nb.ca

FACT

◼ You're not obliged to use an immigration consultant, and applications handled by consultants don't receive preferential treatment – nor are they processed more quickly.

QUEBEC: Your gateway to a new life

The following information, direct from Immigration Quebec, gives more detail on what types of immigrants Quebec is seeking, why moving to Quebec is an attractive option, and explains the five-step application process.

Quebec, a stimulating place to live, work, learn, and do business

Are you looking to make a fresh start and settle somewhere that is recognised for its quality of life? Do you want to belong to an open and dynamic society?

Quebec welcomes immigrants from all over the world with their know-how, skill, culture and religion. For their part, immigrants must adapt to their new environment to participate fully in Quebec society. They must be ready to discover and respect the fundamental values of their host society.

Quebec is a North American society that lives in French. It boasts a safe environment, a modern education system and quality health services. In Quebec, education in the public system is free at the elementary, high school and college levels.

Quebec, a francophone space in North America

Québec enjoys a dynamic economy with free access to the vast market of its most important trading partner – the United States. In addition, NAFTA, the Free Trade Agreement between Canada, the United States and Mexico, has intensified trade within North America.

Montreal, the economic capital, with a population of 3.64 million, is proud of its multicultural society on the cutting edge of science, technology and the arts. A hub of the knowledge economy, it is also a world leader in the aerospace, life sciences, and information and communications technology sectors.

Quebec's various regions offer interesting and varied job prospects, a welcoming living environment and comprehensive health and education services.

French, the official language and the main common language of Quebecers, is also the language of employment, trade and business. Knowledge of French is therefore essential. In some sectors, knowledge of English is an important asset for certain jobs, particularly in the Montreal area.

Quebec, a society that openly embraces initiative and creativity

Do you have a university, technical or vocational degree? Quebec is seeking skilled workers who are ready to meet new challenges.

Provided by expert contributor

Quebec's job market, particularly its growing sectors, is looking for skilled workers with technical or university training. It is dynamic and rewards people who show initiative and imagination. This often requires refresher training in order to fulfil the requirements of the job market and, for some professions and trades, membership in a professional order or other regulatory bodies. Continuing education programmes within the Québec education system offer professional development courses.

Quebec's main selection criteria

The immigration candidates sought are evaluated in terms of their training, work experience, age, knowledge of French and English and their capacity for socioeconomic adaptation.

Quebec offers the possibility of a fresh start!

A five-step procedure

1. Evaluate online your chances of being selected by Québec. The answer is immediate and free of charge. Simply complete the Preliminary Evaluation for Immigration (PEI) available at www.immigration-quebec.gouv.qc.ca/en

2. If your evaluation is positive, print the Application for a Selection Certificate directly from the site. Complete it and return it with the required supporting documentation and payment of the file processing fees.

3. You may be called in for an interview or selected simply on the basis of your file. If the review of your file is conclusive, you will receive a Québec Selection Certificate (CSQ).

4. Once you have been selected by Québec, you must transmit your file to the Canadian Embassy in Paris, France. The Government of Canada will evaluate your medical file and those of any accompanying family members. A security check will be conducted for each person. If you successfully pass this stage, the Government of Canada will issue a permanent resident visa.

5. Take advantage of the waiting period for the permanent resident visa to start preparing for your new life in Québec. Learn more about subjects that affect you directly: the Québec job market and how to find a job, conditions for admission to professional associations and how to find accommodation. For more information, visit www.immigration-quebec.gouv.qc.ca/en

Provided by expert contributor

Your gateway to a **new life**

www.immigration-quebec.gouv.qc.ca/en
The official Québec government Website

Québec 🏵

Law Society of Newfoundland and Labrador: 1 709 722 4740; janice.whitman@lawsociety.nf.ca; www.lawsociety.nf.ca
Law Society of the Northwest Territories: 1 867 873 3828; LSNT@TheEdge.ca; www.lawsociety.nt.ca
Nova Scotia Barristers' Society: 1 902 422 1491; info@nsbs.org; www.nsbs.ns.ca
Law Society of Nunavut: 1 867 979 2330; lawsoc@nunanet.com; www.lawsociety.nu.ca
Law Society of Prince Edward Island: 1 902 566 1666; jwyatt@lspei.pe.ca; www.lspei.pe.ca
Barreau du Québec: 1 514 954 3400 or 1 800 361 8495; infos@barreau.qc.ca; www.barreau.qc.ca
Chambre des notaires du Québec: 1 514 879 1793 or 1 800 668 2473; admin@cdnq.org; www.trouverunnotaire.com (French only)
Law Society of Saskatchewan: 1 306 569 8242 or 1 800 667 9886; reception@lawsociety.sk.ca; www.lawsociety.sk.ca
Law Society of Upper Canada (Toronto): 1 416 947 3300 or 1 800 668 7380; lawsociety@lsuc.on.ca; www.lsuc.on.ca
Law Society of Yukon: 1 867 668 4231; lsy@yknet.yk.ca; www.lawsocietyyukon.com

Temporary residents

Temporary work permits

A temporary work permit is exactly what it implies – a permit that allows you to work in Canada on a temporary basis. It is normally a closed permit, meaning it allows you to come to Canada to take a specified job with a specified employer, and it is for a finite period of time (determined by the employer, within certain limits), though extensions may be possible. Your prospective employer applies to hire you on a temporary basis by submitting a request for a Labour Market Opinion (LMO) to Service Canada, part of Human Resources and Social Development Canada (HRSDC). The LMO application must demonstrate that employing you will benefit the labour market, that the job cannot be filled by a Canadian resident, and that reasonable efforts were made to recruit or train Canadians for the position (requirements that can be difficult to meet). Many LMO applications are processed in four to five weeks, but some take much longer. If the request is approved, your prospective employer will send you a copy of the confirmation letter to include with your temporary work permit application. (If you are being hired for a highly skilled position, your employer may be able to request that the LMO and temporary work permit applications be processed concurrently, to speed up processing.) To work temporarily in Quebec you also need to obtain a certificate of acceptance from the province – the certificat d'acceptation du Québec (CAQ).

 Visit Human Resources and Social Development Canada (HRSDC) online at www.hrsdc.gc.ca. Service Canada is at www.servicecanada.gc.ca, or you can phone 1 800 622 6232 within Canada or go to www.servicecanada.gc.ca/en/common/contactus/phone.shtml for international toll-free numbers.

The fee to apply for a work permit is $150. You usually have to apply from outside Canada, but some exceptions do apply, such as if you already hold a valid work or study permit. Also, certain occupations are exempt from the LMO process, or don't require work permits – performing artists, business visitors and public speakers may fall into this category. The CIC website provides further details of exceptions and exemptions.

If you have a temporary work permit for a skilled occupation – one listed under skill type O or skill level A or B in the National Occupational Classification (see p. 47) – and you're authorised to work in Canada for at least six months, your spouse or common-law partner is eligible to apply for an open work permit, which allows him or her to work in any job with any employer without having to go through the LMO process. The validity of this permit will be the same as that of your temporary work permit, and a satisfactory medical examination may be a prerequisite. See the CIC webpage, www. cic.gc.ca/english/information/faq/work/work-faq08.asp for further details.

 CIC's quick reference guide for temporary foreign workers can be downloaded at www.cic.gc.ca/ENGLISH/resources/manuals/fw/index.asp.

Working holiday and work exchange programmes

Working holiday and international work exchange programmes – sometimes called 'work abroad' or 'youth mobility' programmes – are available to students and young workers from many countries around the world. These allow you to work and travel temporarily in Canada, and are a great opportunity to experience a different culture for anything from a few weeks to a couple of years. Countries with working holiday programmes for Canada include (among others) the UK, Ireland, Australia, New Zealand, Germany, France, Italy, Finland, Sweden, Denmark, Austria, Belgium, Switzerland, the Netherlands, Sweden, the Ukraine, Korea, Japan, South Africa, and the USA. Most require you to be aged between 18 and 30, though some set the limit at 35. Most also limit the number of places each year, so it's important to apply early. Duration, work restrictions, eligibility requirements, and fees differ considerably for each.

The website for the Canadian consulate, embassy or high commission in your region should give details of the programmes offered for your country (though this information is not always straightforward to find), as well as links to the organisations overseeing them if they're not administered directly through the government office. Depending on the options available to your country you may be required to apply through a specific programme, or you may have a choice between a work exchange programme and a working holiday programme. Working holiday programmes usually just process your visa; work exchanges provide you with support services in Canada. Some programmes are basically 'add-on' services built around a working holiday permit, and can cost significantly more than the permit alone. The UK offers student, non-student and employer-specific work abroad programmes, which are arranged by the British Universities North America Club (BUNAC) or directly through the High Commission in London. Ireland's programmes are operated by USIT. BUNAC also operates a six-month programme for students from the USA in conjunction with Canada's SWAP Working Holidays, and various work exchange programmes for Australians and New Zealanders through International Exchange Programs (IEP). (Links to other international affiliates can be found at www.bunac.org.) The SWAP exchange programme caters to applicants from many countries. For details and contacts visit www.swap.ca. Some travel agencies also have arrangements with these organisations and offer packages for working abroad. The World Youth Student and Educational Travel Confederation, which promotes international work exchanges, study, and travel through its WYSE Work Abroad Association, provides information on different types of programmes for young people. A list of association members and their programmes, searchable by country, is available on the website.

> *i* To find the Canadian consulate, embassy or High Commission in your region, visit the Foreign Affairs and International Trade Canada website at www. international.gc.ca and go to *Canadian Offices Abroad.*

◼ Useful contacts for working holidays and exchanges

BUNAC: www.bunac.org
BUNAC UK: 020 7251 3472 (UK); enquiries@bunac.org.uk; www.bunac.org/uk
BUNAC USA: 203 264 0901 (USA); info@bunacusa.org; www.bunac.org/usa
USIT: 01 602 1906 (Ireland); canada@usit.ie; www.usit.ie
IEP Australia: 03 9329 3866 or 1300 300 912; info@iep.org.au; www.iep.org.au
IEP New Zealand: 09 366 6255 or 0800 443 769; info@iep.co.nz; www.iep.co.nz
SWAP Working Holidays: 1 416 646 7927; toronto@swap.ca (details are for Toronto SWAP; for Vancouver, Montreal or Calgary contacts, visit website)
WYSE Work Abroad: 20 4212800 (Netherlands); mailbox@wyseworkabroad.org; www.wyseworkabroad.org
ASSE International Student Exchange Programs: Exchange programmes for secondary school students worldwide. Main website www.asse.com.
ASSE Canada: 1 204 376 3625 or 1 800 361 3214; assecanada@asse.com

◼ Work-abroad programmes for students with specific interests

International Association for the Exchange of Students for Technical Experience: info@iaeste.org; www.iaeste.org (visit website for country-specific contact details)
Association for International Practical Training: 410 997 2200 (USA); aipt@aipt. org; www.aipt.org

> **TIP**
>
> ◼ Most working holiday programmes limit the number of places each year, so it's important to apply early.

> " There were several forms to complete and documents to provide in support of our application, and once lodged, it was simply a waiting game to see if we had been lucky enough to secure places in the limited quota for that year.
> **Andrea Crengle** "

> " **Christina Chiam talks about her experience of coming to Canada through Australia's Working Holiday Program:**
>
> Initially, I moved to Canada on a one-year working holiday permit, which allows you to work in most sectors without additional approval – this made it straightforward for me to find employment in the arts. The Australian and Canadian governments have since changed the terms of the visa, which allowed me to apply for a second permit for another two years. The immigration process was very straightforward. I had to submit an online application form and send the Canadian Consulate a processing fee and passport photos. They say the process can take up to six to eight weeks but I received both my permits within a month of applying. As yet, I don't intend to change my status to anything more permanent, but from what I've heard, the process for obtaining permanent residency is quite expensive and involved. "

Students

In most cases, if you're coming to Canada to study and taking a course that lasts longer than six months, you need a study permit. In order to get one, you have to be formally accepted into a school, college or university, have a clean criminal record, be in good health, and have adequate finances to support yourself (and any family members who come with you), pay your fees, and get home afterwards. If you're coming alone, you'll need funds of about $10,000 per year on top of your tuition fees. The fee for the study permit is $125. Depending on the visa office processing your application, the permit may take a month or more to be issued. Even if you aren't required to have a study permit, it's a good idea to apply for one. That way, if you decide you want to take another course later, you can apply to renew your permit without having to leave Canada. It also means you can legally work part-time on campus, provided you're a full-time student at an approved institution.

There are various options for foreign students who also wish to work. Finding employment on campus is one. Three other student work programmes are available, all of which require specific work permits: the Off-Campus Work Permit Program allows certain full-time students to work off campus while studying; the Co-op Work Program allows you to gain work experience when this is a required part of your study programme; and the Post-Graduation Employment Program enables graduating students to work for up to three years to gain Canadian experience. Restrictions and eligibility criteria apply to all student work permits (see www.cic.gc.ca/english/study/work.asp for further information).

Education in Canada is regulated at the provincial or territorial level, so the institution you plan to attend will be able to give you details about the living expenses and healthcare costs in that territory or province – medical costs aren't necessarily covered for students (see p. 177). As with other immigration categories, if you want to study in Quebec you need a certificate of acceptance from the province (see p. 56 for MICC contact details). If you're a minor (either under 18 or under 19, depending on the province) and are coming to study in Canada without a parent or legal guardian, you must have an appointed custodian who is legally responsible for you in Canada.

 The CIC webpage at www.cic.gc.ca/english/study/schools.asp lists information and contacts to help you choose a school. Study in Canada, a federal government website at www.livelearnandsucceed.gc.ca, has information on all elements of coming to Canada as a foreign student.

If you'd rather study in Canada as part of a work abroad or student exchange programme, this can usually be arranged through your school or university in your home country, or through outside organisations (see p. 62 for more details).

Live-in Caregiver Program

In 2008, up to 9,000 people were admitted to Canada as live-in caregivers for children, elderly people or people with disabilities. Though these workers are initially granted entry on a temporary basis, the programme is structured so participants can go on to become permanent residents. If you want to work as a nanny or caregiver but have no intention of seeking permanent residence, you would normally come to Canada on a standard temporary work permit, or under a work exchange programme.

(If you do this, though, you're not considered part of the Live-in Caregiver Program, and therefore can't apply for permanent residence under its provisions if you change your mind later on.)

The process for being hired as a live-in caregiver is much the same as that for other temporary workers. A family or other employer who wishes to hire you must get job approval in the form of a positive Labour Market Opinion (LMO) in order to employ a foreigner (see p. 61). Employment can be arranged independently or through an agency such as those listed below. A signed contract with your prospective employer is mandatory. Requirements include completion of the equivalent of Canadian secondary school education, and at least six months' full-time training in the caregiving field, or at least one year of directly relevant, paid, full-time employment within the last three years (of which at least six continuous months must have been with the same employer). Good knowledge of either English or French is essential, as you will usually work unsupervised and must be able to read medication labels, communicate with people who call or visit the house, and respond to emergencies. You must live in the home of the person you are caring for, and conditions for quitting or changing your job (unless there is a situation of abuse) are strict – you can be removed from the programme if you live elsewhere, or if you work in any other job without a valid permit. Any new caregiving job requires its own positive LMO, contract and work permit, which must be arranged before your current permit expires. If you lose your job you may be eligible for Employment Insurance (EI) (see p. 193).

Live-in caregiver work permits are now valid for up to three years and three months, and can be extended if you have a renewed job offer and new contract from your employer. After two full years of full-time work you are eligible to apply for permanent residence. You and all your family members (even those not accompanying you) must pass a medical examination for residence to be granted. If it is, you can work in any field in Canada. (You can also apply for an open work permit at the time you apply for permanent resident status, to give you this flexibility sooner.) Processing fees are $150 for the live-in caregiver work permit, and $550 for the principal applicant if you apply for permanent residence (with the $490 Right of Permanent Residence fee also payable if you are approved.)

Domestic caregivers often work very hard and are poorly paid, but they are protected from exploitation by laws regulating minimum wages, overtime pay, days off, and vacation time. If you seek work as a caregiver via an agency, make sure they screen families and clients carefully – your job satisfaction may depend on it.

> The CIC webpage at www.cic.gc.ca/english/work/caregiver/arriving.asp lists the offices responsible for labour or employment standards in each province and territory, as well as caregiver associations that can help with any questions or concerns you may have in your job.

FACT

■ Though live-in caregivers are initially granted entry on a temporary basis, the programme is structured so participants can go on to become permanent residents.

■ Useful contacts

Family Caregiver International Services: 1 416 283 9127; info@familycaregiver.ca; www.familycaregiver.ca
Canadiannanny.ca (Canadian Sitter Incorporated): 1 905 465 2883 or 1 866 221 7918; info@canadiannanny.ca; www.canadiannanny.ca

Select Nannies Inc.: 1 905 327 4000 or 1 866 710 1287; info@selectnannies.ca; www.selectnannies.ca

The following associations have members worldwide and provide listings for a range of agencies in Canada that recruit nannies and homecare providers internationally.

International Nanny Association: 1 713 526 2670 or 1 888 878 1477; www.nanny.org

International Au Pair Association: 45 3317 0066 (Denmark); pb@iapa.org; www.iapa.org

Better Business Bureau: www.ccbbb.ca. (Contact details for bureau offices are available online.)

Free trade agreements

Canada is a partner in various free trade agreements, including the North American Free Trade Agreement (NAFTA), the Canada–Chile Free Trade Agreement (CCFTA) and the General Agreement on Trade in Services (GATS), all of which allow business people to temporarily enter the country for business purposes. The first, NAFTA, is outlined in some detail in the section below. It allows for the temporary entry of four categories of business people: business visitors, professionals, intra-company transferees, and traders and investors. The CCFTA follows the same structure, with some minor differences in the specifics of the business visitors and professionals categories. The GATS, which has 150 World Trade Organization members, also has similarities to NAFTA, but does not have the traders and investors category. It also has different – and far more limited – regulations for professionals (the maximum stay is 90 days within any 12-month period). Additional information on intra-company transferees can be found on p. 68. While these agreements don't have specific provisions allowing spouses or common-law partners to work in Canada unless they qualify separately, this may be possible under CIC's policy for skilled temporary foreign workers (see p. 50).

 Information on how these agreements affect business visitors can be found on the CIC webpage www.cic.gc.ca/english/work/special-business. asp. For full details on Canada's trade agreements, visit Foreign Affairs and International Trade Canada (FAITC) at www.international.gc.ca/trade-agreements-accords-commerciaux/agr-acc.

Regulations for US and Mexican business people

Under NAFTA, citizens of the USA and Mexico may be granted temporary entry to Canada for business purposes without having to obtain a Labour Market Opinion (LMO), provided they meet health and security requirements and the general provisions set by CIC on temporary entry. NAFTA is not for people who want to move to Canada or look for a job in Canada. Many people believe there are no restrictions on moving between Canada and the USA to work or live, but this is not the case. US citizens are subject to the same Canadian immigration requirements as citizens of any other country. However, NAFTA (and the advantageous proximity of the USA to Canada) may help streamline the immigration process in some instances.

(An immigration newsletter available at www.mccrealaw.ca/law/news_4.htm – though not official documentation – provides some useful examples.) If you enter Canada through NAFTA provisions, you can bring your spouse and children: as mentioned above, they can't normally work in Canada unless they qualify independently under NAFTA or other exemptions, or go through the standard immigration process for temporary foreign workers. However, check p. 50 to see whether the skilled temporary foreign worker policy applies to your situation.

If your spouse or children plan to study in Canada they need student authorisations – it's best to apply for these in advance. Publications related to NAFTA can be ordered from any of the three governments involved, or from Foreign Affairs and International Trade Canada (FAITC). FAITC also provides an informative document, *Cross Border Movement of Business Persons*, online at www.international. gc.ca/trade-agreements-accords-commerciaux/agr-acc/nafta-alena/cross. Though aimed at Canadians travelling to the United States or Mexico, it's highly relevant for those coming into Canada as well. If you're planning to travel under NAFTA, it's a good idea to contact the port of entry where you'll be crossing the border, to confirm that you have all required documentation. Each category has different rules governing how you apply and how long you can stay. To qualify, you must meet the following conditions:

■ You must be a US or Mexican citizen (not just a permanent resident).

■ You must be seeking temporary entry only – you cannot gain permanent residence through a NAFTA visa.

■ You must meet the universal security and health requirements that apply to all temporary visitors to Canada.

■ You must qualify under one of four categories of business people (described below).

■ Business visitors

Business visitors do not require a work permit. A business visitor practises one of the following activities on behalf of a US or Mexican company: research and design; growth, manufacture and production; marketing; sales; distribution; after-sales service; or general service. You would be in this category if you were doing a research project, attending a trade fair, selling goods or services (non-Canadian only) to Canadians or setting up and servicing a computer system sold by your company to a Canadian company (note that after-sales personnel have to meet additional requirements). Your principal place of business must be the USA or Mexico. You should apply at the border (port of entry), and bring a letter from your employer stating the purpose of your visit. The letter should also state that the business's main activities and remuneration (i.e. profits) are outside Canada. You'll usually get access for six months.

■ Professionals

If your job classification has well-established education and certification standards, and you're seeking entry with the intention of working at a professional level, you're likely to fit this category. Examples include accountants, registered nurses, librarians, lawyers, and university professors. Employment authorisation is required, but unlike traditional immigration procedures, your employer doesn't have to prove that no Canadian could do the job. You can enter Canada as a professional if you have a pre-arranged job with a Canadian company. An example would be a CEO hired to run

FACT

■ Many people believe there are no restrictions on moving between Canada and the USA to work or live, but this is not the case. US citizens are subject to the same Canadian immigration requirements as citizens of any other country.

a Canadian company or a doctor doing a residency at a Canadian hospital. You can either complete your application for employment authorisation at a port of entry, or apply at a Canadian consulate or embassy in the USA, Mexico or elsewhere before you depart for Canada. In either case, you must present a letter from your employer and proof of your qualifications for the job. Authorisation granted at the time of entry is valid for one year, but you can apply for yearly extensions for as long as your work in Canada retains its 'temporary' nature.

■ Intra-company transferees

This category includes people transferred temporarily to the Canadian operations of an international company. You can apply at the port of entry or in advance at a Canadian consulate or embassy. You must present a letter from your US or Mexican employer confirming that you've worked for them for at least one year within the past three, and outlining the work you'll be performing and your qualifications for the job. This category would include a US executive sent to oversee a Canadian office, or a scientist with specialised knowledge going to a company lab in Canada. Managerial and executive transferees can stay for a maximum of seven years; transferees with specialised knowledge have up to five. Employment authorisations issued at the time of entry allow a maximum of three years but may be extended in two-year increments.

■ Traders and investors

Traders and investors either carry on substantial trade of goods and services between Canada and the United States or Mexico, or establish and invest in a business in Canada. You can be trading on your own behalf or on behalf of a company. You need to apply for employment authorisation at a Canadian consulate or embassy before you leave for Canada, and provide evidence of your proposed investment or details of your trading plans. You can only be admitted as either a trader or an investor, not both. There's no time limit on your stay in Canada, though your initial employment authorisation is for a maximum of one year, and can then be renewed in two-year increments.

■ Useful contacts:

Foreign Affairs and International Trade Canada: (Enquiries service): 1 613 944 4000 or 1 800 267 8376; enqserv@international.gc.ca; www.international.gc.ca

NAFTA Secretariat: www.nafta-sec-alena.org. 1 613 992 9388 (Canada); canada@nafta-sec-alena.orgweb. 202 482 5438 (USA); usa@nafta-sec-alena.org. 55 5629 9630 (Mexico); mexico@nafta-sec-alena.org

Canadian Embassy in the United States: 501 Pennsylvania Avenue NW, Washington DC 20001; 202 682 1740; www.canadianembassy.org

Canadian Embassy in Mexico: Schiller 529, Col. Polanco, 11560 México, DF; 55 5724 7900; www.dfait-maeci.gc.ca/mexico-city

The Embassy of the United States of America in Canada: 490 Sussex Drive, Ottawa, Ontario K1N 1G8; 1 613 688 5335; web1@ottawa.usembassy.gov; http://ottawa.usembassy.gov

Embassy of Mexico in Canada: 45 O'Connor St. Suite 1000, Ottawa, Ontario K1P 1A4 1 613 233 8988; info@embamexcan.com; www.sre.gob.mx/canada (English website available)

Becoming a Canadian citizen

Permanent residents have the same right to work as Canadian citizens and can make use of most social services, though they cannot stand for office, vote in Canadian elections or work in certain high-security positions (such as some federal government roles). A permanent resident qualifies to apply for Canadian citizenship after spending three of the preceding four years (1,095 days) in Canada, though children are exempt from this requirement. Canada permits dual citizenship, as do many other countries including the USA (with some limitations), the UK, Ireland, New Zealand and, since 2002, Australia, so it may be possible to become a Canadian citizen without losing your existing citizenship. To become a citizen, you must complete an application, pay a fee of $200 for processing and 'right of citizenship' ($100 for children under 18), and take a citizenship test. In most cases the test is written, but you may be asked to take an oral test instead (which takes the form of an interview with a citizenship judge). Only people aged 18–54 have to take the test. You are assessed on your knowledge of Canadian history, politics, and geography, and on whether you understand the rights and responsibilities of a Canadian citizen. Questions are based on information in a booklet provided by CIC when you first apply. You also need to show that you have language abilities in either English or French. If you fail the written test, you're given the opportunity to go for an interview and take the test orally instead.

Approved applicants aged 14 or over have to attend a public ceremony where they take the oath of citizenship and receive their certificates of citizenship. While citizenship doesn't confer substantial benefits or rights denied to permanent residents, many immigrants eventually do become Canadian citizens. Love of their adopted country, the desire to vote or obtain a passport, or simply the wish to give customs and immigration officials less reason to delay them at the US–Canada border, leads immigrants to seek Canadian citizenship.

New citizenship rules will come into effect on 17 April 2009. These are primarily to do with restoring citizenship to certain people who lost it due to previous laws, and to restricting citizenship for children born abroad to Canadians who were also born abroad. They are not likely to directly affect the majority of immigrants.

 For more information on citizenship processes and regulations, visit the CIC website at www.cic.gc.ca or phone the CIC Call Centre from within Canada on 1 888 242 2100.

> As soon as I could I became a Canadian citizen, and my Australian citizenship was eliminated. We had burnt our boats; there was no returning.
> **Gerald Garnett**

FACT

▪ Canada permits dual citizenship, as do many other countries including the USA, the UK, Ireland, New Zealand, and Australia, so it may be possible to become a Canadian citizen without losing your existing citizenship.

▪ LANGUAGE

Languages spoken in Canada

Canada has two official languages, English and French, though according to the 2006 census only 17.4% of Canadians are bilingual. There is essentially a geographic divide between francophones and anglophones, with French predominating only in the province of Quebec. Quebec does have English-speaking communities in areas such as Montreal, the Eastern Townships, the Gaspé region, and the Ottawa Valley.

Product labels and many signs are displayed in both English and French

If you wish to immigrate to the province, though, you're expected to be able to speak some French already, or to be willing to learn it in order to make the move. Children of immigrants are generally required to attend French schools, and most business affairs are conducted in French. Francophones make up 80% of Quebec's population, with New Brunswick, the only officially bilingual province, following with 33%. Ontario is home to half a million francophones – more than twice as many as New Brunswick – but these make up a much smaller proportion of the province's overall population. Many other provinces and territories, including Nova Scotia, Manitoba, Saskatchewan, Alberta, and BC, have notable communities of French speakers, but these represent relatively few of the nation's 6.9 million francophones. Few Canadians would argue against bilingualism, but some have strong political or ethnic prejudices against those who don't speak their own mother tongue. This attitude has only been worsened by the ongoing tension between Quebec and the rest of Canada.

For those contemplating the move to Canada, there are a few facts to consider from a language perspective. First, the current immigration system gives preference to those who speak either English or French. Independent applicants are granted up to 16 points in the language category of the points system if fluent in one of these languages. Bilingual applicants do have a clear advantage here in terms of points, as the full 24 points can only be scored by those fluent in both English and French.

FACT

Francophones make up 80% of Quebec's population, with New Brunswick, the only officially bilingual province, following with 33%.

PARLEZ-VOUS QUÉBÉCOIS?

The French spoken in Canada is a little different to that heard in France (particularly in Paris) or taught in most classrooms. *Québécois*, the French language of Quebec, can require some adjustment on the part of newcomers. The colloquial variant, *joual*, is heard mostly in Montreal: slang, commercial terms and Anglicisms abound, with English words frequently adopted and conjugated as French verbs. Among English-speaking Canadians, *Québécois* is best known for two things: its unique collection of powerful, religious-based swear words (a product of the province's repressive Catholic past), of which *tabernac* is the most quoted example; and *poutine*. The latter refers to a strangely alluring, heart-attack-in-a-bowl concoction of fries, squeaky-textured cheese curds and gravy, which has made its way – generally in poorer form – into restaurants and diners around the country, and even onto fast-food menus. Regional French dialects exist as well – particularly in northern Quebec where the English influence is less, and in the northeast of bilingual New Brunswick, where the early French settlers known as Acadians sent the language in a different direction.

Provided you have sufficient points in other areas, though, knowing only one of the official languages is not a bar to immigrating.

Secondly, knowing both languages can be an advantage in terms of finding a job. Many government and public sector jobs across Canada require employees to be bilingual, and some companies – both public and private – have preferential hiring or promotion policies for those who speak both languages. This is more important in the city of Ottawa in Ontario (where the federal government is a major employer) and in New Brunswick, and tends to be less of a factor in the western parts of the country. Therefore, while French isn't essential outside Quebec, if you have the time and inclination to improve your French language skills you may find it opens doors. Even if your fluency isn't enough to impress a prospective employer, you'll be able to visit Quebec and enjoy its considerable charms with more confidence. From a more cultural perspective, some anglophone Canadians choose to learn French on principle, or as a show of support for Canada's bilingual heritage.

Language study

The Canadian government offers free basic language training in French and English to adult permanent residents, through its Language Instruction for Newcomers to Canada (LINC) Program. In Quebec, various French courses are available free of

TRUNKS IN THE BOOT, OR BOOTS IN THE TRUNK?

Canadian English has its own charms and peculiarities. Most notable (and most stereotyped) is the elusive, almost indefinable *eh?* Not quite question, not quite statement, it finishes sentences, can't be faked (not well, anyway) and will pinpoint a Canadian in a line-up. Many Canadian words are variations on an international theme: cars have trunks, not boots; people wear sweaters, not jumpers; a woollen hat is not a beanie, but a tuque (it rhymes with juke); and if you need a toilet you ask for the washroom, not the bathroom. Others – gas station, law enforcement – most likely migrated from the States. Accents and lexicons shift around the country, with Newfoundland's English–Irish-descended dialects and extensive slang the most distinctive regional example. And of course there's the unmistakable 'uwt' in *out and about* – Canadians may deny it, but they say it, and it's one of the defining differences between their own accents and those of their US neighbours.

FACT

 The Canadian government offers free basic language training in French and English to adult permanent residents, through its Language Instruction for Newcomers to Canada (LINC) Program.

charge, with the Ministère de l'Immigration et des Communautés culturelles (MICC) providing financial assistance if you meet certain conditions. Most local libraries have books, audiobooks or interactive CD-ROMs designed to help you learn French. The well-reviewed CD language course *Behind the Wheel French* by Mark Frobose teaches the spoken language and is ideal for commuters, while Living Language's *Ultimate French* includes CDs and a textbook. Both options – and a huge array of others – are available from online retailers. Audiobooks or CD-ROM kits for French study can also be found at most large bookshops, and online or downloadable options also exist.

Part-time or short courses are offered at many tertiary institutes or colleges, as well as from language organisations such as the highly regarded Alliance Française, which has branches in most major centres. Private language schools across Canada are another option, with a range of course lengths, difficulties and levels of immersion available.

i For information on LINC, visit the CIC webpage at www.cic.gc.ca/english/resources/publications/welcome/wel-22e.asp. To find out about learning French in Quebec, contact the MICC (see p. 56 for contact details) or visit www.immigration-quebec.gouv.qc.ca/en/french-language/learning-quebec

◼ BANKING

Banking in Canada is reliable and convenient, though there are fees for everything from withdrawals to money transfers to monthly account keeping. Canada is somewhat behind Australia, Europe, and the UK in the use of electronic banking: debit or 'Interac' cards were only widely introduced in 1994, and paper cheques are still relatively common for paying utility bills and rent. To cash most cheques, you'll need to open a bank account. However, the majority of people have their salaries paid directly into their accounts, and it's now possible to do virtually all banking online. There are 73 banks currently operating in Canada, of which 20 are domestic, and the six largest account for over 90% of the Canadian banking sector's total assets. (These are listed on p. 78 under *Major banks*, along with Canadian Western Bank, the largest domestic bank in Western Canada.) Many European, Asian, and American banks are represented in Canada, but they usually deal with commercial clients only.

 The Financial Consumer Agency of Canada provides simple, helpful guides on various aspects of banking in Canada. See the boxed text on p. 143 for detailed information or visit www.fcac-acfc.gc.ca.

> A key difference I've noticed here is that Canadians still use cheques, which have pretty much been out of commission in Australia for some time!
> **Christina Chiam**

How to open an account

There are a wide variety of banks and financial institutions to choose from in Canada, but the services they offer are much the same. When deciding on a bank, consider

MONEY, MONEY, MONEY

The Canadian dollar is made up of 100 cents. The smaller coins are pennies (1 cent), nickels (5 cents), dimes (10 cents), and quarters (25 cents). The $1 coin depicts an aquatic bird called a loon, and is commonly referred to as the 'loonie'. The $2 coin, introduced in 1996, was immediately dubbed the 'toonie'. Paper bank notes come in $5, $10, $20, $50, and $100 denominations. Once upon a time there were also $500 notes and – up until the year 2000 – $1000 notes. The current bank notes are known as the 'Canadian Journey' series. Before them were the 'Birds of Canada'; these in turn took over from the 'Scenes of Canada' notes, in which portraits of former prime ministers usurped the Queen's position on some denominations. Counterfeiting has been a problem in recent years, and the newest designs have advanced anti-forgery features. Many businesses still refuse to accept the older $50 or $100 bank notes.

Canadian banknotes and coins

whether branches are convenient to your home and place of work, and what their opening hours are. Canadians, like most people, are usually dissatisfied with their bank, so if someone you trust actually recommends one you may want to heed their advice. Anyone can open an account – you don't need to be employed to do so, and no minimum deposit has to be made. Two pieces of identification (originals, not photocopies) are usually required, such as a passport, immigration papers, a driver's licence issued in Canada, or a Social Insurance Number (SIN). Full lists of acceptable ID are available on each bank's website or from branches. Some banks allow you to complete some of the application process online, but it's usually simplest – particularly for new arrivals – just to go into a branch to open an account. How long this takes depends on the complexity of your account requirements and how busy the branch is, but it's usually under an hour. Your debit card (the same as a handycard or access card) is given to you on the spot, and you'll normally be supplied with a sheet of complimentary cheques (even if you don't have a chequebook connected to your account) or a temporary chequebook. Your account can also be set up for online and telephone banking, which is particularly convenient if you won't normally be able to make it to a branch during working hours.

If necessary, you may be able to open an account in Canada before you leave your home country. Some Canadian banks allow this, such as BMO and RBC, and provide online instructions (see p. 78 for website details). If a Canadian bank has

A local branch of the Canada-wide TD Canada Trust, one of the country's largest retail banks

branches in your country, or your current bank has branches in Canada, it may be possible to set up a Canadian account through them.

Banking procedures

Types of accounts

There are two basic types of bank account: general transaction accounts, known as chequing accounts (though they may or may not include a chequing facility), and savings accounts. Chequing accounts are used for daily banking needs, such as

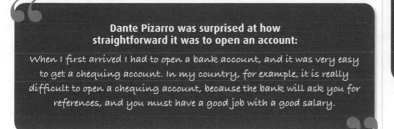

Dante Pizarro was surprised at how straightforward it was to open an account:

When I first arrived I had to open a bank account, and it was very easy to get a chequing account. In my country, for example, it is really difficult to open a chequing account, because the bank will ask you for references, and you must have a good job with a good salary.

We were incredibly lucky in that my company helped with many things, especially with an introduction to the bank (RBC). Even so, getting store cards was hard. We knew we'd finally made it when we were given a Sears card!
Steven Maine

depositing and withdrawing money or paying bills, and generally don't pay interest. Savings accounts are designed to help you build up your funds. They usually pay interest of between 0.5% and 2.5% depending on your account type and balance, but you pay higher fees if you need to make withdrawals or other transactions. Look at the range of accounts offered by each bank to find one that best suits your needs. Consider how many transactions you'll make each month, whether you'll be needing to write cheques, and what your lowest monthly balance is likely to be – your choice of account, and the monthly fees you'll pay, will correspond directly to these factors. In many cases the monthly fee is waived if a minimum balance is maintained throughout the month. Other services can be added to your account, such as overdraft protection. Many banks also offer high-interest, monthly-fee-free 'virtual' savings accounts that link to your main account. You can transfer funds to and from these free of charge using internet or telephone banking, but fees generally apply for other transactions.

Internet and telephone banking

Convenience, efficiency, and 24-hour availability are the main attractions of banking online or by telephone. You can set up access to these facilities when you open your account. Both use a log-in number – usually the number on your access card – and a password or PIN for security purposes. They allow you to carry out most banking procedures (with the exception of withdrawing cash) without going to a branch or ATM, including funds transfers, bill payments and account balance enquiries. Telephone banking works through an automated system. Internet banking enables you to track your spending by viewing a detailed payment record online. You can also choose to receive your bank statements online rather than on paper.

ATMs (automated teller machines)

ATMs are available in most parts of Canada. Allowing for some regional variation, ATMs for the major banks can be found in most towns and commercial centres. Many gas stations and convenience stores also have bank machines, though these are generally third-party owned. Depending on your account limitations you can make a certain number of monthly withdrawals from your own bank's ATMs without being charged. For any additional withdrawals you will be charged a fee. Most ATMs in Canada are connected to other systems via the Interac network (and outside Canada through the PLUS and CIRRUS networks), which allows you to withdraw money from a machine belonging to another bank – but expect to pay a fee of $1.50 or more each time.

If you have an access card for a foreign bank account you can usually withdraw funds from a machine in Canada. Some fee for currency conversion will apply, and this can be substantial if you withdraw large amounts. High fees charged by the foreign bank – usually in the range of $5 per withdrawal – add to your costs and make it an uneconomical solution in the longer term. (The Canadian ATM may also levy a service charge.) It's worth finding out whether your home bank – or other banks in your home country – have reciprocal agreements with any Canadian banks. Scotiabank, for example, has such an arrangement with Westpac Bank in Australia. Although this won't allow you to use the Canadian 'partner' as your own bank, you may be able to make withdrawals from their ATMs without incurring hefty withdrawal fees (though conversion fees will most likely still apply). Many supermarkets, drugstores and other stores also allow you to withdraw cash when you make a purchase using your debit card.

Paying bills

Most bills can be paid from your account using internet or telephone banking or an ATM, or by going into a branch. Direct debit or pre-authorised payment plans can also be set up with companies you receive regular bills from, so that payments are made automatically. Automated electronic payment facilities are now common at retail outlets, and many utility bills can be paid at Canada Post outlets, online on the biller's website, or by posting a cheque. Instructions and detailed payment options are usually outlined on the bill itself. Cheques are generally not accepted for general purchases in stores (cash, Interac or a credit card would normally be used), but many organisations still allow them for paying bills and rent. If you maintain a fairly low account balance you might want to add overdraft protection to your bank account – this is not automatic, and fees can be nasty if you overdraw your account or bounce a cheque.

TIP

◼ Cheques are generally not accepted for general purchases in stores (cash, Interac or a credit card would normally be used), but many organisations still allow them for paying bills and rent.

THE TROUBLE WITH CREDIT CARDS

When you move to a new country, your credit record may not move with you. Many immigrants, even those from the USA, will have difficulty getting a Canadian credit card until they establish a new credit record in Canada. If you are in the country on a temporary or open work permit (such as a working holiday permit) you may have additional trouble. Most banks will allow you to set up a credit card if an amount equal to the card's limit is paid up front as security. This is held by the bank, and you can apply to have it returned once your credit record is established (though this can take a year or more). There are several other ways around the problem:

◼ Ask your home bank to transfer your credit card to a Canadian bank.

◼ Ask a Canadian bank if you can set up a credit card account that uses your savings account as collateral.

◼ Ask a Canadian bank if you can set up a credit card with a very low limit (for example, $500) in order to build a credit record. Apply later to have this limit increased.

◼ Apply for a credit card with an organisation such as President's Choice Financial or a store such as Canadian Tire, which may not have such stringent conditions.

◼ Sign up for newspapers, magazines and frequent-flyer programmes, and wait for the credit card offers to start rolling in.

> My bank account was simple to set up, but credit cards aren't easily issued to those on working holiday permits.
> **Christina Chiam**

Transferring money overseas

There are no foreign exchange controls in Canada. You can send money internationally using an online or wire transfer, bank draft or certified cheque. Fees apply to each of these services and vary considerably, from around $7.50 for an international bank draft to $30 or more to send money by wire transfer (receiving wired funds usually costs around $10). Fees also vary between banks, so check online or with a branch for details.

◣ Major banks

BMO Bank of Montreal: 1 416 286 9992 or 1 877 225 5266; www.bmo.com
Canadian Western Bank: 1 780 423 8888; www.cwbank.com
CIBC Canadian Imperial Bank of Commerce: 1 902 420 2422, 1 800 465 2422 or 1 800 872 2422 (international toll free, select countries); www.cibc.com
HSBC Bank Canada: 1 888 310 4722 (for international numbers see website); www.hsbc.ca
National Bank of Canada: 1 514 394 5555 or 1 888 483 5628; www.nbc.ca
RBC Royal Bank: 1 800 769 2511 or 1 506 864 2275 (international collect); www.royalbank.com
Scotiabank (The Bank of Nova Scotia): 1 416 701 7200 or 1 800 472 6842; www.scotiabank.com
TD Bank Financial Group (TD Canada Trust): 1 866 222 3456 or 1 800 222 3456 (international); www.tdcanadatrust.com

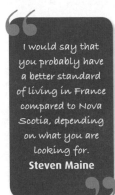

> ❝ I would say that you probably have a better standard of living in France compared to Nova Scotia, depending on what you are looking for.
> **Steven Maine** ❞

> ❝ The standard and cost of living seems to me to be slightly better than Australia or England. Mind you, houses have to be built more robustly to withstand the climate.
> **Gerald Garnett** ❞

◼ COST OF LIVING

On a global scale, living in Canada is considered to be relatively affordable, with a low inflation rate a key factor. Even Toronto, Canada's most expensive city, comes in well below London, Hong Kong, Singapore, and Sydney in terms of pressure on the wallet. The cost of living varies depending on which part of Canada you settle in, and whether you're based in a city or a rural area. It's also affected by the size of your family, your lifestyle, where you shop, and whether or not you own a car. As a general rule, over half your after-tax income (and sometimes much more) will go towards household expenses, including rent or mortgage payments, utilities, food, clothing, transportation (car, bicycle or public transit), communications (telephone and internet), and insurance of various types such as home and contents, health, and car (which is required by law). You also need to budget for other significant but less frequent expenses, such as medical bills, school fees, and car or home repairs. For immigrants and travellers, visiting or staying in touch with those at home often represents additional costs.

BASIC COSTS	
Dinner for two	$40–$60
Lunch for two	$20–$40
Cinema ticket	$11
Single journey on public transit	$2.75

Local phone call (from public phone)	$0.50
Cup of coffee	$1.50
Pint of beer	$5.00
Loaf of bread	$2.50
Litre of milk	$2.10
Litre of gas (petrol)	$1.05
Load of washing at laundromat	$1.75
Haircut	$20–$60

Your income will be the primary factor in determining how you can live. There are a number of ways in which you can keep living costs down, such as finding a home on the outskirts of the city or in a less expensive neighbourhood, using public transit rather than a car, and shopping at markets and discount department stores. Community and thrift stores sell used clothing and furniture at very low cost, and eating at home, rather than at restaurants, can mean substantial savings. Organisations that provide settlement services can help you find affordable housing and living options when you arrive.

 The Going to Canada website at www.goingtocanada.gc.ca has a useful outline of living costs. Select *Move to Canada* for the link. For details of immigrant-serving organisations across Canada see the CIC webpage www.cic.gc.ca/english/resources/publications/welcome/wel-20e.asp.

Coloured and patterned pasta on sale at the Granville Island Public Market, Vancouver, BC

> **Working in a fairly low-paying job, Christina Chiam found Toronto's cost of living a bit of a challenge:**
>
> The cost of living in Toronto is slightly higher than in Melbourne. Public transport is more expensive as it's charged on a per-use basis, rather than a time limit. The cost of consumables and services seems fairly similar initially, but taxes are added at the time of purchase rather than included on the price tag, plus a service tip has to be added for restaurants, hairdressers, and taxis. This slight increase in my living expenses, combined with a low arts salary, has made for a difficult juggling act financially.

▚ PETS

Attitudes to pets

Canada is a nation of pet lovers: there are approximately 3.5 million dogs and 4.5 million cats across the country, with over half of all households having at least one pet. Cats have the greatest popularity in the Atlantic provinces, while the Prairies have the highest proportion of dog owners. Pet ownership has increased significantly in the last decade, as has the number of pampered pooches and coddled kitties – the retail pet market is now worth around $4.5 billion a year. Some people even take out pet insurance to cover their furred or feathered friends against unexpected medical expenses. Veterinarians are widely available: most provinces have a veterinary medicine association that includes a directory of clinics or can help you find a vet. Dogs and cats are licenced through the local city council. Fees vary, but are often substantially lower for sterilised pets. Dogs are generally required to be kept on a leash at all times except in designated off-leash areas. There are dog-friendly parks or beaches in almost every region, and dogs are also permitted (though only on a leash) in most regional, provincial and national parks. If you take your pet outside, though, you're expected to clean up after it – it's good etiquette, and in many cities it's also the law.

Taking your pet abroad

The Canadian Food Inspection Agency (CFIA), under the National Animal Health Program, oversees all animal imports. Pet dogs and cats can be brought into Canada without quarantine, from any country, for any period of time (including permanent stays and temporary or in-transit visits). The one requirement is that your pet is proven to be free of rabies, which is a federally regulated animal disease in Canada. Dogs or cats under three months of age are exempt from this requirement. For pets over this age you need to provide either an original, valid rabies vaccination certificate issued by a licenced veterinarian, or, if your home country is considered to be rabies free, an export certificate signed by an official government vet, which certifies that the country has been rabies free for at least six months and that your

FACT

▪ Canada is a nation of pet lovers: there are approximately 3.5 million dogs and 4.5 millions cats across the country, with over half of all households having at least one pet.

pet has been in the country for all of that time, or since birth.

Pet birds can be imported, but a number of restrictions apply. Outbreaks of the highly contagious 'bird flu' mean that importation from certain countries has been suspended. Even if your home country is not among these, you must obtain an import permit from the relevant CFIA regional office. Birds must be isolated in the lead-up to departure, and will be further quarantined for at least 45 days on arrival in Canada. Rules for importing pet birds from the USA are less rigorous, though importation of all birds is regulated by the Canadian Wildlife Service's Convention on International Trade in Endangered Species. A range of other pet animals can also be imported – see the CFIA website for more information and specific regulations.

If you're not planning on bringing your pet to Canada permanently, check your home country's import regulations as well for any restrictions on returning. Contact your consulate or embassy to get details of the department responsible for imports and exports.

One of Canada's 3.5 million dogs takes a winter walk with his owner in northern Ontario

 Canadian Food Inspection Agency (CFIA)
- Pet imports: www.inspection.gc.ca/english/anima/heasan /import/petse.shtml
- Import contacts: www.inspection.gc.ca/english/anima/heasan /import/conpere.shtml
- Rabies-free countries: www.inspection.gc.ca/english/anima/heasan/ import/rabies_freee.shtml

Convention on International Trade in Endangered Species (CITES)
- Travelling, importing and exporting: www.cws-scf.ec.gc.ca/theme. cfm?lang=e&category=13

HAVE PET, WILL TRAVEL

If you have concerns about arranging your pet's export, or are unable to oversee it yourself, a number of independent, third-party 'pet movers' offer relocation services for a fee. They take care of the paperwork and logistics, and usually provide door-to-door service. The Independent Pet and Animal Transportation Association (IPATA) provides a comprehensive list of pet-relocation services worldwide, and allows you to custom search by location and pet type. See the website at www.ipata.com.

■ GETTING THERE

However you travel to Canada, you will have to present at a point of entry in order to go through immigration. You'll need your passport or other travel documents, proof of funds, and any visas or additional documentation that the Canadian visa office has instructed you to bring.

Air

The vast majority of people coming to Canada from overseas travel by aeroplane. The price of tickets varies hugely depending on where you're flying from, and is higher during peak travel times – in Canada, this is usually from June to September and over the Christmas–New Year period. Certain destinations are also more expensive during the snow season. The national carrier, Air Canada, struggled with bankruptcy a few years back but is considered one of the safest in the world. Most major US airlines and numerous international carriers fly to Canada, and the Canadian-based charter airline Air Transat also serves a number of international destinations.

Most flights from Asia arrive in Vancouver. Those originating in Europe tend to come in through Toronto, though direct flights to other Canadian cities are also possible from many parts of the UK and continental Europe. Non-stop flights from Australia and New Zealand to Vancouver (and on to Toronto) have recently become available, though others still stop over in Asia or the United States. If your home city doesn't offer flights to your specific Canadian destination, you can travel via the USA and transfer there, or catch a connecting domestic flight within Canada. If you do transit through the States, make sure you have a US visa if one is required.

> *i* If you're transiting through the United States, the American Consular Services website at www.amcits.com provides information on visa requirements for nationals of various countries.

Do some searching to find the most competitive fare. Round-trip or round-the-world tickets are economical options, but generally only valid for up to 12 months. These are worthwhile if you're a traveller or temporary visitor, or anticipate a trip back to your home country within the year. Otherwise, you'll probably need a one-way fare. Booking well in advance, travelling midweek and being flexible about airlines and flight times can help keep costs down. The internet is a mine of information, and many search engines will trawl through other sites to find the best available price. Their results are not always comprehensive, so search and compare a range of sites. These sites usually add commission for their services, so if you do find a low fare through a search engine, check it against the relevant airline's own website. Sometimes the best offers come from the airlines themselves, particularly during seat sales or other promotions. Also talk to a travel agent, or check the advertisement sections of newspapers and backpacker magazines for special deals.

You can book tickets through flight-search websites, directly with the airline either online or by phone, or with a travel agent. Travel agents or specialist cut-price ticket consolidators can also provide you with schedules and prices for charter airlines. Always check your fare's terms and conditions, the airline restrictions on luggage weight and carry-on items, and whether additional taxes or fees are applicable (such as departure or airport-improvement taxes), before you pay.

 A comprehensive list of all airlines operating out of Toronto's Pearson International Airport can be found at www.gtaa.com, under *Travellers*

◼ Airline contacts

All numbers are toll free within Canada.
Air Canada: 1 888 247 2262; www.aircanada.com
Air New Zealand: 1 800 663 5494; www.airnewzealand.com
Air Transat: 1 866 847 1112; www.airtransat.ca
American Airlines: 1 800 433 7300; www.aa.com
British Airways: 1 800 247 9297; www.britishairways.com
Cathay Pacific: 1 800 268 6868; www.cathay.ca
China Airlines: 1 800 227 5118; www.china-airlines.com
Continental Airlines: 1 800 231 0856; www.continental.com
Delta: 1 800 241 4141; www.delta.com
Japan Airlines: 1 800 525 3663; www.japanair.com
Northwest/KLM: 1 800 225 2525; www.nwa.com or www.klm.com
Qantas: 1 800 227 4500; www.qantas.com
Singapore Airlines: 1 800 387 0038; www.singaporeair.com
United Airlines: 1 800 621 5647; www.united.ca
US Airways: 1 800 428 4322; www.usairways.com

Land

If you're moving from or via the USA, travelling by car, bus or train may also be an option. Canada and the States share 8,890km of border, with 22 official points of entry dotted along its length. Some car rental companies have restrictions on cars crossing the border between the States and Canada, and on one-way travel, so if you're planning to drive to Canada in a rental car, clarify this when booking. It's also possible to cross the border by bus or train. Greyhound is the major bus line and operates across Canada, the USA, and Mexico. Amtrak offers train services to Toronto and Montreal, both departing from New York, and from Eugene to Vancouver, via Portland and Seattle. Both Amtrak and VIA Rail websites provide detailed information on requirements for crossing the border by train. Be aware that buses and trains won't take responsibility for getting you past the border or through Immigration, and won't necessarily wait for you if you're detained.

 The Canada Border Services Agency provides a list of all Canada–US land border crossings and the anticipated wait times at each (updated hourly) on its website, www.cbsa-asfc.gc.ca.

TIP

◼ Booking well in advance, travelling midweek and being flexible about airlines and flight times can help keep costs down.

> **Gerald and Mary Garnett flew to the United States in the middle of winter, then drove into Canada:**
>
> We landed at JFK airport near New York City and crossed into Canada by land on Christmas Eve, 1975. It was intensely cold, with deep snow, yet the houses were so warm that inside you went around in a shirt. We drove north to Mary's parents' house near Barry's Bay. I was quite scared, as we had gambled everything, jumping into the dark with a three-year-old child and no jobs in a new country.

■ Train, bus and border services contacts

Amtrak: 1 800 872 7245; www.amtrak.com
VIA Rail: 1 888 842 7245; www.viarail.ca
Greyhound: 1 214 849 8100 or 1 800 231 2222; ifsr@greyhound.com; www.greyhound.com
Greyhound Canada: 1 800 661 8747; www.greyhound.ca
Greyhound Mexico: 1 800 710 8819; www.greyhound.com.mx

VIA Rail takes passengers across Canada, and – in connection with Amtrak – across the US border

Canada Border Services Agency: 1 204 983 3500, 1 506 636 5064 or
1 800 461 9999; CBSA-ASFC@canada.gc.ca; www.cbsa-asfc.gc.ca
US Customs and Border Protection: 1 703 526 4200 or 1 877 227 5511;
www.cbp.gov

Sea

For most people, immigrating to Canada by ship or ferry is neither practical nor
convenient. If you're moving up the coast from the USA, however, a ferry is
theoretically one way to travel. Various companies make regular trips along the east
and west coasts of Canada, many of which originate in the States. Bay Ferries has
services from Maine to Nova Scotia; the Victoria Express, Victoria Clipper and others
make trips from various points in Washington State to Victoria on Vancouver Island;
and ferry travel to Canada on Alaska's Marine Highway System is also possible.
Passenger-carrying freighters are another by-sea option and connect with a greater
number of countries, including the UK, Europe, Australia, New Zealand, South
America, Africa, and Asia. Though a great way to see something of the world, it's
not a fast way to travel, departure and arrival dates are fluid, and fares can wind up
being quite expensive. You may or may not be able to travel with your freighted
belongings (and will most likely have to pay more if you do). Maris and The Cruise
People are two companies that arrange freighter travel.

■ Ferry and passenger freighter contacts
Bay Ferries Ltd: 1 902 566 3838 or 1 877 359 3760;
comments@canadaferry.com; www.nfl-bay.com
Victoria Express: 1 250 361 9144 (Canada) or 1 360 452 8088 (USA);
info@victoriaexpress.com; www.victoriaexpress.com
Alaska Marine Highway System: 1 907 465 3941 or 1 800 642 0066;
dot.ask.amhs@alaska.gov; www.dot.state.ak.us/amhs
The Ferry Traveller: 1 604 733 9113 or 1 800 686 0446;
mailto:info@ferrytravel.com; www.ferrytravel.com
Maris: 1 800 996 2747; www.freightercruises.com
The Cruise People: 1 416 444 2410 or 1 800 268 6523;
cruise@thecruisepeople.ca; www.tcpltd.com

■ PLANNING AN INTERNATIONAL MOVE

Making the move

Moving to another country, where new opportunities and different experiences
await, is hugely exciting. It can also be disorienting, demanding, and exhausting.
Planning the requirements of the move in advance, and being as organised as
possible, will help things run smoothly. Selling property, tying up bureaucratic
loose ends, and putting your legal affairs in order are one part of the equation. You
also have to think about how you and your family will travel to Canada, what you
need or want to bring with you, and how you'll transport it. Many online resources

TRAVEL INSURANCE

If you're a working traveller, or on a speculative job-hunting trip to Canada, make sure you arrange comprehensive travel insurance before you go. The number of insurers and insurance brokers is endless; here are just a few:

- Atlas Direct Travel Insurance: 1 800 335 0611 or 1 317 575 2652 (North America), 020 7609 5000 (UK); www.atlasdirect.net
- Columbus Direct: admin@columbusdirect.com; www.columbusdirect.com
- Cover-More Travel Insurance (Australia): 1300 72 88 22; enquiries@covermore.com.au; www.covermore.com.au (also available in the UK, and as Travelsure in New Zealand)
- Expatriate Insurance Services: 1 800 341 8150 (North America), 0700 340 1596 (UK); www.expatriate-insurance.com
- PHA Travel Club: 0845 634 2502 (UK); www.phatravel.com
- Travel Insurance Quotes Canada: 1 866 219 7953; www.travelinsurancequotes.ca
- Travelex: 1 800 228 9792; www.travelex-insurance.com

and checklists can help you prepare for the move: a couple of examples are at www.sefco-export.com/moving.htm and www.movingto.com.

 The Going to Canada website is aimed at people moving to, living in and working in Canada: visit www.goingtocanada.gc.ca or email Questions-goingtocanada@cic.gc.ca. *A Newcomer's Introduction to Canada,* available on the CIC website, also provides useful advice on making the move (go to www.cic.gc.ca and select *Publications*).

Customs regulations

If you have permission to enter Canada as a permanent resident, you're entitled to bring household and personal goods over duty-free on one occasion only. You need to give the customs official a detailed list of all items, including their value, and keep a copy for your own records. A specific form – the Personal Effects Accounting Document – is available from the Canada Border Services Agency (CBSA) for this purpose and can be downloaded at www.cbsa-asfc.gc.ca/E/pbg/cf/b4. Alternatively, you can provide a typed list to the border officer, who will complete the form on your behalf.

CBSA provides a range of helpful publications for newcomers at www.cbsa-asfc.gc.ca/publications/help-aide/topic-sujet/10-eng.html.

Importing goods

Items that are being shipped to you are included in the one-time exemption, provided you also present the customs officer with a detailed list of these goods when you first arrive in Canada. Include model and serial numbers, list clothing by individual item, and state how much the goods are worth. If these items are being sent by mail they can sometimes be taxed by accident – see the CBSA webpage at www.cbsa-asfc.gc.ca/import/postal-postale/person-eng.html for advice on what to do if this occurs. Canada has strict regulations about the types of items that can be brought into the country. The CBSA publication Settling in Canada, at www.cbsa-asfc.gc.ca/publications/pub/rc4151-eng.html, outlines these. If you have concerns, contact the CBSA for more information.

Importing a car

No import duty is levied on cars, motorcycles, boats or other vehicles that you bring as part of your one-time settler's effects, provided you use them for non-commercial purposes. However, Transport Canada has strict safety and pollution standards, and many vehicles cannot be imported. Those manufactured to meet US safety standards don't comply with Canadian standards, but may be able to be

Importing goods into Canada means careful planning and packing, and adherence to Canadian import laws

modified to do so. If your vehicle was manufactured to meet the safety standards of a country other than Canada or the USA, you won't be permitted to bring it to Canada (unless it is over 15 years old or is only being imported temporarily). Exceptions may apply for vehicles that were originally manufactured in line with Canadian or US standards, have not been altered, and bear a label of compliance from the original manufacturer. You can contact the Registrar of Imported Vehicles (RIV) to find out whether your vehicle is admissible. If it is, you have 45 days from the date of arrival in Canada to bring it into compliance. The province or territory you move to may impose its own requirements and charge you sales tax when you licence your vehicle. Check also whether your home country sets export conditions. You may decide that it's easier – and quite possibly cheaper – to purchase a car in Canada instead. For information on buying a car, driving in Canada and car insurance, see *Cars and motoring* on p. 195.

> *i* For more information regarding admissibility and compliance, see the CBSA document *Importing a Vehicle into Canada* at www.cbsa-asfc.gc.ca/publications/pub/bsf5048-eng.html, or call the Border Information Service (BIS) for a copy.

◼ Useful contacts
Canada Border Services Agency: 506 636 5064 (local), 1 204 983 3500 (international) or 1 800 959 2036; www.cbsa.gc.ca
Border Information Service (BIS): 24-hour automated system with agents available 8 am to 4 pm. Call 1 204 983 3500 or 1 506 636 5064 (international), or 1 800 461 9999
Transport Canada (Road Safety and Motor Vehicle Regulation Directorate): 1 613 998 8616 or 1 800 333 0371; www.tc.gc.ca/roadsafety
Registrar of Imported Vehicles: 1 416 626 6812 (international) or 1 888 848 8240; www.riv.ca

Relocation and removal companies

If you're moving from Europe, the UK, Australia or somewhere similarly distant, the high cost of transporting your possessions overseas may make it more economical to purchase new goods and furniture in Canada. If you do plan on bringing a substantial amount of your belongings, you should hire a reputable international removals firm that can help you with the practicalities and all the paperwork. It's always best to get quotes from at least three companies, so you can make a comparison between their fees and services. Many association websites provide searchable lists of international movers, and indicate which industry standards they meet. If you're relocating from the United States, most companies will happily move your goods to Canada. The cost will depend on the total amount being shipped and the distances involved at both ends.

Many businesses employ relocation firms to help settle executives who are being transferred. A good relocation firm will not only find you a house and arrange utilities, but will also advise on education, spousal employment, local regulations, and community facilities. Make sure any firm you hire is a member of the Association of Relocation Professionals, which has ethical guidelines for its members.

FACT

◼ Transport Canada has strict safety and pollution standards, and many vehicles cannot be imported.

◼ Useful contacts

British Association of Removers: 01923 69 9480 (UK); info@bar.co.uk; www.removers.org.uk

Canadian Association of Movers: 1 905 848 6579 or 1 866 860 0065 (Canada); admin@mover.net; www.mover.net

Household Goods Forwarders Association of America, Inc.: 1 703 317 9950 (USA); info@hhgfaa.org; www.hhgfaa.org

Professional Movers Association of South Africa (PMA): 086 138 6506 (South Africa); info@pmamovers.co.za; www.pmamovers.co.za

Federation of International Furniture Removers: 2 426 51 60 (Belgium); services@fidi.com; www.fidi.com

Overseas Moving Network International (OMNI): 01306 889218 (UK); omnihq@omnimoving.com; www.omnimoving.com

Australian International Movers Association: 02 9659 4299 (Australia); admin@aima.com.au; www.aima.com.au

Latin American and Caribbean International Movers Association: 360 2083 or 360 2084 (Panama); lacma@lacmassoc.org; www.lacmassoc.org

European Relocation Association: 08700 726 727 (UK); enquiries@eura-relocation.com; www.eura-relocation.com

The Association of Relocation Professionals: arp.relocation@gmail.com; www.arp-relocation.com

Setting
Up Home

BEAR MOUNTAIN RESORT
VICTORIA, BC • CANADA

Canada's Only Year Round Golfing Destination

WESTIN RESORT HOTEL • NICKLAUS GOLF • SANTÉ SPA • ATHLETIC CLUB • VILLAGE

A TRUE WORLD CLASS RESORT

Situated on the southern tip of scenic Vancouver Island, is Canada's premier master planned resort community, Bear Mountain Resort.

Discover Bear Mountain today and you'll understand why Condé Nast Traveler Magazine has consistently rated Victoria as one of the most liveable cities in the world.

Offering a wide range of fully-serviced properties and individual housing styles. Everything from:

• Exclusive gated estates
• Spacious fairway properties
• Town homes
• Luxury condominiums
• Fractional vacation ownership properties

CONDOMINIUMS FROM $369,500 • BUILDING LOTS FROM $250,000

BEAR MOUNTAIN GOLF·RESORT·PROPERTIES | THE WESTIN BEAR MOUNTAIN VICTORIA Golf Resort & Spa

BEARMOUNTAIN.CA/UK | 866-391-6100

Advertisement feature

A World Class Resort

Victoria, British Columbia, is located on the sunny southern tip of Vancouver Island and has been consistently rated one of the most liveable cities in the world by *Conde Nast Traveler Magazine*.

This historic capital city is a world-renowned tourism destination that is blessed by beauty and magnificent nature in every direction. Downtown is a quaint walkable city that will lead you past galleries, cafes, heritage storefronts and modern shops alike and Victoria is acclaimed for its many fine restaurants, pubs, vibrant nightlife and a full compliment of cultural events.

Just 20 minutes from downtown Victoria you will discover Bear Mountain Resort. Rugged yet pristine, Bear Mountain is setting the course to become one of the world's finest luxury mountainside resort communities. As Canada's only resort featuring 36 holes of Nicklaus Designed golf, Bear Mountain can also claim Starwood Hotels & Resorts first Westin Hotel property on Vancouver Island. Exquisite restaurants, a premiere fitness club, a luxurious spa, and a vibrant village complete this master planned community that offers a wide range of properties and individual housing styles.

A world class resort in a world class destination.

Master-Planned Community

Bear Mountain Resort is a great place to visit, but an even better place to call home. The real estate investment opportunities are many and varied and each exceptional property has been thoughtfully sited to take full advantage of the natural terrain and rugged beauty that makes Bear Mountain such an incredible place to live.

Gated Estate Homes – spectacular views perfect for the seekers of the good life; exclusive & grand
Townhomes – beautifully crafted homes of traditional design and elegant architecture
Single Family Lots – a variety of choices to build a home that suits your family's needs
Condominiums – a luxurious second home or a lock & leave residence
Fractional Vacation Ownership – offering flexibility and hassle free living with a world renowned brand – Westin Hotels & Resorts.

With Health and wellness at its heart, Bear Mountain offers a lifestyle with a variety of activities to be enjoyed year-round. In addition to the programmes and classes offered at the Mountainside Athletic Club, there are many hiking trails, landscaped parks and pedestrian walkways surrounding the resort that offer a fabulous chance to get back to nature. If golf is not your game, there is also tennis, squash, volleyball and mountain biking.

Bear Mountain Resort is not just building another residential development – this is a community.

Nicklaus Design Golf

As the only resort in Canada featuring 36 holes of Nicklaus Design golf, Bear Mountain Resort is first and foremost a premiere golf experience. Both the Mountain Course co-designed by Jack Nicklaus and his son Steve and the Valley Course a Nicklaus Design, strike the perfect balance between playability and a truly challenging year-round golf experience for golfers of all skill levels.

The prestigious Bear Mountain Golf & Country Club has a variety of membership opportunities that are tailored to meet your specific needs – be it individual, family, corporate, social or fitness.

The Bear Mountain Golf & Country Club with all its features and services will ensure that Bear Mountain Resort takes its rightful place among the leading golf destinations in the world.

A Luxurious Getaway

The Westin Bear Mountain Victoria Golf Resort & Spa is a luxury hotel that welcomes you with a premium level of style, sophistication and elegance.

The Westin Bear Mountain features 156 contemporary traditional guest rooms and one-bedroom suites boasting expansive views of the golf course fairways, Mount Finlayson and Mount Baker. All guest rooms and suites feature Westin's signature Heavenly Beds®, well appointed bathrooms complete with Heavenly Shower®, high speed internet access and balcony with patio chairs and table. Those looking for a home away from home will appreciate the kitchenettes in all traditional guest rooms and full kitchen, dining rooms and separate living area with sofa bed in all suites.

From the moment you arrive, our friendly and knowledgeable staff will take care of your every need making your weekend getaway or family holiday the perfect escape.

The Village

At the heart of Bear Mountain Resort you will find the Village. Bear Mountain has carefully selected their tenants to offer a variety of services and amenities to complete the sense of community and ensure the highest standard of living.

The Mountain Market grocery store specializes in everyday essentials to gourmet meals made for one. It features some of the finest products, specialty items and a few hard to find delicacies. Best of all it's within a 10-minute walk from most residences.

The many and varied dining options make it difficult to choose, but rest assured there is something for everyone. Located in the Westin hotel you will find fine dining at Panache, casual all day dining at the Copper Rock Grill with extensive selection of west coast fare, and the Masters Lounge an opulent lounge offering a relaxed ambience. Within the Village you will find Jack's Place, a sports pub that offers up billiards, darts & chance to watch your favourite game or Kuma Sushi with offerings of delectable sushi and sashimi dishes.

Soon you will be able to catch a show or listen to music playing from the outdoor plaza, but the Village already features the Mountain Bean Coffee Company with its unique blend of coffees, Galerie Sorance a fine art gallery, BFL Insurance to look after all your insurance needs and Lilypad a specialty home furnishings and décor store.

A Premiere Fitness Facility

Health, fitness or relaxation – whatever you desire, you'll find it at the Mountainside Athletic Club. The goal is to provide a fun, safe environment, complete with professional and friendly staff to assist you with achieving your goals or simply trying something new for the first time.

The MAC has everything from Paramount fitness equipment in both the co-ed and ladies-only gyms to a fitness studio offering yoga, pilates, spinning, bosu and swiss ball programmes, as well as step and body sculpting workouts.

The year-round heated outdoor salt water pool and hot tub, seasonal outdoor pool cabana, infrared sauna and tanning bed are just a few of the specialty features within this world class facility.

■ CHOOSING WHERE TO LIVE

Canada has quite a mobile population, with people frequently moving from house to house, city to city or province to province. As a result, the housing market is fluid and there are many companies dedicated to buying, selling, and renting property.

Costs

Living in one of Canada's major cities is much more expensive than living in a suburban or rural area. The average Canadian household spends almost 20% of its budget on shelter costs, such as mortgage payments or rent. As a general rule, 30% of pre-tax household income is considered the upper limit of affordability, and around one-quarter of households spend this amount or more on shelter. In Vancouver and Toronto, 33% of households spend at this level. Proportions are also higher for renters than for owners; two out of five spend 30% or more of their income on rent.

Home ownership is still the ideal, and increasing numbers of Canadians buy their own homes: on average, only three in 10 households rent. The rate is higher in cities than in other regions, with 37% of city households renting (compared with 28% elsewhere). Ontario and Quebec account for two-thirds of Canada's total rental expenditure. Of those who buy their homes, a little under half own them outright as opposed to having a mortgage. The real estate market boomed for most of the last decade, with houses in urban areas routinely selling above their list price after fierce bidding wars. This had a direct impact on the mortgage market. The share of household income required to cover mortgage payments rose to levels considered 'undesirable' by the lending industry: 38% for a five-year mortgage and down payments, up from 28% just four years ago. Many buyers opted for lengthy mortgages – up to 40 years in some cases – to soften the impact. With affordability continually decreasing, the market was inevitably going to run out of fuel: even before the current global financial crisis, ID Bank economists were predicting a substantial drop in home price growth. According to the Canadian Real Estate Association (CREA) the soaring prices of recent years have now come down to ground: growth has not only slowed but reversed, with national averages declining monthly since June 2008 (these figures are skewed somewhat by price drops in the most expensive markets – notably Vancouver). A US style housing collapse is not

FACT

■ According to TD Bank economists, the national average rate for home price growth – 11% in 2007 – is forecast to drop substantially to 2% in 2008, rising to just 3.5% in 2009.

FACT

■ The average Canadian family spends almost 20% of its income on shelter costs, such as mortgage payments or rent.

> ## Christina Chiam explains why she chose Toronto as her place of residence:
>
> My goal was to work for Canada's major film festival, so the decision of where to live was dictated by that. When my first contract finished I looked for work outside Toronto, but by that stage I'd been living in the city for three to four months and had begun establishing friendships, and I'd grown accustomed to the city. The thought of moving and starting all over again was not so appealing. Thankfully I secured a permanent job in Toronto so the decision to stay paid off.

anticipated by CREA – 17 out of 25 major markets were still reporting price gains in September 2008 – though buyers may still have to contend with rising mortgage rates. See *House prices in Canada*, on p. 138, for average purchase prices in specific cities.

Other considerations

Canada is a hugely varied country, and different locations hold different appeal: Vancouver, Victoria, and the west coast for their natural beauty and milder climate; Alberta and the Prairies for their growth and job opportunities; Quebec for its strong French identity and cosmopolitan flair. The Atlantic provinces, with their stunning, rugged coastlines and moody weather, attract more newcomers from the UK and Europe than from anywhere else in the world. Ontario is always popular – particularly Toronto, with its big-city status and multicultural reputation. If you're making the move with a pre-arranged job offer in hand, your destination will largely have been decided. If not, your choice may be based on employment or education prospects, on family already in Canada, or on lifestyle.

Unless you're very familiar with the area in which you plan to live and work, it's best not to purchase a home before you arrive. The average vacancy rate across Canada's metropolitan areas is under 3%, but has remained relatively stable for the last year. Specific vacancy rates vary considerably between cities – Kelowna and Victoria, both in British Columbia, have the lowest vacancy (both at 0.3%), and

> If possible, try to rent a house when you first get here, so you can get a feel for the area, especially if you have young children at school.
> **Alan Critchley**

IMMIGRATION AND THE INCOME GAP

Three-quarters of immigrants make their homes in Canada's three largest cities: Toronto, Montreal, and Vancouver. However, the number heading to outer regions, particularly the Greater Toronto Area (GTA), is on the increase. The distinct ethnic communities that have developed in these parts are an incentive for some. Other newcomers deliberately live away from those who share their culture and language, believing this encourages them to acclimatise to their new home more quickly. The proportion of newcomers living in rural areas or small towns is low – under 3%. Interestingly, immigrants in small urban centres and regional areas have a much higher chance of earning an income on par with their Canadian-born neighbours. Even after four years in Canada, those in the biggest cities earn 22% less, on average, than their Canuck counterparts; in smaller urban centres, they earn 2% more. For those who settle in rural or small-town Canada the gap is even further in their favour – on average, their wages exceed those of Canadians by 4% after just one year.

Vancouver's is also low (0.9%) but expected to increase. Windsor, Ontario, has the highest (13.2%). Despite the low average, rental properties in most cities are not difficult to find (though it can take some time), and after several months in Canada you'll have a much clearer idea of which region and neighbourhood is most suitable for you and your family. Aside from affordability, key factors to consider are proximity to your workplace (or the region you expect to work in) and access to public transport – particularly if you don't plan to drive. Though many Canadian cities have regular and efficient public transit systems their comprehensiveness and quality varies, so this is worth looking into, especially if you're thinking of living in one of the smaller cities. The crime level of a given area can also be important. Other considerations include the location of schools, grocery stores and amenities, restaurants, doctors and dentists, libraries, pools, sporting centres and parks, as well as your own lifestyle preferences. If you have young children, for example, you may not want to live in an inner-city high-rise or by a busy major road but; if you work and socialise downtown you might not be keen to commute from the suburbs each day.

Types of properties

More than 80% of Canadians live in urban areas with a density of at least 400 people per sq km. The largest of these – Vancouver, Montreal, and southern Ontario – are home to just under 14 million people, close to half the country's population. Almost one-third of dwellings are apartments, with single-family homes making up most of the remainder. These may be detached, semi-detached, duplexes, or row- or townhouses. The average occupancy per house is two or three people; occupancy for apartments is one to two. Apartment or condominium living is an increasing reality for city-dwelling Canadians, and many prefer the associated convenience and security. 'Condominium' ('syndicate of co-ownership' in Quebec, or 'strata' in BC) is a specific type of ownership in which you own an individual apartment or unit, but share all other facilities and components of the property with the owners of the other units. Any type of property can be part of a condominium, but the most common are purpose-built, high-rise apartments – these dot the landscape in some neighbourhoods and dominate entire streets in others. A monthly maintenance fee is paid to the condominium board on an ongoing basis. Condominiums represent

> **Steven Maine and his family initially lived in a rental property, which gave them a chance to find a suitable home to buy:**
>
> We didn't get much of a choice on where in Canada to live – because of the work the company does, it's based in Nova Scotia. The company was very good and provided furnished rental accommodation for the first three months we were here. This meant we had time to look around for a house to buy – essential, as we had brought our pets with us, and many rentals won't consider tenants with animals. One thing we didn't realise is that there aren't many houses for sale around September to November, when we were looking, so we had only a handful to choose from in our price range that had the number of bedrooms we needed, etc.

an affordable alternative for many first-home buyers and retirees, and are also gaining popularity in the luxury sector of the market. Vancouver is particularly condo minded, with around 60% of home sales falling into this category in 2008.

Recent years have also seen a trend towards the 'monster home' in Canada, and newer subdivisions are often crowded with enormous houses separated by tiny strips of lawn. Even in more modest developments the emphasis is on bigger being better. These are usually situated on city outskirts, where large tracts of land are still available for development. Older neighbourhoods typically have larger gardens and backyards. Traditional brick housing prevails across much of Canada, and basements are common throughout. Front porches feature frequently, and sloping roofs – generally steeper in mountainous areas – are a necessity for reducing snow build-up. Montreal is known for its gracefully curving external staircases, while east-coast houses tend towards simple design, weatherboard siding, and careful colour. Toronto's housing style is related throughout many neighbourhoods, following a basic theme of two or three storeys (often main floor, second floor, and gabled top storey) plus basement. These homes are either occupied by a single resident, couple, family, roommates or divided into separate apartments. Most regions offer a range of property types for rent or sale.

Real estate agents

You can usually engage a Canadian real estate agency to search for a house on your behalf, particularly if you're looking to buy. You may wish to use a REALTOR®, an agent who is a member of the Canadian Real Estate Association (CREA). CREA requires its members to adhere to strict ethical guidelines and professional standards. Realtors also have access to the Multiple Listing Service® (MLS®), a national

> " We moved into a one-bedroom condo, which was a new experience for us as apartment living is not that typical in New Zealand. We loved it – although cannot see wanting to do it as a longer-term lifestyle.
> **Andrea Crengle** "

HIBERNATION, SWEET HIBERNATION

Buildings in Canada tend to be much better heated and insulated than those in many other countries – Canadian winters are cold, and Canadians prepare accordingly. Home becomes a haven during the winter months, and the creature comforts of the typical house reflect this: more than one in two Canadian households have a dishwasher, 94% have a microwave oven, two-thirds have at least two televisions (and the same proportion have cable or satellite TV), 83% have a DVD player, and 75% have home computers, with the majority connected to the internet. A clothes dryer, of course, is a necessity – things take a long time to dry on an outside line if they're frozen as stiff as a board. To guard against the summer heat – and summers can be surprisingly warm and unpleasantly humid in some parts of the country – almost half of all households have air conditioning.

property database. Most Canadian real estate firms offer assistance to buyers free of charge; agents' fees are based on commission and are normally paid by the seller, sometimes as a flat rate but usually as a percentage of the sale price. It's always in the agent's interest to sell you a home, so bear this in mind when considering a purchase. Don't let a pushy agent convince you to buy if you're not ready, or if the price feels too high.

 You can find out more about realtors and real estate in Canada on the CREA website, www.crea.ca. Visit www.realtor.ca to search for a property or realtor.

The sales commission is generally split between the agent who lists the property for the seller and the agent who brings in the buyer. One agent or firm can play both parts, though it isn't advisable – this is known as multiple representation or 'dual agency'. When seller and buyer are represented by the same agent, conflicts of interest are a considerable risk. Unless the agent you're using clearly states that he or she is working exclusively in your interests (operating as a 'buyer broker'), chances are he or she is a sub-agent of the seller, with duties first and foremost to them. This is often defined in terms of the difference between being a customer (receiving all care, but no ultimate responsibility) and being a client (guaranteed exclusivity and confidentiality). Regulations do vary between provinces: in Ontario, you need a Buyer Representation Agreement to ensure your agent works solely for you, rather than for the seller (this also commits you to using that agent's services for the term of the agreement); in many other provinces the relationship is automatic, and no agreement is required. You never pay an agent for finding you a home if they're a sub-agent of the seller. If using a buyer broker you may either negotiate to pay them a fee yourself, or specify that they receive their commission via the seller's agent. Agents often have to negotiate – unless you're certain your agent is bound by confidentiality, be wary about the information you share. Otherwise, key details (such as your upper price limit) might be reported to the seller in order to close a deal more quickly.

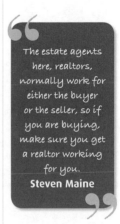

> The estate agents here, realtors, normally work for either the buyer or the seller, so if you are buying, make sure you get a realtor working for you.
> **Steven Maine**

You can investigate housing costs and opportunities on the realtor website above, and on those of the real estate companies listed under *Useful contacts*, below. These firms are nationwide and have branches in most cities and many smaller towns. Their websites or your local phone book will list the branches nearest you. For other agencies in your area, contact the local real estate board and request a list of members, or check the *Yellow Pages* (also available online at www.yellowpages.ca). Further information on how properties are advertised can be found in the *Finding a property* and *Buying a home* sections later in this chapter.

 The Real Estate Institute of Canada (REIC) includes lists of Canadian real estate boards and associations on its website, www.reic.ca (select Industry Links on the home page).

■ Useful contacts

Canadian Real Estate Association (CREA): 613 237 7111; info@crea.ca; www.crea.ca

Real Estate Institute of Canada (REIC): 416 695 9000 or 1 800 542 7342;
infocentral@reic.com; www.reic.ca
Century 21: 604 606 2100 (Vancouver), 416 491 6232 (Toronto) or
1 800 446 8737; info@century21.ca; www.century21.ca
Coldwell Banker: info@coldwellbanker.ca; www.coldwellbanker.ca
Prudential: 1 800 387 5946; www.preacanada.com or
www.prudential.ca/intl/canada/cacrea1000.html
Re/Max Canada: 250 860 3628 or 1 800 563 3622 (Western Canada),
1 888 542 2499 (Ontario and Atlantic Canada), 450 668 7743 or 1800 361 9325
(Quebec); www.remax.ca
Royal LePage: 1 877 757 4545; www.royallepage.ca
Real Estate Council of Ontario (RECO): 416 207 4800 or 1 800 245 6910;
communications@reco.on.ca; www.reco.on.ca

◼ Useful newspapers

Calgary Herald: 403 235 7323 or 1 800 372 9219;
calgaryherald@reachcanada.com; www.calgaryherald.com
Edmonton Journal: 780 429 5100; www.edmontonjournal.com
Halifax Chronicle-Herald: 902 426 2811; reception@herald.ca;
www.thechronicleherald.ca
Montreal Gazette: 514 987 2222; www.montrealgazette.com
National Post: 416 383 2500; www.nationalpost.com
Regina Leader-Post: 306 781 5211; classifieds@leaderpost.canwest.com;
www.leaderpost.com
St John's Telegram: 709 364 6300; telegram@thetelegram.com;
www.thetelegram.com
Toronto Star: 416 367 4500 or 1 800 268 9213; circmail@thestar.ca;
www.thestar.com
Vancouver Sun: 604 605 2000, 604 605 7381 or 1 800 663 2662;
circservice@png.canwest.com; www.vancouversun.com
Victoria Times Colonist: 250 380 5211; www.canada.com/victoriatimescolonist
Winnipeg Free Press: 204 697 7000; www.winnipegfreepress.com

◼ NEIGHBOURHOODS AND CITIES

Pricing estimates in this section are based on monthly rent for a two-bedroom apartment (non-basement unless otherwise indicated) in an apartment building or house, with utilities included. Rent in every neighbourhood varies widely depending on the type of apartment, location, and facilities. These figures are an approximation of the most common rental price for each area.

Neighbourhoods of Toronto

The Greater Toronto Area (GTA) is made up of four regions (Durham, Halton, Peel, and York) plus the City of Toronto, covers an area of 7,000 sq km, and is home to over 5.1 million people. The City of Toronto alone has more than 2.5 million residents. Based on 2006 census results, more than 45% of the GTA population is immigrant based. In Toronto itself, that figure is 50%. Throughout the metropolitan

CANADA

TORONTO

GREATER TORONTO AREA

PEEL

YORK

DURHAM

CITY OF TORONTO

HALTON

EAST YORK

DANFORTH VILLAGE

UPPER BEACH

THE BEACH

RIVERDALE

LESLIEVILLE

SOUTH EGLINTON

MOORE PARK

ROSEDALE

CABBAGE-TOWN

REGENT PARK

CHAPLIN ESTATES

DEER PARK

SUMMERHILL

DOWNTOWN

FOREST HILL

SOUTH HILL

NORTH MIDTOWN

YORK-VILLE

HARBOURFRONT

CEDAR-VALE

HUME-WOOD

HILLCREST

CASA LOMA

ANNEX

SEATON VILLAGE

UNIVERSITY OF TORONTO

CHINA-TOWN

ORANGE PARK

KING/SPADINA

OAKWOOD VAUGHAN

REGAL HEIGHTS

DOVER-COURT PARK

CHRISTIE PITS

BICKFORD PARK

PALMERSTON

SUSSEX ULSTER

LITTLE ITALY

KENSINGTON

ALEXANDRA PARK

TRINITY BELLWOODS

DUFFERIN-DAVENPORT

EARLSCOURT

WALLACE EMERSON

BROCKTON VILLAGE

BEACONS-FIELD

LIBERTY

NIAGARA

CARLTON VILLAGE

JUNCTION

RONCESVALLES

NORTH PARKDALE

SOUTH PARKDALE

ST CLAIR

HIGH PARK

BLOOR WEST VILLAGE

SWANSEA

LAKE ONTARIO

NORTH

NEIGHBOURHOODS**OF**TORONTO

Typical homes in the tree-lined Annex, Toronto

area there are well over 100 suburbs, neighbourhoods, and districts, all with their own characteristics and features. The following examples represent just a few of the many facets of Canada's largest city.

 The Toronto Neighbourhood Guide, available free online at www. torontoneighbourhoods.net, covers 157 neighbourhoods in the City of Toronto and is a great place to find basic information.

The Annex

The attractive Annex, centred on lively Bloor Street in the region around Bathurst Street and Avenue Road, is home to some of Toronto's best-known artists, academics, and writers, including Canadian literary legend Margaret Atwood. Most of the neighbourhood's multi-storey houses – which range from modest to grand – were built over 100 years ago. The majority are now single-family homes, or are divided into apartments for young professionals or students from the nearby University of Toronto. Close to public transport and walkable from downtown, the Annex is both a local hangout and a destination, with renowned sushi, multiple health-food stores, bookshops, restaurants and bars, and the historic repertory Bloor Cinema. Koreatown's stores and culinary charms are a literal stone's throw away, while Honest Ed's – Toronto's carnivalesque bargain-hunter's maze – stands like a beacon on the corner of Bathurst.

The Beach

The Beach (often referred to as the Beaches) lies east of the city along the shore of Lake Ontario, stretching north to Queen Street East. The tree-lined streets, resort-town feel, and architecturally diverse houses make this one of Toronto's most popular neighbourhoods. Young professionals and their families (think baby strollers and sleek pooches) are particularly well represented. Though pollution from Canada's largest city means it's not always safe to swim, the Beach provides numerous other options for the sports minded. And with a 3km boardwalk, waterfront trails, and plenty of green space, it offers some respite from Toronto's humid summers and a psychological escape from the city. On the hottest days, however, you'll find a good many others escaping with you – the main street, with its funky cafes and ice-cream shops, restaurants, bars, art-supply stores, and boutiques, can become horrendously overcrowded.

TIP

With a 3km boardwalk, waterfront trails, and plenty of green space, the Beach offers some respite from Toronto's humid summers and a psychological escape from the city.

Best for: young, affluent couples or families
Less good for: traffic congestion on Queen Street East in summer
Expect to pay: $1,600

Boardwalk view at the Beach, Toronto

Bloor West Village

The Eastern European influence of this popular neighbourhood's first residents is firmly entrenched – between Jane and Runnymede stations, Bloor Street West's Ukrainian and Polish pastry shops and delicatessens sell authentic pierogy, paska, sausage, borscht, and cheese. Each summer, the village hosts the annual Ukrainian Festival – the largest Ukrainian street party in North America. Close to the tree-filled expanses of High Park, Bloor West combines a village-like atmosphere with easy accessibility to downtown. Families appreciate the proximity to good schools (both public and private) and recreation centres. Many of the businesses in the lively shopping district are family owned, and more than 70% of the homes along its well-cared-for streets are owner-occupied. Prices for the houses – mostly two-storey detached or semi-detached, and built primarily in the decade after 1912 – range from around $350,000 to over $1 million. Condos, of which there are a growing number, are priced more affordably between $220,000 and $550,000.

> **Best for:** village atmosphere
> **Less good for:** encroaching condo developments
> **Expect to pay:** $1,600

The Danforth

Alternatively known as Greektown or Danforth Village, this pleasant neighbourhood occupies the area north of Danforth Avenue – the east-side continuation of Bloor Street. Famed for its multitude of long-established Greek and Mediterranean restaurants, the Danforth now boasts Cuban, Mexican, Indian, Thai and sushi options, plus bars, a cluster of Irish pubs and a range of specialty stores and boutiques. A seemingly disproportionate number of dentists and bridal shops also do business here – perhaps due to the relative affordability of the houses (typically built in the 1920s or 1930s, which makes this area a popular choice for families and first-time homebuyers. Public transport is particularly convenient: with the east-west subway line running directly underneath the street, downtown Toronto is just a few minutes away. The Danforth's culinary multiculturalism is celebrated each year with a weekend-long festival, Taste of the Danforth, which closes the street to traffic and draws over a million visitors.

FACT

The Danforth's culinary multiculturalism is celebrated each year with a weekend-long festival, Taste of the Danforth, which closes the street to traffic and draws over a million visitors.

> **Best for:** families and first-time homeowners
> **Less good for:** condo-lifestyle addicts
> **Expect to pay:** $1,200

Forest Hill and Casa Loma

Roughly divided by St Clair Avenue West, Forest Hill (to the north) and Casa Loma (to the south) form part of Toronto's established and elite residential identity. Affluent and showy, Forest Hill boasts two of Canada's most exclusive private schools, as well as the quaint Forest Hill Village shopping district. The gracious homes and gardens of Casa Loma – named for the medieval-style castle (still in existence) whose once extensive grounds it grew from – make this a pleasant place to wander, even if you can only window shop. Homes here can easily surpass $800,000, while those in Forest Hill tip over the $1 million mark or even $2 million. The ethnic make-up of both areas is predominantly Jewish, Canadian and English, though the nannies who bring their small charges down to the playground in the afternoons are a lot more multicultural than the families who employ them.

Best for: wealthy professionals
Less good for: the rest of us
Expect to pay: $1,650

Kensington Market

South of College Street, and rubbing shoulders with Chinatown at Spadina Avenue, Kensington Market is a colourful, casual sprawl of narrow streets and small Victorian row houses. Its bohemian sensibility and laid-back community attitude attract a range of residents, including singles, families, students, and professionals. The neighbourhood's 'market' identity was established in the 1920s by Toronto's Jewish immigrant population, and it now reflects a huge range of later influences: Ukrainian, Hungarian, Italian, Portuguese, Chinese, Vietnamese, South American, African and Caribbean food and culture have all played a part. Stores and open-air stands cater to both locals and tourists, selling fresh produce, spices, organic foods, cheap empanadas, and the usual tacky hats and t-shirts. Vintage-clothing devotees come for the numerous eclectic boutiques, and Augusta Avenue and its cross-streets offer a choice of clubs and unpretentious bars.

Best for: shopping purposefully or browsing aimlessly
Less good for: finding peace and quiet on weekends
Expect to pay: $1,400

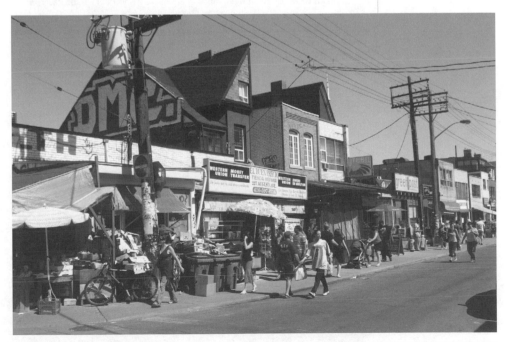

Blue skies over the colourful, eclectic Kensington Market, Toronto

Leslieville

Once thoroughly down at heel, now increasingly hip and desirable, Leslieville sprouted up around the Toronto Nurseries in the 1850s and was named for the nursery owners, George Leslie and sons. The older, shabbier storefronts along Queen Street East are now interspersed with chic cafés, bakeries and restaurants, antique stores and eco-conscious boutiques. A younger crowd colonises the two distinct generations of residences – the cottages, row houses, and Victorian homes of the late 1800s, and the modest bungalows and semi-detached dwellings of the early 20th century. Toronto's film industry is equally attracted to the district, with studios occupying the industrial locale around Eastern Avenue. Gerard Street, Leslieville's northern perimeter, hosts the largest East Indian market in North America, and Chinatown East's restaurants and grocery stores add extra flavour. Streetcars, buses, and the subway are all within reach, and recreational opportunities abound, with bike paths, swimming pools, basketball courts, baseball diamonds, and an ice rink nearby.

Best for: diversity and convenience
Less good for: the nearby waste treatment plant
Expect to pay: $1,200

Little Italy

Toronto's best-known Italian neighbourhood, Little Italy owes its cultural identity to the Italian immigrants who moved into the area in large numbers in the early 1900s. The traditional Italian vibe is still in evidence – distinctive architecture, formal front gardens, and religious statues grace many homes – but the Portuguese influence is now also strong, and younger residents and urban professionals are an increasing part of the mix. Condos and lofts have joined the older-style apartment buildings and the area's predominating two-storey, semi-detached Victorians. Chic College Street West offers trendy shopping as well as cafés, crèperies, martini bars, and a wealth of Italian eateries. The wide, curving street is a place to see and be seen, with patios filled to bursting in the warmer months.

> **Christina Chiam enjoyed getting to know Toronto and its many distinct neighbourhoods, and found that many things about her new home felt familiar.**
>
> I was struck by the similarities between Toronto and my hometown of Melbourne, Australia. Toronto's downtown streets form a grid, as do Melbourne's, so I could easily navigate my way around. The similarities extend to the different cultural pockets of the city. Like Melbourne, Toronto has little communities dotted around the city that celebrate particular ethnicities and cultures, such as Chinatown, Little Italy, and the Danforth with its strong Greek influences.

Parkdale

Lying west of downtown, east of High Park, and north of Lake Ontario, this was once an elite suburb boasting large homes, bay-and-gables mansions and the Sunnyside Complex (Toronto's answer to Coney Island). The Second World War delivered an economic blow, and Parkdale fell further from grace in the 1950s with the Gardiner Expressway development: houses were demolished, Sunnyside closed, and the new highways cut off the suburb's defining lake access. Parkdale has struggled with what are euphemistically termed 'big city social problems', but is steadfastly building a new identity for itself with condos, trendy artist lofts, and the restoration of original houses. Affordable rents and housing prices appeal to young families and professionals as well as new immigrants. Impressive architecture, treed streets, proximity to the markets, and delicatessens of the Polish-dominated Ronscesvalles Village, and eclectic shopping, eating, and drinking options are undeniable draws. Streetcars provide easy access to downtown or to the Bloor-Danforth subway line.

Greater Toronto Area (GTA)

The five-million-plus residents of the GTA live in a rapidly expanding network of towns, farms, and urban and rural communities in what is the largest metropolitan region in Canada and the country's business and manufacturing epicentre. Aside from the City of Toronto itself, the GTA includes 24 municipalities across four regions. Affordability, work opportunities and lifestyle are some of the incentives that lead many – including a growing number of immigrants – towards cities like Brampton, Mississauga, Markham, Richmond Hill, Oshawa, and Burlington. According to the 2006 census, almost half of all GTA residents identify themselves as visible minorities, defined in Canada's Employment Equity Act as 'persons other than Aboriginal peoples, who are non-Caucasian in race or non-white in colour', with the largest groups identifying as South Asian (14%), Chinese (10%), and black (7%). The Greater Toronto Marketing Alliance, which promotes the GTA to potential businesses and investors, provides regional profiles, economic and industry overviews, and a range of useful information on education, housing, recreation, and more.

FACT

Affordability, work opportunities and lifestyle are some of the incentives that lead many – including a growing number of immigrants – towards cities like Brampton, Mississauga, Markham, Richmond Hill, Oshawa, and Burlington.

 Visit the website for the Greater Toronto Marketing Alliance at www.greatertoronto.org.

Neighbourhoods of Vancouver

The City of Vancouver is made up of 23 communities, but like Toronto, the borders aren't always set in stone. Over 2.1 million people live in the census metropolitan

NEIGHBOURHOODS **OF** VANCOUVER

NORTH →

CANADA

VANCOUVER

UNIVERSITY ENDOWMENT LANDS

WEST POINT GREY

DUNBAR – SOUTHLANDS

KITSILANO

KERRISDALE

ARBUTUS RIDGE

SHAUGNESSY

FAIRVIEW

STANLEY PARK

MARPOLE

OAKRIDGE

SOUTH CAMBIE

MOUNT PLEASANT

WEST END

DOWNTOWN

RILEY PARK – LITTLE MOUNTAIN

SUNSET

DOWNTOWN EASTSIDE

STRATHCONA

KENSINGTON – CEDAR COTTAGE

VICTORIA – FRASERVIEW

GRANDVIEW WOODLAND

RENFREW – COLLINGWOOD

KLLARNEY

HASTINGS – SUNRISE

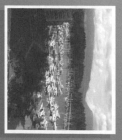

The view to Stanley Park and beyond, from a Coal Harbour condominium balcony, Vancouver

area, and many get to enjoy the stunning water, forest, and mountain views that define Vancouver – and BC – in so many ways. The following neighbourhoods and districts are just a selection from the many residential areas available.

Coal Harbour

Officially part of the West End, Coal Harbour comprises its own community, both visually and culturally distinct from its flamboyant and colourful neighbour. This brand-spanking-new residential region faces north-east, claiming the waterfront stretch between the downtown financial district and Stanley Park. Within 20 years, Coal Harbour has transformed from an industrial spread of concrete, car parks, railway yards, and floatplane terminals into a glistening collection of contemporary high-rises. (The floatplane terminals remain, with regular appearances of the little aircraft adding to the area's affluent charm.) Urban professionals, including a good proportion of empty nesters, are the primary inhabitants, and, providing they're not facing another building, enjoy fabulous views: pleasure craft moored in the harbour's marinas; the deep greens of Stanley Park; and the gorgeous North Shore mountains. A $20m complex, opened in 2007, provides mixed-income housing for seniors and people with disabilities. Coffee shops, grocery stores, retail shops, and restaurants – albeit high-end ones – have increased the community identity of this once slightly soulless district, and the waterfront

Coal Harbour Community Center, complete with gym, dance studio, and rooftop green space, plays an important role.

> **Best for:** the views
> **Less good for:** the bills
> **Expect to pay:** $2,500

Commercial Drive

Hop on the SkyTrain in downtown Vancouver and you can be at 'The Drive', in the east end of the city, in around 10 minutes. An eclectic collection of stores stretch out along the 21 blocks between Venables Street and 13th Avenue, drawing an eclectic crowd with a left-wing bent: artists, musicians, environmental activists, eco-lifestylers (unkindly referred to in Canada as 'granola munchers'), and a sizeable portion of Vancouver's gay and lesbian population are among the hood's residents. Once best known as Vancouver's little Italy, Commercial Drive is now startlingly diverse, with an energetic multitude of cultures, ethnicities, restaurants, grocers, bakeries, coffee bars, furniture, and clothing boutiques. Heritage homes and commercial buildings, many of which are now being restored, are a defining part of its identity. Fans like to compare The Drive to New York's Greenwich Village, or even the Rive Gauche in La belle Paris. Its alternative vibe is accompanied by some of the grittier elements of city life: homelessness, drugs, and prostitution are still realities in the area, despite surging housing prices (which tripled in the last decade) and the consequent, inevitable yuppification.

> **Best for:** lively street culture
> **Less good for:** panhandlers and prostitution
> **Expect to pay:** $1,400

Gastown

This little pocket of cobbled streets and painstakingly restored heritage buildings is where Vancouver began, thanks to the whisky-serving services of saloon-keeper 'Gassy Jack' Deighton in 1867. Razed by fire in 1886, Gastown was rebuilt but the Great Depression of the 1930s hit hard: neglect, drugs, and prostitution took a severe toll, and the area was eventually threatened with demolition. Saved and revitalised through the efforts of concerned citizens, it's now a declared historic area hugely popular with tourists. Restaurants, bars, intriguing shops (tourist traps and otherwise), and hanging flower baskets in spring and summer characterise the district, though the trickle-over effects of its indisputably skid-row neighbour, the Downtown Eastside, are still felt at times. The Gastown Business Improvement Society takes an active role in keeping things clean, safe, and friendly, and Gastown is becoming increasingly popular as a residential area, with 'urban heritage' the defining style, and lofts, condominiums, and studio warehouses available for discerning renters and buyers (the thicker your wallet, the better).

> **Best for:** living in a heritage site
> **Less good for:** living with tourists day in and day out
> **Expect to pay:** $2,100

Tourists stroll through Vancouver's historic Gastown district

Kerrisdale

Quiet, safe, and famously stable, this upscale residential neighourhood west of Marpole is popular with well-off families and older residents – an above average number of over-40s call Kerrisdale home. The bustling, prosperous Kerrisdale Village, anchored on 41st Avenue, is the commercial heart of the community, and proud of its old-school values and charm: the Kerrisdale Business Association promises a welcome 'as warm as a Norman Rockwell postcard'. A range of schools, parks, recreational facilities, and other community amenities service the tree-lined neighbourhood, which is defined primarily by large single-family homes. Almost half Kerrisdale's residences were built before 1960. Apartment buildings – the bulk of them low-rise – make up just over a third of all dwellings, and the percentage of rentals in this homeowner-heavy region is roughly the same. Like West Point Grey, the demographic is predominantly moneyed – average household earnings are well above $110,000 – and white, though about a third of Kerrisdale's residents have Chinese as their mother tongue.

Best for: families with money, or those who are happy to live in the basements of families with money
Less good for: families without money
Expect to pay: $1,200 for basement suite; $3,500 for house

Kitsilano

Formerly affordable, 'Kits' (as it's known by the locals) has undergone a price explosion in recent years. With trendy shopping, fantastic proximity to downtown Vancouver, loads of recreation options, and the gorgeous outlook afforded by Kitsilano Beach (which also boasts a heated saltwater pool), it's no surprise Kitsilano is one of the city's most desirable addresses. The highly educated population (close to 90% have some level of post-secondary education) is comprised essentially of generation-X yuppies, with a decent dose of retirees thrown in for good measure. Fewer residents have children than in other parts of Vancouver (and those that do, have fewer children), and renting is common: many people move on after a few years. Housing is diverse in style – from California-style bungalows to row houses – but is predominantly apartment based; only 10% of properties are semi-detached or detached family homes. The densely packed neighbourhood is ethnically diverse, but far less so than most areas of the city, and the proportion of recent immigrants is also lower.

Best for: the beach
Less good for: families and those with no tolerance for yuppie couples
Expect to pay: $1,600

Marpole

In the 1860s, a vast expanse of forest lay between the tiny town of Marpole (then called Eburne) and Vancouver. Now, this modest neighbourhood on the north shore of the Fraser River is part of the city, and there's a bustling expanse of homes and businesses instead. Marpole is known for its strongly multicultural (particularly Chinese) community and its relatively affordable housing – condos begin at around $200,000, though a single-family home will set you back $650,000 or more. Residential rezoning in the 1960s saw stucco-coated low-rise apartments replace older homes in some areas, and population density continues to increase. Around 21,000 people, including many families, now live in the neighbourhood. Sliced through by the southern ends of Granville and Oak streets (and the heavy traffic they carry), Marpole functions as the gateway to the city. Beautification efforts have been stepped up with the 2010 Winter Games – and the vast number of anticipated visitors travelling through from Vancouver International Airport – on the horizon.

Best for: affordable housing
Less good for: constant traffic
Expect to pay: $1,400

FACT

Mount Pleasant is now a real-estate hot ticket, particularly among young professionals, though there are fears that rampaging gentrification will force out those who've depended on the neighbourhood's low-cost housing.

Mount Pleasant

Once intended to become Vancouver's modish uptown district, Mount Pleasant was both defined by, and suffered from, industrial development throughout the 1900s. Dropping property values and industrial expansion in the 1930s saw its finesse as a residential zone wear off, though many homes and heritage buildings from before this period remain (the gracious, red-roofed Heritage Hall – now a community meeting hall – was formerly a post office and dates to 1915). 'Eclectic' and 'diverse' are terms often applied to Mount Pleasant, with its artists' studios, converted warehouses, notoriously seedy past, and a richly multicultural mix encompassing

Chinese, Filipino, Vietnamese, German, and Spanish residents. It's defined by its high number of of renters, lots of common-law couples and single-parent families, and lots of young residents. Appealingly close to downtown – just 10 minutes by car – and with expensive new condo developments adding to the concentration of apartment residences, there's been rapid transformation here in recent years. It's now a real-estate hot ticket, particularly among young professionals, though there are fears that rampaging gentrification will force out those who've depended on the neighbourhood's low-cost housing.

> **Best for:** its downtown proximity and reputation as an up-and-coming area
> **Less good for:** low-income earners
> **Expect to pay:** $1,600

West End

Perhaps best known for being the hub of Vancouver's gay population – particularly Davie Village, with its fashionable clothing stores, hip restaurants, high-energy clubs, and iconic rainbow banners – the West End provides everything a Vancouverite could ask for. This upbeat, diverse, and densely populated region extends from Downtown to Stanley Park and offers beaches, parks, shopping, nightlife, lively entertainment, and non-stop action in general. The population ranges widely, from young residents and recent immigrants (substantially more in both categories than the Vancouver average) to retirees. Families with young children are much less common. Household incomes tend to be lower here than elsewhere in the city, with around half of all West Enders working in sales, service, business, and administration. Over 80% rent their homes. Apartments make up the vast, vast majority of housing – almost four-fifths of residences were built between the 1940s and 1990, with the late 1950s and the 1960s seeing phenomenal densification. The Vancouver Pride Parade, which celebrates its 30th anniversary in 2008, is held in the West End each summer.

> **Best for:** those who like a gay-friendly and diverse community
> **Less good for:** families
> **Expect to pay:** $1,800

FACT

■ The West End is perhaps best known for being the hub of Vancouvers gay population – particularly Davie Village, with its fashionable clothing stores, hip restaurants, high energy clubs and iconic rrainbow banner.

West Point Grey

The westernmost neighbourhood in Vancouver, West Point Grey nestles comfortably between Kitsilano and the parklands surrounding the University of British Columbia (UBC), with a prime view across English Bay. Upscale and well established, this hilly neighbourhood offers tree-lined streets and large, luxurious homes (more than 40% of which were built before 1946), and is a far cry today from its early existence as logging camp and whaling station. Single-detached homes make up more than half of all residences, with low-rise apartment buildings accounting for around a quarter. The 12,000 residents themselves are predominantly high-earning anglophones – both singles and families – with an average household income easily clearing $100,000. The second most common language group, as in Vancouver generally, is Chinese. Point Grey Village, with its old-town style and family-run businesses, promotes a strong community spirit, while numerous parks – among them the extensive, waterfront Jericho Beach Park – make living in West Point Grey a pleasure (if an undeniably indulgent one) for those who can afford it.

Glistening condo towers in Yaletown, Vancouver

Best for: prestige and prime views
Less good for: lower-income earners
Expect to pay: $1,200 for basement apartment; $3,500 for house

Yaletown

Having morphed from a neglected warehouse district to a high-rise heaven for young to middle-aged professionals, Yaletown – technically part of downtown – presents a pleasingly architectural mix of a little heritage with a lot of shiny and new. Glassy apartment towers and converted lofts – many owner-occupied – comprise 98% of dwellings. Prices are high, but that hasn't stopped rapid residential growth. Bang in the centre of Vancouver, the neighbourhood is characterised by relatively affluent residents with plenty of disposable income, and with waterside restaurants and bars along False Creek, hip boutiques boasting local designers, a strong arts presence, and even its own magazine (see www.yaletownmagazine.ca), it's easy to see why. The mobile population includes a considerable proportion of high-earning science, business, management and finance professionals, as well as an above-average percentage of recent immigrants. Yaletown's mix of ethnicities is a defining feature: the locals have Spanish, Serbian, and Persian origins, as well as Korean, Chinese, and British.

City guides

Montreal (Quebec)

Situated on the Island of Montreal, overlooking the St Lawrence River, Montreal is a dynamic, cosmopolitan city – the largest in Quebec, and second largest in Canada. Almost half the province's 7.5 million residents live in Montreal and the surrounding metropolitan area; the city itself is home to 1.6 million people, 30.8% of whom are foreignborn. (In some regional municipalities this figure is as high as 45.4%). Not surprisingly, more immigrants with French as their mother tongue come here than to any other part of Canada. Hugely popular with tourists, the city boasts world-class art museums, festivals, restaurants and infinite opportunities to wander and absorb. Montreal drivers have a reputation – at least partially deserved – for being assertive and unpredictable, so driving is not always the most relaxing way to get around. In any case, this is a place best explored on foot, whether you're shopping along Rue Sainte-Catherine, strolling through the grounds of the renowned McGill University,

An overview of Montreal from the Mount Royal lookout

or perusing the bistros, restaurants, cafés, and boutique stores of Rue Saint-Denis. Mount Royal Park (parc du Mont-Royal), beloved of Montrealers, sprawls over 101 hectares (250 acres) of forested parkland near the downtown core, its peak rising to 233m (764 ft). The park's picnic areas, playgrounds, and winding paths for joggers and cyclists (and cross-country skiers in winter) are a natural escape for both city-dwellers and visitors. Particularly lovely in spring and autumn, it offers fine views of the city skyline. The Champlain Bridge – the busiest in Canada – provides another outlook on this striking assortment of buildings and office towers. (The second-busiest bridge, the Jacques Cartier Bridge, is also in Montreal.)

Montreal is made up of a number of distinct districts and *arrondissements* (boroughs or municipalities). Old Montreal, the city's birthplace, is distinctly European in feel, with cobbled streets, stone buildings, and the dramatic Notre-Dame Basilica, as well as the Bonsecours Market, where a range of artisans sell locally produced crafts and goods. This town knows how to eat and drink better than most, and Little Italy and the diminutive Chinatown are both on the menu, as is the Latin Quarter with its restaurants, cafés, bars, and theatres, and The Village – Montreal's vibrantly proud gay district. The Plateau Mont-Royal, primarily francophone and once a working-class neighbourhood, is now trendy, arty, and much sought after, with eclectic shopping, lively nightlife, and picturesque residential streets. In broad terms, the west side of Montreal is more English than the east, which is almost completely francophone. Notre-Dame-de-Grâce (or the NDG), a large, suburban residential area, is predominantly anglophone, as is the well-to-do Westmount. One of the most racially and culturally diverse districts is Côte-des-Neiges. It is part of the same administrative borough as the NDG, but a francophone neighbourhood with a large immigrant population. City transport in Montreal is based around buses and the metro subway system, while VIA Rail, intercity bus services and Greyhound Canada connect to more distant points including Quebec City, Ottawa and Toronto. Two international airports cater to domestic and international travellers.

Ottawa (Ontario)

Canada's fourth-largest city is proud of its role as the nation's capital. Ottawa's impressive Parliament Buildings – the domain of the Government of Canada – sit high on their hill with a clear view across the wide Ottawa River to the Quebec

> **Dante Pizarro, who came to Montreal from Chile in 1996, was impressed by the city's amenities, and by his introduction to snow:**
>
> There are so many different cultures and people from different countries; this was something I wasn't used to. Some areas of Montreal I liked very much – there are some very beautiful neighbourhoods. I also liked the parks, there are so many of them and they are all very clean and well kept. There are many shopping centres too, all very clean, even the washrooms. The public transit system is very good, with schedules posted in the bus stops. The buses are comfortable, and the drivers are very polite. In general, people here are very polite. In Montreal I saw snow for the first time, and it was a great experience.

shore. The Senate, the House of Commons and the Supreme Court of Canada also call this prime location home. The capital region, which includes the city of Gatineau in Quebec, has a population of 1.13 million. Ottawa's identity is undeniably public-service-based – dozens of federal government organisations and 110 foreign embassies cluster along its streets – but the city is also a major centre for business, technology, research, and academia. It boasts the most highly-educated workforce in Canada, and an enviable, admirable collection of cultural attractions including the Royal Canadian Mint and the Canadian Museum of Civilization. Chief among its 30 museums and 50 galleries is the impressive National Gallery of Canada, a showcase for both Canadian and international art. Numerous festivals are held each year, including winter celebration Winterlude, and the Canadian Tulip Festival (the largest such festival in the world). The dominant federal government presence and Ottawa's extreme proximity to Quebec mean that many services are provided in both English and French; close to half a million 'Ottawans' speak both languages.

Ottawa prides itself on being a great place for families, with a multicultural community and easy and prolific access to the outdoors. Nearby parklands, forests and waterways offer many opportunities for sports and exploration, and the 36,131 impressive hectares (89,280 acres) of Gatineau Park are a short trip northwest of the city. Many people commute into town each day from rural communities such as Lanark County and Renfrew. The Rideau Canal, the oldest 19th-century canal still in operation (with most of its locks still cranked by hand), is surrounded by a hugely popular recreational area. In winter the canal becomes a skate path, which

FACT

■ Chief among Ottawa's 30 museums and 50 galleries is the impressive National Gallery of Canada, a showcase for both Canadian and international art.

Ottawa, as seen from the steps of the Parliament Buildings

currently holds the title of largest outdoor ice-skating rink in the world (a position that Winnipeg is threatening to usurp). The canal isn't Ottawa's only ice-related asset: in 2007, the city's hockey team – the aptly named Ottawa Senators – held the hopes of the nation in their hockey-stick-wielding hands when they battled California's Anaheim Ducks in the last few games of the Stanley Cup. But it was not to be: Anaheim took home the cup, and the States chalked up another year of NHL domination (an outcome that was repeated, sadly, in 2008, with reduced resistance from Canada).

Just two hours' drive from Montreal and five from Toronto, Ottawa offers the benefits of life in a smaller city, with realistic access to the country's biggest. An international airport, VIA Rail and Greyhound bring the rest of Canada (and parts of the outside world) to the door, and the city itself enjoys the convenience of an intra-city bus service, a light rail and a dedicated bus-only roadway system. Summers here are mild, but like most of Canada, Ottawa can get chilly in the winter. Average temperatures then are about −10°C, but extreme lows can drop to −40°C. The city sees around 235cm of snow on an annual basis, and uses between 140,000 and 190,000 tonnes of salt each year to clear it from roads and sidewalks – more than anywhere else in the country.

Calgary (Alberta)

A combination of wild-west landscape, downtown commercialism, and urban sprawl, Calgary's one-million-plus population makes it the largest city in Alberta, beating Edmonton, the capital, by a short half-head. The province is considered a Canadian Texas by some, due to its enduring cowboy image and oil-related wealth though the global economic crunch of October 2008 is currently reigning this in. The benefits of Alberta's financial strength have been shared among Albertans, and are reflected in the province's low income taxes and lack of provincial sales tax (PST). Calgary's economic growth, like Edmonton's, has been tied up until now to Alberta's seemingly inexhaustible natural resources, and many oil companies have their headquarters in the city. Much of the highly educated population works in energy-related fields, though high-tech and agricultural industries are also strongly represented. Tourism has been another growth industry, thanks primarily to the majestic and conveniently located Rocky Mountains, which are just an hour away. The influx of new residents to this true boomtown – more than 340,000 people since 1991 (130,000 of them within the last five years) – has not been without its problems. Housing construction and infrastructure have struggled to keep pace, and homelessness is an ongoing concern. In the last few years the demand for office space has outstripped supply – more than half the office construction across Canada has been occurring in Calgary – and shiny new condos have sprung up out of the prairie soil.

Despite its awe-inspiring mountain backdrop and a skyline defined by the torch-like Calgary Tower, Calgary hasn't always been known for its architectural sensitivity. Most historic buildings have been torn down, and the modern streetscapes that now exist don't have quite the same soul. The city's physical footprint is on par with New York's; its ecological footprint is the largest in Canada. Yet Calgary is kicking back at its 'non-cultured' reputation. While still best known for the annual Calgary Stampede – a cowboy-hat-and-boot-wearing, testosterone-laden, crowd-drawing celebration of all things rodeo, where you 'drink until you fall down or foolishly hit on your co-worker' (as one Calgarian summarised) – a vibrant new theatre scene

FACT

■ While winters are cold (and exceptionally dry), Calgary is sporadically thawed by chinook winds – warm, dry winds off the eastern slopes of the mountains.

The city skyline stretches out behind the carnival rides of Calgary's famous Stampede

has started to make its mark, with a range of companies drawing attention for their cheeky and often impressive productions. The Globe, The Uptown, and The Plaza – three art-house cinemas – serve tasty flicks as well as delicious popcorn. The city is divided into four compass-related quadrants, and the Northeast (NE) offers great ethnic dining, with Indian, Filipino, Italian, Thai, and Japanese among its many choices. Mission (also known as 4th Street SW) is home to the Lilac Festival and its accompanying crowd of 100,000 in late May. With funky boutiques and diverse restaurants, it gets the vote for coolest neighbourhood. Kensington's diverse shops and café lifestyle bring it in second. Chinatown is the hub of Calgary's Chinese community, which number more than 50,000. And if the Rockies are just a little far for that outdoor endeavour, you can head to the Douglas Fir Trail, an arduous walking trail shrouded by fir trees, many over 400 years old (and one of the few historic features of Calgary that remain standing). Or take a stroll, run or ride along the city's 600-km-long system of paved pathways – the largest in North America and a blessing for cyclists, rollerbladers, joggers, and dog walkers. While winters are cold (and exceptionally dry), Calgary is sporadically thawed by chinook winds – warm, dry winds off the eastern slopes of the mountains, that raise the temperature, melt the snow and make the rest of the Prairies jealous.

Edmonton (Alberta)

Attractively situated on the North Saskatchewan River, Edmonton offers historic neighbourhoods, beautiful parks, and proximity to stunning wilderness (Jasper

> **Andrea Crengle explains why she and her husband chose Calgary as their Canadian home:**
>
> For us, the main deciding factor was simply that a very good friend of my husband's from New Zealand has been living in Calgary for many years now, with his wonderful Canadian partner. So Calgary was always to be our starting point and we would 'go from there'. However, having arrived and seeing how close to the Rocky Mountains Calgary is, we decided to stay put. Weekends were filled with short trips to the Rockies for hiking and car trips to the many nearby regions.

National Park is a four-hour drive). It promotes itself as a centre for creativity and innovation: its strong arts culture and community-based approach earned it a designation as a Cultural Capital of Canada in 2007. With an industry based around oil and natural resources, the city has been right in the centre of Alberta's various energy booms. The demand for workers, professionals, supplies, and administrative services has attracted job seekers from around the country and the globe, and the population is now just over one million. Like much of the country, the population

Victoria's unmistakable Inner Harbour

here comprises Aboriginal peoples, European immigrants and their descendants, and newcomers from around the world, and the city has Eastern European, German, Chinese and Arabic communities. Winters are undeniably frigid, but you can always escape to the phenomenally oversized West Edmonton Mall: mini-golf courses, bungee jumping, live sea lions, a casino, and a five-acre water park are just some of the diversions available.

Halifax (Nova Scotia)

Not everyone who comes to Canada makes it to the port city of Halifax, the largest city in Atlantic Canada, but it has a habit of charming those who do. Like much of the country, it's a place layered in history, from the tragic harbour explosion in 1917 – which caused 1,500 deaths and wiped out 13,000 homes and businesses – to its role in the aftermath of the *Titanic* sinking. Halifax offers city-style living without the big-city population – just 373,000 according to the last census; about 40% of all Nova Scotia's residents. Artists and students are especially drawn to the area, which offers an eclectic culture, active nightlife and music scene, and dozens of art galleries and museums, along with several universities – chief among them the highly regarded Nova Scotia College of Art and Design (NSCAD). Heritage homes, pleasant residential areas, and a carefully developed waterfront make it an attractive place both to visit and to live.

FACT

■ Artists and students are especially drawn to Halifax, which offers an eclectic culture, active nightlife and music scene, and dozens of art galleries and museums, along with several universities.

Wandering through the Historic Properties near the Halifax waterfront

The Saint John lifestyle

Saint John is the largest city in New Brunswick with a population of 124,000. Although many residents have family roots due to generations of history in the area, newcomers from across Canada and around the world are drawn to the opportunity and lifestyle of the region. The area is very attractive to new immigrants who desire a high quality of life and a variety of services while settling in a smaller, quieter urban setting.

East Coast Canadians are famous for their friendly, welcoming attitude and this characteristic is particularly pronounced in Saint John. You can expect a warm greeting from strangers on the street, have doors held open for you, be invited to social activities by people you've just met, and generally receive a great welcome. Many local residents are intrigued by newcomers and will quickly offer to show you around the area and introduce you to their friends, making it fast and easy to integrate into the community.

Surroundings

Saint Johners enjoy a wide variety of choice in crafting their lifestyle. The natural environment of the area is incredibly varied: stunning rugged ocean coastlines, three picturesque river systems and the Appalachian mountain range and pastoral farmland, surround the urban city and its suburbs perched on the Saint John Harbour. This diverse topography allows residents to choose from almost any outdoor activity imaginable, and with the majority of natural surroundings untouched by man, exploring the natural world in all its forms is still a centrepiece to active life in the region. A host of maintained parks and trail systems exist within city limits, including Rockwood Park which is 2,200 acres of wooded trails and lakes, and is the largest municipal park in Canada.

Accommodation

Housing options in the Saint John Community are just as diverse as its surroundings. The oldest incorporated city in Canada, the urban heart of the community is famous for possessing the largest inventory of heritage buildings in the country (approximately 75% of the registered heritage properties in Canada). In recent years many of these heritage buildings have been renovated, and now typically have street-level shops and restaurants and loft apartments or unique commercial spaces on the upper floors. The city also offers a large contingent of affordable multi-unit housing, making Saint John an ideal opportunity for those interested in becoming landlords, and a huge variety of choice in single-family homes, townhouses and condos.

Around Saint John, quiet, peaceful suburbs are geared towards families and those looking for a quieter life. Everything from large waterfront mansions to mobility-friendly bungalows exist along the rivers and coastline of the suburbs. Travel times into the heart of the city range from 10 to 45 minutes.

Education

Educational institutions in Saint John include all levels of elementary and secondary schools, the largest community college campus in the province, the University of New Brunswick and many professional training institutes.

Provided by expert contributor

Curriculum is provided in Canada's two official languages English and French. Options for apprenticeship and training for skilled trades-people in the area continue to increase, driven by an incredibly strong residential and commercial construction market and large industrial projects.

Healthcare

Healthcare is also provided in both English and French, and offered through Saint John's two hospitals and many community health clinics. Although all of Canada is experiencing a shortage of family doctors, Saint John has successfully increased its number of general practitioners per capita. The region also has an established system of healthcare support for residents waiting for a family doctor, and a proven method of matching residents to new doctors as soon as a new practice is started. The Saint John Regional Hospital – a recognised leader in a variety of medical specialisations – houses the New Brunswick Heart Centre and is complimented by wide-ranging community programming and services offered by Saint Joseph's Hospital.

Activities

With the region's extreme geographic diversity outdoor activities also offer a lot of choice. Water-based activities like kayaking, fishing, kite-surfing, etc. are a central to the Saint John way of life. Choices for non-water lovers also exist – the challenging coastal roadways are catnip to local and international cyclists, fitness activities of all kinds are gaining immense popularity in the community and rock-climbing, hiking and geo-caching are all common to the area. Wildlife watching opportunities abound in the community, and Saint John is a hotspot for whale and bird enthusiasts.

New retail developments continue to pop up in Saint John, making it the new shopping centre of the province. Night hawks enjoy everything from the traditional pub scene to contemporary nightclubs and martini bars, and the indoor ped-way system in the Uptown core allows for an enjoyable evening out even in the worst of winter's storms. Sporting events and major concerts are common at the city's biggest indoor entertainment venue Harbour Station, as well as the Canada Games Aquatic Centre. Volunteering and community involvement is also a large part of the lives of many Saint John residents, where the sense of community and togetherness dominates.

Provided by expert contributor

Victoria (British Columbia)

Lovely seaside Victoria, with its distinctive Legislative Buildings, picturesque Inner Harbour, and romantic, ivy-strewn Empress Hotel, could have been lifted straight from Victorian–Edwardian England. Originally a trading post for European settlers and the local Lekwammen people, Victoria grew rapidly during BC's mid-1850s gold rush, with the passage of miners and prospectors heading to the mainland. In 1868, a wealthy city, it became the capital of British Columbia. Though hugely popular with retirees and seniors, its temperate climate, stunning location, and proximity to endless recreational and adventure opportunities pull in a much younger crowd as well; the population is now upwards of 330,000. Ferries connect to Vancouver and the mainland in a matter of hours, or let you island-hop through the picturesque Gulf Islands. As for most large urban centres, homelessness is a concern – like Vancouver, the milder temperatures here make winter on the streets more survivable than in other parts of Canada. But Victoria is defined by its strong community focus, exceptional natural beauty, and quality of life – if you can afford the housing prices.

Winnipeg (Manitoba)

Situated at the geographic midpoint of Canada, Winnipeg sits in the south of the province where the Assiniboine and Red Rivers converge. A total of 60% of all Manitobans live in the capital city, which has a broadly multicultural population (Aboriginal, French, Ukrainian, Italian, and Chinese) just shy of 700,000. Winnipeg is renowned for many things: its long-established and extraordinarily prolific arts scene, which has spawned such talents as The Guess Who, alt-rock favourites The Weakerthans, and Canadian film legend Guy Maddin; its notorious mosquitoes in summer; its cold, sunny, and sometimes brutal winters (characterised by wind, extreme cold snaps and enduring snow); and its status as the birthplace of rebel Métis leader Louis Riel, whose controversial actions led to Manitoba joining the fledgling Dominion of Canada in 1870. Architecturally, Winnipeg has been strongly influenced by contemporary and modernist styles: its angular buildings and skyscrapers form an intriguing contrast to the surrounding prairie farmland.

Quebec City (Quebec)

Arriving in Quebec by night, with the light from street lamps bouncing off the cobblestone roads, or by day, with fog softening the sharp points of the Château Frontenac's roofline, you could be forgiven for thinking you were in old-world

The extraordinary Château Frontenac dominates a picture-postcard view of Quebec City

Europe. Perched on a cliff above the St Lawrence River, the walled city of Quebec – a UNESCO World Heritage site – is perfectly positioned to survey its surroundings. In one direction is the river and the facing shore of Lévis; in all others, a spreading cloak of churches, chimneys, heritage rooftops and homes. Just outside the wall is Battlefields Park, once the site of a desperate battle between the French and English armies, and France's eventual defeat. Now, its gently undulating grassy expanses see tourists, dog-walkers, and joggers instead, and lead to the quiet treasures of the excellent Musée des beaux-arts du Quebec. The city of Quebec itself (La Cité) is surrounded by seven other arrondissements, or boroughs: Beauport, Charlesbourg, La Haute-Saint-Charles, Laurentien, Les Rivières, Limoilou, and Sainte-Foy–Sillery; and the metropolitan area is home to around 715,500 residents. Immigrant numbers are low, something the city – which offers culture, recreation, excellent education, and a welcoming attitude – is actively working to address.

Saskatoon (Saskatchewan)

Some clichés must have been made for Canada. From the air, Saskatoon is surrounded by a mosaic of tiny green, beige, and brown squares, and the broad South Saskatchewan River snakes – literally – through the city. The parklands and trails surrounding the river are a feature of the city, which is liberally dotted with neighbourhood parks, provides treed residential areas, and boasts many beautiful heritage buildings. While Regina – less than three hours' drive away – is Saskatchewan's capital city, Saskatoon is the province's largest, with around 234,000 residents, based on current census figures. Like Regina, immigrants make up a relatively low proportion of the population, at just 7.7%. In Saskatoon's case this translates to around 18,000 people, around 3,300 of whom arrived between 2001 and 2006. Earlier immigration from Eastern Europe, including people from religious groups such as the Doukhobors, Mennonites, and Hutterites, has influenced the city's cultural make-up, as has more recent immigration from China, India, Pakistan, the Philippines, and Vietnam (among others).

■ SHORT-TERM STAYS

Hostels

TIP

If you're travelling solo or with a partner or spouse, and don't have a huge amount of luggage, hostels can be a cheap and convenient place to stay while you get your bearings in a new place. Some also accept family groups. Either independently run, or affiliated with Hostelling International (HI), hostels exist in all large cities in Canada and in many smaller towns and regional areas as well. Prices vary with location and with the facilities and amenities offered, and standards differ considerably. Hostels in the HI network (known in various other countries as YHA, DJH, FUAJ or AIG) often charge slightly more than their independent counterparts, but are required to meet certain standards of cleanliness and safety – if you become an HI member you're eligible for lower rates and other discounts. Backpackers Hostels Canada is a network of independent hostels across the country. Dorm accommodation (usually sleeping four to 10 people) is standard in hostels, though many also offer private rooms. The majority of hostels are youth oriented. They cater primarily to travellers and are not usually intended for long-term accommodation, so there are often limits on how long you can stay. You can find details of most hostels on the internet, and in many cases make your bookings online as well.

 Search for HI hostels Canada-wide at www.hihostels.ca. To ask about membership, contact HI in your country, call 1 800 663 5777, or email info@hihostels.ca. For Backpackers Hostels Canada, visit www.backpackers.ca, phone 1 807 983 2042 or 1 888 920 0044, or email info@backpackers.ca.

Bed-and-breakfasts

Bed-and-breakfast accommodations range from good old-fashioned comfort, to high-priced luxury, to a cosy spare room in a family home. The owners usually run the business and live on the premises. Rates are often lower than those for comparable hotels, and breakfast is part of the deal. Most B&Bs target couples, though singles are always welcome and some establishments offer larger rooms for family groups. Children are not always encouraged or permitted, so confirm this in advance. Bathrooms may be private or may have to be shared with other guests – this is often reflected in the price. As with hostels, standards and facilities vary widely, so find out as much as possible before booking to make sure you'll be staying somewhere that suits your needs. BBCanada.com is a useful, searchable website listing Canadian B&Bs. There are numerous others, including *The Canadian Bed and Breakfast Guide* which is available in both English and French versions. Bookings are made through individual businesses.

◣ Useful contacts

BBCanada.com: www.bbcanada.com
BBSelect.com: 1 800 741 1617; www.bbselect.com
CanadianBedBreakfast.com: 250 477 7970 or 1 877 477 7970;
www.canadianbedbreakfast.com
The Canadian Bed and Breakfast Guide: 905 262 4597 or 1 877 213 0089;
info@canadianbandbguide.ca; www.canadianbandbguide.ca

Apartment hotels

Apartment hotels can suit various budgets; they range from discount hotels with basic self-catering facilities to upscale executive serviced suites with fully equipped kitchens. Standards, accommodation styles, and rates vary significantly. Private and furnished (to differing degrees), they usually offer a more cost-effective short-to-mid-term solution than staying in conventional hotels – though finding a short-term apartment rental, sublet, or furnished room might be cheaper again. Many apartment hotels offer competitive rates, which often operate on a sliding scale depending on the length of your stay. Some require a minimum number of nights. A major advantage – and a potentially significant saving – is being able to prepare your own food. Search the internet for apartment hotels, serviced apartments, rental suites or discount hotels in the city or area in which you'll initially be staying, or check under 'Apartments', 'Apartment Hotels' or 'Tourist Accommodation' in the local *Yellow Pages* (or online at www.yellowpages.ca). Settlement or other immigrant-serving organisations can often give you information as well – go to www.cic.gc.ca for details of organisations across Canada.

■ Some Canada-wide contacts

Accommodations Canada: www.accommodationscanada.com
ARC Corporate Housing & Serviced Apartments: 700 598 0735; www.arc-corporate-housing.com
Boardwalk Rental Communities: 403 531 9255 or 1 800 310 9255; www.bwalk.com
Executive Hotels & Resorts: 604 642 5250 or 1 888 388 3932; www.executivehotels.net

■ RENTING

It isn't always easy to find something you like, in an area where you want to live, at a price that fits your budget. You might be lucky and secure something within a few days, or it may take weeks or even a couple of months. If possible, don't rush the process: allow yourself time to find a place where you think you can comfortably live for a while. It might take a little longer at the initial house-hunting stage, but it means you'll be less likely to have to move again within your first year in Canada.

Before you start looking, familiarise yourself with your rights as a tenant. It's illegal for landlords to discriminate based on race, religion, ethnicity, age, gender, sexual orientation or disability, or to refuse to rent to you because you have children. They are also prohibited from asking you certain personal questions relating to these matters, and cannot request your Social Insurance Number. If you're concerned about your rights in any of these areas or want more information, the Canadian Human Rights Commission lists contact details for its provincial and territorial offices at www.chrc-ccdp.ca/about/reach-us_en.asp. Landlords are allowed to ask about where you work, what you earn, whether you smoke or own pets, and who will be living in the apartment. They also can – and most likely will – carry out credit and reference checks, and may ask for personal or business references as well as details of your rental history.

 For more information on the Canadian Human Rights Commission, visit the website at www.chrc-ccdp.ca, or phone 613 995 1151 or 1 888 214 1090.

Landlords can check the credit rating of prospective tenants by applying to one of Canada's official credit bureaus, as long as the tenant consents. Your credit rating is tied to any loans, credit cards or other money you have borrowed in Canada, and is calculated based on your success in paying it back. Without a Canadian credit rating or a Canadian rental history, being approved by a landlord can be difficult (even if you have stellar ratings or references in your home country). Without a job, or some other form of income, it can be almost impossible. This is a particular issue – and often hugely frustrating – for new immigrants, who may not have employment when they arrive, and haven't yet had the chance to build up a credit rating in Canada. Finding a job, if possible, should be at the top of your list. If proving income is a problem and you have a willing relative or friend in Canada, they may be able to act as your co-signer or guarantor – this means they are legally responsible for your rental and lease obligations if you are unable to pay. Settlement, community, and religious organisations can often provide newcomers with practical support and help with obtaining housing.

 The Citizenship and Immigration Canada webpage at www.cic.gc.ca/english/resources/publications/welcome/wel-20e.asp#ontario includes contact details for settlement organisations across Canada.

Types of properties

You can rent most types of property, though the majority on offer are apartments. Entire houses are harder to find in many areas and are usually more expensive. Many apartments are in divided houses (called duplexes or triplexes in some provinces), while more conventional options are walk-up (older, low-rise buildings without elevators) or high-rise apartments. Basement apartments are the most economic

TIP

Settlement, community, and religious organisations can often provide newcomers with practical support and help with obtaining housing.

> **For Andrea and Stefan Crengle, having references and a sympathetic landlord made renting their condo a fairly smooth process.**
>
> Renting was the only option for us as we knew we would be moving on sooner rather than later. The internet was the way we found our condo, and renting it was relatively simple, with our Canadian-based friends and new employers being referees for us. I think we were lucky in that our new landlord was not from Canada either and so understood our position.

rental option; beneath the main floor of a house (or sometimes of a walk-up apartment building), they may offer as much floor space as the apartment above and usually have their own entrance. The downside is that ceilings are generally low, windows (where they exist) are high and relatively small, and most – if not all – of your living space is below ground. If you crave natural light this can be an issue, particularly during the long months of winter when days are darker and accumulating snow at ground level can further block any outside views. Most rental properties are not furnished, though partially or fully furnished places can often be found if necessary. Even unfurnished apartments should come with a stove and fridge installed. Central heating is standard, and many cities have by-laws that require landlords to provide a minimum level of heat through the winter months.

Short-term renting

Though most rental agreements are for 12 months, it's usually possible to find short-term sublets or properties with shorter fixed-term leases, or weekly or monthly periodic leases. You can search for temporary rentals using the same methods outlined in *Finding a property*, below. Both on- and off-campus student housing often becomes available for subletting when long-distance students return home for two or three months during the summer – campus housing offices at local universities should be able to provide information. Many apartment-listing websites and other online search sites advertise short-term rentals and sublets, including Sublet.com and the ever-useful Craigslist, which is a trading point for everything from kitchenware to cars. As always, have your wits about you when using online posting sites – while the majority of advertisers are legitimate, scammers do unfortunately exist. If you're interested in a property, arrange to see it in person and take someone with you when you do, make sure to get any rental agreement in writing, and never hand any money over in advance (or without getting a reciept).

Imagining yourself into an empty apartment is one of the challenges of house hunting

 Sublet.com at www.sublet.com and Craigslist at www.craigslist.org are two helpful websites for finding short-term rentals, but keep an eye out for fraudulent advertisements.

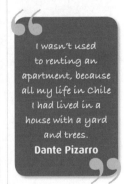

> I wasn't used to renting an apartment, because all my life in Chile I had lived in a house with a yard and trees.
> **Dante Pizarro**

Finding a property

Apartments, rooms, and houses are advertised in a variety of ways on the internet, and in the classifieds section of print and online newspapers such as those on p. 166. Many free neighbourhood papers and ethnic community papers list rentals as well. It's also common for properties to be advertised casually in shop windows or on houses (look for small black signs with orange lettering), on signs outside apartment buildings, or on community bulletin boards. Real estate agents may be able to help you find a property from among those on their lists – any commission is paid by the landlord, not by you. Rental locators are another option, though in this case you do pay a fee – usually somewhere between $50 and $100. If you use a locator, make sure the company is reputable before handing over any money or signing any papers. If you're house hunting from overseas and have friends or relatives already living in or near an area in which you're looking, they may be able to give you details of available rentals, as well as some insider information on the neighbourhood and its suitability for your needs.

 There are endless internet options for finding properties – two of the most useful are Craigslist, noted on the previous page, and www.viewit.ca.

Unless you're rolling in cash, you'll most likely have to make some compromises when it comes to finding a property. Make a list of the things that are essential in your new home; then list items of secondary importance. Try to be flexible when matching your preferences to available properties. If you're a smoker or have pets (or plan to have pets), take this into account – look for rentals without anti-pet or anti-smoking policies, rather than disregarding the landlord's wishes. However, some apartments that don't allow dogs will accept cats, and many non-smoking properties allow smoking on the front porch, so it's worth asking for clarification. When it comes to inspecting an apartment or house, take detailed notes – if you look at more than a couple of places they can quickly mesh together in your memory. *Your Guide to Renting a Home* from the Canada Mortgage and Housing Corporation (CMHC) (see p. 127) includes a useful Rental Unit Evaluation Worksheet that you can print out and take with you. The early bird really does get the worm – especially in busy rental markets – so search often, visit available properties as early as possible, and be clear about what you want so you can act swiftly when the right opportunity arises.

> **Christina Chiam initially stayed with friends in Toronto, then sublet a room for her first summer in Canada before moving into longer-term accommodation in a shared apartment.**
>
> Craigslist.com is an excellent website for share housing, rentals and sublets, and has become my main resource for house hunting. Having so few belongings lessens the challenge of moving but also limits the types of places I can look for. Given the temporary nature of my stay, I'm only interested in renting and don't want to invest in large pieces of furniture, so I've been living in shared accommodation. I was accustomed to share-house living in Australia but generally with friends, so I've had to adapt to living with strangers, and accept the pitfalls (and joys) that come with it!

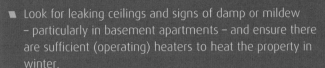

TIPS FOR THE CAREFUL RENTER

- Look for leaking ceilings and signs of damp or mildew – particularly in basement apartments – and ensure there are sufficient (operating) heaters to heat the property in winter.
- Check that windows open enough to allow airflow in the hotter months, and that they close and latch properly.
- Make sure all windows and doors lock securely, and that entranceways and stairs to upstairs or downstairs apartments can be safely accessed.
- Check whether the kitchen has a working exhaust fan.
- Smoke detectors should be installed where they can be heard from the bedrooms.
- Ask about parking options and laundry facilities. If you have to use a laundromat, is it walkable or would you need to drive or take public transit?
- Look for evidence of cockroaches, silverfish or other bugs. These pests are generally more prevalent in the warmer months, and more active at night.
- Consider whether traffic, nearby construction sites or even other tenants (such as the rowdily playing kids next door) are likely to be a noise issue.
- Walk around the neighourhood to get a feel for the area. Do you feel safe in the property, and in the surrounding streets? What's the crime rate like? Would you be comfortable walking home from the shops or the bus at night? Is there adequate lighting in the street, and at the property entrance?

Rental laws and costs

Rental conditions in Canada are regulated at the provincial level, and aim to protect both tenants and landlords. Each province or territory has its own Residential Tenancies Act (or its equivalent), and a regulatory body that oversees and administrates it. The laws that govern property rental vary considerably between provinces, so if you're planning to rent, it's important to find out the facts relevant to where you'll be living. The CMHC's invaluable Provincial and Territorial Fact Sheets are a terrific first stop in learning about your prospective province's rental regulations. These fact sheets include details of organisations and contact points that relate to tenant and landlord rights, housing assistance, and other information services, and also provide information on ordering provincial or territorial government publications.

The CMHC's Provincial and Territorial Fact Sheets are available online at www.cmhc-schl.gc.ca/en/co/reho/yogureho/fash/index.cfm

■ The laws that govern property rental vary considerably between provinces, so if you're planning to rent, it's important to find out the facts relevant to where you'll be living. The CMHC's invaluable Provincial and Territorial Fact Sheets are a terrific first stop.

■ If you have a fixed-term rental agreement and need to leave your tenancy before it expires, subletting or assigning your apartment may be a possibility.

Rental agreements

In most provinces, leases can be either fixed term (usually for 12 months, with the tenancy ending on a specific date) or periodic (week to week, month to month or sometimes year to year). A 12-month fixed-term lease is the most common rental agreement, and usually converts automatically to a month-to-month agreement at the end of the term. Regulations vary, though – in some provinces, a fixed-term lease will simply come to an end if a new lease or new terms are not negotiated in advance. Periodic leases (including year-to-year tenancies) often renew automatically for another period of the same length if neither the tenant nor the landlord give notice of termination. Knowing the rules that apply to your province is the best way to protect yourself against losing a property you want to keep living in, or ending up with unplanned rental obligations. If you have a fixed-term rental agreement and need to leave your tenancy before it expires, subletting or assigning your apartment may be a possibility. Subletting means that you find someone else to 'let' the property to, but you are still financially responsible if that person causes damage to the apartment or fails to pay rent – this is not really an advisable course of action unless you know and trust the person replacing you (or plan to return to the property after a certain period). Assigning your lease means that you legally transfer your obligations to another person. Either option has to be negotiated with your landlord. The fact sheets mentioned above include further details and specific provincial and territorial guidelines.

Most rental agreements begin on the first day of the relevant calendar month. The first month's rent is generally required upfront, with subsequent rent payable on the first day of each following month. Post-dated cheques are a common method of payment and are preferred by many landlords. These are standard cheques made out with a future date and given to the landlord in advance, often for a number of months at one time (though the landlord is not able to cash a given cheque until the date indicated). Tenants are not necessarily obliged to comply with requests for post-dated cheques – check the fact sheet for the province or territory that relates to you. In some provinces, late payment of rent (which may be as little as one day after the due date, or as many as 30 days, depending on the province) may incur a late penalty fee, or be grounds for eviction.

Security deposits

In addition to the first month's rent, landlords in most provinces may request a security deposit to protect them against the cost of damage (beyond reasonable wear and tear) caused by tenants, or failure to pay rent. If the tenant is in the clear at the end of the tenancy, the deposit is returned – and in most provinces, the landlord is obliged to pay interest on the amount. The security deposit normally equates to either half or a full month's rent (less for week-to-week periodic leases). In Ontario, landlords cannot request a security deposit for damages. They can ask for a rent deposit of up to one month's rent – thus the standard requirement in Ontario of 'first and last months' rent' – but this can only be used to cover outstanding rent, never damages. In Quebec, deposits of any kind are illegal. Rules differ significantly between provinces in terms of the amount that can legally be requested as a security deposit, the interest rate that applies, and the person or organisation permitted to hold the deposit (which may be the landlord, a bank or trust account, or a rentalsman office). Each province and territory also has specific regulations that dictate whether security deposits can be retained to cover damages or rent, or whether your landlord must apply to the rental regulatory body in order to keep any of your money. Key deposits are prohibited in most provinces, as are all other deposits aside from the security deposit. Saskatchewan and the Yukon are exceptions, and do allow key deposits to be requested.

Rent and other expenses

Rent varies widely according to property size and location. Average monthly rent for a two-bedroom apartment (non-basement) ranges from around $500 in some smaller urban centres to over $1,000 in Toronto, Vancouver, Calgary or Edmonton. As in most countries, rent is almost always higher in the cities than in the suburbs and some smaller cities, where housing demand is booming for employment or education reasons, it can also be expensive. Tenants don't pay property taxes, and rent is exempt from GST. Utilities (heat, water, gas, and hydro) may or may not be included in the monthly rate. This is usually specified in the rental advertisement and is crucial to know – heating, especially electric heating, can be a nasty extra cost in winter if it's on top of your rent. Internet and cable are sometimes included too, though telephone connection fees and bills are almost always the responsibility of the tenant. If utilities are not included in the rent, ask the landlord for an estimate of the average monthly costs. If he or she can't provide these details, the companies that provide each service to that property may be able to. As a rough example of costs, service and utility bills for a three-bedroom city apartment with electric heating and stove, washer, dryer, and wireless internet might come in at around $210 each month. Bills go to your landlord if utilities are part of your rent; if not, they go directly to you.

As with most other rental regulations, those governing rent increases and related notice periods are provincially based. Rent increases are generally only allowed once each year, and landlords have to provide substantial notice. Though many provinces terminated rent-control programmes in the 1990s, they are still in effect in others. These controls regulate the amount by which rent can be increased – landlords wishing to levy a higher increase have to apply for special permission in order to do so. All notices (such as notice of termination, rent increase or eviction) must be in writing, whether from you to the landlord or from the landlord to you. The required notice period for lease termination differs between provinces, and may also vary depending on whether the lease is fixed-term or periodic. Landlords usually have to give more extended notice than tenants.

Signing the lease

Some provinces and territories require leases to be signed by both the tenant and the landlord; others permit verbal or implied rent agreements. For your own protection, it's best to get everything in writing in case disputes arise later on – but whatever type of lease you have, it's a binding agreement between you and your landlord in which both parties have obligations and responsibilities. Checklists or signed inspection reports that record the condition of the property on moving in and again on moving out are not required in the majority of provinces. However, they

ADDING UP THE COSTS

Rent isn't the only cost to consider when deciding whether a house or apartment is affordable. Utilities, if not included, are an obvious one. Telephone, cable, and internet can quickly run up substantial bills. Parking needs to be factored in – if the property doesn't include a car space you may have to pay to park elsewhere, or purchase a resident permit from the local council in order to park on the street. Public transit or other transportation costs (such as petrol or gas) need to be calculated, especially if you'll be commuting some distance. Not all apartments – nor all apartment buildings – provide washing machines and dryers; whether you're feeding your building's machines or those at a laundromat, a weekly coin-operated wash and dry can easily drag a few hundred dollars from the kitty over a year. Tenants' or contents insurance is another big financial hit, though worthwhile, to protect yourself from liability and your belongings from harm. And you can never be sure when a landlord will decide to up the rent: if your expenses are so borderline that a small rent increase will break the bank, it might be best to contemplate a more budget-friendly housing option.

TIP

In Toronto and many other cities, home and business owners are required by law to clear snow that falls on the sidewalk outside their property. If you're a tenant, clarify whether you or your landlord has to do the shovelling.

are mandatory in some, and recommended by most. Even if this isn't a requirement where you plan to live, it's wise to document and photograph any areas of damage or concern for your own records.

Clauses prohibiting pets and smoking are often written into rental agreements and can be cause for eviction if tenants don't comply. Depending on the province, your landlord may have to prove that that your pet has caused damage to the property or disturbed other tenants, that your smoking contravenes safety regulations or is a fire-insurance issue, or that your pet or smoking has caused a serious injury, in order to evict on this basis. In some parts of the country, public housing rentals are exempt from no-smoking or no-pet clauses. Read all clauses in your lease thoroughly before signing, and make sure you understand them. Find out who has responsibility for maintaining areas of the premises such as gardens or lawns. In Toronto and many other cities, home and business owners are required by law to clear snow that falls on the sidewalk outside their property. If you're a tenant, clarify whether you or your landlord has to do the shovelling.

When you meet with your landlord to sign the lease you'll hand over the first month's rent and any required (and legally permitted) security deposit. In return, you'll get the keys to the property. You may need to cut additional copies for other people living with you at your own expense. Make sure you get a signed copy of the lease for your records, as well as dated receipts for any payments made.

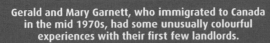

> **Gerald and Mary Garnett, who immigrated to Canada in the mid 1970s, had some unusually colourful experiences with their first few landlords.**
>
> Unknown to us, our first landlord was a major marijuana grower for the Saanich Peninsula and our second landlord, we discovered later, was an armed bank-robber. My cousin's first husband was looking after a house for the owner, who lived in Kitimat. He offered to rent us the unfinished basement cheaply while I looked for a job. He seemed to be able to have a car and a motorbike, but no visible means of support. It was only later that we discovered he was growing marijuana in a shed at the bottom of the property. Eventually the real owner retired from his work at Kitimat, but let us stay on in the basement until we found a duplex in Victoria. When we returned for a visit two years later we found the owner was in prison. He had been reluctant to dip into his savings, so over the course of a year had committed 11 armed bank robberies on the mainland, returning by ferry. Our next landlord was a Scottish shipyard worker, who lived through the thin walls of our duplex; we used to hear his drunken raving on Friday nights.

◼ Provincial and territorial regulatory bodies and tenancy acts

Alberta: Residential Tenancies Act www.qp.gov.ab.ca
Alberta Government Services: 780 427 4088 or 1 877 427 4088; www.servicealberta.gov.ab.ca
British Columbia: Residential Tenancy Act www.qp.gov.bc.ca
Residential Tenancy Head Office: 604 660 1020 or 1 800 665 8779; www.rto.gov.bc.ca
Manitoba: The Residential Tenancies Act web2.gov.mb.ca
Manitoba Consumer and Corporate Affairs — A Division of Manitoba Finance, Residential Tenancies Branch: 204 945 2476 or 1 800 782 8403; rtb@gov.mb.ca; www.residentialtenancies.mb.ca
New Brunswick: Residential Tenancies Act www.gnb.ca
Department of Justice, Office of the Rentalsman: 506 453 2557; www.gnb.ca
Newfoundland and Labrador: Residential Tenancies Act www.assembly.nl.ca
Department of Government Services — Consumer & Commerical Affairs Branch, Trade Practices Division, Residential Tenancies Section: 709 729 2610, 709 729 2608 or 1 877 829 2608; www.gs.gov.nl.ca/cca/tp/residential-tenancies
Northwest Territories: Residential Tenancies Act www.justice.gov.nt.ca/PDF/ACTS/Residential_Tenancies.pdf
NWT Rental Office: 867 920 8047 or 1 800 661 0760; www.justice.gov.nt.ca/RentalOffice/rentalofficer.htm
Nova Scotia: Residential Tenancies Act www.gov.ns.ca
Service Nova Scotia and Municipal Relations — Residential Tenancies, Public Enquiries — Service Nova Scotia & Municipal Relations: 902 424 5200 or 1 800 670 4357; www.gov.ns.ca

Nunavut: Consolidation of the Residential Tenancies Act (Nunavut)
(http://action.attavik.ca/home/justice-gn/attach-en_conlaw_prediv/Type1701.pdf)
Nunavut Housing Corporation, Rentals Officer: 867 975 7291;
rentaloffice@gov.nu.ca; www.nunavuthousing.ca
Ontario: Residential Tenancies Act and Regulations www.e-laws.gov.on.ca
Landlord and Tenant Board: 416 645 8080 or 1 888 332 3234;
www.ltb.gov.on.ca
Prince Edward Island: Rental of Residential Property Act www.gov.pe.ca/law/
statutes/pdf/l-04.pdf
Office of the Director of Residential Rental Property: 902 892 3501 or
1 800 501 6268; www.irac.pe.ca/rental
Quebec: Loi sur la Régie du logement and the Civil Code of Quebec www.rdl.gouv.
qc.ca/fr/droits/lois.asp
Régie du logement: 514 873 2245 or 1 800 683 2245; www.rdl.gouv.qc.ca
Saskatchewan: Consolidation of the Residential Tenancies Act, 2006
(www.qp.gov.sk.ca/documents/english/Statutes/Statutes/R22-0001.pdf)
Office of Residential Tenancies: 306 787 2699 or 1 888 215 2222;
www.saskjustice.gov.sk.ca/Rentalsman
Yukon: Landlord and Tenant Responsibilities general summary of the Yukon
Landlord and Tenant Act www.community.gov.yk.ca/consumer/landtact.html
Government of Yukon, Consumer & Safety Services, Community Services:
867 667 5111 or 1 800 661 0408; www.gov.yk.ca

■ BUYING A HOME

To get detailed information on all aspects of buying a home in Canada, spend some
time exploring the Canada Mortgage and Housing Corporation (CMHC) website,
www.cmhc.ca. *The Newcomer's Guide to Canadian Housing* is concise and helpful,
and a good starting point. CMHC publishes many other documents for homebuyers,
including *Settling in Canada, Homebuying Step by Step*, and the *Condominium
Buyers' Guide* (all available online or for download free of charge). A mortgage
calculator is also provided, to help you estimate what size mortgage you're likely
to be eligible for. See www.cmhc.ca/en/co/buho/index.cfm for links and details.
Canadian banks, financial institutions, and settlement organisations are also useful
sources of information on homebuying – overviews and guides can be found on
many of their websites.

There are many factors involved in finding the right house to buy. As with
renting, you need to identify your priorities and calculate what you can afford to
spend. Only in this case, the financial commitment you make is much more serious,
and much longer term. A key part of your housing choice is deciding where you
want to live. Once you've spent some time in Canada you'll have an idea of which
areas or neighbourhoods appeal. Explore these areas as thoroughly as possible
and consider how well they'll fit with your living requirements. If you're looking to
buy a new property, visit development sites in different areas and examine model
homes. Properties are advertised through real estate agents, online, in major and
local papers, and in free promotional magazines and booklets in most cities. See
Real estate agents on p. 98 for useful websites, agency contact details, and relevant

TIP

■ To get detailed
information on all
aspects of buying
a home in Canada,
spend some time
exploring the Canada
Mortgage and
Housing Corporation
(CMHC) website,
www.cmhc.ca.

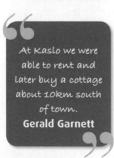

At Kaslo we were
able to rent and
later buy a cottage
about 10km south
of town.
Gerald Garnett

Chloe is a native Calgarian with a degree in Social Work and a keen interest in helping families relocate. Chloe's services are designed to guide, educate and reduce the stress of moving abroad. She is sensitive to the newcomer's desire to settle in a neighbourhood that will accommodate their lifestyle and long term goals, the first task in relocating a family is to help them find a community where they can feel a sense of belonging.

After being personally escorted through various properties, Chloe will guide them through the negotiation process, preparing a written 'Offer to Purchase' contract and advising them on 'Conditions' to the Offer for their protection; a 'possession date' is selected. If the Contract is accepted by the Sellers, the property is then called 'Conditionally Sold' and is no longer available to other purchasers. **There is no gazumping in Alberta!** She then guides you through the steps to 'Waiving the Conditions' and when complete, the status changes to Sold and the documents are executed by a Lawyer. Unlike the UK, the negotiation process is very rapid and the 'possession date' is arranged for a future date, usually within 45 days. Your future living situation is predictable and organized.

Chloe and her team love guiding newcomers through real estate transactions and helping them learn how different the process is from the UK practices. Chloe facilitates introductions to the other members of www.AlbertaRelocations.ca, team members that have been hand picked for their professionalism; knowledge and experience in helping people from the UK relocate to Alberta. And Chloe's services do not stop there! She helps new families establish social networks in their new community by offering several events each year geared toward helping newcomers make friends and contacts in their newly chosen home.

Accredited Buyer's Representative
001-403-650-0888/c21gold@telus.net

A for-sale sign advertises a home on the market

newspapers. A huge number of real estate publications are available online, in stores or by mail order. The Homes Publishing Group's range includes city-specific issues for people relocating to or within Canada (see p. 88). Many real estate firms publish their own listing papers or deliver flyers in nearby neighbourhoods. Settlement organisations for immigrants may be another avenue of information and assistance (see p. 99 for a link to organisations across the country).

House prices in Canada

According to real estate industry estimates, the average purchase price for an existing Canadian home was $340,390 in the first half of 2008. Global economic downturn has softened prices since. There's a dramatic range across the country, with Vancouver at the high end, averaging $536,000 in September 2008, and Fredericton at the low end, averaging $138,000. Prices change considerably from month to month, as well. PEI and New Brunswick currently have the lowest average home prices, at around $130,000–$140,000, while BC still leads the pack with an average of $412,000 though dropping prices (and sales) are being felt by the province. Alberta, the Northwest Territories, and Ontario are next in line, with average prices between $290,000 and $345,000. A house in Newfoundland and Labrador will set you back around $178,000; one in Quebec, about $210,000. In terms of cities, the Toronto average is $386,000, with Ottawa at $291,000, Montreal at $270,000, Calgary at $391,000, Edmonton at $325,000, Victoria at $477,000, Regina at $236,000, and Halifax at $240,000.

 The Canadian Real Estate Association (CREA) website at www.crea.ca provides statistics on monthly average sale prices for Canada's provinces and major cities. For data on Montreal, visit www.cigm.qc.ca

Taxes and fees

When buying a home in Canada, an assortment of taxes and other fees apply on top of the actual purchase price. Property taxes are paid annually by the owner and go to the local council to help pay for things like fire services, police, education, road maintenance, and garbage collection. They vary between municipalities but are usually under 1% of the taxable value of the property (based on estimated market value). In Toronto you'll pay around 0.8% for a residential property, while taxes in Montreal and Vancouver are around 0.5%. Land transfer tax – also known as land registration tax, property transfer or property purchase tax, or a deed registration fee – is paid on closing the sale. Normally provincially based (though not levied in all provinces), this is calculated on a percentage of the property's sale price, usually between 1% and 2%. First-home buyers may qualify for an exemption. The City of Toronto controversially introduced a Municipal Land Transfer Tax in 2008 in addition to the provincial levy (though first-home buyers are eligible for a rebate on this). New homes are also subject to a goods and services tax (GST), reduced to 5% as of 1 January 2008 – this comprises part of the 13% harmonised sales tax (HST) in some provinces. Existing homes don't attract GST or HST.

 The Canada Revenue Agency (or Revenu Québec, in Quebec) provides partial GST or HST rebates for new homes. See the webpage at www.cra-arc.gc.ca/E/pub/gp/rc4028/rc4028-e.html for details.

A home inspection usually costs in the vicinity of $500, and is highly recommended so you know exactly what you're in for when you take on a particular property. It can also protect you if the inspector fails to report an existing problem that requires costly repairs after you move in. (Ensure the inspector you use has errors and omissions insurance, as he or she can be held financially liable.) An appraisal is different – this estimates the value of the property, and is often required (at your expense) before a lender will approve your mortgage. You'll most likely need to pay between $250 and $350 for this. If you're buying in a rural or regional area that depends on well water and a septic system rather than mains water and sewage, you'll need a certificate showing water availability and quality – the vendor might cover the cost; otherwise, you're looking at $50 – $100. For purchases of existing condominium units (except in Quebec) there might be a charge of up to $100 for the 'estoppel certificate', which gives financial and legal details about the property. You'll also have to pay a monthly fee to the condominium board for maintenance of shared areas and facilities. If you take out a mortgage, as most homeowners have to do, there'll be fees and charges associated with that, as well as an initial down payment. (See p. 142 for more details on mortgages.) And lastly, don't forget to pay your lawyer or notary: legal fees will be at least $500 (before taxes), and may be substantially more.

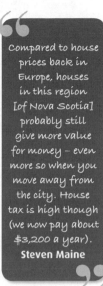

TIP

A home inspection usually costs in the vicinity of $500, and is highly recommended so you know exactly what you're in for when you take on a particular property.

Purchasing and conveyancing procedures

Professional assistance

Many different professionals can assist you in buying a home. A mortgage lender can help you work out what kind of mortgage you can afford, so you can set a purchase budget. Real estate agents or realtors can guide you through the house-hunting and purchasing processes. A lawyer (or notary, in Quebec) is invaluable in dealing with the legalities of the purchase and protecting your interests: he or she will ensure that the title on the house is clear, that there are no outstanding work orders or unpaid back taxes, and that your offer to purchase – when you're ready to make one – is in order. Real estate agents can help you prepare the offer to purchase, but as it becomes a legally binding document once accepted by the vendor it's best to have your lawyer involved as well. Lawyers will also take care of closing the sale. Law societies or bar associations in your region can supply you with details of lawyers specialising in real estate. Home inspectors and appraisers have specific roles, as outlined previously under *Taxes and fees*. It's wise to take advantage of their expertise – the financial outlay this requires is negligible next to the expense they may save you in the long run. The Canadian climate can be hard on houses: piled-up snow puts pressure on roofs, and when melting can leak through in unexpected places; pipes freeze and burst; temperature extremes cause timbers to shift, shrink, and expand. Older homes may use lead plumbing or lead-based paints, or contain asbestos; termites are destructive and expensive to get rid of; salt in coastal areas can be damaging. Your real estate agent might recommend a home inspector, or you can find one through a local or national association such as the Canadian Association of Home and Property Inspectors (CAHPI). A trained appraiser's main advantage to you (other than helping secure your mortgage) is in giving you a clear idea of the value of the property you're considering. Many appraisers are members of the Appraisal Institute of Canada (AIC) or similar associations.

 You can find the Canadian Association of Home and Property Inspectors (CAHPI) online at www.cahpi.ca, and the Appraisal Institute of Canada (AIC) at www.aicanada.ca. See p. 144 for phone and email details.

The sale agreement

An existing house is usually purchased in a personal arrangement between the buyer and the owner, with the real estate agent (in combination with your lawyer) acting as a formal go-between. When you find a house you want to buy, you need to prepare, and then make, an offer to purchase (or an agreement of purchase and sale). You can specify that the offer is conditional upon a satisfactory home inspection, the completion of certain repairs, selling your own home or receiving mortgage approval. As mentioned above, an agent can assist with this, and it should ideally be checked by a lawyer. Your offer should also include a deposit: this demonstrates that you're a serious buyer and holds the property for you if the offer is accepted (if it's rejected, your deposit is returned). The seller has a limited period of time in which to accept or reject the offer or to make a counter offer requesting certain amendments – this is specified in your offer, and is usually between 48 and

72 hours. Sellers are not obliged to accept an offer, even if it's at the asking price (though the agent's commission may still be payable if the seller rejects an offer at asking price, which can be an incentive for them to sell).

Buyers of brand-new homes often deal directly with the development company or builder. Most builders offer an after-sale warranty that covers you against defects in workmanship or materials for one year. Builders may also provide a New Home Warranty through an independent, third-party warranty corporation, which provides more extensive protection and quality control. Third-party warranties are compulsory in Quebec, Ontario, and BC, and optional elsewhere (though currently unavailable in Nunavut or the Northwest Territories).

 The Canada Mortgage and Housing Corporation (CMHC) webpage lists New Home Warranty Program contacts at www.cmhc-schl.gc.ca/en/co/buho/hostst/hostst_007.cfm≠whome. More details on warranties and sales contracts can be found at www.cmhc-schl.gc.ca/en/co/buho/buho_004.cfm.

Buying a condominium

Though the processes are related, there are key differences between buying a condominium (whether an apartment or another type of residence) and buying a house. For this reason, although the professionals involved are much the same as those discussed on p. 98, it's recommended that you choose people who specialise in condominiums. Each province or territory has its own legislation for condominium operation, and every condominium corporation has different regulations. (CMHC's *Condominium Buyers' Guide* has more information and provincial contact details – see p. 136).. The obvious distinction is the monthly (and mandatory) maintenance fee levied by the condominium board. Individual apartment owners have joint ownership of the land and are responsible for the shared costs of communal facilities – your ownership percentage and the fees you pay each month are normally based on your unit's value in proportion to the whole corporation. Fees cover operations, maintenance and cleaning of the building and grounds, and may include utilities. Some condominiums have services such as gymnasiums and swimming pools, and these add to your monthly charges. In luxurious condominiums the maintenance fee can equal the monthly rent of a smaller apartment, but for convenience, location, and resale value, buying a condo can be a wise investment. Relative affordability and minimal maintenance obligations are also advantages. There are disadvantages too: all condominiums have rules that must be followed; noise from nearby neighbours can be an issue; and there are often restrictions on pets, renovations, and general activities. The estoppel certificate (see p. 139) is crucial if buying a resale condo. This is a financial statement that tells you what your monthly fees will be and whether the seller has any outstanding payments, and it will need to be shown to your mortgage lender. Existing condominiums also have a reserve fund to cover major or unexpected repairs – make sure you know how much money it contains, to protect yourself against unwelcome extra bills in the event of a shortfall. If the condominium is brand new there won't yet be an estoppel certificate – you'll need to obtain a disclosure statement from the developer instead. The information provision in Quebec differs again – refer to the *Condominium Buyers' Guide* for details.

Mortgages

Mortgages with Canadian companies

Virtually every homebuyer will need to take out a mortgage, and competition between financial institutions makes it relatively straightforward to find one that suits your situation. In Canada, mortgages can be issued by chartered banks, trust companies, finance companies, insurance companies, credit unions, and private lenders. Mortgage brokers are not usually lenders, but can help you locate one if you need assistance – in most cases the lender pays their fees. You can take out either a conventional or a high-ratio mortgage, depending on what you can afford as a down payment. A conventional mortgage requires at least 20% of the purchase price to be paid up front. A high-ratio mortgage lets you put down as little as 5%, but the lender will require you to take out mortgage loan insurance to protect their investment in case you can't pay them back. (Zero-down mortgages have also been possible, though a recent crackdown means this is no longer permitted for government-backed mortgages, including those insured by the government-owned CMHC.) As for any insurance, premiums apply. You can apply through CMHC, which has a 60%–70% share of the market, or through one of Canada's private mortgage loan insurers, Genworth Financial Canada, AIG United Guaranty Canada or the PMI Group, Inc. Canada (see p. 144 for contacts). You should also consider mortgage life insurance, which pays off your remaining mortgage if you or your spouse dies.

The primary consideration when selecting the lender and term of your mortgage is the level of interest you have to pay. Interest rates for most mortgages are in the vicinity of 5% to 8%. Rates are generally higher for long-term mortgages, so a shorter term is usually more economical overall. Each repayment you make will be higher, but you'll pay the loan off sooner, with less interest. An open or variable mortgage is an option if you want to pay off your debt more quickly or make additional repayments, though interest rates may not be as competitive. Closed mortgages give you security and lower rates, but there's often a penalty for making extra payments or paying your mortgage in full before the end of the term. Mortgage options are many, varied, and can be quite complex, so talk to a broker or a number of lenders about possible options, and do some research of your own. (Be aware that your credit score can be affected to some degree when a lender or mortgage broker checks your credit history.) Company websites are a good place to start. To find out about mortgages offered by banks, check the contact details under Major banks, p. 78.

> The CMHC webpage at www.cmhc.ca/en/co/moloin/index.cfm links to a comprehensive list of National Housing Act (NHA) approved lenders. The Canadian Equity Group has a similar listing at www.canequity.com/mortgage-resources/cmhc_approved_mortgage_lenders.stm.

> We managed to get a mortgage with RBC easily, mainly because we asked for less than we qualified for, put down a decent deposit, and had permanent residence. We also used the branch that my company banks with.
> **Steven Maine**

Repayment conditions

Mortgages can be negotiated for any length of time, but the majority have terms of six months to 25 years. The term of your mortgage doesn't refer to how long you have to pay off your home, but to how long you're expected to make a specific

repayment at a specific interest rate. The actual time over which you repay the loan
is known as the amortisation period. For example, you might choose a three-year
mortgage, with a repayment schedule geared to amortise the cost of your home
over 30 years. Your monthly repayment would be established at the beginning of
the term, and the interest rate would remain the same for all three years (unless
you have a variable or multi-rate mortgage). At the end of three years you would
have the opportunity to renew or renegotiate your mortgage, or pay off the loan in
full. Your lender will likely offer to renew your mortgage if your financial situation is
stable, but you also have the option of moving to another financial institution if you
can negotiate a better deal elsewhere. Lenders use specific formulae to determine
how much they will lend you, based predominantly on your household income.

 Websites such as www.mymortgagecanada.com, www.mortgagesincanada.
com, and www.canequity.com offer rate comparisons and tools to calculate
mortgage payments.

TIP

■ At the end of
your mortgage term
you would have the
opportunity to renew
or renegotiate your
mortgage, or pay off
the loan in full.

Offshore mortgages

Some international banks and financial institutions provide mortgages for the
purchase of overseas properties, but homes intended for use as a primary residence
are often excluded. You may be able to re-mortgage or take a second mortgage on
property in your home country in order to finance a purchase in Canada, but if part of
your original mortgage was used for home improvements or capital raising you may
lose some tax relief. Some offshore financing companies have an online presence

only, making it difficult to validate their legitimacy (and the legality of many online advertisers in this field is questionable). If you're considering an offshore mortgage, talk to reputable banks or lending institutions only, and consult with an independent lawyer.

Canada itself offers little scope for offshore mortgages. Strict regulations and careful enforcement rule out any other schemes designed to make mortgage interests and costs tax-deductible, and it's wise to be wary of any scheme or company that suggests otherwise.

■ Useful contacts for homebuyers

AIG United Guaranty Canada: 416 640 8924, 1 866 414 9109 or 1877 244 8422 (for underwriting inquiries); info@aigug.ca; www.aigug.ca

Appraisal Institute of Canada (AIC): 613 234 6533; info@aicanada.ca; www.aicanada.ca

Canada Mortgage and Housing Corporation: 613 748 2000 or 1 800 668 2642; chic@cmhc-schl.gc.ca; www.cmhc-schl.gc.ca

Canada Revenue Agency (CRA): 1 800 959 8281; www.cra-arc.gc.ca

Canadian Association of Home and Property Inspectors (CAHPI): 613 839 5344 or 1 888 748 2244; info@cahpi.ca; www.cahpi.ca

Canadian Equity Group Inc. (CEG): 1 888 818 4262; www.canequity.com

Financial Consumer Agency of Canada (FCAC): 613 996 5454 or 1 866 461 3222; www.fcac-acfc.gc.ca

Canadian Real Estate Association (CREA): 613 237 7111; info@crea.ca; www.crea.ca

Genworth Financial Canada: 1 800 511 8888; mortgage.info@genworth.com; www.genworth.ca

Homes Publishing Group: 905 479 4663 or 1 800 363 4663; info@homesmag.com; www.homespublishinggroup.com

PMI Canada: 416 607 4400 or 416 607 4401 (President and CEO); www.pmicanada.ca

Revenu Québec: 418 659 6299 or 1 800 267 6299; www.revenu.gouv.qc.ca

■ SERVICES AND UTILITIES

TIP

Many companies give you the option of averaging out your estimated usage over the year, to reduce the financial strain of peaks in particular months (such as hefty heating bills over the winter).

All but the most remote communities in Canada are already hooked up to electrical, sewage, and telephone systems, and dealing with utility companies is generally straightforward. Bills are issued monthly, bimonthly or quarterly, depending on the company and on the service provided. Charges may be either estimated or based on actual usage. Many companies give you the option of averaging out your estimated usage over the year, to reduce the financial strain of peaks in particular months (such as hefty heating bills over the winter). You can also set up authorised payment plans, so your bills are paid automatically from a designated bank account. Actual meter readings might be carried out every two months, quarterly or just twice a year again, this varies between providers. Discrepancies in estimated billing (such as under or overpayment) are corrected in the bill that follows the reading.

Electricity, natural gas and water services are regulated to varying degrees in each province, usually through independently operated government agencies or boards (see below for contact details). This means that a specified local provider delivers these utilities to your property at set rates. Deregulation and restructuring are changing the face of the Canadian energy market however – particularly in Alberta. While customers continue to have electricity and gas delivered by the regulated provider for their area, they can now often choose to pay a competitive retailer for the energy they actually consume. These retailers do sometimes offer a better deal; in other cases you're better off sticking with your original provider. You should be able to get details of energy retailers in your area from the relevant provincial regulatory body (see below), and some will be listed in the local *Yellow Pages*. (They're also highly likely to phone you at home – regularly – in an attempt to solicit your business.)

When moving into your first home or apartment in Canada, you'll have to make credit arrangements with the utility companies. This may involve making a deposit on future charges. In the case of your telephone company, you may need to provide a deposit against long-distance bills. Your landlord – or agent, if you're buying a property – will tell you who your utility companies are so you can arrange for any necessary connections. (If all basic utilities are included in your rent, you'll only need to connect your telephone, and internet or cable television if you want them.) Arrange to have the meters read on or before the day you take responsibility for the property, so you're not held liable for the previous tenant's expenses. Make appointments for meter readings as far in advance as possible. If you're moving into accommodation that has been vacant for a while, the power and gas may have been turned off. Call a few days in advance to arrange for reconnection. Note that in rented accommodation, repairs to the central heating or hot-water heater should be dealt with by the landlord. You must also inform your landlord if you plan to change the power supply or install any major appliances.

This section covers the major utilities and services you are likely to need or want in your Canadian home. Property tax, another periodic expense for homeowners, is covered on p. 133.

■ Public utilities boards

Alberta Utilities Commission: 780 427 9362; info@auc.ab.ca; www.auc.ab.ca
British Columbia Utilities Commission: 604 660 4700 or 1 800 663 1385; Commission.Secretary@bcuc.com; www.bcuc.com
The Public Utilities Board, Manitoba: 204 945 2638 or 1 866 854 3698; publicutilities@gov.mb.ca; www.pub.gov.mb.ca
New Brunswick Energy and Utilities Board: 506 658 2504 or 1 866 766 2782; general@nbeub.ca; www.pub.nb.ca
Newfoundland and Labrador Board of Commissioners of Public Utilities: 709 726 0742 or 1 866 782 0006; ito@pub.nl.ca; www.pub.nf.ca
Northwest Territories Public Utilities Board: 867 874 3944; www.nwtpublicutilitiesboard.ca
Nova Scotia Utility and Review Board: 902 424 4448; uarb.board@gov.ns.ca; www.nsuarb.ca
Ontario Energy Board: 416 314 2455 or 1 877 632 2727; www.oeb.gov.on.ca
Prince Edward Island Regulatory and Appeals Commission: 902 892 3501 or 1 800 501 6268; info@irac.pe.ca; www.irac.pe.ca
Régie de l'énergie Québec: (Montreal) 514 873 2452 or 1 888 873 2452, (elsewhere in Quebec) 418 646 0970 or 1 888 527 3443; secretariat@regie-energie.qc.ca; www.regie-energie.qc.ca

FACT

■ When moving into your first home or apartment in Canada, you'll have to make credit arrangements with the utility companies. This may involve making a deposit on future charges.

Saskatchewan Rate Review Panel: 306 934 1948 or 1 877 368 7075; input@saskratereview.ca; www.saskratereview.ca
Yukon Utilities Board: 867 667 5058; yub@utilitiesboard.yk.ca; www.yukonutilitiesboard.yk.ca

Electricity

Canada uses 110-volt electricity at 60 hertz. If you're coming from a country where the standard voltage is 220, 230 or 240, such as the UK, Australia or most parts of Europe, you may be able to use voltage converters or transformers on some appliances. Many mobile phones, MP3 players, and camera chargers are designed to work on a range of voltages (though you'll still need a converter to fit Canadian wall sockets), but energy-sucking items like hairdryers or large appliances are unlikely to run efficiently, and may pose a safety hazard. When you add the expense of transporting heavy appliances (and the risk of damage) to the potential difficulty of using them in Canada, it's probably simpler and more practical to purchase new equipment when you arrive. You can find advertisements for cheap used appliances in the local press or on websites such as Craigslist (www.craigslist.org), though high repair costs can be a risk. Canadian discount electronic stores or department stores often sell affordable appliances as well. According to the Canadian Centre for Energy Information, about 19% of Canadian households are heated with electricity. Thermal and nuclear stations generate around a third of Canada's electricity; almost all the rest is produced from hydroelectric projects such as Hydro-Québec's massive James Bay development. (Thus the common use in Canada of 'hydro' to refer to electricity, rather than water.) Wind, solar, and biomass energy industries are also growing.

 The Canadian Centre for Energy Information provides extensive explanations, analysis and data on Canadian energy sources and their use. Visit www.centreforenergy.com, call 403 263 7722 or 1 877 606 4636, or send an email via the website.

Gas

The use of piped-in natural gas has been promoted in Canada in recent years, and it currently supplies more than half the energy used to heat Canadian homes. Prices can be volatile and spiked in the winter of 2000–2001, causing such hardship that many governments were forced to offer rebates. To avoid dramatic fluctuations, customers can lock in a contract setting the price of their gas for up to five years, though the price you pay to begin with will be higher than going market rates. (Watch out for the hard sell from telemarketers or door-to-door contract salespeople as well; they often present themselves quasi-officially, asking to speak with the bill payer, and may try to press you into signing a contract that's not necessarily in your best interests.) The government and some utility companies offer financial incentives to switch to gas, and if you're building your own home it's often preferable to electricity for heating, cooking and hot water. Bottled propane and butane are less common fuels, but widely available for use in camping equipment or mobile homes.

TIP

Many mobile phones, MP3 players, and camera chargers are designed to work on a range of voltages, but energy-sucking items like hairdryers or large appliances are unlikely to run efficiently, and may pose a safety hazard.

TIP

In Canada, 'hydro' is commonly used to refer to electricity, rather than water.

Oil

Oil is still a common fuel for heating, particularly in the Atlantic provinces, and is used in 11% of households. Oil heating is generally via either a forced-air or a hot-water (hydronic) furnace. Oil is stored in large tanks that hold around 1000 litres (220 gallons) of fuel, is delivered to most residences by truck, and is priced by the litre. Leaks and spills are an ongoing environmental concern. If you're moving into a home heated with oil, arrange to have the fuel in the tank measured so you won't end up paying the previous tenant's bill as well. The price of heating oil has climbed steadily over the last few years. Costs have a tendency to increase with demand in the colder months, and drop back as things warm up – locked-in contracts or capped rates are often possible. Major petroleum companies and other fuel distributors will deliver oil. Some monitor your estimated usage and deliver replacement fuel automatically. If your distributor doesn't, check how far ahead you should place your order to ensure you don't run out – especially in winter.

> *Oil to heat the house is very expensive now – we pay around $250 a month all year for this.*
> **Steven Maine**

Water

Water and sewage services are supplied through the municipality you live in – for example, the City of Ottawa or the Town of Innisfail. You can find their contact details online, or under *Water* in the blue (government) pages of your local *Yellow Pages*. You may be billed on either a flat or a metered rate, and minimum charges apply in some municipalities. Bills are normally issued monthly or every second month. Unless your water supply comes from a well, tap water is generally safe to drink (and usually palatable, if a little fluoride-flavoured in some parts of the country), but many people prefer to filter their water. If the mains supply springs a leak you should contact the water company, but to install appliances or fix related problems, call a plumber.

Telephone

In 1876, Alexander Graham Bell placed the first long-distance telephone call from tiny Paris, Ontario, to his father, just 12km away in Brantford. These days, phone services in Canada are efficient and not overly expensive, and you can have a line installed within days. Handsets can be purchased at hardware or electronics stores (the cheapest are around $20) or rented from your phone company. The installation of a new telephone line can cost around $100 (though prices vary substantially between service providers), but most homes with previous tenants will already be wired for at least one. You may still need to pay a re-connection fee of around $55. Unlike the per-call or timed-call systems in many countries, in Canada you pay a flat monthly fee that includes all local calls. Depending on the provider and package you opt for this can range from about $20 to $50, but you'll need to allow for taxes and surcharges too. Bills are issued monthly. Features such as call waiting, call forwarding, and call screening are included in some packages, or otherwise available for small monthly fees. Long-distance and overseas charges are not included in the flat rate, and can be expensive. Calls from one part of a large region to another can sometimes be long distance even if the phone numbers use the same prefix.

FACT

In 1876, Alexander Graham Bell placed the first long-distance telephone call from tiny Paris, Ontario, to his father, just 12km away in Brantford.

Canada's largest communications companies include Bell Canada, Telus, Rogers Communications, and Bell Aliant, and they dominate heavily. Local markets were opened to competition for long-distance business in the mid 1990s, and dozens of other companies have entered the scene since, providing both local and long-distance services. This has led to much lower long-distance pricing from players such as Primus, Phonetime, and Globealive (which operates Yak, LooneyCall and other discount services). VoIP-based outfits like Vonage, which work through a broadband internet connection, provide both local and long-distance services, and can easily out-price the big kids. If you prefer, you can use one provider for local calls and a more competitively priced company for long-distance and international calling. If you do change to a cheaper carrier you'll most likely find your current provider approaching you with ever-cheaper rates as well. With plenty of choice out there it's not hard to find services offering rates of just $0.02 or $0.03 per minute for calls to the UK, Australia, New Zealand, and most parts of Europe. Fax machines and dial-up internet modems are available at business supply or electronics stores, and can be plugged into any phone jack.

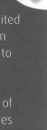

DON'T CALL ME

Most of us have experienced the annoyance of the unsolicited telemarketing call: the long pause before the caller clicks in and speaks; the difficulty pronouncing names; the request to speak to 'Mrs' Smith when you've never been married (or to 'Mr' Smith when you've never been a man). Rarely do telemarketers in Canada introduce themselves at the start of the call, though the law, under the Competition Act, requires it. And while the majority of call recipients understand that telemarketers are just doing a job, they'd usually prefer that that job wasn't being done on their time. If this sounds like you, Canada's new National Do Not Call List should have you jumping for joy. Launched in September 2008, under the operation of Bell Canada, this nationwide registry allows you to register your telephone number for three years at a time, reducing (if not completely eliminating) unwanted calls. For more details, see the Canadian Radio-television and Telecommunications Commission fact sheet at www.crtc.gc.ca/eng/INFO_SHT/t1026.htm. For information on telemarketing under the Competition Act, visit the Competition Bureau webpage at www.competitionbureau.gc.ca/epic/site/cb-bc.nsf/en/01228e.html.

Mobile phones

With prices falling rapidly over the past few years, mobile or cell phone usage among Canadians has become increasingly common. More than two-thirds of households have at least one. Most wireless network providers offer a range of monthly plans and prepaid service options. Plans generally begin at $20 or $25 per month. Service and emergency 911 access fees usually add another $7–$10 each month, and some providers charge an activation fee. You can generally choose not to have a contract, or can sign a one, two or three-year agreement. Various incentives are offered to encourage you to sign, and handsets are usually included free or at low cost. Without a contract, you'll normally have to buy a handset outright unless you bring your own (see below). To get a contract you'll need to show that you're living in Canada (not just travelling through) and you'll be asked to provide identification. A passport and your visa (or Permanent Resident Card, if you have one) will probably suffice, though the provider may also want to see your SIN (see p. 193). Prepaid plans are great if you're a minimal to moderate cell user, like to control what you spend, or want to avoid being locked into a monthly rate or plan. You top up your account with vouchers or by credit card, and there's no contract or monthly bill. Standard call rates are generally higher – usually $0.20 to $0.30 per minute – but many prepaid plans offer cheap rates at certain times of day (evenings and weekends, for example), or other deals. Depending on your provider, your prepaid start-up kit may or may not include an initial credit towards calls. Calls are usually charged per minute for both monthly and prepaid plans, though 'unlimited' or flat-rate options are sometimes possible. You pay to receive calls on your cell phone, as well as to make them. Some services such as caller ID, voicemail, and call waiting may be included in your wireless plan; in other cases you pay extra to use these.

Major wireless providers using GSM technology are currently limited to Rogers Wireless and Fido (which is owned by Rogers). If you're bringing a GSM-standard handset from home (which you can use with either a contract or a prepaid plan), check it has the correct band frequencies for North America – generally GSM-1900 and GSM-850 – otherwise it won't operate. You may be able to set up global roaming from your home country so your existing number continues to work in Canada, but call rates make this prohibitively expensive for anything more than very short-term use.

In Canada, your mobile phone number normally has the same area code as landline numbers in your region – calls to your cell phone within that region are therefore considered local. Make sure your new cell-phone number has the correct area code for the city or region you'll be residing in – otherwise, every call you make and receive 'locally' will be billed as long distance.

> ❝
> **Christina Chiam was surprised to discover that in Canada, cell-phone users pay for both incoming and outgoing calls:**
>
> I find that some everyday needs are not as well serviced in Canada as they are in Australia. For example, cell-phone users are charged to receive calls. Cell-phone coverage is province specific, so if you travel outside of Ontario, you're charged a long-distance rate.
> ❞

Most of the telecommunications companies listed on p. 151 provide wireless services, as do Virgin (www.virginmobile.ca, partnered with Bell), Solo (www.solomobile.ca, owned by Bell), and new-kid-on-the-block Koodo (www.koodomobile.com, owned by Telus).

Internet

Whether planning a trip, researching a paper, emailing family overseas or just checking the weather, using the internet has become an everyday part of life. In most Canadian workplaces internet access is a given, and of the three-quarters of the population with a home computer, almost all are connected. Various types of internet connections are used in Canada, including dial-up, DSL (digital subscriber line), cable modem, satellites and wireless. In some areas you can also get portable internet plans which allow you to connect to your service anywhere in your coverage area. Internet performance and cost depend on which service you choose, and availability may be restricted by where you live, particularly in remote or less populated regions.

 Major internet service providers (ISPs) include Rogers, Bell, Telus, and Shaw, though you can choose from numerous others as well. The website at www.canadianisp.com lets you search for providers in each province in Canada.

Monthly plans with the big-name companies start at around $20 (before taxes) for basic service (normally dial-up), with top-of-the-range connections costing upwards of $80. Smaller providers often price more cheaply. In either case, check what you'll be paying and what you'll get for it carefully – there are often hidden costs to do with service or access fees, modems, and taxes. Minimum contract terms can apply, especially for bundled services. If you're not able (or don't wish) to get your own connection, most cities have internet cafés where you can pay to go online. Public libraries normally allow free use of their computers (including internet access) for a limited period of time each day, and some have wireless access (Wi-Fi) for visitors with their own laptops. You can also take your laptop along to one of the increasing number of coffee shops that offer wireless to customers. The larger chains still tend to make you pay, but many independent coffee shops let you connect for free. Just order your latte, open your computer and you're on your way.

Cable television

Around 65% of Canadian households have some type of cable television, and hundreds of channels are available to subscribers for different monthly fees. Services may be supplied via analogue cable (though this will be phased out in the next few years) digital cable (which offers additional channels and better clarity), or direct-to-home satellite. In some areas, connection is available through multipoint distribution systems (which use a rooftop aerial) or telephone lines. Installation can cost around $30-$100, and monthly charges range from under $30 for some basic packages to up near $100 for those with all the bells and whistles. Subscriptions to extra channels or value packages are also possible for added fees, and many companies offer video-on-demand or pay-per-view for digital viewers. The six largest providers in Canada are Rogers, Bell ExpressVu, Shaw, Cogeco, Star Choice, and Videotron. They supply service to almost 10 million people, though many smaller outfits also offer cable services. For information on some of the cable channels available in Canada, see p. 171.

■ Major communications companies

Rogers: 416 935 5555 or 1 888 764 3771; www.rogers.com
Bell: 310 2355 (from any area code in Canada); www.bell.ca
Shaw: 403 750 4500 or 1 888 750 7429; www.shaw.ca
Cogeco: 1 866 427 7451; www.cogeco.ca
Star Choice: 1 866 782 7932; www.starchoice.com
Vidéotron: 514 281 1711 or 1 888 433 6876; www.videotron.com
Telus: 1 866 558 2273 (wireless) or 1 877 310 4638 (internet); www.telus.com
SaskTel: 1 800 727 5835; www.sasktel.com
Aliant: 1 866 425 4268; www.aliant.net
NorthernTel: 1 800 360 8555; www.northerntel.ca
Telebec: 1 888 835 3232; www.telebec.com
MTS (Manitoba Telecom Services Inc.): 204 225 5687; www.mts.ca
B2B2C: 514 908 5420 or 1 800 965 9065; www.b2b2c.ca
Fido: 1 888 945 3436; www.fido.ca

■ MOVING IN

Furniture

Unless you bring your household contents with you, you'll need to acquire at least some new furniture when you arrive. How you go about this will depend on your budget, home size, and style. Stores like The Brick (www.thebrick.com), Leon's (www.leons.ca), Home Furniture (www.homefurniture.ca) or United Furniture Warehouse (www.ufw.com) sell a large selection of mid-range furniture and cater to a variety of tastes and budgets, as do department stores such as The Bay (www.thebay.com), Sears (www.sears.ca) or Zellers (www.zellers.com), and numerous independent stores. Payment plans or deferred terms may be available to approved customers. If you're after something more exclusive, like a down-filled leather sofa or a designer lamp, high-end retailers like DeBoer's (www.deboers.com), Koolhaus (www.koolhausdesign.com) or Livingspace (www.livingspace.com) could be more your style. Furniture rental or rent-to-own companies like Insta-rent (www.insta-rent.ca), which operates through The Brick and United Furniture Warehouse, can be practical if you're staying short term or don't want to buy items outright. Consignment or resale stores often sell quality furnishings at reasonable prices, and thrift stores can be a great source of bits and pieces at very low cost. Some have regular cut-price sales (often midweek) to encourage customers. Dining tables, chairs, cabinets, dressers, bed ends, and various electrical items can be found at Value Village (www.valuevillage.com), Goodwill (www.goodwill.on.ca), and the Salvation Army (www.thriftstore.ca), as well as second-hand and junk stores. Quality varies of course, and you may need to visit multiple times to stumble across the

TIP

■ Furniture rental or rent-to-own companies like Insta-rent can be practical if you're staying short-term or don't want to buy items outright.

perfect sidetable, but these are definitely avenues worth exploring if affordability is a consideration. The ubiquitous Ikea (www.ikea.com) offers the same practical, attractive, flat-packed solutions in Canada's major cities as it does worldwide, while vintage and antique stores provide options for more eclectic tastes.

Home insurance

Property or home insurance protects you against financial loss relating to your home and its contents, and against personal liability if someone is injured on your property. It generally covers the structure of your home and your personal effects, but not the building's foundation or the land. Most lenders require you to have property insurance in order to approve a mortgage. If you're renting, your landlord should have insurance on the building, but this won't normally cover your belongings or protect you from personal liability. Tenant's insurance (which is much cheaper than homeowner's insurance) is available to cover you in this situation. Condominium owners usually need insurance to cover contents and personal liability, and may also be responsible for insuring fixtures and fittings or unit improvements – this varies between provinces, so check the relevant legislation for details (government contacts can be found in the *Condominium Buyers' Guide,* mentioned on p.141. The condominium board normally covers the building and common areas.

Insurance in Canada is reasonably priced, with competition keeping premiums quite low. Policies are usually both flexible and generous, with many extending coverage to personal belongings stolen from cars or hotel rooms, or to dependent students living away from home in order to study. You determine the dollar amount or 'replacement cost' to insure your property for. No insurer will cover you against

GET MOVING

Most rental tenancies begin on the first of the month, which means most people move on or around this date. Apparently, moving on the first is also popular among homebuyers, particularly in the summer months. In Montreal, so many people move house on the first of July – which is also Canada Day and a national holiday – that it's regarded as a quasi-official moving day (in fact it's a hangover from a rental-lease law change in the 1970s). If you're renting, and the previous tenants have already moved out, your landlord might be willing to take an extra week's rent and let you move in early. If you must move on the first, make sure to book a moving van or truck (if you need one) and get yourself organised well in advance. Otherwise, you might find yourself stuck on the day with no way to move your belongings. If you hire a moving company, you may also want to take out insurance against the potential loss or breakage of your belongings during the move.

TIP

■ Most lenders require you to have property insurance in order to approve a mortgage.

overland flooding, but you may want to include coverage for serious water damage or sewer backups, particularly if you're living on the main floor or in a basement apartment – heavy rain or sudden snowmelts can sometimes overload home or municipal plumbing systems, with costly consequences. Items such as jewellery, art, bicycles, and musical instruments usually have to be insured separately, which can add to your premium. Keep a record of your possessions and any serial numbers. Photographing the furnished rooms of your house will also help if you ever need to make a claim.

Insurance can be purchased directly from an agency or through a broker. Most banks also offer coverage. It pays to compare, as policies and premiums vary considerably between companies. Brokers work on your behalf to find the most competitive policy, but charge a fee. The Insurance Brokers Association of Canada website (www.ibac.ca) has links to provincial broker associations, which contain member lists. You can also reach them by phone on 416 367 1831 or send an email to ibac@ibac.ca. If you're looking for an agent, the Insurance Bureau of Canada – to which 90% of insurance agencies belong – includes a directory of members at www.ibc.ca, or you can call them on 416 362 2031.

 Websites such as www.myinsuranceshopper.ca and www.kanetix.ca search online for the best insurance rates.

Daily Life

■ CULTURE SHOCK

A change might be as good as a holiday, but it can also be a lot more confronting. Depending on where you're moving from, what languages you speak, and where you settle, your first impressions of Canada will vary greatly. Isolation is a common problem for newcomers, due sometimes to geographical location and sometimes to a lack of friends and social contacts. There will inevitably be cultural differences – and this is the case between different parts of the country as well. You may end up living in a much bigger city or a much smaller town than you're used to. If you're from a southern-hemisphere country like New Zealand or Australia, the seasons will be back-to-front. Supermarkets and other stores won't stock all the brands or types of products you use back home. Social expectations and behaviours, and ways of forming friendships, may be different as well.

Prepare a little before you leave by learning about Canada's history and current political, economical, environmental, and cultural scene. Once you arrive, start exploring: walk, visit sights, use the transit system, eat the food. The best way to start creating a new network is to get involved. Join local clubs, organisations or sporting teams. Use immigrant-serving publications and organisations as a way to meet people, but make efforts to get to know Canadian-born residents as well. Look for points of commonality and shared interests, and try to avoid dwelling on things that seemed better in your own country – clichéd as it sounds, a positive, open attitude is crucial. Expat forums can be helpful sources of advice from others who've been in the same situation (see p. 136). Children tend to adapt more quickly than adults; if you have kids, you'll have opportunities to meet the parents of those they befriend. Finding a job is a huge help; obviously, it brings in income, but it also produces a sense of achievement and validity. If you're unable to work, or are having trouble getting a job, consider taking a short course at a local college or institution, or even studying long-term. This can be a great way to meet similarly minded people, while improving your employability.

Give yourself time – Canada is a very different place at different times of year, and you need to let a full cycle of seasons pass to really experience it. Winters can be long and tiring, particularly if you're unused to so many months of snow and cold – and there's no denying that they're cold. While Toronto generally stays

> **Christina Chiam moved from Melbourne, Australia, to Toronto. The cultural parallels between the two countries helped keep the culture shock to a minimum.**
>
> Moving to any new country requires an adjustment period, but given Canada and Australia's close ties and cultural similarities, this wasn't overwhelming. There are no language barriers, except for the occasional confused look when slang terms are bandied about! Their currency is straightforward, their obsession with sport entertainingly familiar and their pop-culture references – while heavy on the North-American side – are easily translatable for Australians.

above −10°C or −15°C (Vancouver is warmer still), northern Ontario and the Prairies frequently register in the minus 20s or 30s. Cold snaps of −40°C are not uncommon here, nor in Ottawa or Quebec (and there's no describing that kind of cold until you've felt it). Navigating icy roads and sidewalks, wearing cumbersome gear and having your outdoor activities restricted are all things you'll need to adjust to. Make sure you have the appropriate clothes: a coat designed for the Canadian climate, along with lined and waterproof boots, will go a long way to ensuring a happy first winter.

Innocent-faced bandit: a bold raccoon poses for the camera in Vancouver's Stanley Park, BC

TIP

▪ Unless you have an excellent long-distance phone carrier, keep a stock of phone cards on hand so you don't run up horrendous bills.

LOST IN TRANSLATION

Unless you sound peculiarly Canadian already, your accent can quickly flag you as a foreigner. This doesn't mean you should start shifting your vowels, emphasising your r's and dropping the occasional 'eh?' in an effort to blend in – most Canadians are friendly and open-minded, and they'll probably be interested to know where you're from. But it's good to be aware that the way you speak (and some of the words you use) might trip up communication now and then. You may not even notice your own accent until you're surrounded by people who speak with a different one, and it's possible you won't always understand everything they say. If you're worried about your abilities in either English or French, and you need to be able to read, write, and speak competently in that language, a programme at a language school – or through the federal government's LINC Program (see p. 71) – is a good option.

Family and friends back home – the people who've known you longer than anyone else – will be an ongoing source of support. Stay in touch. If you can afford to buy a home computer and connect to the internet this is invaluable: it allows you both to search for information (and you'll have plenty to search for in the first few months), and to keep up regular contact with those on the other side of the globe. Unless you have an excellent long-distance phone carrier, keep a stock of phone cards on hand so you don't run up horrendous bills. Keep in touch through letters and photos as well – these are more personal than emails, and will help you feel more connected.

▪ FOOD AND DRINK

Canadian cuisine

Certain aspects of Canadian cuisine are homogenous across much of the country, and reflect a traditional, westernised approach to food: hearty fried breakfasts, roast dinners, baked beans, and fruit pies. Home fries (baked or fried cubes of potato) appear as a side on almost every diner-style dish, and maple syrup is a breakfast-table standard. But this is only a part of the picture – food in Canada is influenced by a huge range of traditions, cultures, and ethnicities, and boasts incredible regional variation. The geographical locations and resources of different provinces contribute to this: the Maritime provinces and BC draw on their coastal positions for culinary ingredients and inspiration, with outstanding mussels, oysters, scallops and lobster coming from PEI and Nova Scotia, and salmon a specialty of the west coast.

While the classic Canadian breakfast may be eggs and peameal bacon, there are options to suit just about any taste

Newfoundland has its own unique, time-honoured oceanic fare. Alberta produces famously high-quality beef as well as leaner, finer buffalo meat. Freshwater fishing is a key industry in Manitoba, where the influence of Ukrainian immigrants is also well and truly entrenched, and Canada's National Ukrainian Festival is held each year. Quebec is a gourmand's heaven – duck, apples, and fine cheeses are among its many specialties (and who can forget poutine?) – with Montreal its fine-food nucleus. Berries, both wild and cultivated, grow in great variety from coast to coast, and are frequently sold at roadside stalls during summer. Saskatoon berries are a traditional First Nations food, along with wild rice, fish, and bison. The Okanagan Valley in BC is a key fruit- and wine-producing region, as is Ontario's Niagara Peninsula. The unique position and climatic conditions of the Niagara Escarpment create an enviable growing environment here, and wines from the region are gaining increasing recognition worldwide. Particularly famous – and delectable – are the ice wines, made from grapes picked in −8°C temperatures. They can be tasted (for a small fee) at many of the peninsula's numerous wineries, and range in price from the justifiable to the sublimely ridiculous.

Traditional holidays are often celebrated by family gatherings in which food plays a major and cohesive role. Christmas, Thanksgiving, and Easter are excuses to eat yourself into a near-comatose state, with turkey, ham, and multifarious side dishes, followed by substantial desserts – pumpkin pie is standard at Thanksgiving.

FACT

■ Food in Canada is influenced by a huge range of traditions, cultures, and ethnicities and boasts incredible regional variation.

Maple syrup is a perennial favourite, and well stocked by every Canadian grocery store

Restaurants and bars

Eating and drinking are central to Canadian social life, and both are enjoyed immensely. Eating-out options range from the usual fast-food culprits to expensive gourmet affairs, and include everything in between: market stalls, greasy-spoon diners, family restaurant chains (of both uninspiring and surprisingly decent varieties), low-key cafes, trendy brunch nooks, and lively restaurants with atmosphere and affordable menus. Increasing immigration has brought many more dishes to the table, and Canadian food – particularly in larger cities – is in a constant state of evolution. Almost every type of international cuisine can now be found, including Thai, Chinese, Korean, Japanese, Mongolian, Cantonese, West Indian, East Indian, Ethiopian, Middle Eastern, Italian, French, Croatian, Pakistani, Portuguese, Greek, Ukrainian, Polish, and Mexican (and the list goes on). The English, Irish, and Scottish influence is well represented in some of the more traditional aspects of the Canadian diet, as well as in pubs serving Irish beer or British fare, and the occasional upmarket tearoom. One quirk of Canadian menu customs is the use of the word 'entrée', which in North America actually refers to a main course. 'Appetizer' is used for what non-North Americans might know as an entrée. (Except in Quebec, where, logically enough, the French term *entrée* is used to mean entrée.)

Drinking venues include casual lounges and live-music venues, clubs, classy martini bars, funky bars and less classy sports bars and the aforementioned pubs.

A local café or restaurant is a great place to dissect the newspaper over a coffee, or linger over Sunday brunch

Liquor licensing is regulated at the provincial level – in most provinces the legal drinking age is 19; in Alberta, Manitoba, and Quebec it's 18. Import restrictions can be frustrating, especially if you're after a drop of a familiar wine from your own country – the options on sale don't always reflect the quality available back home. Canada has a well-respected brewing industry, with local boutique and microbreweries producing excellent beers and nosing out market space around Labatt and Molson, the brewery giants. Steam Whistle in Ontario, the Granville Island Brewery in Vancouver, and the Microbrasserie La Diable in Quebec are just a few of the many.

Tipping is expected in restaurants and bars. The standard tip is 15%; tip more if the service is better than average; in general you only tip less (or not at all) if you want to make a point. Leave your bartender a dollar per drink if you're buying by the glass (same goes for bottles of beer).

Health and nutrition

There's a strong and increasing emphasis in Canada on eating fresh, nutritious produce, though a considerable variety of refined, sugary, and fatty foods still line supermarket shelves and find their way into many homes. This may not seem extreme in comparison to the United States (which has a severe addiction to these foods and an obesity problem to match), but the North American capacity to indulge

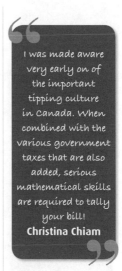

I was made aware very early on of the important tipping culture in Canada. When combined with the various government taxes that are also added, serious mathematical skills are required to tally your bill!
Christina Chiam

TIMBITS AND PIECES: CANADIAN FOOD ODDITIES

Canadians like peanut-butter-filled chocolate; they like crackers crumbled in their soup; they don't seem to mind the ubiquitous bright-orange cheese; and most really do enjoy their maple syrup, the majority of which is extracted and manufactured in Ontario and Quebec at the tail end of winter. They buy their milk in plastic bags (cartons only go up to two litres). They call tomato-based pasta sauce 'marinara', though there's nothing fishy about it, other than the name. The Nanaimo bar – a delicious, biscuity, creamy-filled, chocolate-topped slice named for a city on Vancouver Island – is a nostalgic favourite. And they have an insatiable appetite for donuts: Tim Hortons – established in 1964 by hockey legend Miles Gilbert (Tim) Horton – is the most well-known coffee and donut chain in the country. It has 2,750 stores in Canada and over 350 creeping southward into the United States, and is probably responsible for more drive-thru traffic in the country than McDonalds. If you don't know what a double-double is – and it may indeed mean toil and trouble – you soon will. And you can't have one of those without a Timbit or two – bite-sized donut balls that cost just $0.16 a piece.

is alive (if not so well) on the northern side of the border too. Offsetting this is the large and growing range of organic produce that is now readily available in many parts of the country (though fresh – particularly organic – foods can be harder to obtain in small towns and remote areas). The federal government promotes healthy eating through Health Canada, and publishes *Canada's Food Guide* to provide practical help in eating a more balanced diet. The Health Canada website at www.hc-sc.gc.ca provides a link to the guide, which can be downloaded or ordered as a hardcopy.

> We found food prices generally pretty high here [in Bedford, Nova Scotia], and the standard of food is not as good – especially the fresh fruit and vegetables, mainly because much of it has to travel quite a distance before it gets here.
> **Steven Maine**

◼ SHOPPING

Opening hours

In larger cities, most retail stores have fairly generous hours. Box stores (large, box-shaped mega-stores that congregate in suburbs and on city outskirts), department stores, and major chains usually open around 10am and don't lock their doors until 9pm or 10pm on weekdays and Saturdays; Sunday hours tend to be shorter. Small businesses and mom-and-pop establishments often close around 6pm, and are more likely to be shut on Sunday or Monday (or both). The Monday closure is also common for hairdressers, many of whom work Saturdays and sometimes Sundays. The bigger malls may stay open until 9pm on weekdays, with an earlier close on the weekend. Some supermarkets and drug stores let you shop until midnight, or 24 hours a day. Restaurants generally close up between 9pm and 11pm, though this varies widely: a busy eatery on a bustling big-city street will be open much later than a small-town diner. Some fast-food chains and Tim Hortons outlets stay open around the clock, for those with the midnight munchies or a caffeine craving, or for those heading home after a long night. Standard closing time for bars is 2am.

Food shopping

Most people shop at supermarkets for at least some of their food items, but fresh-food markets are also popular and often provide greater choice and fresher, cheaper produce. Small local grocery stores may also be able to meet many of your food needs. Specialty stores – those that haven't been squeezed out by the supermarkets – offer extra choice, and thrive in communities with an emphasis on local business. Pastry shops, butchers shops, bakeries, organic-produce stores, health-food stores, kosher and Asian grocery stores, delicatessens... (the list goes on). Food is not generally expensive, though if you're on a tight budget cutting down on meat and certain dairy products like cheese can be a cost saver. Mainstream organic products can be found without too much trouble even in supermarkets – the President's

Supermarkets in Canada offer the usual array of fresh, frozen and pre-packaged produce, as well as homewares, household supplies, books and magazines, and in some cases, in-store pharmacies

Choice Organics label, available through selected retailers including Loblaws, Dominion, and No Frills, is quite extensive and encompasses everything from carrots to cookies to baby food. You can often find independent organic stores that will home deliver weekly food hampers with a mix of fresh fruit and veggies (handy for those who have trouble getting to the store themselves, or keeping to a healthy-eating plan!). Most supermarkets also have home-delivery options. Farms sell a range of seasonal, freshly grown products – normally for less than you'd pay in a store – and sizable farmers' markets draw customers from near and far. These are an important source of income for area farmers and businesses, and some sell renowned sausage and cheese products from local Mennonite communities. Take-out restaurants are a handy option for grabbing a quick meal to go (and if you're sitting down to eat, most restaurants will happily package up whatever you can't finish so you can take it home). Liquor isn't cheap, but it's not exorbitant either. You can buy a bottle of local or imported wine for $10–$15 (possibly even less), a six-pack of imported or boutique beer for around $13, and a bottle of quality vodka for about $25. In some provinces alcohol can only be bought from special government stores or government-licenced outlets, though rules vary. In Quebec, beer and wine are readily available from corner stores and supermarkets as well.

FACT

In some provinces alcohol can only be bought from special government stores or government-licenced outlets, though rules vary.

Other shopping

Shopping in Canada is characterised by a combination of independent retailers, chain stores, department stores, and an increasing number of North-American-style box stores.

Chains, department stores, and malls

Major box-store retailers include Wal-Mart (low prices for almost anything you can think of), Staples (office and business supplies), Future Shop (electronics – everything from cameras to computers and CDs), Best Buy (similar to Future Shop), Canadian Tire (auto products, plus everything from tents to ice skates to bocce balls), Home Depot (hardware, tools, and building supplies), The Brick (furniture and home décor), Chapters/Indigo (books, magazines, and gifts; often with a coffee shop as well) and Shoppers Drug Mart (everything from prescriptions and pills to cosmetics, books, chocolates, and basic groceries – see p. 182 for more on drugstores). Many homeware and furniture retailers belong to the box-store market as well (see p. 151).

The Hudson's Bay Company (HBC) – the oldest corporation in Canada – has moved a long way from its fur-trading past: its primary company, now just known as The Bay, is a mid-range to high-end department store with outlets in most provinces. HBC also operates Zellers, its mass-market alternative, and Home Outfitters, a superstore selling homewares and furnishings. Specialty department store Holt Renfrew – another long-established Canadian company – prides itself as Canada's 'luxury-goods giant' and has stores in each major city. With designer fashions and luxury beauty products it caters to a classy clientele (or at least one with expensive taste). Sears is a huge, mainstream retailer and can be found in numerous locations throughout the provinces (but not in the three territories). Catalogue and online sales form a substantial component of its business. For bargain hunters, Winners is a favourite, with clothes, shoes and accessories – including those from designer brands – at significantly discounted prices. Canadian clothing company Roots sells bags, yoga

Shoppers and commuters navigate busy Yonge Street, Toronto

wear, and accessories, but is best known for its range of highly branded sweaters and track pants, much desired (and worn) by the preppy university crowd.

Malls are an inevitable feature of North America's shopping culture, and Canada has no shortage of supply. Some are mega malls like Vancouver's Pacific Centre, the Eaton Centres in Toronto and Montreal and the gargantuan West Edmonton Mall. They often include outlets for some of the companies listed above. Others are small, community-based malls filled with local retailers or anything in between. Relished by some people and considered a consumerist nightmare by others, malls do offer convenience, as well as a handy, heated escape during the winter.

Independent stores

Independent retailers come in every shape, size, and variety: clothing stores for all ages, tastes and budgets; boutiques selling apparel and accessories by local designers; hairdressing and beauty (or 'esthetics') salons; baby merchandise stores; florists; pet stores; computer and electronics stores; quirky gift stores; galleries; toy stores. You can find great eclectic bookshops that offer a pleasant alternative to the chains (and allow you to feel virtuous for supporting small business), and excellent music stores, many of which do an active trade in new and pre-loved records as well as the standard CDs. Souvenir stores display their tacky wares in shop fronts across the country (higher quality examples as well), and convenience or corner stores (known by some non-Canadians as milk bars) sell the basics – bread, milk, cat food, ice cream, cigarettes – in almost every locale. Vintage and second-hand stores offer a wealth of discoverable treasures for penny-pinching students and savvy fashionistas alike, ranging from true bargain-bin territory to marked-up old-school couture. Toronto's Kensington Market and Gastown in Vancouver are a couple of well-known hunting grounds for vintage wear, while Value Village and other thrift stores have extensive selections from the shabby to the chic. (See Furniture, p. 151, for more on thrift stores.)

 Websites for some of these stores are listed on pp. 151–152, and on p. 363 of the Appendices. Others can be easily found online.

■ MEDIA AND COMMUNICATIONS

Newspapers

There are two national newspapers in Canada: the generally centrist Globe and Mail, and the conservative National Post (founded by former media baron Conrad Black who was recently – and famously – jailed for fraud). The main French-language papers are La Presse and the tabloid Le Journal de Montréal, both published in Montreal. Most large cities offer two or more daily papers tailored to left-or right-leaning audiences. Though colourific television news reports and the convenience of the internet have impacted on newspaper readership in recent decades, the Canadian Newspaper Association (CNA) reports that more than half of all adults still read the paper every day. Most newspapers have embraced the electronic medium and provide online versions as well.

 The CNA website at www.cna-acj.ca provides links to newspaper websites, and you can search for daily papers by city or region. Select the relevant link under *About Newspapers* on the homepage.

Newspapers rely on subscriptions and advertising for their income. An annual print subscription can cost $300 a year (more for the Globe and Mail), while single issues are normally around $1 on weekdays and up to $2.75 on weekends. Metro, a free daily paper for commuters, is published in Calgary, Edmonton, Halifax, Montreal (in French), Ottawa, Toronto, and Vancouver. You can also explore the Metro website or read the print edition online by going to www.metronews.ca. Some international papers are available from Canadian newsstands, and a considerable number can be sourced online. The website www.newsstand.com, searchable by country and category, sells digital versions of print editions for around $2–$3 per issue and offers various subscription options. Sites such as Press Display (www.pressdisplay.com/pressdisplay/viewer.aspx) give you a choice of subscriptions for online browsing and viewing, while the print-on-demand service at www.newspaperdirect.com can supply printed editions of international newspapers on the day of publication.

■ Major newspapers

National
The Globe and Mail: www.theglobeandmail.com
National Post: www.nationalpost.com

Western Canada and the Prairies

Vancouver Sun: www.vancouversun.com
Calgary Herald: www.calgaryherald.com
Winnipeg Free Press: www.winnipegfreepress.com
The Edmonton Journal: www.edmontonjournal.com

Central Canada

Toronto Star: www.thestar.com
Toronto Sun: www.torontosun.com
The Montreal Gazette: www.montrealgazette.com
La Presse: www.cyberpresse.ca
Le Journal de Montréal: www.journaldemontreal.com
Le Devoir: www.ledevoir.com
Ottawa Citizen: www.ottawacitizen.com

Atlantic Canada

St John's Telegram: www.thetelegram.com
Halifax Chronicle-Herald: www.thechronicleherald.ca
New Brunswick Telegraph Journal: www.telegraphjournal.com

Magazines

Canadians have access to a wide variety of American publications, but many of the most popular titles are specifically Canadian. *Maclean's* is a widely read current-affairs weekly; *TIME Canada* offers world news plus Canadian content; and *Châtelaine* (also published in a French edition in Quebec) is the top-selling women's magazine, ahead of US competitors such as *Vogue* and *Cosmopolitan*. Canadian magazines in both English and French are available on business, health, home and garden, lifestyle, travel, and family. *The Walrus* is the country's premier literary magazine; *Canadian Geographic* is a consistent favourite; *Toronto Life* and other city and provincial regulars explore their own regions of the country; and *The Beaver* provides a bi-monthly dose of Canadian history. For sensationalism and celebrity gossip, Canadians turn to US magazines. Various free alternative magazines are also available, such as the monthly Canada-wide music mag *Exclaim!* and entertainment papers including Toronto's *Now*, Vancouver's *Georgia Straight*, (often just the *Straight*) and Montreal's *Hour Magazine* (English) and *Voir* (French). These can usually be picked up at music stores, cafés and bars, and sometimes from street-side newspaper boxes. Magazines from many countries can be found at international newsstands, specialty stores and mega-bookstores like the Chapters/Indigo chain.

 The Magazines Canada website at www.magazinescanada.ca lists hundreds of Canadian titles on almost every topic.

Books and bookshops

It's a source of frequent infuriation among Canadian book buyers that the prices they pay tend to be substantially higher than in the United States. (And it doesn't help that the US price is blatantly visible on the book's cover.) A lower Canadian dollar helps even out (or at least explain) the disparity, but in late 2007, when the

US dollar dropped, and the Canadian loonie charged above parity, customer squawks started changing to shrieks. Various booksellers sucked up the financial margin and dropped their prices. Some Canadian publishers, though feeling the pinch also started to close the gap, in some cases selling at one price in both countries. It's unclear what impact the current economic climate will have on the industry. Despite the mammoth Chapters/Indigo chain that dominates much of the Canadian market, and the growing ease of online ordering, many excellent independent, specialty, and second-hand bookstores still exist. US and other international titles are widely available, but Canadian literature is strongly and proudly promoted, and Canadian novels usually feature among the bestsellers. Famed and respected authors include Margaret Atwood, Michael Ondaatje, and Alice Munro; an enormous number of other writers – both established and up-and-coming – also contribute to Canada's thriving literary scene. The Giller Prize and the Governor General's Award for fiction are two of the most prestigious literary prizes.

> ### FACT
>
> ■ The Governor General's Award for fiction and the Giller Prize are two of Canada's most prestigious literary prizes.

> *i* The Canadian Bookseller's Association website, though intended for bookselling professionals, allows you to search for bookstores by entering your city or town name. Visit www.cbabook.org.

Independent bookstores provide a pleasant haven for browsers and buyers

Websites

A vast array of websites supply information on Canadian life, media and entertainment:

- News and current affairs sites include those of CBC News (www.cbc.ca), The Canadian Press – a non-profit, multimedia news agency. (www.thecanadianpress.com) and Macleans magazine (www.macleans.ca).

- Maple Leaf Web (www.mapleleafweb.com) provides independent political education and information.

- Many local or free publications, such as those noted in the previous Newspapers and Magazines sections, have excellent websites as well. Try Exclaim.ca (www.exclaim.ca) for music news and reviews, Maple Music (www.maplemusic.com) for Canadian acts and releases, MuchMusic (www.muchmusic.com) for information and concert listings, or Inside E Canada (www.insideeonline.com) for mainstream entertainment information and celebrity gossip.

- Xtra.ca (www.xtra.ca) provides gay and lesbian news, views, culture, and entertainment.

- The Media Alliance for New Activism (MANA) is a network of independent and alternative media groups and publications – their site at www.independentmedia.ca includes an extensive list of these, along with website links.

- TSN (www.tsn.ca) is dedicated to sports news and information, while NHL.com (www.nhl.com) has all the action on the National Hockey League.

- The Canadian Living magazine website (www.canadianliving.com) covers food, health, family, crafts, and exercise.

- Leading social networking sites include Facebook (www.facebook.com), which is hugely popular in Canada, and Myspace (www.myspace.com).

- Canada.com (www.canada.com) offers media, news, and information, including guides to the major cities. If you're looking for something to do, Canada Events (www.canadaevents.ca) can tell you what's on in various cities, and Where – a publisher of visitor information magazines – also maintains a website (www.where.ca) with listings for major cities and regions.

- Government resources include Going to Canada (www.goingtocanada.gc.ca), with information on attractions and activities, and the events webpage at www.canada.gc.ca/whats-quoi/newevent.html, which gives details of government- and non-government-related events and exhibitions across the country.

- If you have an urge to know the finer statistical details of the Canadian population, visit Statistics Canada at www.statcan.ca.

■ For weather updates and environmental information, go to The Weather Network (www.theweathernetwork.com) or Environment Canada (www.ec.gc.ca).

Radio

Canada has over 900 government, commercial, and community radio stations on both AM and FM frequencies, as well as satellite radio services. The federally funded Canadian Broadcasting Corporation (CBC) – in French, the Société Radio-Canada Television – is the national public broadcaster. The CBC offers programming in English, French, and eight Aboriginal languages, with additional language services provided through Radio Canada International (RCI), its international broadcasting service. The nationwide CBC Radio One offers excellent news and arts programming; CBC Radio 2 provides a broad range of music including live concerts, classical, and jazz; and CBC Radio 3 – a satellite station – promotes new, independent Canadian music.

 You can stream CBC content online, or tune in to listen through your radio. Visit www.cbc.ca/frequency for channels and frequencies, and for links to each CBC channel website (including Radio Canada International).

Canadian radio stations are regulated by the Canadian Radio-television and Telecommunications Commission (CRTC), which grants licences and enforces Canadian content regulations. A certain percentage of all songs played on music stations must be by Canadian artists; Toronto and Vancouver have built thriving alternative music industries with the help of this airplay. In addition to news and sports networks, most cities have their own commercial classical, country, pop, and rock music stations.

 The website www.canehdian.com includes a radio guide that's searchable by major city, while www.radio-locator.com lists hundreds of stations in smaller towns and regional areas.

Television

Both free-to-air and cable services (analogue, satellite or digital) are available in Canada. However, analogue transmission of all over-the-air television stations will cease by 31 August 2011, in a nationwide switch to digital broadcasting. Viewers with conventional analogue television sets will need a set-top converter box (details can be found at www.ic.gc.ca/epic/site/oca-bc.nsf/en/caq23362.htm). As with radio, all broadcasting is regulated by the CRTC. The CBC provides English- and French-language television programming across Canada, and has regional stations from coast to coast. It offers a higher level of Canadian-produced content than its major national rivals CTV and Global, and broadcasts the popular Hockey Night in Canada weekly during the NHL hockey season (CBC also airs the British Coronation Street, with which many Canadians have long been obsessed). CTV is the largest independent broadcaster and the forerunner for national news and prime-time viewing; both CTV and Global air a lot of US programmes. Quebec's French television network, TVA, is the largest independent producer of French-language news and entertainment programming in North America. Virtually all free-to-air and cable stations run advertisements. (One exception is the US network PBS, which is dependent on viewer contributions.)

Public phones can be found on most major streets

Cable stations include include local networks and educational, news, lifestyle, movie, and music channels (such as MuchMusic, Canada's version of MTV). Lists of available channels can be found on the websites of cable television providers (some are included in the list on p. 151). Most major newspapers publish a weekly TV guide listing programming for free-to-air and cable television stations, and online guides (such as www.tvguide.ca) are also available.

Telephones

Telephone installation and billing is covered on p. 147. Call costs from your home phone depend on your carrier and long-distance plan. Some plans offer a flat rate applicable at all times, while others have discounts during evenings and weekends but a higher rate during the day. Depending on where you're calling to, the time of day, and any applicable discounts, a three-minute call can cost anywhere from a few cents to quite a few dollars.

FACT

The price of a local call from most pay phones doubled to $0.50 in 2007 – it had been just a quarter ($0.25) for the previous 25 years.

Public phones have dwindled to some extent with the prevalence of cell phones, but they can still be found in most public areas such as shopping centres and major streets. Coins are standard; some also take credit cards. The price of a local call from most pay phones doubled to $0.50 in 2007 – it had been just a quarter ($0.25) for the previous 25 years.

Convenience stores and drugstores sell prepaid long-distance phone cards, which can be used from private or public phones by dialling an access number. Some major phone carriers also offer calling cards, but their rates are rarely as competitive. Be wary of cards issued by small, unknown companies, and read the fine print. Many have hidden access fees, pay-phone surcharges or short-term (or single-call) expiry policies that can eat up your fantastic per-minute rate surprisingly fast. The good ones, however, provide great value for money. Some, such as CiCi cards, can programme the numbers you call into your phone so you don't have to dial the access number and PIN every time.

The website www.ontariophonecards.ca provides useful comparisons and information on Canadian phone cards.

TIP

Convenience stores and drugstores sell prepaid long-distance phone cards, which can be used from private or public phones by dialling an access number.

AREA CODES FOR MAJOR CITIES	
City	**Area code**
Toronto, ON	416, 647
Vancouver, BC	604, 778
Montreal, QC	514, 438
Ottawa, ON	613
Calgary, AB	403
Edmonton, AB	780
Quebec City, QC	418
Winnipeg, MB	204
Saskatoon, SK	306
Victoria, BC	250
Halifax, NS	902

Visit the Canadian White Pages website at www.whitepages.ca/maps for an interactive map showing all area codes in Canada.

■ POSTAL SYSTEM

Post offices

Canada Post, a crown corporation, is Canada's national postal system. There are 6,600 post offices delivering to 14 million Canadian addresses, and processing 11.6 billion pieces of national and international mail each year. The postal system is partially privatised: Canada Post operates 60% of the post offices, with other outlets operated by private businesses. These may be independent retailers, or large-scale franchises such as Shoppers Drug Mart. Many post offices offer fax, postal money orders, and electronic mail services, as well as private post-office boxes and bill-payment facilities.

Delivery and rates

The Canadian postal system is not super efficient. Next-day delivery is uncommon, even between cities in the same region, and it can take four days or longer for mail to be delivered to another province (or even to a distant location in the same province). Next-day delivery can be arranged through Canada Post's Priority Courier service (or Expedited Parcel service, for business account holders), but this costs considerably more than regular delivery. Xpresspost, which delivers packages within a couple of working days, is often only a dollar or two more than regular mail for items sent within Canada. Other courier services such as FedEx are also available in Canada (see www.fedex.ca). In most cases these are not operated via Canada Post, however FedEx and Canada Post Express launched a combined Priority Worldwide service for urgent or critical international delivery in September 2008.

The standard red Street Letter Box from Canada Post

 The Canada Border Services Agency provides detailed information on import duty and taxes for mailed items at www.cbsa-asfc.gc.ca/import/postal-postale/duty-droits-eng.html.

Stamps are available from all post offices as well as many variety, convenience, and drug stores. It currently costs $0.52 to send a standard letter within Canada, and $0.96 to send one to the United States. International airmail of up to 30 grams costs $0.96, but is faster than the national service speed would suggest. Standard letters sent internationally take seven to 10 business days to arrive. Parcels are priced by dimensions and weight, and can be quite costly to send internationally. The Canada Post website at www.canadapost.ca provides details of rates and services. At the time of writing, price increases were being proposed that would bring those figures up to $0.54, $0.98 and $1.65 respectively, effective 12 January 2009.

Import duty may be payable on any parcels sent to you from overseas, though exemptions apply for gifts and low-value items.

POSTAL ABBREVIATIONS

Alberta	AB
British Columbia	BC
Manitoba	MB
New Brunswick	NB
Newfoundland and Labrador	NL
Northwest Territories	NT
Nova Scotia	NS
Nunavut	NU
Ontario	ON
Prince Edward Island	PE
Quebec	QC
Saskatchewan	SK
Yukon	YT

■ WASTE AND RECYCLING

Each municipality is responsible for its own garbage collection and recycling services, and household collection is usually provided on a weekly or alternating-weekly basis. (In the City of Toronto, for example, garbage is collected one week and recycling the next.) Garbage is put out for collection in garbage cans, carts (wheeled, lidded bins) or heavy-duty plastic bags, depending on the regulations of the council. Carts are becoming more common as a tidy, efficient method of storage and collection. Environmental awareness among Canadians is reasonably strong – though there's still an astounding amount of Styrofoam use – and people are recycling in increasing numbers. Around 93% of households have access to some type of recycling programme, and over 95% of those make use of them. The majority of Canadian residential waste still goes to landfill or is incinerated, but over a quarter is now recycled. A greater emphasis is also being placed on organic waste: some municipalities offer reduced-price backyard compost bins to encourage residents to compost their own waste, or they collect organic waste separately so it can be composted at a municipal facility. Leaf and yard waste is usually collected on specified days. Collection of large household items such as couches, mattresses, and other furniture varies – in some places these can be put out on the curb on regular collection days; in others they must be taken to a depot. You can contact the local council for your area or visit their website for specific information.

FACT

■ Each municipality is responsible for its own garbage collection and recycling services, and household collection is usually provided on a weekly or alternating-weekly basis.

Many municipalities collect garbage, recycling and organic waste separately, and specific bins are used for each

◾ HEALTH

The Canadian national health system

Healthcare in Canada is administrated by the provincial and territorial governments, though the federal government sets national principles and standards through the Canada Health Act and contributes funds. Pre-payment is collected from workers and employers through taxes or monthly premiums. For medically necessary treatment there is normally no charge to patients, as doctors bill the Ministry of Health directly. The overall system – known as Medicare – is similar to Australia's version of Medicare or to the UK's National Health Service. It has received much attention (both favourable and critical) in recent years, as the United States looks for alternative approaches to its own beleaguered system. However, unlike those in many other countries, Canada's system is not tiered: there is no private-health option as an alternative to the public system. The Canadian system is both cheaper and more humane than that in the States, but it's plagued with long queues for some treatments and operations. People who can afford it sometimes choose to travel to the States for faster treatment.

The main focus of the publicly funded system is on providing primary care, which allows people who need healthcare to go to a doctor or other health professional.

PUBLIC, ACCESSIBLE, UNIVERSAL

Canada is proud of its non-profit healthcare system, which is based around five core principles:

- Public administration: operated by public authorities in each province or state with accountability to their own government
- Accessibility: access to medical and health services for all insured residents
- Universality: the same health coverage terms and conditions apply to all
- Comprehensiveness: coverage for all medically necessary services provided by medical practitioners or within hospitals
- Portability: coverage under each provincial or territorial plan for insured residents who move provinces or travel abroad (limitations apply)

Services such as dental care, optometry, prescriptions, hospital upgrades, and ambulance transport are considered to be additional or supplementary, and are not generally covered under the provisions of the system. The specifics vary between provinces, however: for details of included and excluded services under a particular province's health plan, contact the provincial department or ministry of health, or check their website. Many Canadians have additional insurance to cover supplementary services, either through the employee benefits plan or group plan offered by their workplace (which may cover some or all of these extras), or through their own private insurance (see p. 178). The Provincial governments usually cover the costs of supplementary health services for groups such as seniors, children and social-service recipients. Health Canada's main website is at www.hc-sc.gc.ca, or you can find out more about the healthcare system at www.hc-sc.gc.ca/hcs-sss/index-eng.php. The Citizenship and Immigration Canada (CIC) website is also helpful: see www.cic.gc.ca/english/resources/publications/welcome/wel-06e.asp for a useful breakdown of information.

 Though published a few years ago, a publication entitled Canada's Health Care System (downloadable at www.hc-sc.gc.ca/hcs-sss/pubs/system-regime/index-eng.php) provides an excellent overview.

Most newcomers aren't eligible to apply for coverage under their provincial health-care plan until permanent resident status is granted (or, in some cases, until they receive confirmation from CIC that they've met the medical requirements for landing). Even then, BC, Ontario, Quebec, and New Brunswick have a waiting period of around three months. This is less of a problem if you're already a permanent resident when you arrive, but if you come over to be with a Canadian spouse or partner you may have a considerable wait until your permanent residence comes through. Temporary residents and foreign workers may be eligible, depending on the type and length of their permit, but visitors and those on working holiday permits are not. International students are eligible for cover in some provinces but not in others (in which case private insurance is required in order to attend college or university). To find out whether you qualify for cover, contact the department of health in your province. If you're not eligible, or if there's a waiting period, you'll need to take out private medical insurance to cover yourself for as long as necessary.

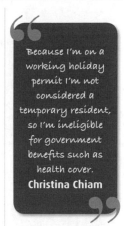

Because I'm on a working holiday permit I'm not considered a temporary resident, so I'm ineligible for government benefits such as health cover.
Christina Chiam

◼ Provincial and territorial departments of health
Alberta Health and Wellness: 780 427 1432; www.health.Alberta.ab.ca
British Columbia Ministry of Health: 1 800 465 4911; www.gov.bc.ca/health
Manitoba Health: 1 800 392 1207; www.gov.mb.ca/health
New Brunswick Department of Health: 506 457 4800; www.gnb.ca
Newfoundland and Labrador Department of Health and Community Services: 709 729 5021; www.gov.nl.ca/health
Northwest Territories Department of Health and Social Services: 1 800 661 0830; www.hlthss.gov.nt.ca
Nova Scotia Department of Health: 902 424 5818; www.gov.ns.ca/health
Nunavut Department of Health and Social Services: 1 867 975 5700; www.gov.nu.ca/health
Ontario Ministry of Health and Long-Term Care: 800 268 1153; www.health.gov.on.ca
Prince Edward Island Department of Health: 902 368 6130; www.gov.pe.ca/health
Quebec Ministry of Health and Social Services/Ministere de la Santé et services sociaux du Québec: 418 266 7005; www.msss.gouv.qc.ca
Saskatchewan Health: 1 800 667 7766; www.health.gov.sk.ca
Yukon Health and Social Services: 1 867 667 3673 or 1 800 661 0408; www.hss.gov.yk.ca

◼ Canada-wide health agencies and associations
Health Canada: 416 973 4389 or 1 866 999 7612 (Ontario headquarters); Info@hc-sc.gc.ca or medicare_hc@hc-sc.gc.ca; www.hc-sc.gc.ca
Royal College of Physicians and Surgeons of Canada: 613 730 8177 or 1 800 668 3740; info@rcpsc.edu; www.rcpsc.medical.org
Canadian Medical Association: 1 888 855 2555; cmamsc@cma.ca; www.cma.ca
Canadian Dental Association: 613 523 1770; reception@cda-adc.ca; www.cda-adc.ca
Public Health Agency of Canada: www.phac-aspc.gc.ca
Canadian Institute for Health Information (CIHI): 613 241 8120; communications@cihi.ca; www.cihi.ca

Health cards

As soon as you've established that you're eligible for healthcare, you need to register with the relevant department of health and obtain a health card. This shows healthcare providers that you're entitled to receive care under the provisions of your province or territory's health system. Each province has its own requirements for issuing health cards, and its own application processes, so you need to familiarise yourself with the rules and regulations of the province you plan to live in. Depending on the province, you may need to complete information online, send in documentation, or go into a provincial health office in order to complete the registration process. Once you receive your health card, carry it with you at all times.

 The Health Canada webpage at www.hc-sc.gc.ca/hcs-sss/delivery-prestation/ptrole/index-eng.php provides links to the health-card sections of each provincial department of health website.

Reciprocal health agreements

As portability is one of the five provisions of the Canada Health Act, all provinces and territories take part in reciprocal billing arrangements. These allow Canadians who are insured under their own province's health plan to receive healthcare in another province without having to pay at the point of service. The reciprocal arrangements cover in-patient and out-patient hospital care in all provinces, as well as medical or physician's services in all provinces but Quebec. Some limits and exclusions are imposed on the services that qualify for out-of-province coverage, and non-emergency treatment may need to be approved in advance. As mentioned previously students and temporary workers are not covered in all provinces, or under all circumstances. Quebec, however, has social security arrangements with Denmark, Finland, France, Greece, Luxembourg, Norway, Portugal and Sweden, so students or temporary workers who happen to be nationals of these countries are usually eligible for the provincial health plan. If you're moving to Quebec permanently from one of these countries, the normal three-month waiting period for health cover is waived. Visit the Régie de l'assurance maladie du Québec webpage at www.ramq.gouv.qc.ca/en/citoyens/assurancemaladie/arriver/ententes_ss.shtml for details.

Private health insurance

If neither your employer nor the provincial government provide you with health coverage for dental care and other supplementary services (such as those outlined on p. 181), you may need or want to take out private health insurance to cover the gap. Even if you don't get sick often, medical or dental emergencies can be phenomenally expensive if you're not insured. Insurance plans usually provide for private or semi-private rooms and include additional benefits. Many insurers have policies specifically for visitors (including foreign workers, foreign students, and new immigrants) who are not covered by a provincial health plan, though these are emergency based and won't give you the same kind of routine coverage as the public system. Online insurance brokers like HealthQuotes.ca (www.healthquotes.ca) offer comparison services to help you find the best policy for your budget and needs. Many banks also offer health insurance. Alternatively, you can take out expatriate insurance, either directly through an international insurance agency, or through a broker such as Expatriate Insurance Services who specialises in arranging international health, travel, and life insurance. (See also Travel insurance, p. 86.) The Consumer

Assistance Centre at the Canadian Life and Health Insurance OmbudService provides consumers with information and publications relating to the insurance industry, and provides links to a large range of participating companies. Visit www.clhio.ca, or phone 416 777 2344 or 1 800 268 8099. A Manulife-sponsored website, Canada Health Insurance (www.canada-health-insurance.com), gives a clear and helpful overview of the Canadian healthcare system and the role of private insurance.

■ Health insurance companies

Canada Protection Plan: 1 877 528 6060; web www.cpp.ca
Expatriate Insurance Services: 1 800 341 8150 (North America), 0700 340 1596 (UK); info@expatriate-insurance.com; www.expatriate-insurance.com
Great-West Life: 416 492 4300 (Toronto office); www.greatwestlife.com
Green Shield Canada: 1 888 711 1119; www.greenshield.ca
Ingle International: 416 640 7863 or 1 800 360 3234; helpline@ingleinsurance.com; www.ingletravelinsurance.com
Manulife Financial: 1 877 268 3763; www.coverme.com
Medavie Blue Cross: 1 800 355 9133 (Ontario office); www.medavie.bluecross.ca
Ontario Blue Cross: 1 866 732 2583; bco.indhealth@ont.bluecross.ca; www.useblue.com;
Sun Life Financial: 1 877 786 5433; service@sunlife.ca; www.sunlife.ca
TIC Travel Insurance: 604 986 4292 or 1 800 663 4494; pr@travelinsurance.ca; www.travelinsurance.ca

Doctors

Most Canadians have a regular family doctor. However, a shortage of physicians has been an issue for some time, particularly in rural and regional areas, and it can be difficult to find one with space for new patients. Word of mouth is often the most effective approach to seeking out an available doctor. A family member, friend, neighbour or co-worker may know of someone who is accepting new patients, as may immigrant-serving organisations in your area. If you have contact with other health professionals such as pharmacists or sports trainers, or a doctor at a walk-in medical clinic, it's worth asking them as well. Not all doctors who are prepared to take on new patients will advertise the fact, so your personal contacts can be valuable. Provincial medical associations are another useful resource: each province and territory has its own regulatory authority (in most cases a college of physicians and surgeons) that licence medical practitioners, and these associations can often

> **Steven Maine and his family live in Bedford, near Halifax, Nova Scotia, a region that definitely isn't immune from Canada's doctor shortage.**
>
> Many of the facilities are old and out of date; it's difficult to find a GP that will take new patients in the area around Bedford; and the waiting list at the hospital is so long for certain procedures that patients are being told they can be treated in places like Toronto as long as they can pay to get there. We didn't realise there's no private healthcare system here, so you just have to wait until you can get an appointment.

help you find available doctors in your area. Most include physician details and listings on their websites, and many offer 'doctor search' functions – some even allow you to search specifically for physicians accepting new patients.

The Ministry of Health in your province may also be able to help – some provide

 The Royal College of Physicians and Surgeons of Canada provides contact details for each province's medical association at www.rcpsc.medical. org/links/provli_e.php. Health Canada includes links to these and to other online healthcare resources (such as hospital wait-time lists) at www.hc-sc.gc.ca/hcs-sss/medi-assur/res/links-liens-eng.php.

contact phone numbers or online search functions to help locate doctors. The Yellow Pages (online at www.yellowpages.ca) lists doctors under Physicians and Surgeons. A number of provinces provide a nurse-on-call or telehealth services.

If you don't have a regular doctor and need to see a physician, walk-in medical clinics offer medical services without an appointment – though you'll spend more time in the waiting room. Walk-ins are normally listed under Clinics – Medical in the Yellow Pages. Another option is to ask a hospital in your area whether you can receive treatment there as an out-patient, or if they can refer you to a nearby doctor. In an emergency, or if no other option is available, you can go to a hospital emergency room – without a health card, however, this can cost around $350 for just the basics, with diagnostic procedures adding to the bill. If you're not covered by a provincial health plan, a doctor's visit is likely to be around $130. Some community and sexual-health clinics provide free services even if you don't have a health card, with some catering specifically to uninsured immigrants and refugees. Settlement services in your area may be able to help you locate a free clinic, if necessary. Bring your medical and dental records with you when you move to Canada, so you can provide a full history to your new healthcare providers.

Dentists

Routine dental care is not normally covered under provincial medical plans, but many employers offer dental plans as part of their benefits package, which may cover some or all of your treatment. If you're not covered through your employer and don't have your own insurance, dental treatment can be expensive. For a general check-up and cleaning you can pay $100 or more. Seniors, children, and social-service recipients may qualify for government funding or assistance. Most people use a regular dentist, though walk-in clinics are widely available in most cities. Dental schools (where treatment is provided by supervised dental students) offer an affordable option and can be a good solution, especially for less complex procedures such as check-ups and fillings, though there can be long wait times for a student to become available. The process for finding a dentist is much the same as that for finding a doctor – a recommendation from someone you know is often helpful, and it's a good idea to find a dental surgery that's convenient to your home or your work. The Canadian Dental Association provides links to provincial and territorial dental associations on the webpage at www.cda-adc.ca/en/oral_health/faqs_resources/reg_authorities.asp. Most associations have websites with dentist search features or directories. Settlement organisations can provide assistance, or you can look under Dentists in your local *Yellow Pages* (or at www.yellowpages.ca) for practitioners in your area.

Opticians

The provisions for (and restrictions on) optometric care are similar to those for dental care. Services are included as additional benefits under some provinces' health plans, but not under all. In many cases the cost of routine eye exams is covered (either partially or totally) for seniors and children, and sometimes for those receiving low-income assistance. Other residents have to pay their own fees, however, either out of their own pocket or through separate insurance. You can usually get private insurance to cover eye examinations as well as the cost of glasses and contact lenses. If treatment is considered medically necessary for an eye-related medical condition such as glaucoma or cataracts, you would normally be covered under the provincial plan. The Canadian Association of Optometrists (www.opto.ca) provides information on how optometrists operate in Canada, as well as a search service to help you find one in your area. You can also contact the Association by phone on 1888 263 4676 or by email at info@opto.ca. The webpage at www.opto.ca/en/public/links.asp links to the individual associations and regulatory bodies for each province.

Alternative healthcare

Depending on the province or territory, some forms of alternative healthcare may be covered, or partially covered, under the provincial health plan. For example, Manitoba insures chiropractic services for spinal or pelvic adjustments, but doesn't cover acupuncture, podiatry or services that are not considered medically necessary. British Columbia provides some scope for acupuncture, chiropractic care, physiotherapy, massage therapy, naturopathy, and non-surgical podiatry, but only for low-income earners, who receive assistance with their premium payments. A wide range of alternative and complementary health services are available in Canada outside of the Medicare system, and you can take out private insurance to cover (or partially cover) these. Many health providers in these fields belong to professional associations – some are listed below. Canadian Wellness, an online directory, lists health-related professionals at www.canadianwellness.com, while the non-profit Consumer Health Organization of Canada educates people on alternative and holistic options.

■ **Alternative healthcare organisations**
Canadian Massage Therapist Alliance: 604 873 4467;
locke@massagetherapy.bc.ca; www.cmta.ca
Consumer Health Organization of Canada: 416 924 9800;
info@consumerhealth.org; www.consumerhealth.org
Homeopathic Medical Council of Canada: 416 788 4622;
Ontario@HMCC.ca; www.hmcc.ca
Natural Health Practitioners of Canada: 780 484 2010 or 1 888 711 7701;
admin@nhpcanada.org; www.nhpcanada.org

The Canadian Association of Naturopathic Doctors: 416 496 8633 or
1 800 551 4381; www.cand.ca
The Canadian Chiropractic Association: 416 585 7902 or 1 877 222 9303;
www.ccachiro.org

Hospitals

FACT

■ Under the Canada Health Act, provincial health plans cover medically necessary services in hospitals for both in-patients and out-patients.

If you become very ill, need surgery or require specialised care, you may have to go to a hospital. In most cases your doctor or other primary-care provider will refer you, though in a severe accident or other emergency you would go straight to the emergency room (or may be taken there by ambulance). Under the Canada Health Act, provincial health plans cover medically necessary services in hospitals for both in-patients and out-patients. This includes nursing services, drugs administered in the hospital, accommodation in standard (public) hospital wards, and diagnostic procedures such as X-rays and blood tests. If surgery is required, you're also covered for the use of operating rooms and access to anaesthetics. Most hospitals in Canada are operated by local boards of trustees, municipalities or voluntary organisations. Provinces are responsible for funding and governing their own hospital systems, though the federal government makes financial contributions. You can find out more about hospitals and hospital management in your province or region by contacting the provincial health ministry or department (see p. 181 for contact details).

Pharmaceuticals and pharmacies

Spending on prescription and non-prescription drugs in Canada totals about $22 billion each year – around one-sixth of the country's overall health expenditure. The national health system covers the costs of necessary drugs given to patients within Canadian hospitals. For non-hospital situations, publicly funded drug programme are administered by the provincial and territorial governments. Costs of prescription medicines are covered for certain eligible groups. For example, provincial or territorial governments may provide coverage or payment assistance for seniors, those in low-income brackets or people with certain medical conditions that involve substantial drug expenses. The federal government covers around one million Canadians in specific groups, including Aboriginal Canadians, members of the military and the Royal Canadian Mounted Police (RCMP), and veterans. If you're not covered by the public system you can usually obtain coverage for prescription medicines through private insurance.

 Health Canada has detailed information on pharmaceuticals on the webpage at www.hc-sc.gc.ca/hcs-sss/pharma.

Drugstores or pharmacies fill prescriptions, and are easy to find in most regions. Vitamins, supplements, painkillers, and non-prescription drugs are also available from pharmacy shelves, though certain medications must be bought over the counter. Some drugstore locations are open late, or even 24 hours. Common companies include Rexall, Guardian, Pharmasave, and PharmaChoice, as well as the pervasive Shoppers Drug Mart. Many supermarkets also contain pharmacy outlets, and various online pharmacies also exist.

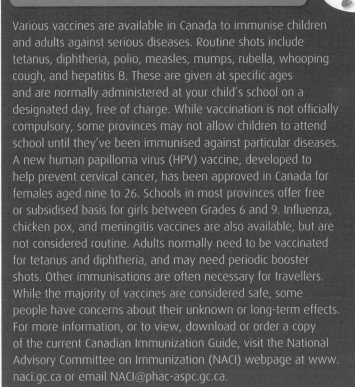

PREVENTION IS BETTER THAN CURE

Various vaccines are available in Canada to immunise children and adults against serious diseases. Routine shots include tetanus, diphtheria, polio, measles, mumps, rubella, whooping cough, and hepatitis B. These are given at specific ages and are normally administered at your child's school on a designated day, free of charge. While vaccination is not officially compulsory, some provinces may not allow children to attend school until they've been immunised against particular diseases. A new human papilloma virus (HPV) vaccine, developed to help prevent cervical cancer, has been approved in Canada for females aged nine to 26. Schools in most provinces offer free or subsidised basis for girls between Grades 6 and 9. Influenza, chicken pox, and meningitis vaccines are also available, but are not considered routine. Adults normally need to be vaccinated for tetanus and diphtheria, and may need periodic booster shots. Other immunisations are often necessary for travellers. While the majority of vaccines are considered safe, some people have concerns about their unknown or long-term effects. For more information, or to view, download or order a copy of the current Canadian Immunization Guide, visit the National Advisory Committee on Immunization (NACI) webpage at www. naci.gc.ca or email NACI@phac-aspc.gc.ca.

Emergencies

Dialling 911 will connect you with an emergency operator, though many regions also have specific numbers for health emergencies. The first page of your local *Yellow Pages* should list emergency numbers and hospitals in your region. Most hospitals have emergency departments, which have clearly marked entrances. Wait times can be long – sometimes many hours – so if your complaint is less severe, a local clinic might be a better option. Many clinics offer immediate treatment of urgent medical complaints. The cost of ambulance transport varies. In BC, if you're covered by provincial healthcare you pay a flat rate of $80. In the Prairies, an ambulance ride can set you back between about $250 and $350, while Ontario charges $45 for transport deemed medically necessary ($240 otherwise). In Quebec and Atlantic Canada, fees range from $115 to $150, though there's no fee in New Brunswick. Higher fees apply if you don't have a health card or if you use ambulance services outside your own province, and charges for air transport are usually different as well. In some cases a third party – such as workers' compensation, an acute-care hospital or your employer – might cover your ambulance fees. Unless you're certain of this, it's best have your own insurance to cover yourself, particularly if you'll be travelling out of province. (See p. 178 for insurance information and contacts.)

■ EDUCATION

Moving from one education system to another can be stressful for both children and parents. Choosing a school, adjusting to a different curriculum and making new friends is often challenging, particularly for older children and teenagers. If you have children, a great way for them to start learning about Canada and preparing for the move is to spend some time on the internet. Canadian websites designed specifically for children (or with youth-oriented content) abound, and can be a great resource. A sample of the most useful sites – both government and non-government – is included in the internet resources for children box.

> *i* For a more comprehensive list of resources for kids and teenagers, click on the links at the Library and Archives Canada (LAC) Learning Centre webpage, at www.collectionscanada.gc.ca/education/008-2010-e.html.

Education is a high priority in Canada, with around 5.3 million elementary and secondary students attending 15,500 schools, and over a million Canadians enrolled in full-time or part-time university studies. Government spending on education in 2005–06 came in at almost $76 billion. In the 2006 PISA survey (Program for International Student Assessment), undertaken through the OECD (Organisation for Economic Co-operation and Development), Canadian students ranked fourth for reading skills, seventh for math and third for science. The Canadian Council on Learning projects that by the year 2015 around 70% of new jobs in Canada will require post-secondary education or training. Almost 49% of Canadians have a post-secondary qualification; more than a third of those are university degrees. Canada has excellent, fully funded, non-denominational public schools. In BC, Alberta, Saskatchewan, Manitoba, and Quebec, funding (or partial funding) is also given to independent schools. The majority of these are religious or faith-based schools, most commonly Roman Catholic. There is also a network of highly regarded private schools. French speakers have the right to be educated in French anywhere in Canada, and French-language school boards exist in each province outside Quebec to oversee the management of French-language public schools. A similar (but opposite) set-up operates in Quebec for the provision of English-language public schools, though these have diminished in number over the years, and there are restrictions on who can attend. Children of immigrants are almost always required to attend French schools if they want to be educated in Quebec's public system, though they can go to an English private school if they wish – and can afford – to. (*Questions and Answers about Quebec's Language Policy*, referred to on p. 56, helps explain the rules regarding education in Quebec.)

The provincial and territorial governments are responsible for education, which means there are 13 different education systems across the country. Funding is provided through transfer taxes from the federal government, provincial income taxes and municipal property taxes. School boards or other local authorities govern the schools in different districts, and school-board members are elected by the

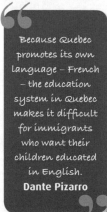

Because Quebec promotes its own language – French – the education system in Quebec makes it difficult for immigrants who want their children educated in English.
Dante Pizarro

A typical public school classroom

community. While the provincial school systems are similar in many ways, there are certain differences in terms of content, programme structure, and compulsory schooling ages. Each is regulated and administered through the province's department or ministry of education, which also develops and sets the school curriculum. Some provinces have a separate department or ministry for post-secondary education. The Council of Ministers of Education, Canada (CMEC), is an intergovernmental body that operates as a connection point and forum for the education ministers in each province. CMEC maintains a detailed website at www.cmec.ca.

 Full website and contact details for each education ministry are listed on the webpage at www.cmec.ca/educmin.en.stm. For comprehensive and specific information on the education system in a particular province, follow the links to the relevant ministry site.

The vast majority of Canadian public schools are coeducational, though some offer single-sex programmes or classes. School uniforms generally aren't worn in the public system, being more traditionally associated with private schools. However, some public schools prefer to have their students dress in uniform, believing it improves security and encourages school pride. Even if a uniform isn't required, there will be a dress code of some sort that students must adhere to. Students either bring lunch from home or purchase food from the school cafeteria.

RESOURCES FOR CHILDREN

- www.artsalive.ca – Arts Alive, National Arts Centre. Information and resources on music, dance, and theatre.
- www.collectionscanada.gc.ca/hockey/kids – Backcheck: Hockey for Kids. Hockey history, stories, and information.
- www.cbc.ca/kids – Canadian Broadcasting Corporation for Kids. Games, reviews, video submissions, downloads, and a section for preschoolers.
- www.collectionscanada.gc.ca/childrenliterature – Children's Literature Service. Canadian fiction and non-fiction collection with literature resources for children.
- www.collectionscanada.gc.ca/confederation/kids – Confederation for Kids. Teaches kids about how Canada became a country.
- www.ecokidsonline.com/pub – EcoKids. Fun, funky, environmentally themed, with games, activities, contests, and blogs.
- www.ainc-inac.gc.ca/ks/index-eng.asp – Kids Stop, Indian and Northern Affairs Canada. Culture, history, art, and language of Aboriginal Canadians.
- www.space.gc.ca/asc/eng/youth – KidSpace, Canadian Space Agency. Puzzles, projects, printable colouring books, and interactive displays.
- www.nrcan-rncan.gc.ca/kids – NRCat's Scratching Post, Natural Resources Canada. Natural resources games, quizzes, facts, and website links.
- www.collectionscanada.gc.ca/explorers/kids – Passageways: True Tales of Adventure for Young Explorers. Canadian exploration from the first inhabitants to the 20th century.
- www.atlas.nrcan.gc.ca – The Atlas of Canada. Maps, facts, and statistics.
- www.canadianencyclopedia.ca – The Canadian Encyclopedia. Online encyclopedia for older children and adults. Also includes a Youth Encyclopedia.
- www.vancouver2010.com – Vancouver 2010 Olympic Winter Games. Official site, with mascot-themed games and activities.
- www.virtualmuseum.ca/English/Games – Virtual Museum Canada. Play games on everything from shipwrecks to butterflies, or create an online museum with My Personal Museum.
- www.pc.gc.ca/apprendre-learn/jeunes-youths – Youth Zone Adventure, Parks Canada. Interactive games and activities on Canadian nature and history.

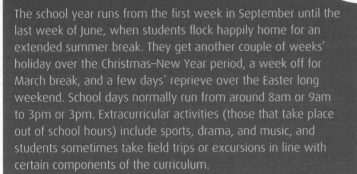

SCHOOL'S OUT

The school year runs from the first week in September until the last week of June, when students flock happily home for an extended summer break. They get another couple of weeks' holiday over the Christmas–New Year period, a week off for March break, and a few days' reprieve over the Easter long weekend. School days normally run from around 8am or 9am to 3pm or 3pm. Extracurricular activities (those that take place out of school hours) include sports, drama, and music, and students sometimes take field trips or excursions in line with certain components of the curriculum.

French immersion schools

Schools offering French immersion or intensive French programmes are popular in Canada as a way of helping non-francophone students gain a functional knowledge of the French language. School boards normally offer French immersion programmes as an alternative to the standard English-taught curriculum; most or all subjects are taught in French, with the exception of English language arts. Programmes may be based on early immersion (starting in Kindergarten or grade one), middle immersion (beginning in or after Grade 3) or late immersion (beginning in or after Grade 6). To find out more about the opportunities offered by French immersion programmes and schools, contact your district school board. The Canadian Parents for French (CPF) website at www.cpf.ca may also be useful. You can also contact CPF by phone on 613 235 1481, or by email at cpf@cpf.ca. CPF membership costs $25 per year ($60 for three years), and members have access to various resources including the *CPF Guide*, a comprehensive, pan-Canadian list of immersion and extended core-French programmes for elementary and secondary students.

The structure of the education system

Education in each province and territory essentially works on a three-tiered system, based around elementary, secondary and post-secondary schooling. Many children also attend pre-elementary school. In most provinces, education is provided for 12 years over the elementary and secondary levels; Quebec uses an 11-year programme.

As a general rule it's compulsory to attend school until the age of 16, but students in New Brunswick have to stay until they either complete high school or turn 18. Students generally attend a designated school for the catchment area or neighbourhood they live in, based on their residential address. It is possible to attend a different school, provided that school has places in its programme for outside students and your application is accepted by the principal. Regulations for registering your child vary between provinces and between district school boards. Contact details and websites for each school board can be obtained through the

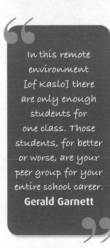

FACT

■ School boards normally offer French-immersion programmes as an alternative to the standard English-taught curriculum; most or all subjects are taught in French, with the exception of English language arts.

> In this remote environment [of Kaslo] there are only enough students for one class. Those students, for better or worse, are your peer group for your entire school career.
> **Gerald Garnett**

provincial ministry of education. Visit www.cmec.ca/education.en.stm the Council of Ministers of Education, Canada, website for links to each ministry. Your local school board will be able to provide details of registration times and locations, and inform you of what documentation you need to bring to enrol your child.

Pre-elementary

Publicly funded kindergartens are available for five-year-olds in each province, and offer a year of education before beginning elementary school. Kindergarten is not compulsory except in BC, New Brunswick, and Nova Scotia; however, it is considered a key part of early childhood development. Junior kindergartens and pre-schools offer programmes for four-year-olds – and sometimes for even younger children – in several provinces. More than 40% of four-year-olds in Canada attend junior kindergarten. Provision for this age group varies considerably across the country and is often limited (though places are widely available in Ontario). Kindergartens may operate on a part-day or full-day basis, and are usually closed over the summer months, from late June until early September. Licenced day-care centres and nursery schools can also give children under the age of five basic social and reading skills.

Elementary

The elementary school system normally begins at Grade 1 and continues to the end of Grade 6 or Grade 8, depending on the province. In some provinces, students move on to a different school or campus for their junior-high or middle-school years, which often encompass grades 7 through 9. This helps ease the transition from elementary education to the secondary-school environment. In other cases, students simply make the shift from elementary to secondary in Grade 7, Grade 8 or Grade 9. A variety of subjects are taught at the elementary level, including English language arts, mathematics, science, social studies, art, music, information and communication technology, health studies and physical education, core (non-immersion) French, other languages (including Aboriginal languages), business skills, and drama. Some subjects may be optional.

Secondary

Secondary schools can be academic, vocational or both. Some form of streaming exists in most systems – students can take courses geared to prepare them to enter the workforce, or to move on to post-secondary study at a community college or university. Some students choose to undertake programmes that lead them towards an apprenticeship in a particular trade, while others attend schools with specialised programmes in visual or performing arts or other specific disciplines. Secondary school is organised around a core curriculum of compulsory courses with various options, and students need to complete a certain number of courses to graduate. Depending on the province, completing secondary school takes four to six years (though some of this may overlap with junior high or middle school). In Quebec, once students complete their 11th year of schooling they move on to a Collège d'ensignement général et professionnel (Cégep). Here, they have the option of taking either a two-year academic programme, as a pathway to university, or a three-year technical programme, which can progress to vocational work or to higher-level post-secondary study.

> **Gerald Garnett, recently retired after teaching in Kaslo, BC, for almost 30 years, shares some of his experiences of the education system:**
>
> In the early days it was tremendously challenging. I had to teach Grade 10 Business and was barely a chapter ahead of my students the whole year. It was useful though. The pupils were not interested, but I, at 28, needed to know about mortgages, insurance, and tax returns.
>
> Then I had lots of Grade 8 classes of English, Guidance, Physical Education. I had never taught any of these before and had never been in the public school system at all.
>
> I often lost the discipline battles in those early years and would reach the end of the day like a punch-drunk boxer just hanging on to the end of the round. But I had chosen this. It fitted in with my left-wing ideals. I could not throw in the towel. When I retired a couple of years ago, I was teaching the children of those earlier students and had learnt to handle them a bit more like an experienced bee-keeper. No bee veil, no smoker, a quiet voice, but underneath a hardened will and a discipline plan.

Community colleges

There are more than 150 recognised community colleges in Canada, which encompass everything from the aforementioned Cégeps to applied-arts colleges, to institutes of technology. These institutions have relatively low tuition fees in comparison to universities – around $2,400 annually on average – and are vocationally based. (There are no fees for Quebec residents to attend Cégeps.) They provide a broad range of options for professional and technical training, and also offer programmes in academic areas of study to enable students to upgrade their skills and transfer to university. To many employers, specialised job training is at least as important as a university degree. Many students choose to attend community colleges for the practical, industry-focused nature of the programmes, which cover social services, hospitality, applied and creative arts, business, agriculture, and technology. Most qualifications take the form of certificates (for one-year programmes) or diplomas (for two- or three-year programmes), though some colleges also have provisions to offer and confer associate or applied degrees (two years or four years, respectively). The Association of Canadian Community Colleges provides a full list of member colleges and institutions on its website, as well as a searchable programmes database.

 Visit the website of the Association of Canadian Community Colleges at www.accc.ca, or reach them by phone on 613 746 2222.

Universities

Canada is home to around 90 fully fledged universities, many of which have an international reputation for excellence. McGill University in Montreal and the

University of Toronto – Canada's largest, with over 62,000 students – are world famous (and aesthetically impressive as well). Queen's University (Ontario), Dalhousie University (Nova Scotia), the University of Western Ontario, and the University of British Columbia (UBC) are widely respected. Institutions with strong arts, design, and media courses include the Ontario College of Art and Design and Ryerson University in Ontario, Simon Fraser University and the Emily Carr Institute of Art and Design in BC, and the Nova Scotia College of Art and Design. Along with those first mentioned, McMaster University (Ontario) and the University of Alberta rank highly for their medical courses, while the University of New Brunswick, University of Ottawa (Ontario), and Université de Montréal are strong in law. Many of the above universities have highly regarded business schools, including York University's Schulich School of Business, UBC's Sauder School of Business, and Queen's School of Business. *Maclean's Guide to Canadian Universities*, updated annually and published in November each year, is a comprehensive and anxiously awaited evaluation of Canada's major universities, with profiles, rankings, programme details, and information on scholarships. An adjunct to their main website at www.macleans.ca, Maclean's 'campus' website, http://oncampus.macleans.ca, provides post-graduate news, updates, and various rankings.

Canada's university structure has three levels. The undergraduate or bachelor's degree, which may be in a general or specialised programme, takes three to four years of full-time study to complete. A master's degree normally requires two further years; and a doctorate – in most cases a PhD – takes three to five more. Each level of qualification acts as a stepping stone to the next, though it's occasionally possible to circumvent the master's degree requirement if you have an honours-level bachelor's degree. Entrance to university is normally based on successful completion of a certain number of subjects, with a specified minimum average score – requirements vary between institutions and courses, and satisfying the requirements doesn't necessarily ensure admission.

 For detailed information on Canada's universities and degree-level colleges, visit the website of the Association of Universities and Colleges of Canada at www.aucc.ca (or phone 613 563 1236). Three online databases allow you to search for post-secondary programmes from over 10,000 listings.

Post-secondary funding

Tuition is heavily subsidised by the government, and fees are a fraction of their US equivalents. The average undergraduate programme cost across the country is around $4,500 annually, though figures vary considerably between provinces and programmes. Quebec's fees are the lowest (out-of-province students don't get the benefit of this perk, however), and Nova Scotia's the highest. Fees for international students are higher again, with $14,000 the average annual price tag for an undergraduate degree. Various federal and provincial student loans and grants help post-secondary students cover their college and university costs, and most educational institutions have facilities that provide funding assistance and help with financial planning. Nonetheless, few students can afford to enter full-time education without some parental support. It's standard practice for Canadian students to finance their education and living expenses with summer and part-time jobs, and many continue to live at home while studying in order to save money. A brand-new, consolidated Canada Student Grant is currently in the works, however, and will e introduced in the fall of 2009. This is aimed at assisting students from lower- or middle-income families who are undertaking a trade-school, college or undergraduate programme. Eligibility is tied to the student's eligibility for the Canada Student Loan.

 The federal government website CanLearn (www.canlearn.ca) is the place to go for information on fees, bursaries, loans, and financial planning for education expenses. See www.canlearn.ca/eng/main/spotlighton/bdg2008/csg.shtml for details of the new Canada Student Grant.

To find out about provincial loans that you or your child may be eligible for, contact your provincial government or visit their webpage (see p. 364 for contact details). Foreign students – who have to demonstrate sufficient finances in order to be issued a study permit – are likely to be ineligible for government funding programmes, though they may be able to obtain financial assistance through their university. Most universities offer scholarships and hardship funds. The federal government's Study in Canada site lists scholarships and bursaries open to international students, and StudyinCanada.com (a different entity to the government site) has a useful webpage, www.studyincanada.com/english/finance, which outlines various funding possibilities. Foreign students admitted on student visas have restrictions on employment, but some work options do exist – see Students on p. 64 for these, and for further details on coming to Canada as a foreign student.

Private and international schools

Private schools have to meet provincial curriculum requirements and follow provincial regulations, though they usually claim to offer smaller classes and better instruction. Canada has quite a number of residential private schools, with both day and boarding facilities, though the vast majority are regular schools. There are approximately 1,700 private and independent schools across the country. They receive less provincial funding than public schools – many people dispute whether they should receive funding at all – and fees are usually steep, ranging from $10,000 to $28,000 per year.

 A directory of private schools in each province is available on the Canadian Association of Independent Schools website, www.cais.ca (or you can phone 705 652 1745).

Many private schools – and some public schools – also provide facilities to prepare students for the International Baccalaureate (IB) exam. This internationally recognised programme is regarded across North America as being equivalent to the first year of university (though minimum scores may be a requirement for university admission, depending on the course), and can be an excellent alternative to the conventional school programme. Courses can be taken at either standard level or higher level (which provides additional credit). For students wanting a universally recognised educational qualification the IB holds obvious appeal, though it shouldn't be

FACT

■ Many private schools – and some public schools – also provide facilities to prepare students for the International Baccalaureate (IB) exam.

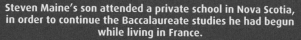

> **Steven Maine's son attended a private school in Nova Scotia, in order to continue the Baccalaureate studies he had begun while living in France.**
>
> Our youngest was 16 when we arrived. We were lucky that we could afford for him to go to the Halifax Grammar School. We felt this was important as they sit the International Baccalaureate exam, instead of the Canadian leaving exams. He had already been studying for the French Baccalaureate when we were living in France, so the move wasn't too disruptive for him. He found the other children very friendly and helpful, and although he has now finished school and is at university, he still keeps in touch with many of his school friends.

undertaken lightly: academic standards are high and the programme can be very demanding.

■ International Baccalaureate schools

Branksome Hall: 10 Elm Avenue, Toronto, Ontario, M4W 1N4; 416 920 9741; www.branksome.on.ca

Champlain College Saint-Lambert (Cégep): 900 Riverside Drive, St-Lambert, Quebec, J4P 3P2; 450 672 7360; www.champlaincollege.qc.ca

Elmwood School: 261 Buena Vista Road, Ottawa, Ontario, K1M 0V9; 613 749 6761; www.elmwood.ca

Saint John High School: 170–200 Prince William Street, Saint John, New Brunswick, E2L 2B7; 506 658 5358; www.sjhigh.ca

Toronto French School: 306 Lawrence Avenue East, Toronto, Ontario, M4N 1T7; 416 484 6533; www.tfs.ca

Upper Canada College: 200 Lonsdale Road, Toronto, Ontario, M4V 1W6; 416 488 1125; www.ucc.on.ca

St John's School: 2215 West 10th Avenue, Vancouver BC V6K 2J1; 604 732 4434; www.stjohns.bc.ca

Meadowridge School: 12224 240th Street, Maple Ridge BC V4R 1N1; 604 467 4444; www.meadowridge.bc.ca

Strathcona-Tweedsmuir School: RR 2, Okotoks, Alberta T1S 1A2; 403 938 4431; www.sts.ab.ca

Sir Winston Churchill High School: 5220 Northland Drive N.W., Calgary, Alberta T2L 2J6; 403 289 9241; http://schools.cbe.ab.ca/b857

■ SOCIAL SERVICES

Canada has a generous social security system, but like the medical system it comes at a high cost to workers. Contributions to the Employment Insurance programme (EI) and the Canada Pension Plan (CPP) are deducted from workers' income. Employers match their employees' CPP contributions and pay EI premiums at 1.4 times their employees' rate. Various benefits, allowances, supplements, and pensions are available through a range of programmes, for the unemployed, children, seniors, veterans, and people with disabilities. For complete details see the Service Canada website at www.servicecanada.gc.ca. Select Income Assistance on the left-hand side of the homepage for a full list of available benefits and programmes.

If you're unemployed, not eligible for EI and in urgent financial need, provincial governments do have their own social-service provisions, aimed at providing immediate income assistance and helping you find work as quickly as possible. Your provincial government will be able to tell you which ministry or department is responsible for social services. In most cases you can find this information easily on the relevant government website (see p. 364 for contact details), though it's not always immediately obvious which department to look under – in Alberta, for example, social services are divided among a number of ministers.

Social insurance number

In order to work in Canada, or to make use of government programmes and other benefits, you need a Social Insurance Number (SIN), which is a nine-digit identifying number. You can apply as soon as you arrive by visiting a Service Canada Centre – see p. 230 for more details. There is no fee to apply (though if you lose your card there's a $10 replacement fee), and the process is straightforward. You'll need to provide immigration documents such as a visa, work or study permit, or permanent resident card, and you may need to show your passport or other identification. Protect both your SIN and your card very carefully, and be aware of the risk of identify theft. It's best to memorise your SIN and keep your card in a secure place, rather than in your wallet. If you're using government services, opening a bank account or completing your income tax return, you may need to provide your SIN, but be extremely cautious about revealing it in other circumstances. SINs for temporary residents begin with a 9 and have an expiry date – people in this category need to supply evidence of their immigration status in order to start a job or apply for benefits such as Employment Insurance.

> *i* A list outlining who is and is not entitled to request to know your SIN can be found at www.servicecanada.gc.ca/en/sin/protect/provide.shtml.

Employment Insurance

Canada's Employment Insurance (EI) programme provides financial assistance to Canadians who are temporarily unable to work. You may qualify for EI if you lose your job or are laid off without being at fault, or if you become sick or injured. (For information on workers' compensation for workplace injuries, see the boxed text on p. 257.) Maternity and parental benefits, compassionate care benefits, and family supplements for qualifying low-income families with children are also provided. The Service Canada webpage at www.servicecanada.gc.ca/en/ei/menu/eihome.shtml provides information and links. Maternity and parental benefits in Quebec are provided through the Quebec Parental Insurance Plan (Régime québécois d'assurance parentale), under the Ministère de l'Emploi et de la Solidarité sociale – see Useful contacts, below, for details.

Contribution and payment rates

Canadian workers pay $1.73 in EI premiums for every $100 earned annually up to $41,100; employers contribute $2.42. Premiums are lower in Quebec. If you change employer during the year, your payments start over again (overpayments are refunded at tax time). Depending on the unemployment rate where you live, you need to have worked for 420 to 910 hours in the last 52 weeks (or since the start of a previous claim, if this time period is shorter) in order to be eligible for EI benefits. Applications should be made within four weeks of your last day at work, either online at the Service Canada website, or in person at a Service Canada Centre. Required documentation includes identification, a Record of Employment (ROE) from any employers you've worked for in the last 52 weeks, and details about why you're no longer able to work. No benefits are paid for the first two weeks of unemployment. Rates are normally based on 55% of your average weekly earnings, which are calculated using a number of factors. The maximum amount payable is $435 per week (unless you also qualify for the Family Supplement), and tax is deducted from this.

Regular, sickness, maternity and parental benefits

Regular EI benefits are paid for up to 45 weeks, but you're expected to be actively looking for work during this time. Sickness benefits are paid for a maximum of 15 weeks. Maternity and parental benefits in Canada are particularly generous. Birth or surrogate mothers who've worked at least 600 hours in the last 52 weeks can receive up to 15 weeks of maternity benefits, followed by up to 35 weeks of parental benefits. Fathers and adoptive parents can also qualify for parental benefits, but the combined leave for both parents can't be more than 35 weeks. If you work while on maternity or sickness benefits, your payments are reduced by an equivalent amount; however, you can earn up to $50 (or 25% of your weekly benefits) each week while on regular or parental benefits. People living in specific economic regions are currently permitted to earn up to $75 per week (or 40% of their weekly benefits).

FACT

Maternity and parental benefits in Canada are particularly generous. Birth or surrogate mothers can receive up to 15 weeks of maternity benefits, followed by up to 35 weeks of parental benefits.

Pensions

Service Canada administers both the Canada Pension Plan (CPP) and the Old Age Security Pension (OAS). Benefits under the CPP include retirement pensions, benefits for spouses and children of deceased contributors, and disability benefits. The Service Canada webpage at www.servicecanada.gc.ca/en/isp/cpp/cpptoc.shtml provides further details. People who work in Quebec contribute to the Quebec Pension Plan – you can find out more at www.rrq.gouv.qc.ca/en/programs/regime_rentes. Contributions to the CPP for 2008 are based on 4.95% of all income between $3,500 and $44,900, which constitutes a maximum annual contribution of $2,049.30. Your employer must contribute an equal amount on your behalf. Self-employed workers contribute both portions. Canadians are eligible for the OAS pension once they turn 65, and may be able to receive it even if they are still working or have never had a job. Whether you qualify for full or partial payment depends on how long you've lived in Canada – the minimum length of time for eligibility is 10 years after the age of 18. As government pensions are rarely sufficient to support people in retirement, private savings, investments and pensions also play an important role. Registered

Retirement Savings Plans (RRSPs) are one such option, and are discussed on p. 212 under Income tax. Page 294 under Retirement includes more on pensions, including maximum monthly payment amounts. Social security agreements between Canada and various other countries mean you may be able to claim benefits from your home country – see the boxed text on p. 294 for further details.

■ **Useful contacts**

Service Canada: 1 800 622 6232 (general enquiries), 1 800 206 7218 (Employment Insurance), 1 800 277 9914 (Canada Pension Plan) or 1 800 277 9914 (Old Age Security) (all phone numbers are toll free within Canada and the United States – see p. 230 for international toll-free details); www.servicecanada.gc.ca

Quebec Parental Insurance Plan (Régime québécois d'assurance parentale): 416 342 3059 or 1 888 610 7727; www.rqap.gouv.qc.ca

Association of Workers' Compensation Boards of Canada: 905 542 3633; contact@awcbc.org; www.awcbc.org

People with disabilities

Canada promotes accessibility for people of all abilities, and considerable efforts are made to ensure people with physical or mental disabilities have access to services, buildings, employment, and all other opportunities. Most stores, restaurants, theatres, and offices (and all government offices) have wheelchair access, and purpose-designed buses or paratransit vehicles often provide door-to-door transportation. Guide dogs are permitted in shops, restaurants, taxis, and aeroplanes, and laws have been passed in some cities making it compulsory for subway and bus stops to be announced, for the benefit of visually impaired passengers. People with disabilities are also eligible for various government benefits, pension plans, rebates, and credits. Service Canada provides details of these on the webpage at www.servicecanada. gc.ca/en/audiences/disabilities/benefits.shtml. Other useful websites include Persons with Disabilities Online (www.pwd-online.ca), the Canadian Abilities Foundation's EnableLink (www.enablelink.org), and the Ontario-specific (but widely relevant) AccessON.ca (www.accesson.ca).

■ CARS AND MOTORING

Driving in Canada

Canadian drivers benefit from an extensive and mostly toll-free system of expressways, highways, and roads. These are generally well maintained, though winters are hard on road surfaces and some stretches are notorious for their potholes and patches. Road signs appear in English or English and French in all provinces but Quebec, where they are in French only. Though a testament to Quebec's determination to avoid its French heritage being diluted by English Canada, it can make for disconcerting driving if you don't read any French.

Canadians drive on the right-hand side of the road. This requires a bit of adjustment for British or Australasian drivers, though a bigger concern tends to be learning to drive on snowy or icy roads. Accidents and pile-ups are very common during snowstorms, and you should reduce your speed by at least 20km/hr if

> There were new driving skills to learn on our twisting, icy mountain roads: do everything in slow motion, especially braking. If you make any abrupt move, it's possible to be caught in a relentless skid.
> **Gerald Garnett**

driving in snow (much more at times). 'Black ice' – ice that forms on the road but is completely invisible – is particularly treacherous. Most Canadian drivers use all-season tires, which give better grip than standard tires, or they switch to snow tires in the winter – these have deeper treads that provide traction on snowy roads. In some regions you can use tires with metal studs, which reduce the chance of sliding on ice. If you're not used to driving on snow and ice it helps to have an experienced Canadian driver or instructor teach you about steering and braking techniques.

Canadian drivers aren't overly aggressive, though city drivers can be pushy and impatient at times – particularly during peak hour – which makes navigating

DRIVING ON ICE AND SNOW

- Don't drive in (or just after) a snowstorm unless you absolutely have to.
- Drive slowly and carefully and be aware of potential dangers like black ice (which is impossible to see).
- Freezing rain and cars don't mix. You'll know it by the ice that clumps on your windshield (instead of brushing off like snow). Don't drive in it, or on it.
- Watch out for dangerous drivers or cars that are too close – they can slide into you or go into a spin without warning.
- Give yourself lots of room, and don't follow too closely.
- Every time you brake you risk losing control, so do it slowly, gently, and carefully – stopping on snow or ice is difficult (sometimes impossible).
- Corners are hazardous – keep your speed down and try to avoid braking, so you don't spin out.
- If driving in a snowstorm where visibility is poor – the worst kind is called a 'whiteout' – use your hazard lights to help other drivers see you.
- Carry a shovel (to dig your car out of snow banks) and an ice-scraper and brush (to clear snow and ice from the windows and roof). Credit cards are handy for scraping ice off the inside of windows.
- Make sure you have antifreeze in your windscreen-wiper fluid, or you'll end up with frozen lines and a trip to a heated garage for some thawing time.
- If you break down or have to pull over, get as far off the road as you safely can – parked cars are at risk of being hit by passing traffic, particularly if visibility is bad.
- Keep your emergency roadside assistance up to date (see p. 178).

A peaceful late-afternoon scene in St Andrews By-the-Sea, New Brunswick

the larger cities less than completely relaxing. The occasional hoon will weave precariously through traffic, garnering looks of disgust from other drivers, but for the most part the road rules are obeyed. As everywhere, the price of gas here has been climbing relentlessly, and currently sits at around $1.35 per litre.

Driving regulations

Depending on which province you live in, traffic violations may be dealt with by up to three different police forces. The Royal Canadian Mounted Police (RCMP) work under contract in most provinces to monitor motorways and remote areas. Ontario and Quebec's provincial forces, the Ontario Provincial Police (OPP) and the Sureté du Québec, have a marked presence on highways in these provinces. Municipal or regional police forces handle the bulk of traffic violations, prowling roads and using radar to catch speeders. Roadside photo radar is used in some areas to issue speeding tickets by mail. (See p. 178 for more details on policing in Canada.)

Roundabouts are uncommon in Canada; traffic lights appear frequently. When turning a corner on a green light, you must give way to pedestrians. A flashing green light is an advance-turning light (the same as a green arrow), normally used to allow left turns. Lights change to amber before going red. You can turn right on a red light (unless it's signed otherwise), except on the Island of Montreal, where this is prohibited. Parking is regulated by ticket machines, coin-operated meters, and residential parking permits, and fines are issued for overstaying. Wheel clamping is seldom practised, though if you park illegally in a busy area your car may be towed. Check signs carefully when parking on the road – on many streets parking is only legal between certain hours, or is restricted to residents. Parking on 'snow routes' – roads that must be kept clear for emergency vehicles – is banned at designated

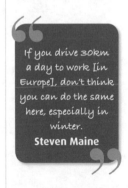

If you drive 30km a day to work [in Europe], don't think you can do the same here, especially in winter.
Steven Maine

FACT

In Nova Scotia, BC, and Ontario it's now illegal to smoke in a vehicle if you're carrying any passengers under the age of 18.

Heading towards a midday snowstorm on a winter highway in Ontario

times (usually when there's a significant snowfall, though in Winnipeg the ban applies every night from December to March).

In Nova Scotia, BC, and Ontario it's now illegal to smoke in a vehicle if you're carrying any passengers under the age of 18, and fines apply if you break the rules. Other provinces are considering similar legislation.

Driver's licences

Foreign driver's licences are valid (provided they haven't reached their expiry date) for anywhere from 30 days to six months for new residents, depending on the

THE SPEED'S THE LIMIT

Speed limits are posted in metric figures. The limit on major expressways is usually 100km/h (some have a limit of 110km/hr), and highway speeds range from 60km/h to 100km/h. In built-up areas the limit ranges from 30km/h to 60km/h. Faster drivers use the left lane on expressways; though speed limits are enforced and fines are substantial, many drivers still hit 120km/hr or more on highways or open roads and tend to get away with it.

FOREIGN LICENCE VALIDIY AND PROVINCIAL LICENSING CONTACTS

Province	Validity period	Contact
Alberta	90 days	Service Alberta: www.servicealberta.gov.ab.ca/Drivers_MotorVehicles.cfm
British Columbia	90 days	Insurance Corporation of British Columbia (ICBC): www.icbc.com/Licensing
Manitoba	three months	Manitoba Public Insurance: www.mpi.mb.ca
New Brunswick	six months	Service New Brunswick: www.snb.ca
Newfoundland and Labrador	three months	Government of Newfoundland and Labrador: www.gs.gov.nl.ca/gs/mr/dl.stm
Northwest Territories	30 days (90 days for tourists, visitors and US residents)	Northwest Territories Department of Transportation: www.dot.gov.nt.ca/_live/pages/wpPages/newDLandGIC.aspx
Nova Scotia	90 days	Service Nova Scotia and Municipal Relations: www.gov.ns.ca/snsmr/rmv/licence
Nunavut	not valid	Department of Economic Development and Transportation: www.edt.gov.nu.ca
Ontario	60 days	DriveTest: www.drivetest.ca
Prince Edward Island	120 days	Government of PEI: www.gov.pe.ca/infopei/index.php3?number=60699&lang=E
Quebec	90 days	Société de l'assurance automobile du Québec (SAAQ): www.saaq.gouv.qc.ca
Saskatchewan	90 days	Saskatchewan Government Insurance (SGI): www.sgi.sk.ca
Yukon	120 days	Yukon Department of Community Services: www.community.gov.yk.ca/motorvehicles/mvdrlic.html

province. If you're in Canada as a visitor, or have an International Driving Permit, you may be able to drive for between three and 12 months on your current licence. Before the applicable period is up, contact the licensing organisation in your province to find out if your licence qualifies for exchange or whether you need to take additional tests. Do this as soon as possible after you arrive, as wait times can be lengthy. Most provinces allow experienced drivers from specific countries to surrender their existing licence in exchange for a Canadian provincial licence (though you may need to meet medical standards and pass a vision test). Inexperienced drivers, or those from non-qualifying countries, normally have to complete certain components of the province's standard licensing programme. If you don't have a licence and want to get one in Canada you have to complete all licensing requirements. This usually involves obtaining a learner permit, completing a probationary period, passing vision, knowledge and practical tests, and paying fees.

Buying a car

New and second-hand cars are widely available in Canada. Look in the classified section of major newspapers (both print and online editions) or online magazines such as www.autotrader.ca or www.carpages.ca. *Auto Trader Magazine* is also sold in print editions (with separate issues for different vehicle types and price brackets) at Canadian Tire and many convenience stores. New and used cars are sold through car dealerships or private sellers. When buying a used car, look for one that already has a safety standards certificate or certificate of inspection. If you buy without a certificate you'll have to get the car certified before you can drive it. Some provinces also require used cars to have passed an emissions test. If you want, you can order a CARFAX vehicle history report (which tells you about the car's history and any substantial damage) for about $30 on the CARFAX website, www.carfax.com. Canadian Automobile Association (CAA) members can order this via the CAA website at www.caa.ca. A vehicle inspection by a licenced mechanic costs around $90–$150 and is advisable if buying a used car – the fee is minimal compared with what you might otherwise spend on repairs. Various organisations can perform these, including the CAA and the Automobile Protection Association (APA) (visit www.apa.ca). If you're thinking of bringing your car with you to Canada, check p. 87 for information on the significant restrictions that apply to imports.

TIP

When buying a used car, look for one that already has a safety standards certificate or certificate of inspection.

Car registration

All cars must be registered with the provincial Transportation Ministry at the time of purchase, and provincial sales tax and licence fees apply. (If purchased through an authorised dealer, the tax may already have been paid.) Various documentation is required: you may be asked to show identification (normally your driver's licence), proof of ownership (such as a bill of sale), and proof of insurance. Rules are not uniform across Canada: in Alberta, the car must be insured before you can register it; in BC, it must be registered in order to be insured. Registration fees vary considerably between provinces (and in some cases within provinces as well). As a general rule, they're low: in southern Ontario you'll pay an initial $20 for your vehicle permit and number plates, then $74 per year to register your vehicle. (Fees in northern Ontario are just $37 per year.) Passenger-vehicle registration in Nova Scotia ranges from $125 to $290 for a two-year period.

Car insurance

Car insurance is compulsory in Canada. Rules and rates vary by province. All require a minimum level of insurance, which includes third-party liability up to $200,000 ($50,000 in Quebec – $500,000 for off-road vehicles – and $500,000 in Nova Scotia), and covers you in the United States as well (but not in Mexico). Most also provide accident benefits coverage to protect you if you're injured and unable to work. Fire, theft, and other forms of insurance are optional. Ontario has no-fault insurance, which means you always make claims through your own company, regardless of who caused the accident. New Brunswick, Nova Scotia, and PEI have liability caps to prevent excessive payouts for minor injuries. In BC, Saskatchewan, and Manitoba, mandatory insurance is sold through government-run agencies, while private companies compete for optional extras. Your insurance documents must be kept in your car and shown to the police on request, or you can be ticketed. The cost of insurance depends on your car's make, model and value, your driving record, and in some cases, your age and gender. If your spouse or partner has a licence, you have to include them on your policy as well, which can increase your premium. In addition to government-run and private insurance companies, most banks also sell auto insurance. A comprehensive policy will cost around $1,000–$3,000 annually. InsuranceHotline.com (www.insurancehotline.com) is a useful site for insurance comparisons; some others are listed under *Useful contacts for drivers,* overleaf. Entering your details brings up the three lowest quotes – you do need to provide an email address and phone number, but a bogus number works just as well.

Motoring associations

Motoring associations offer 24-hour roadside assistance if you have a flat tyre or battery, run out of fuel or need to be towed. Some will carry out minor repairs to get you back on the road, and assist with accommodation and travel costs if you're stranded away from home. Various grades of coverage are available. Canada's largest assistance service is the Canadian Automobile Association (CAA) (www.caa.ca), with 148 offices across the country; it's affiliated with AAA in the United States and with a number of international automobile associations. Many other private companies and banks also offer roadside assistance programmes, and car dealers often include coverage when you purchase a new car.

 Visit the Canadian Automobile Association (CAA) website at www.caa.ca, or reach them by phone on 613 820 1890 or 1 800 267 8713.

Breakdowns and accidents

If you have an accident in which someone is injured or substantial damage is caused, you must dial 911. Police and an ambulance will come to the scene. In some provinces you need to call the police after every collision, though if damage is minimal you would generally call the local police rather than the emergency number. The police may come to the scene to establish how the accident occurred (and possibly ticket one or more of the drivers), or may send you to a

SHOW ME THE WAY

Google Maps (www.maps.google.com), with its literal monopoly over the globe, is the automatic route planner of choice if you're looking for the quickest way from A to B. (It's also great fun for satellite-stalking your friends back home by zooming in on their rooftops.) Mapquest (www.mapquest.com) does an okay job as well, but it's not as quick, intuitive or detailed. If you're planning to travel cross country, either on or in the vicinity of the Trans-Canada Highway (and it can be hard to avoid), check out the Trans-Canada Highway Trip and Vacation Planner (www.transcanadahighway.com). This handy, fact-filled, and clearly laid-out site provides information on pretty much everything you can see and do along the Trans-Canada route, with detailed city information, sightseeing suggestions, hotel listings, maps, and travel tips. Spend some time exploring the site, and don't be surprised if your feet start itching to get back on the road.

The Granville Bridge in Vancouver, BC, gives motorists a unique perspective on the city

collision-reporting centre, where you'll complete a police report. This report is important as evidence for your insurance company. Make sure to exchange insurance information with any other drivers while at the scene of the accident, and contact your insurance company as soon as possible.

If you break down on a motorway, try to get your car well out of the way of passing traffic. Turn on your hazard lights or emergency flashers. If you don't have a mobile phone or there's no reception, you can walk to a gas station or restaurant to call your motoring association or the police. It may be safer to leave your car, depending on its location and the conditions (night, rain, snow, below-freezing temperatures). Keep a first-aid kit, blankets, water, flashlights, spare batteries, booster cables, candles, and matches in your vehicle. (If you're stuck without heat in very cold climes, a single lit candle can warm your car enough to stop you freezing.) Roadside emergency telephones are also available in some regions. If you can't get to a phone, a passing driver will usually notify the police of your location if you lift the hood and trunk of your car.

■ Useful contacts for drivers
Canadian Automobile Association (CAA): 613 820 1890 or 1 800 267 8713; www.caa.ca
Insurance Bureau of Canada: 416 362 9528 or 1 800 387 2880; www.ibc.ca
Insurance Corporation of British Columbia (ICBC): 604 661 2800; www.icbc.com

TIP

■ Keep a first-aid kit, blankets, water, flashlights, spare batteries, booster cables, candles, and matches in your vehicle.

IF YOU DRINK AND DRIVE ...

The war against drinking and driving in Canada has included grisly commercials, well-publicised prison sentences, community initiatives, and spot-check programmes such as Ontario's RIDE (Reduce Impaired Driving Everywhere) and Alberta's Checkstop. These programmes, which operate throughout the year, involve setting up temporary police checkpoints where drivers can be pulled over at random, and questioned or required to take a breath test. Checkpoints can be set up at any time, but are particularly common on holidays and long weekends. You must stop if pulled over, and if you refuse a breath test you may be charged, or your licence may be suspended. The blood alcohol concentration (BAC) limit in Canada is 80mg per 100mL (.08). In some provinces you can be charged even if your BAC is below .08. Impaired driving is a criminal offense: penalties can include licence suspension for a set period (normally one year for a first offence) or for life, as well as fines and prison sentences. Transport Canada's document Smashed (available online at www.tc.gc.ca/roadsafety/tp/tp1535/menu.htm) provides more information on the government's approach to drinking and driving.

Manitoba Public Insurance (MPI): 204 985 7000 (Autopac Line) or
1 800 665 2410; www.mpi.mb.ca
Saskatchewan Government Insurance (SGI): 306 751 1200 (Customer Service
Centre) or 1 800 667 8015; sgiinquiries@sgi.sk.ca; www.sgi.sk.ca
Financial Services Commission of Ontario: 416 250 7250 or 1 800 668 0128;
contactcentre@fsco.gov.on.ca; www.fsco.gov.on.ca
The Société de l'assurance automobile du Québec: 514 873 7620 or
1 800 361 7620; www.saaq.gouv.qc.ca
Insurance-Canada.ca: Quote comparisons, online only. www.insurance-canada.ca
Kanetix.com: Quote comparisons, online only. www.kanetix.com
Belairdirect: 1 888 280 8549; belairdirect.ontario@belairdirect.com;
www.belairdirect.com
AXA Financial Protection: 1 877 292 4968; www.axa.ca
The Co-operators: 519 824 4400 or 1 800 265 2612; service@cooperators.ca;
www.cooperators.ca

■ TRANSPORT

Public transport

Urban transport is a municipal responsibility. There are a huge number of transit systems across Canada, of which more than 120 are members of the Canadian Urban Transit Association (CUTA) – see www.cutaactu.ca. Around 15% of total federal, provincial, and local government spending on transportation ($3.7 billion annually) has been directed towards public transit in recent years. As concerns about the world's environmental future increase, so too do the number of Canadians choosing to take transit to work: while the vast majority of workers still drive, 2006 census figures indicate that 11% now regularly opt for the public system, up from the 10.5% recorded in 2001. In major cities, where public transportation systems are more extensive and easier to access, the average proportion of passengers increased from 14.4% to 15.1%.

The majority of transit systems are based around bus services, but larger cities normally have a range of vehicle options. Toronto's distinctive red-and-white streetcars crisscross the city, while both Toronto and Montreal have subway systems that operate in conjunction with buses and commuter trains. Vancouver provides monorail-style rapid transit with its SkyTrain, and ferries form a regular part of the transit network. Halifax also offers an integrated ferry system. Most cities either operate specific paratransit services for people with disabilities, or have wheelchair-accessible buses or other accessible transport options available on their normal routes. Night buses often operate on specific routes.

A flat fee is normally charged per trip, regardless of length, though additional fares may apply if your journey covers multiple zones or takes you across a municipal boundary. Most single adult fares cost between $2.00 and $2.75. Buses often require exact change or tokens (sold at stations, and sometimes at newsstands). You can normally purchase tickets in multiples (generally in batches of six or 10), or buy daily, weekly or monthly passes. This tends to be more economical than paying for single fares if you plan to use public transport on a regular or semi-regular

> *I've also found the transport system frustrating.*
> *In Toronto, it's expensive without being extensive – only three subway lines for over 5 million people!*
> **Christina Chiam**

PUBLIC TRANSPORT SYSTEMS IN MAJOR CITIES

Alberta	Calgary Transit	www.calgarytransit.com	bus, light rail
	Edmonton Transit System	www.edmonton.ca (select the Transit tab)	bus, light rail
British Columbia	Greater Vancouver Transit Authority	www.translink.bc.ca	bus, commuter train, monorail, ferry
Manitoba	Winnipeg Transit	www.winnipegtransit.com	bus
New Brunswick	City of Fredericton Transit Division	www.fredericton. ca/en/transportation/ transportation.asp	bus
Newfoundland and Labrador	St. John's Metrobus	www.metrobus.com	bus
Northwest Territories	Yellowknife Transit	www.yellowknife.ca/ Residents/Bus_Schedules. html	bus
Nova Scotia	Halifax Metro Transit	www.halifax.ca/ metrotransit	bus, ferry
Ontario	Toronto Transit Commission	www.ttc.ca	bus, subway, streetcar, commuter train, paratransit
	OC Transpo, Ottawa	www.octranspo.com	bus, light rail
Prince Edward Island	Charlottetown public transit	www.city.charlottetown. pe.ca/residents/transit_ routes.cfm	bus
Quebec	Société de transport de Montréal	www.stcum.qc.ca	bus, subway, commuter train, taxibus, paratransit
	Réseau de Transport de la Capitale, Québec City	www.rtcquebec.ca	bus, taxibus, paratransit
Saskatchewan	Regina Transit	www.reginatransit.com	bus
Yukon	Whitehorse Transit	www.city.whitehorse.yk.ca (select City Departments, then Transit)	bus

basis. Semester passes (for students) and annual passes may also be available. Discounted fares usually apply for students, seniors, and passengers with disabilities who have (and can show) the requisite identification card. In some cities, such as Toronto and Regina, an entire family can travel on a standard adult day pass on Saturdays, Sundays, and public holidays. Vancouver offers a similar deal for monthly ticket holders. Some cities also have free travel initiatives to promote use of their transit systems: Halifax offers free rides downtown in the summer months, Calgary provides free use of its light rail system within a designated downtown zone, and seniors in Ottawa can travel without charge on Wednesdays during summer.

Contact your municipal Department of Transportation for transit schedules and fares, or visit the CUTA webpage at www.cutaactu.ca/en/member_transit_systems to find links to the websites of transit systems in your province.

TIP

▪ A flat fee is normally charged per trip, regardless of length, though additional fares may apply if your journey covers multiple zones or takes you across a municipal boundary.

FACT

▪ The federal government recently introduced tax credits to encourage transit use and to help ease costs to commuters.

The boxed text on p. 205 provides details of systems in major Canadian cities in all provinces and territories except Nunavut – a public bus service was briefly introduced in Nunavut's capital, Iqaluit, as part of a transit trial, but was cancelled in 2005 due to lack of use. Air transportation represents the main mode of 'public' transit in this remote territory, and taxi service (often shared) is available in many communities.

The federal government recently introduced tax credits to encourage transit use and to help ease costs to commuters. Passengers who buy monthly passes can claim the credit. (Regular commuters who buy weekly passes or pay with electronic payment cards may also be eligible.) To do so, you must keep all expired transit passes (and receipts, if applicable) and may need to provide other supporting information. The government, in collaboration with the Canadian Urban Transit Association, maintains a specific transit credit website with full details at www.transitpass.ca. You can also visit the Canada Revenue Agency (CRA) website at www.cra-arc.gc.ca/transitpass.

Trains

A substantial amount of Canadian taxpayers' money goes towards subsidising rail services. Much is used to sustain little-used lines in remote areas – more than four-fifths of rail travel in Canada occurs on just one-third of tracks. The Canadian National Railway (CN) and Canadian Pacific Railway (CPR) – both freight carriers – own or lease 75% of Canada's railway tracks. Between them they bring in almost 90% of the country's annual railway revenue. Other companies including VIA Rail, the national passenger service, pay trackage rights to run on CN or CPR tracks. VIA Rail provides coast-to-coast transportation with 480 departures each week, as well as tour packages and value passes like the 'Canrailpass' (12 days of travel for $549 off peak or $879 in season). A 35-minute ride from Toronto to Brampton costs around $17, while a seven-hour trip between Ottawa and Quebec City is $107. Various regional companies also cater to passengers and tourists, including Ontario Northland Rail Transportation Services and BC's Rocky Mountaineer. The First Nations-owned Keewatin Railway and Tshiuetin Rail Transportation provide access to remote areas of Newfoundland and Labrador, Manitoba, and Quebec. US railway Amtrak also serves some Canadian cities (see p. 83). Train tickets can normally be booked online, by phone or at station ticket counters (except at some smaller stations), and must be bought before boarding the train. Discounts are often available for children, students, and seniors, and you can reduce costs by booking in advance. (If you plan to travel first class, in a sleeper car or on a popular route, it's always best to book ahead.)

VIA Rail: 1 888 842 7245; www.viarail.ca
Amtrak: 1 800 872 7245; www.amtrak.com
Ontario Northland: 705 472 4500 or 1 800 363 7512 (ext. 0); www.ontarionorthland.ca
Rocky Mountaineer: 604 606 7200 or 1 877 460 3200; www.rockymountaineer.com

Buses

Greyhound is the largest intercity bus company in Canada, and regularly serves almost 1,100 locations. Greyhound also operates throughout the USA and in parts of Mexico. An eight to 10-hour trip from Montreal to Toronto costs $93; the fare from Edmonton to Calgary (around four hours) is $47. Acadian operates in the Maritimes – PEI, New Brunswick, and Nova Scotia – and is a subsidiary of Orléans Express, Quebec's major intercity carrier. Intercar operates in regional areas of Quebec. Coach Canada connects to parts of southern Quebec and south-eastern Ontario, the Saskatchewan Transportation Company (STC) carries people and freight in that province, and DRL Coachlines provides service in Newfoundland and Labrador. Pacific Coach Lines links Vancouver with Victoria and Whistler in BC, and, through Cantrail, with Seattle in the USA. Local or regional bus companies operate in many areas, particularly those less well serviced by Greyhound. Brewster, for example, will shuttle you from Jasper to Banff in the Rocky Mountains in half the time and distance of Greyhound's circuitous route (and for considerably less money). Charter bus lines, tourist coaches, and backpacker services also operate across the country – for a list of privately run companies, see the Motor Coach Canada website at www.motorcoachcanada.com or visit the Canadian Business Directory webpage at www.canadianbusinessdirectory.ca.

Greyhound Canada: 1 800 661 8747; www.greyhound.ca
Acadian: 1 800 567 5151; www.smtbus.com

FACT

■ Greyhound is the largest intercity bus company in Canada, and regularly serves almost 1,100 locations.

A local transit bus pulls up alongside an intercity Greyhound at a downtown Toronto intersection

Pacific Coach Lines: 604 662 7575 or 1 800 661 1725; www.pacificcoach.com
Orléans Express: 514 395 4032 or 1 888 999 3977; www.orleansexpress.com
Intercar: 418 547 2167 or 1 888 547 6784; www.intercar.qc.ca
Coach Canada: 705 748 6411 or 1 800 461 7661; www.coachcanada.com
Saskatchewan Transportation Company (STC): 1 800 663 7181;
www.stcbus.com
DRL Coachlines: 709 263 2171 or 1 888 263 1854; www.drlgroup.com
Brewster Inc.: 403 762 6700 or 1 866 606 6700; www.brewster.ca

Air travel

There are over 1,700 aerodromes in Canada, including land airports, water bases, and heliports, but around 94% of passengers and cargo are handled through 26 major airports. Air Canada dominates the market, having taken over (and subsequently closed) its major rival, Canadian Airlines, at the end of 1999. The lack of competition drove prices up, although low-cost airline WestJet is growing steadily and challenging Air Canada on many Canadian and US routes. Various discount airlines such as Porter Airlines or Air Canada Jazz also compete on certain routes, and some airlines offer tiered pricing systems that include cheaper, 'no frills' options. City-to-city rates are still high in comparison to Europe or the United States (though the distances between Canadian cities are comparatively high as well). Return flights from Toronto or Montreal to Vancouver vary widely in cost. Special offers can start from as low as $400–$500 (including taxes), but lowest available fares can easily reach more than $1,000. Round-trip flights between Toronto and Montreal cost anywhere from $275 to $700, similar to the cost of one- or two-hour flights to US destinations. See p. 83 for more information on air services, and for contact details for international airlines.

Air Canada: 1 888 247 2262; www.aircanada.com
WestJet: 1 888 937 8538; www.westjet.com
Air Canada Jazz: 1 888 247 2262 www.flyjazz.ca
Porter Airlines: 416 619 8622 or 1 888 619 8622; www.flyporter.com

Ferries

On Canada's west coast, BC Ferries connects Vancouver and the lower mainland regions of BC with Vancouver Island and the Gulf Islands. The meditative Inside Passage trip, which meanders up the coast to Prince Rupert, is also under BC Ferries jurisdiction. On the eastern side of the country, Marine Atlantic travels from Nova Scotia to two locations in Newfoundland and Labrador (one only operational in summer), while Bay Ferries and Northumberland Ferries link Nova Scotia with New Brunswick and PEI. CTMA, based in Quebec's stunning Magdalen Islands, has a range of ferry and cruise services connecting with PEI and Montreal. Many other operators offer transportation, cruises, and lake crossings. The majority of ferries are equipped to transport vehicles as well as passengers, though you need to book well ahead to ensure space for your car. If you're on foot, you'll normally have little trouble getting on board, unless you're on a high-demand route or it's the peak of summer. See p. 85 for additional ferry information.

British Columbia Ferry Services Inc. (BC Ferries): 1 888 223 3779;
www.bcferries.com
CTMA Group: 418 986 3278 or 1 888 986 3278; www.ctma.ca

Ferries negotiate the docks at the BC Ferries terminal in Tsawwassen, BC

Marine Atlantic: 902 794 5200; www.marine-atlantic.ca
Bay Ferries Ltd: 902 566 3838 or 1 877 359 3760; www.nfl-bay.com
Northumberland Ferries: 902 566 3838; www.peiferry.com

Taxis

Taxi service is widely available in Canada, and in many small towns and remote areas it functions as a stand-in for public transport. Drivers must be licenced, and services and fares are generally regulated by the municipality. Airport taxi and limousine services provide fixed-fare travel to various destinations, but most regular cabs charge a metered rate. This normally includes a flag-fall of $2.75–$3.50, then a per-minute rate of anywhere from $0.30 to $1.60. Tax is included in the fare, but your driver will expect an additional tip of around 15%. You can dial 310 TAXI (310 8294) from anywhere in Canada to be connected with one of a range of partner taxi companies. No area code is required. Similar services exist in the Toronto area on 416-TAXICAB (416 829 4222), and through some wireless phone companies.

FACT

■ Taxi service is widely available in Canada, and in many small towns and remote areas it functions as a stand-in for public transit.

The website www.taxiwiz.com lets you estimate the cost of trips in Toronto, Vancouver, and Montreal. TakeaTaxi.ca (www.takeataxi.ca) lists taxi services and contact phone numbers for every province, and is searchable by city within each province.

Cycling

Cycling for sport and recreation is popular in Canada, and around 190,000 commuters ride to work (based on 2006 census results). Though this only represents 1.3% of all commuters, the importance of cycling – both for health and as an alternative mode of transportation – is gaining government recognition, with provinces allocating funding to cycling infrastructure or offering sales-tax exemptions on helmets and safety equipment. Helmet laws vary: in some provinces their use is compulsory; in others they're only required for children; and some have no provincial legislation at all (though city by-laws may exist). Many communities have recreational bike clubs or networks, and enthusiasts can get involved in rallies, tours, mountain biking, and competitive sports. Cycle Canada (www.cyclecanada.com) has tour information and a directory of cycling clubs. Bikes can be bought quite cheaply or rented for occasional use. Toronto's Community Bicycle Network (www.communitybicyclenetwork.org) has rentals for $10 a day. Montreal is currently piloting a public bike system, BIXI, to be launched in spring 2009; Toronto has similar plans. Theft is an issue in many cities – never leave your bike unsecured on the street (unless you're prepared to donate it to someone else's cause), and if possible, store it indoors or in your backyard.

> *While I have an international driver's licence, a separate Canadian licence is required. I decided to buy a bike instead, as the streets are fairly well equipped for cyclists.*
> **Christina Chiam**

 The Canadian Cycling Association (www.canadian-cycling.com) offers courses for children and adults through the CAN-BIKE programme, covering how to ride, safety and handling, and riding in traffic.

◾ TAXATION

For the average Canadian household, more than 20% of annual expenditures disappear into the tax system. Residents of BC, for example, are subject to income tax, goods and services tax, provincial sales tax, property tax, insurance premium tax, and schools tax, among others. Liquor, tobacco, gas and fuel, passenger vehicles, hotel rooms, gambling, logging, mining, and healthcare may also be taxable, depending on where you live. It's hardly surprising, then, that Canadians unofficially celebrate 'tax freedom day' each year – the day when their salary begins to go into their own pockets instead of into government coffers. This falls on different dates in each province, though the national average is currently June 20. While high taxes are seen by some as a disadvantage of living in Canada, they do play an essential role in providing the services, facilities, and quality of life that Canadian residents enjoy.

Income tax

The Income Tax Act of Canada is a complex document, with provisions that tend to alter on a yearly basis. On the plus side, rates have generally been going down for the last 10 years. Income tax includes both federal and provincial components, which you calculate separately when completing your tax return. Quebec has a separate tax agreement with the federal government and collects provincial income tax from its residents through Revenu Québec. Federal income taxes are calculated based on four income levels, which change regularly. To complicate things further, each province has its own system: Alberta has a flat tax rate of 10%, while all other provinces and territories have incremental tax rates based on income, with differing cut-off points. Ontario, Nova Scotia, PEI, and the Yukon also levy surtaxes on the tax itself. Most charge surtaxes of 5% to 10% and have thresholds in the range of $6,000 to $12,500, but Ontario charges 20% at a threshold of just $4162, plus a painful 36% on anything over $5249.

If you work in Canada, your employer deducts income tax from each pay cheque you receive. Self-employed individuals are expected to pay a certain amount quarterly. Following the end of the fiscal year (1 January to 31 December, in Canada) your employer must issue you a T4 slip, which indicates your earnings and tax payments for the year just passed. If you have earnings from other sources you'll receive separate T4s for those. Various benefits exist for low-income earners and families with children, and if you pay rent or property taxes you can claim some deduction on those.

 For the most up-to-date tax rates and other information, visit the Canada Revenue Agency (CRA) website at www.cra-arc.gc.ca. For provincial income tax in Quebec, go to the Revenu Québec site at www.revenu.gouv.qc.ca).

INCOME TAX GRADUATION

$1 to $37,885: you would pay 15% of your income in federal income tax and a further 4% to 17% in provincial tax.

$37,885 to $75,769: you would pay the federal government a flat tax of about $5,700, plus 22% on the amount of income over $37,885. The provinces would take an additional 5.5% to 19%.

$75,769 to $123,184: you would pay a flat tax of about $14,000, plus 26% on the amount of income above $75,770. The provinces would take around 7% to 21%.

Over $123,184: you would pay a flat tax of about $26,500, plus 29% on any income above $123,184. The provinces would charge you an additional 7% to 24%.

Note: These figures are intended as a guide only, and don't include applicable surtaxes, deductions, benefits or tax credits. Tax-free basic personal amounts apply federally and in most provinces. The federal basic personal amount is currently set at $9,600; provincial rates vary from $7,566 (Newfoundland and Labrador) to $16,161 (Alberta). You may also be eligible for other deductions; availability and rates vary between provinces.

Capital gains, interest, and dividends

Income tax is also payable on capital gains, dividends, and interest earnings, and rates vary by province. The maximum combined federal and provincial marginal tax on interest is between 39% and 48.22%, while that for capital gains ranges from 19.5% to 24.11% (effectively 50% of the full tax rate, as you only pay tax on half the gain). The tax on dividends – such as those from corporation shares – is worked out using a formula and is somewhat complicated, involving grossing up the amount and then applying a discount (called a dividend tax credit). This is calculated on your taxable dividend income, but the actual deduction is applied to the final tax you owe. You receive an additional dividend tax credit from the provincial government. Overall, this works in your favour and reduces the tax you pay on dividend income: as a very rough guide, it equates to a combined maximum marginal rate of around 16% to 30%, depending on the province. (Note that maximum marginal tax rates only apply to the portion of your income that falls into the highest tax bracket.) In each case, Alberta has the lowest maximum taxes and Quebec the highest.

Registered Retirement Savings Plan

Many Canadians take advantage of a tax-reducing pension scheme called a Registered Retirement Savings Plan (RRSP or RSP). Under this government-regulated plan, which is offered by banks, trusts, and other financial institutions, you can contribute 18% of your previous year's earnings (to a set maximum, currently $20,000), towards a special retirement fund. Unused contribution space from earlier years can also be carried forward. Your contribution in a given year is deducted from your taxable income, and may even put you into a lower tax bracket. RRSP money is taxed when it is withdrawn, but in the meantime you'll have earned interest (on

MAXIMUM COMBINED FEDERAL AND PROVINCIAL TAX RATES		
Province	**Interest** Income from interest paid on bank accounts, bonds, term deposits.	**Capital gains** Financial gain from selling a capital asset at a profit; tax payable on half of gain.
Alberta	39%	19.5%
British Columbia	43.7%	21.85%
Manitoba	46.4%	23.2%
New Brunswick	46.95%	23.48%
Newfoundland	45.5%	22.75%
Northwest Territories	43.05%	21.53%
Nova Scotia	46.5%	23.25%
Nunavut	40.5%	20.5%
Ontario	40.16%	20.08%
Prince Edward Island	45.7%	22.85%
Quebec	48.22%	24.11%
Saskatchewan	44%	22%
Yukon	41.76%	20.88%

which the tax is also deferred), and your lower retirement income will usually mean taxes are payable at a lower rate.

 The Canada Revenue Agency (CRA) administers all RRSPs. You can find out more at www.cra-arc.gc.ca/tx/ndvdls/tpcs/rrsp-reer/rrsps-eng.html, or by clicking the RRSP link on the CRA home page.

Tax treaties

Canada has agreements with almost 90 countries (and others pending) to avoid double taxation for people with taxable income in two countries. The CRA webpage at www.cra-arc.gc.ca/tx/nnrsdnts/trty-eng.html provides information, and links to a listing of treaty countries. You can also read the somewhat legalistic treaties online. If your home country has a treaty with Canada, you can get information from the International Tax Services Office (www.cra-arc.gc.ca/cntct/international-eng.html) on 613 952 3741 (international collect calls are accepted) or 1 800 267 5177 (within Canada). Alternatively, your home country's international tax office should be able to provide advice. You also need to check with your home country whether you owe taxes for the portion of the fiscal year preceding your move to Canada.

It's important to note that being a resident of Canada for tax purposes is not the same as being a resident for immigration purposes. Your 'tax resident' status is determined by a range of factors, such as how many days of the year you've spent in Canada, and what economic and social ties you have to the country. While the decision is quite subjective, you can submit a form to the CRA to request their opinion of your status. Links to the relevant forms can be found at the bottom of webpage www.cra-arc.gc.ca/tx/nnrsdnts/cmmn/rsdncy-eng.html. Another webpage, www.cra-arc.gc.ca/E/pub/tp/it221r3-consolid/it221r3-consolid-e.html, provides detailed information on the matter of residence status for tax purposes.

It's important to note that being a resident of Canada for tax purposes is not the same as being a resident for immigration purposes. Your 'tax resident' status is determined by a range of factors.

Filing a tax return

The Canadian tax year runs from 1 January to 31 December, and tax reports must be filed by 30 April each year or you risk a penalty for late filing. If your completed return shows a balance owing to the government, you should also pay this by 30 April. (If you're not able to pay the full amount by this date you should still submit your return, to avoid the late fee.) You'll normally receive a tax refund (or a request for payment, if payment is still owing) four to six weeks after you file your return. The General Income Tax and Benefit package, which includes all information and forms (except those for Quebec's provincial tax), can be obtained in several ways:

The Canadian tax year runs from 1 January to 31 December, and tax reports must be filed by 30 April each year or you risk a penalty for late filing.

Steven Maine and his wife discovered they hadn't quite anticipated the cost of Canada's taxes:

When we moved here, we were really surprised by the level of taxation in Nova Scotia (especially when you compare it to other provinces), to the extent that financially we're not really that much better off here.

print, download or order a copy online at the CRA website; call 1 800 959 2221 (toll free) to have one mailed to you; or pick one up from any post office or Service Canada office between February and the start of May. You'll need to complete the relevant forms, stating any deductions you qualify for and declaring all income, collect the required supporting documentation (such as T4s), and file your return with the CRA. You'll also need to provide your SIN. The CRA website has an onscreen course, Learning About Taxes, that guides you through the process of submitting a return.

 Information guides for newcomers and non-residents are also available: go to www.cra-arc.gc.ca/formspubs/clntgrp/thrs/nn_rs-eng.html. For information on business tax, see p. 289.

Sales taxes

The federal government levies a tax (GST) on most goods and services purchased in Canada, which has recently been reduced to 5%. GST is generally not included in the ticket price, and is added at the cash register. With the exception of Alberta and the three territories, each province also has a provincial sales tax (PST), which ranges from 5% to 10%. In Nova Scotia, New Brunswick, and Newfoundland and Labrador, the GST and PST are combined into a single, harmonised sales tax (HST) of 13%. (In Quebec, GST and QST – Quebec sales tax – are administered by Revenu Québec.) Certain goods and services are usually not taxed, such as basic groceries, prescription drugs, and books. To help offset their tax costs, Canadian residents with low incomes can apply to the CRA for a quarterly GST/HST credit. Short-term visitors to Canada who purchase accommodation as part of a tour package or are involved with a foreign convention may also be eligible for GST/HST rebates. The previous Visitor Rebate Program no longer exists. See the CRA webpage at www.cra-arc.gc.ca/tax/nonresidents/visitors for more information.

Property taxes

Municipal councils charge property owners a tax based on the value of their property. The value is determined by an assessment authority, in line with estimated market value. If you disagree with the assessed value of your property you can file an appeal or request for reassessment with the relevant assessment body. Much of the money raised by property taxes goes towards the public school system, while some is used to fund the local police force and other services – Taxes and fees on p. 139 gives some additional details. Rates vary from one locality to the next. Based on 2008 rates, you'd pay around $3,000 for a house in the City of Toronto with an assessed value of $350,000. A similarly priced home in Vancouver would attract taxes of about $1,510. In Ottawa you might pay $4,350, in Montreal you're looking at around $1,670 and in Calgary about $1,610 would be charged.

Professional tax advice

Most people with straightforward tax returns don't bother engaging a tax accountant, but you may decide it's worthwhile if you're preparing to submit your first tax return in Canada and don't yet feel familiar with the system, or if there are complex aspects to your income, benefits or personal situation. Considerable deductions are available to self-employed people, for example, that you may not be aware you can claim. There are various ways in which your tax bill can be reduced, such as through RRSPs or similar investments, and tax accountants are well placed to advise you on what factors apply to your situation. Fees vary considerably, and may be based on a flat rate or on a percentage of your return. (Accountants who offer an instant cash-back option will often take the fee in this percentage form.)

Information on the three accounting designations available in Canada is outlined on p. 281 under Accountants and on p. 246 under Financial and banking services. The website addresses for the national associations provide links to provincial associations, many of which provide directories or search functions to enable you to find a personal accountant in your area. Contact details for some of Canada's major accounting firms are listed under Accounting and finance, p. 275, however these companies tend to be primarily business focused. The largest tax consultancy firm for personal income tax preparation is probably H&R Block (1 800 561 2154; customer.support@hrblock.ca; www.hrblock.ca), which has numerous offices and also offers an online tax preparation service.

■ INHERITANCE LAWS AND WILLS

There are currently no inheritance taxes or succession duties in Canada (though the New Democratic Party (NDP) unsuccessfully pushed for inheritance tax back in 2004, and some predict the law will change in years to come). You are still taxed after death, though: someone will have to submit a final return on your behalf, and capital gains tax applies to your capital assets (excluding your principal residence), which are taxed as if they had been sold and the gain realised. Provinces also levy probate fees (called 'estate administration fees' in Ontario) to cover the process of having a court verify your will. These are based on the value of assets being transferred, and vary between provinces. There are various ways you can reduce or avoid probate fees, such as transferring your property before death, holding property in a joint tenancy, and establishing trusts, life insurance policies or pension plans (such as RRSPs) that name the intended beneficiary – each has its advantages, disadvantages and potential tax consequences, so professional legal advice is recommended. If you're a Canadian permanent resident, your property and assets will be subject to provincial inheritance laws. These may require that 50% of your assets go to your spouse, or allow your spouse to make a claim to this effect. If you die intestate – without a will – your estate is distributed according to provincial legislation. This normally provides spouses with a 'preferential share,' as well as a share of the balance, known as a 'distributive share'. The remaining distributive shares go to your other descendents. Be aware that if you're in a common-law (either opposite or same-sex) relationship most provinces won't recognise this as 'spousal' under intestate law, even if you are treated as married for tax or immigration purposes. (British Columbia and Manitoba are two exceptions to the rule.) Sound advice on planning your estate can be found in the book You Can't Take it With You: Common-Sense Estate Planning for Canadians (Sandra E. Foster, John Wiley & Sons, 2006).

Though you're not legally required to make a will, it's strongly advised if you're in a non-married partnership, want any control over what happens to your assets

PROVINCIAL PROBATE FEES BASED ON VALUE OF ASSETS

Alberta	$25 if up to $10,000; $100 if up to $25,000; $200 if up to $125,000; $300 if up to $250,000; $400 if over $250,000
British Columbia	No fee on first $25,000; if over $25,000, $208 plus 0.6% up to $50,000, then 0.14% on remainder
Manitoba	$70 on first $10,000; then 0.7% on remainder
New Brunswick	$25 on each $5,000 up to $20,000; 0.5% if value above $20,000
Newfoundland and Labrador	$60 on first $1,000, then $0.50 per $100 on remainder
Northwest Territories	As per Alberta
Nova Scotia	$74.76 if up to $10,000; $187.97 if up to $25,000; $312.92 if up to $50,000; $875.76 if up to $100,000; if over $100,000, $875.76 plus 1.48% on remainder
Nunavut	As per Alberta
Ontario	0.5% on first $50,000, then 1.5% on remainder
Prince Edward Island	$50 if up to $10,000; $100 if up to $25,000; $200 if up to $50,000; $400 if up to $100,000; 0.4% of entire amount if over $100,000.
Quebec	No fee for notarial will (one prepared by notary); $95 fee for non-notarial will
Saskatchewan	0.7%
Yukon	No fee on first $25,000; $140 if over $25,000

when you die, or need to ensure financial support for your dependants. Laws regarding acceptable forms of wills differ between provinces, so check with your provincial ministry of attorney general or justice (the main provincial government website should provide a link to this – see p. 364 for website addresses). If you have a will made under international law it may be taken into account, though provincial requirements may still be enforced. However, making a Canadian will is straightforward, and will help save your family and executors needless complications. Using a lawyer (or notary, in Quebec) will ensure your will is in line with provincial legislation, but you can make your own if you prefer, either through an online service such as Canadian Legal Wills (www.legalwills.ca) or by using a will kit (available at stationery stores). Wills-Net (905 844 6664; info@wills-net.com; www.wills-net.com) also provides useful information and fee-based will preparation. You need to make sure the will you complete is considered legal in your province. It's also possible to create a 'living will' or legal directive that states your wishes regarding medical treatment – and names someone to carry them out – in the extent that you become unable to give informed consent. A living will only applies while you are alive; your last will and testament takes over once you pass away. Self-Counsel Press (604 986 3366; www.self-counsel.com) publishes a number of helpful step-by-step wills guides.

▉ CRIME AND THE POLICE

Crime and safety

Canada enjoys a deserved reputation as a safe and peaceful country. Theft, vandalism, violence, and drug-related crimes do of course occur, but you're generally safe walking alone, often even at night. Most cities have at least some dubious streets or neighbourhoods, so be street smart, especially if you're new to an area. In recent years there has been a rise in inner-city gang violence, but the national homicide rate – despite a slight increase in 2004 and 2005 – has been trending downward overall since the 1970s. At 1.8 homicides per 100,000 people, it's less than a third of the US rate. Higher crime is normally associated with big cities, but a recent study from Statistics Canada indicates that this is not necessarily the case in Canada. While rates for (and instances of) robbery and car theft are higher in larger cities and metropolitan areas (where around two thirds of people live), overall crime rates are actually highest in small urban areas – as a proportion of population – particularly those in western and northern regions of the country. Patterns vary considerably across the provinces: for example, homicide rates in Alberta, Saskatchewan, and Manitoba are highest in rural areas, while in Ontario and BC these crimes occur at a higher rate in cities. Based on figures released in 2007, violent crime levels in larger cities in the provinces of Ontario, Alberta, and Quebec remain below the national average, while Winnipeg, Halifax, and Vancouver reported higher rates. On an overall provincial basis, Saskatchewan has the highest rate of criminal activity, Ontario the lowest.

Unlike the USA, Canada does not have a gun-loving culture. Concealed weapons are prohibited. To possess a firearm you must have a licence, pass a public-safety

The Royal Canada Mounted Police force on parade in Regina, Saskatchewan

check and meet firearms safety training requirements. Canada has three legal classes of firearms: non-restricted, restricted and prohibited. The Canada Firearms Centre, operated by the Royal Canadian Mounted Police (RCMP), is responsible for gun licensing and registration. The Firearms Act was introduced by the Liberal Party in 1995 and included a controversial long-gun registry (for non-restricted firearms such as hunting rifles and shotguns) which proved a debacle: costs spiralled to more than $1 billion and many firearm owners still refuse to cooperate. The current Conservative government, with a stated belief in 'targeting criminals, not duck hunters and farmers', recently renewed efforts to abolish the registry. Public and political opinion remains divided. Determined criminals can still find ways of obtaining guns, but accidental and domestic shootings are relatively uncommon – those tragedies that do occur invariably result in public outcry and pushes to further tighten gun laws.

You're not required to carry an identification card in Canada, and if arrested, you must be told why and be given access to a lawyer. You can apply for legal aid to help pay for a lawyer, and if needed, you have access to a free interpreter. Canada's criminal justice system is based around an approach of eventual rehabilitation and reintegration of offenders into society. Those sentenced to less than two years are a provincial responsibility; all others are dealt with through the federal Correctional System of Canada.

Law enforcement

There are over 64,000 federal, provincial, and municipal police officers in Canada; about one for every 512 people. While law enforcement is still a male-dominated field – 82% of police offers are men – the number of female officers has been steadily growing for the past 40 years. The Royal Canadian Mounted Police (RCMP), an agency of Public Safety Canada, is the national police service and functions on federal, provincial, and municipal levels. It has a force of around 26,300, including 685 officers and 11,118 constables. The RCMP, known as Mounties, are an iconic presence in Canada (and the reason for the hatted, scarlet-coated bears and moose that are sold in every souvenir store in the country). They provide law enforcement and operational support services across Canada, and also police on a contract basis in all provinces and territories except Ontario and Quebec, which have their own provincial forces – the Ontario Provincial Police (OPP) and the Sûreté du Québec. Newfoundland and Labrador's Royal Newfoundland Constabulary is also a provincial force, but only has jurisdiction in certain areas of the province. Many cities and towns have their own municipal or regional police service. Almost 500 exist in total (including those provided through contracts with the RCMP and OPP), and 59% of all police work at the municipal level. Services to Aboriginal communities are provided through a range of agreements, including the First Nations Policing Policy (FNPP), which operates in 405 communities. Most officers in these areas are of Aboriginal descent. Some services are independently run; the majority of others operate through the RCMP.

Other police forces include the Canadian Forces Military Police, who provide services and protection to military communities in Canada and abroad, and auxiliary or reserve police (usually unarmed volunteers) who assist regular officers with certain tasks. Community policing – including Crime Stoppers and various citizens' groups – also plays a role. Border security and cross-border crime is addressed in

A Toronto city policeman on the job

collaboration with the United States. The Canadian agencies involved are the Canada Border Services Agency, the RCMP and various municipal and provincial forces.

As a general rule, Canadian police are reasonable, approachable, non-aggressive law enforcers. While they are not immune from misconduct or corruption (and have received unwelcome public attention for arguably over-zealous Tazer use), the vast majority are dedicated to crime prevention and control, with an increasing emphasis on the community.

 Safe Canada provides a list of police contacts at www.safecanada.ca/link_e .asp?category=4&topic=35. In an emergency, you can reach the police by dialing 911, or 0 for the operator in more remote areas.

FACT

■ There are over 64,000 federal, provincial, and municipal police officers in Canada, about one for every 512 people.

■ Useful contacts

Canada Firearms Centre (Royal Canadian Mounted Police): 1 800 731 4000; cfc-cafc@cfc-cafc.gc.ca; www.cfc-cafc.gc.ca
Public Safety Canada: 613 944 4875 or 1 800 830 3118; communications@ps.gc.ca; www.publicsafety.gc.ca
Canadian Crime Stoppers Association: 1 800 222 8477 (to report information about a crime); ccsa.admin@sympatico.ca; www.canadiancrimestoppers.org
Royal Canadian Mounted Police: 613 993 7267; www.rcmp-grc.gc.ca

Working in Canada

Applying for permanent residence to Canada as a Skilled Worker: Tips and avoiding common mistakes

i

The Immigration and Refugee Protection Act (IRPA) and the Immigration Regulations constantly change, so it is important to keep up to date with any changes or amendments to *the Act* or *the Regulations*.

Education

This is often a factor where applicants rely too much on the interpretation of the immigration case officer. Keep in mind that they are looking for what your qualification is equivalent to in Canada. It is highly recommended that you complete an evaluation of your qualification by a Canadian company, such as International Credential Assessment Services (www.icascanada.ca).

Work Experience

When your work experience is examined, you must remember that your educational background does not need to be directly related to your skilled work experience. In other words, you may have a University degree in Geography, but are now working as a Management Consultant.

You are required to have a minimum of one year's full time, paid work experience in the ten (10) years preceding the submission of your application. Full time is classified as 37.5 hours per week. This work experience must be of a certain skill level to be admissible for consideration, hence the category, *skilled* worker. The determination of whether your work experience is skilled or not is defined by Canada's National Occupation Classification (NOC). This is a dictionary of the all of the occupations in Canada and their definitions. You can view this at: http://www23.hrdc-drhc.gc.ca/2001/e/generic/welcome.shtml

I encourage you to refer to the NOC as your interpretation of work experience may differ from the NOC. For example, many trades people refer to themselves as an "Engineer". In Canada, you are only considered an Engineer if you have completed a University Degree in Engineering. The NOC definitions will give you greater clarity as to the duties you would perform in your occupation. If the NOC definition accurately reflects your day to day duties and responsibilities, then this will be the NOC code to submit under. You must have performed all of the essential duties, a substantial number of the main duties as well as the duties in the lead statement.

Provided by expert contributor

It is your responsibility, as the applicant, to list your four (4) digit NOC code(s) on the application. This must corresponds to each of the occupations under which you have worked. An Immigration officer is *not required* to consider occupations that have not been specified in the application.

You can also claim work experience in more than one admissible occupation. You will be assessed on your work experience during the ten (10) years preceding your application.

The preparation of your application is crucial to the timely completion of your application. You must complete everything in full as this can lead to delays. Remember - You are assessed only on paperwork that you provide, so it is critical that you get it right.

Christopher Willis is a Member in Good Standing with the Canadian Society of Immigration Consultants (CSIC) #M041230 and the Canadian Association of Professional Immigration Consultants (CAPIC). He can be contacted on +1 450 458 2186 or chris@willisbrazolot.com or www.willisbrazolot.com

Provided by expert contibutor

View from the Pinnacle, Lake Lyster, Eastern Townships, Quebec

Canada boasts a buoyant economy. We have excellent healthcare and education systems and an unparalleled overall quality of life. These pull factors continue to attract migrants from all over the world, including the UK, a country that could fit into Canada forty times yet houses twice the population of Canada. The popularity of our country is reflected by the 260,000 new migrants welcomed to Canada in 2007. Many of you who have visited Canada have experienced the opportunities and benefits of Canadian life.

Canada is experiencing a shortage of skills in many key sectors including education, healthcare, construction and transportation. As a result, employment opportunities abound. Many new migrants want the security of employment before relocating. Not only does this give the migrant more security, a validated offer of employment means that their immigration applications will be expedited, so they can be in Canada with permanent residency in a matter of months rather than years.

Willis Brazolot & Co. (WBC) is committed to assisting individuals, families and business people achieve their goals of immigrating to Canada. With over 30 years of combined experience, WBC assist you in every aspect of your move to Canada, including jobs and career assistance, placement with temporary work visas and full relocation services. WBC specialise in trades, professionals, business applicants and family reunifications.

- Christopher Willis, Dennis Brazolot, Louise Willis and Helen Brereton are full, registered members of the Canadian Society of Immigration Consultants (CSIC), and are Certified Canadian Immigration Consultants (CCIC)
- Christopher Willis & Dennis Brazolot are full, registered members of the Canadian Association of Professional Immigration Consultants (CAPIC)
- Christopher Willis & Dennis Brazolot are both Commissioners of Oaths
- Willis Brazolot & Co. is an Authorised Agent for Desjardins Immigrant Investor Programme.

Citizenship & Immigration Consultants

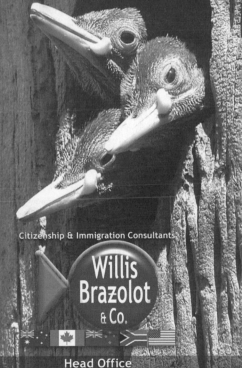

Looking across the Pond?

'Employment opportunities across Canada in all sectors'
Willis Brazolot & Co. (WBC) is committed to assisting
individuals, families and business people achieve their
goals of immigrating to Canada. With over 30 years of
combined experienced, we assist you in every aspect of
your move to Canada.

Citizenship & Immigration Consultants

Willis Brazolot & Co.

Head Office
35 Wharf Rd., Hudson, QC, Canada J0P 1H0
T: +1 450 458 2186   F: +1 450 458 2848
info@willisbrazolot.com   www.willisbrazolot.com
European Office
Fretweide 27, Zoetermeer, 2727 HG The Netherlands
T: +31 79 341 4259

■ FINDING A JOB

A guide to the market

With 16 years of steady economic growth on the books, and unemployment at a 33-year low, Canada was in a strong fiscal position – the strongest, according to the Department of Finance's 2008 Budget, of any G7 country. Since that claim was made, the financial crisis of October 2008 has reverberated around the world, and Canada – while still in a favourable economic position relative to other countries – is preparing for a tight couple of years. International markets have broadened but the Canadian economy is still undeniably affected by that of the USA. The strong Canadian dollar of recent years – which spiked at over US$1.09 in November 2007 before plummeting below US$0.80 in late 2008 – had a detrimental effect on manufacturing, filmmaking, and other industries that provide goods or services across the border. Ontario's auto industry and Montreal's textile and aerospace industries have been hit particularly hard. Forestry has also been badly affected (and BC has felt the pinch more than most), with the US housing collapse reducing demand for lumber. On the plus side there are around 1.5 million more people workinig now than there were at the end of 2002 and although unemployment will inevitably rise to some degree, a dramatic increase is not expected.

There are over 17 million Canadians in the labour force, across a range of industries. The goods-producing sector employs around four million workers, while approximately 13 million work in service industries. Within these categories, around one million work in financial services or real estate; over 1.1 million are in professional, technical or scientific fields; almost 1.2 million work in education; 1.9 million work in health or social services; the construction industry accounts for another 1.2 million workers; around 2 million are employed in the manufacturing sector; almost 2.7 million work in trade; and hospitality and food-service industries employ just over one million people. Around 337,000 people are employed in agricultural fields, with a similar number working across forestry, fishing, mining, oil, and gas industries. Unemployment in Canada has typically been 1%–2% higher than in the USA, and currently sits at around 6%. Economists attribute the traditional discrepancy between the countries partly to strong regional ties in Canada, which reduce the level of labour mobility in comparison to that in the USA; partly to the proportionally higher number of cyclical and seasonal industries such as fishing, which suffer from greater unemployment in the off-season; and partly – in theory, at least – to Canada's higher unemployment benefits, which may tempt some to abuse the system. Alberta, at 3.8%, in September 2008 has the lowest unemployment rate of any province, with Saskatchewan and Manitoba not far behind – their success (at least until now) largely fuelled by booming oil, gas, and resource-based industries and the resulting demands for construction and transportation. Unemployment in BC is also below the national average. Rates are highest in the Atlantic provinces, with Newfoundland and Labrador coming in last at over 13%. While this seems high, it actually represents a period of historically low unemployment for the province, as considerable petroleum and metal resources have enjoyed rapid export growth (and created population growth along with it).

FACT

■ Alberta, at 3.8% in September 2008, has the lowest unemployment rate of any province, with Saskatchewan and Manitoba not far behind.

The Toronto skyline, dominated by the CN Tower, rises above the waters of Lake Ontario

Like the USA, Canada is fast becoming an information society, with information industries predicted to employ a substantial proportion of the future workforce. The country is a world leader in telecommunications, aerospace and nuclear technology, biotechnology and geographical exploration. Natural resource industries, including mining, forestry, and farming, play a significant role in the Canadian economy. Many of these areas hold potential for immigrants with a background in science, engineering or technology. Job opportunities in the service sector are increasing as well.

 The blog website www.canadaimmigrationblog.com provides some useful news and updates on foreign recruitment and labour shortages in Canada.

Job search resources

As discussed in *Before You Go*, if you don't have relatives in Canada your chances of qualifying for immigration are often improved if you have a job lined up. This is especially relevant if you don't have enough points to apply as a skilled worker. You might decide to visit Canada to look for a job before applying for permanent residence. If you do, it's wisest to enter the country as a tourist and keep your other intentions to yourself – visits for the sole purpose of job-hunting aren't smiled upon by immigration officers, who may suspect you'll stay illegally if you find work. If and when you find someone willing to employ you, you'll have to return to your own country before applying to immigrate.

It's pretty hard to get work if you don't speak the official languages, so the best way is through contact with people in your community. When I became more familiar with the city I started looking for myself, by checking ads in the paper and showing up with my résumé.
Dante Pizarro

LABOUR MARKET RESOURCES

- The Going to Canada website (www.goingtocanada.gc.ca) offers specific information for people thinking of working in Canada. As well as general advice about moving to and living in Canada, it provides access to the useful Working in Canada Tool. This allows you to search for your occupation (or find its equivalent) in Canada, and produces detailed labour market reports describing occupational duties, standard wages, regulatory requirements, and job opportunities.
- Human Resources and Social Development Canada (HRSDC) has a range of publications relating to Canada's labour market, including the detailed document *Looking Ahead: A 10-Year Outlook for the Canadian Labour Market* (2006–2015). You can access this online by going to www.hrsdc.gc.ca, selecting *Publications and Resources* from the home page, then *Research*, then *Labour Market* (Employment and Unemployment), then scrolling down the list of publications.

If you're immigrating to Canada without a job, bring copies of any degrees, diplomas or certificates, and records of your school and university results. Written references from past employers may also be useful – make sure these outline your job responsibilities, achievements and work ethic, as well as the period of time you worked for the company.

Relocation agencies may be able to help you find work, though their services tend to be expensive and they're predominantly geared towards executive relocations. Your embassy or consulate in Canada won't be able to assist, but permanent residents can use employment services provided by the Canadian government. Anyone, in fact, can access the government-maintained online Job Bank and other government websites made available through Service Canada centres (see p. 230).

Newspapers

Apart from temporary jobs for nannies or au pairs, Canadian vacancies aren't normally advertised in other countries' newspapers, though international papers based out of North America occasionally carry advertisements for senior-executive posts in Canada. Canada's nationwide *Globe and Mail* carries a multitude of advertisements for jobs across the country, and the *National Post* advertises vacancies in all areas of business and finance. Local newspapers, such as those listed on p. 166, usually include job or employment sections. While the *Globe and Mail* can sometimes be obtained overseas at international newsstands, most others are difficult to get hold of in print outside of Canada. However, newspaper websites normally provide at least as much employment information as the print editions (if not more), and often provide job-search functions as well.

TIP

- If you're emigrating to Canada without a job, bring copies of any degrees, diplomas or certificates, and records of your school and university results. Written references from past employers may also be useful.

Magazines, directories, and other publications

Mediacorp Canada (416 964 6069 or 1 800 361 2580; www.mediacorp.ca) publishes a range of Canadian employment magazines and directories under the *Canada Employment Weekly* umbrella. These include Canada Employment Weekly itself, which is the largest career-focused paper in Canada (available in print or as an online subscription); *The Career Directory* for graduates; and the *Who's Hiring* guide, which profiles the fastest-growing Canadian employers in specific fields. These publications can be bought from various retailers (*Canada Employment Weekly* is widely available at newsstands or at Chapters/Indigo), purchased on the Mediacorp website, or ordered by emailing orders@mediacorp.ca. Mediacorp also produces an annual guide to Canada's top 100 employers, which is featured in *Macleans* magazine each year and which you can view at www.canadastop100.com/national. A search engine on the site – provided by sister company Eluta.ca – allows you to search for available positions with these employers (and with those from a range of provincial and other 'top' lists). *Canadian Business* magazine (416 764 1200; www.canadianbusiness.com) lists executive positions, and is also available in an online edition as *Canadian Business Online*. You can find various directories to Canadian businesses in many public libraries. These include the *Canadian Key Business Directory*, the *Canadian Trade Index* (website at www.ctidirectory.com), *Frasers Canadian Trade Directory* (online directory at www.frasers.com), and the National List of Advertisers (website at www.cardonline.ca). In addition to this title, Crimson Publishing (www.crimsonpublishing.co.uk) has a range of other publications that contain information about working overseas: *Summer Jobs Worldwide* includes information and advertisements for posts in secretarial, agricultural, tourism, and domestic work; *Your Gap Year* and *Gap Years for Grown Ups* have advice for temporary job seekers; *Work Your Way Around the World* includes a chapter on Canada; and *The Directory of Jobs and Careers Abroad* has a section on working in Canada as well as specific career information.

Internet resources

Almost all companies post job opportunities online these days, and for many job-seekers the internet is their primary (or even only) resource. The online job-search giants in Canada are Workopolis and Monster.ca, but an enormous array of others exist, including industry- and location-specific sites. Many allow you to create and post your résumé for viewing by potential employers, and to save your search preferences so you can quickly rerun your search each day. The Going to Canada website (www.workingincanada.gc.ca) provides lots of information and links for newcomers looking for work, and Job Post Canada, which promotes itself as Canada's biggest job site directory, lists a huge selection of websites at www.jobpostcanada.com. Here are just a few:

- **www.workopolis.com:** Canada's biggest job site works with media and newspaper companies to list around 75,000 jobs. It provides free registration and a good resource centre with job-search how-tos. A Quebec-based French edition (click 'Français' on the main site's home page) and a specific site for students (www.workopoliscampus.com) are available as well.

- **www.monster.ca:** part of the international Monster network, Monster. ca has thousands of job listings and other resources.
- **www.jobbank.gc.ca:** Service Canada's Job Bank is a government-operated site listing over 50,000 government and non-government positions.
- **www.theworkplace.ca:** this government site, provides centralised information and links relating to the Canadian labour market.
- **www.mediajobsearchcanada.com:** specialised site listing vacancies in media-related professions (film, television, magazine, newspaper, radio, and advertising).
- WorkInfoNet provides career planning and employment information for each province and territory. Though the Canada-wide site no longer seems to be in operation, the provincial sites provide links to one another. The Ontario site is www.onwin.ca.
- **www.careerbeacon.com:** focuses on recruitment in Atlantic Canada.
- **www.eluta.ca:** monitors job placements by employers across Canada, adding them to a searchable database. Allows specific searches for jobs with Canada's top 100 employers (as mentioned on p. 229), as well as with the top employers in certain regions or categories.
- **www.canjobs.com:** Canadian recruitment network with national, provincial, and city-specific job websites.
- **www.thecanadianimmigrant.com/jobboard:** job board for skilled immigrants; part of *Canadian Immigrant* magazine's website.
- **www.mycanadajobs.com:** easy-to-use job board with searches by sector, location, and job type.

FACT

Almost all companies post job opportunities online these days, and for many job-seekers the internet is their primary (or even only) resource.

Service Canada Centres

Service Canada Centres are available in all provinces and territories, and offer 'single window access' to a range of programmes and services provided by the Canadian federal government. These centres provide free internet access to specific government websites, including the online Job Bank (www.jobbank.gc.ca). This searchable database lists available jobs in your area and provides details on how

> **Andrea and Stefan Crengle found work in Calgary fairly quickly:**
>
> We both used the newspaper and internet for work searches. As we were only after semi-casual employment (as in little responsibility, nine-to-five type jobs, not in our usual profession) we had more options open to us than if we were looking for corporate employment. Our only stipulation was that we didn't work evenings and weekends so that we were free to explore the country and experience it to the max. I secured a receptionist job at a spa within three days of looking for work, and Stefan gained employment with a pellet-making company within a few weeks.

to apply. You don't need to register with Service Canada to use the service or to apply for listed jobs – it's free to the public, which can be helpful if you don't have internet or computer access elsewhere. Other resources for job hunters are usually provided on a provincial or territorial level, through the relevant department or ministry of employment or training. Services may include education and training programmes, résumé and cover-letter assistance, interview practice, job-search strategies, employment counselling, group workshops, and employer presentations. You can contact your provincial government for more information (main contact details are provided in the *Appendices*, p. 364), or ask your local Service Canada Centre for advice on which organisations offer employment services in your area.

 To find your nearest Service Canada Centre, visit www.servicecanada. gc.ca and use the search function on the home page, or phone 1800 622 6232. The website at www.servicecanada.gc.ca/en/lifeevents/job.shtml provides basic, helpful information for job seekers.

Chambers of commerce

Chambers of Commerce are geared to promoting the interests of companies trading in Canada. As a rule, they can't help you find work, but they can be a useful source of information about companies in your area, or of companies based in your home country that also have operations in Canada. The canadian chamber of commerce, which has 170,000 members, maintains a useful website (www.chamber.ca) that provides links to the websites of regional chambers of commerce or boards of trade in each province, as well as to international trade organisations. Each of these websites includes a member directory, which you can use to find contact information for any companies that interest you. If you'd rather contact the Canadian Chamber of Commerce directly, phone 613 238 4000 or send an email to info@chamber.ca.

Company transfers

There are many Canadian firms operating in other countries, and many international subsidiaries operating in Canada. If you work at an international firm you may want to investigate the possibility of being transferred to the Canadian branch. Transfers to Canada are allowed on a temporary basis only, and there are regulations governing which employees qualify, but on the plus side, you don't need to apply for a Labour Market Opinion (LMO) in order to get a work permit. Business people from the United States and Mexico are governed by NAFTA (see p. 66); those from Chile apply under the comparable regulations of the Canada–Chile Free Trade Agreement (CCFTA). The General Agreement on Trade in Services (GATS) allows service providers from World Trade Organization member countries to visit or work in Canada on a temporary basis, and also has similar provisions to NAFTA. In order to be eligible as an intra-company transferee, there must be a legal and qualifying business relationship between the Canadian and foreign companies, and potential transferees must be employed in an executive, senior managerial or 'specialised knowledge' capacity. You must also have worked for the foreign company for at least one out of the previous three years. Work permits are granted for up to three years, with the option to apply for extensions in two-year increments (to a maximum of seven years

ACCELERATE YOUR CAREER. SLOW DOWN YOUR LIFE.

In Ontario, we value a healthy balance between business and pleasure. Here, you can build your career while enjoying a highly satisfying and relaxed lifestyle. Our spirit of innovation and quality of life attracts professionals from around the world, for a wide variety of industries. As a result, we have a diverse, multicultural society that will make you feel right at home. When it comes to recreation and leisure, Ontario's options are second to none. We have over 250,000 lakes for fishing, canoeing, kayaking and swimming; hundreds of golf courses; ski hills; world-class theatre and more. There's no better place in the world to work – and play.

ONTARIO
CANADA

bis@ontario.ca
2ontario.com/balance

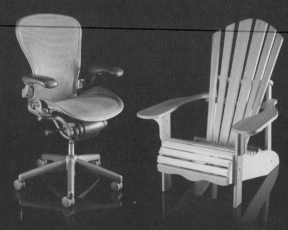

Ontario Paid for by the Government of Ontario.

Advertisement feature

Ontario: Where the World Works

Today, large and small companies set up wherever they find the best combination of talent, cost-efficiencies and market access.

That's why companies and entrepreneurs all over the world choose Ontario as a location to successfully expand or start new businesses, including those in the communications, agricultural, IT, manufacturing, arts and other sectors. Why?

Ontario offers:
- a growing economy
- strong trade partnerships with North America, Europe and Asia
- competitive business costs
- a highly skilled workforce
- streamlined regulations

The main ingredient for success is the vision and work of business immigrants who see the opportunities Ontario offers. Take Andrew and Val Stimpson. More than 10 years after they arrived here from England, their product has become an Ontario brand name.

Bringing with them more than 20 years of experience in the brewing industry, they own and operate Neustadt Springs Brewery, in the village of Neustadt near Hanover, Ontario.

Their increasingly popular products have received rave reviews from consumers, winning several Canadian and international industry awards. A model of success for business immigrants, Val Stimpson shares her experience at seminars organized by the Ministry of International Trade and

Investment to overseas investors interested in Ontario business opportunities.

Government tax incentives and assistance in promoting the industry, flexible legislation allowing access to bigger markets and potential changes that will reduce their shipping costs will help contribute to their success. "We can see great advantages coming," says Andrew Stimpson. "We've had no regrets coming to Ontario."

Are you interested in starting or expanding your business in Ontario? The Business Immigration Section of the Ministry of International Trade and Investment provides a range of services and support to business immigrants.

Our consultants can advise investors on corporate immigration matters such as the guidelines around intra-company transfers and work permits, including information on how spouses and dependents can accompany successful candidates, study or work in Ontario. We can also provide referrals to other organizations and contact information for resources and people who can offer advice.

For more information or to set up an appointment with one of our experienced consultants contact:
Business Immigration Section
Ontario Ministry of International Trade and Investment
Telephone: (+1) 416-325-6777
Fax: (+1) 416-325-6653
Email: bis@ontario.ca
www.2ontario.com/home

Paid for by the Government of Ontario

for executives and managers, or five years for specialised knowledge workers). To be eligible to apply for a new permit after that time, you must first work for the company outside of Canada for at least one year. You can apply for a work permit at the Canadian embassy or consulate in your home country. (For most people it's also possible to apply at a port of entry when you arrive in Canada.)

 Check the Citizenship and Immigration Canada website (www.cic.gc.ca), and specifically the webpage at www.cic.gc.ca/english/work/special-business. asp, for more details on policies, eligibility, regulations, and entry requirements.

Employment agencies

Hundreds of recruitment agencies operate across Canada, helping workers to find temporary, contract or permanent positions, and employers to fill short- or long-term vacancies. Services vary depending on the agency: some focus primarily on placing temporary workers; others spend significant time headhunting candidates for high-level executive or professional roles. Many of the larger companies offer multiple services to meet different employer needs. The company that employs you compensates the agency for their recruitment efforts; however, legislation varies

A MULTINATIONAL MARKET

Companies such as the following, which have an international presence, may offer the option of transfer abroad:

Canadian companies operating internationally

Canadian companies with major overseas enterprises include Royal Bank (RBC), Canada Life, Scotiabank, Air Canada, CAE (Canadian Aviation Electronics), CGI Group, Alcan, Research in Motion (RIM), McCain Foods, Canpotex, Four Seasons Hotels, Fairmont Hotels and Resorts, Nova Chemicals, Nortel Networks, Sun Life Financial, and Travel Cuts (has affiliated offices worldwide).

International companies operating in Canada

Though the USA's huge population base makes it a more obviously attractive site for international companies, most multinational firms are also represented in Canada. The addresses of many of the larger companies are listed in the Directory of Employers on p. 275. Others include Accenture, Apple, Aviva Canada Inc., Amec PLC, British American Tobacco, British Petroleum, Cadbury, Ernst and Young, HMV, IBM, Imperial Chemical, Macquarie, and PepsiCo.

(controversially) between provinces. In some, agencies are expressly forbidden to charge workers for finding them a job (though they may be permitted to levy fees for services such as résumé writing); in others, some agencies do charge for job-finding services. Avoid working with a company that charges for this – members of the Association of Canadian Search, Employment, and Staffing Services (ACSESS), which represents the staffing industry across Canada, do not charge job-seekers for their services. The ACSESS website (www.acsess.org) is an excellent resource that allows you to search for agencies by city, province, industry or service type (i.e. temporary, contract, long-term). You can also look up companies by name through their member directory. Other websites like Recruiter Websites.com (www.recruiterwebsites.com), Jobs in Canada (www.jobsincanada.ca) or the Headhunters Directory (www.headhuntersdirectory.com/canada.htm) may also be helpful. Some of the largest employment agencies are listed here:

- **Adecco Employment Services Limited:** 416 646 3322 or 1 866 646 3322; www.adecco.ca
- **David Aplin Recruiting:** 613 288 2211; www.aplin.com
- **Design Group Staffing Inc.:** 905 829 4848 (Ontario office); www.dg.ca
- **Drake International:** 613 237 3370 or 1 800 463 7253; www.drakeintl.com
- **Eagle Professional Resources Inc.:** 1 800 956 3778; www.eagleonline.com
- **Express Personnel Services:** 416 590 9948 (Toronto office); www.expresspros.com/ca
- **Hunt Personnel:** 613 238 8801; www.hunt.ca
- **Kelly Services:** 416 368 1058; www.kellyservices.ca
- **Manpower:** 416 225 4455; www.manpower.ca
- **Quantum Management Services Ltd:** 514 842 5555 or 1 800 978 2688; www.quantum.ca
- **Randstad Canada:** 613 564 2555; www.randstad.ca
- **Spherion Staffing Solutions:** 905 361 1550; www.spherion.ca
- **The 500 Staffing Inc.:** 604 685 1400 or 1 866 685 1400; www.the500.com

Professional and executive employment agencies

Many agencies provide professional-placement and executive-search services, and can help you look for a permanent or long-term position in Canada. They conduct preliminary interviews and act as a liaison between the company and the prospective employee. If a specific employer declines to hire you, the agency may keep you in mind for another position. You can find companies offering these services through the agencies and recruitment directories listed above, and under *Employment* in your local *Yellow Pages*.

Temporary employment agencies

Employers often turn to temporary employment agencies for their seasonal staffing needs. Though the hourly rate paid to temping agencies is high, employers don't have to pay benefits or give notice. Workers usually earn about half the hourly rate paid to the agency, and while agencies should supply vacation pay, they seldom offer benefits. In addition to the lack of benefits, disadvantages can include periods of unemployment, and (if you don't have a car) difficulties with transportation. Nonetheless, temping can be an attractive and well-paying option – particularly in the short term – and if you're lucky it can lead to a full-time job. You may end up working for the one company for months, though it's equally possible that you'll move from place to place on a weekly or daily basis. It can be a good opportunity to work out the field of business or the company size you prefer.

Most agencies have separate departments for administrative and manual work, and some specialise in placing specific types of workers, such as accountants, medical workers, legal personnel or technical staff. You'll usually need to go in to an agency office for typing, computer and even personality testing, which can take some hours. Don't exaggerate your typing or computer skills as most agencies use programmes to test your abilities in given software applications. Dress professionally for any agency meetings, as this helps assure the agency that you'll fit into a business environment. Most of the firms listed on the previous page can help you find temporary vacancies. You can also check the online recruitment directories noted on the same page, and look under Employment Agencies – Temporary in the *Yellow Pages*.

Agencies may charge the client company a large placement fee if the company wants to hire a temporary worker permanently. When you begin working for an agency you'll often have to sign a contract stating that you won't accept a position without informing the agency.

Outplacement and transition services

Outplacement agencies are often hired by companies when restructuring or large-scale redundancies occur. They assist staff in finding new jobs if they've been laid off, or in upgrading their skills or making the transition to a different position.

Professional and trade bodies

Journals or websites of Canadian professional associations are a good source of job leads. Contact the national professional association for your field in your home country to find out the address of its Canadian counterpart, or look them up in a directory of associations and professional bodies at your local library. *Associations Canada* is the main print directory listing Canadian trade, professional and business associations; it's also available in electronic database format. While these directories aren't generally available on the internet, you can search online for likely suspects (i.e. throw the name of your field and the word 'association' or 'institute' into a search engine like Google).

 The Canadian Information Centre for International Credentials (CICIC) posts a list of national and provincial professional organisations on the webpage at www.cicic.ca/en/profess.aspx?sortcode=2.19.21.21, while Construction Canada.com lists construction-related trade associations at www.constructioncanada.com/Associations.htm#10.

Applying for work

Even for experienced workers, the process of applying for jobs and going to interviews can be daunting, frustrating, and tiring. This is particularly so in another country, where procedures sometimes differ from what you're used to. Having a résumé (CV) – usually written as resumé or resume – that's clear and tightly written is a huge help, and it's worthwhile preparing a 'default' version of this well in advance. That way you can quickly modify the contents to suit specific jobs. The same is true of cover letters (see below for more on these); if you have a basic template worked out, you can adapt this relatively easily for each position you apply for. The government website Going to Canada (www.goingtocanada. gc.ca) provides a useful guide to applying for work, from writing résumés and cover letters to preparing for interviews. To find it, select *Working in Canada* from the home page, then *Find a Job in Canada*, then *Job Application Resources*. A link to Service

City workers begin heading home as 5.00pm approaches

Canada's Training and Careers site provides access to helpful advice on creating your résumé, including a downloadable guide, *Focus on Résumés*.

The résumé

It's standard to provide a typed résumé when you apply for a job, and the majority of employers require it. There's no one absolute style rule to follow in Canada. You might prepare a traditional chronologically ordered résumé, present your experience in a skills-based format, or produce something more innovative to give you a competitive edge. Spellings should be Canadian, not American (The *Canadian Oxford Dictionary* is an authoritative reference, but there are others). The guide mentioned above provides good résumé-writing advice, and you can find helpful tips at Canadian Careers.com (www.canadiancareers.com/resandcl.html) and the Canadian Résumé Writing Service (www.canadian-résumé-service.com/résumé-writing-tips.asp). Publications like *Best Canadian Résumés* (Sharon Graham, Sentor Media Inc., 2007) can also be useful – you can order this, and other career books, at Sentor Media's online store, www.careerbookstore.ca and through Chapters/Indigo (www.chapters.indigo.ca).

However you present your résumé, you need to provide your name, address, and a contact phone number (including international dialling code if you're applying from overseas), but not your age, gender or other personal information. The Going to Canada website recommends briefly stating your 'job goal', and outlining any

> For me, getting this job was easy as the company wanted me to work for them. If I left though, I think it would be very difficult for me to find another job in Canada.
> **Steven Maine**

> **Gerald Garnett explains how he and his wife Mary found their teaching positions in Kaslo, BC:**
> My wife is very organised, confident, and determined and I needed to borrow some of those qualities to be so brazen at getting interviews, following up with phone calls, and knocking at doors. I am naturally quite reserved and shy, but desperation made me push the limits. All I can say is that we had an extraordinary amount of luck. When Mary graduated, we sent out 30 résumés, went to 15 interviews. We very nearly ended up teaching at Quesnel or Masset, but in the end were offered two jobs in Kaslo in the Kootenays. We have just retired after teaching there for nearly 30 years.

skills and abilities you have that are relevant to the job in question. Educational details generally come next, with the most recent course or qualification first. Your employment history – including voluntary work – follows. Make sure to include the name, location, and dates of work for each employer, as well as the major duties you carried out. Details of wages aren't necessary. After this, include any additional skills and experience, especially if you speak other languages or are proficient in using particular computer applications. You can then note your interests or activities, additional volunteer experience, and any prizes or awards you've won. You don't need to include your references at this stage – the company can ask for these later in the process if they're interested in your application. Have your references' names, addresses, phone numbers, and email addresses prepared and ready to go, though, just in case – and make sure you've checked that each of them is willing to speak on your behalf if the need arises. As mentioned earlier, it's a good idea to have written references from your past employers to support your application – despite the ease of communication between Canada and the rest of the world, potential employers won't necessarily want to make international contact in order to check up on your history.

You need to target your résumé for each position you apply for, to convey your skills and qualifications clearly. Make sure it looks professional and has no grammatical or spelling errors (this can mean instant rejection), and keep it concise. Most employers will spend less than a minute deciding whether you warrant further consideration, so make that time count.

The application procedure

Whether you're responding to a job advertisement or writing to find out about general employment opportunities, a concise, convincing cover letter should accompany your résumé. Be enthusiastic (without resorting to exclamation marks) and specific. Briefly state why you're interested in the position and what qualifications, languages, and skills you possess. If you're applying for an advertised position, make sure you address the criteria and requirements outlined in the advertisement. If applying speculatively, explain clearly why you want to work for that particular company, and demonstrate your knowledge of what the company does (you may need to spend a little time researching this; again, showing genuine interest and enthusiasm will always work in your favour. If you're applying from overseas and are in an immigration category that doesn't require an approved job offer, make a point of assuring the employer that he or she won't have to complete any applications or paperwork on your behalf.

Keep your cover letter to a page or less, and include your name and address, the name and address of the company contact person, the date, and a clear reference to the job you're applying for (including a job number, if one is given in the advertisement). Letters should always be typed, and applications to companies in Québec should be written in French. You would normally email or mail your

 The International Federation of Translators (www.fit-ift.org) includes links to member institutes and associations around the world who can connect you with a translator or interpreter in your area (select Members from the homepage, then choose your geographical region). Many colleges of further education also offer translation services.

application, depending on the instructions in the advertisement – many employers now request email submissions only.

Don't expect to hear back from Canadian companies unless you make it to an interview. Though some will acknowledge receipt of your application, most won't, and this policy is often stated in the advertisement itself. This can be frustrating – and sometimes dispiriting – if you feel your life is on hold in the meantime. If you're not contacted within a couple of weeks you can generally assume you won't be interviewed. However, a follow-up call or email after a week or so may prompt a second look at your application, or at least end your suspense.

Interview procedure

If a large national or multinational company asks you to attend an interview in Canada they may reimburse your travel costs – particularly if you're being considered for a senior position. Smaller companies won't necessarily be able to pay for your flight; it's a good idea to find out how many people are being interviewed for the position to see whether you have a reasonable chance of getting the job. Many companies will agree to meet with you if you let them know you'll be in Canada for another reason and don't expect them to cover any of your costs. If you can arrange several interviews, or combine your job search with a holiday or a visit to Canadian friends, it might be worth paying for a journey overseas.

To make a good impression at an interview, be polite, interested, enthusiastic, and sincere. The interviewer will want to know why you're interested in the role, and your answer should show an understanding of both the company and the position. You also need to explain why you feel you're an ideal candidate for the job. A little research into the company and its Canadian operations will impress most interviewers. Most employers will also ask why you want to work in Canada. Not surprisingly, many have concerns about foreign employees leaving after six months or a year to return to their own country, and this can make them reluctant to risk hiring a non-Canadian. If you genuinely intend to remain in Canada, make this as clear as possible to your interviewer.

> The company in Canada flew me and my wife across twice, to look around and for the Provincial Nominee Program interview. We had never been to Canada before. We spent about 5 days here during each trip.
>
> **Steven Maine**

> **Research, research and more research was the key to finding work for Christina Chiam.**
>
> My motivation for moving to Canada was work based so I did a lot of research before I moved, and more when I arrived. Through contacts in Canada I learnt about relevant job websites for employment in the arts, and these became my main source for job vacancies.
> For other young professionals thinking of coming to Canada, I would suggest thoroughly researching your chosen field – the main players, recruitment cycles and so on – especially in the city where you plan to live. Try to establish contacts before arriving, be prepared to befriend strangers and ask their advice, and don't be perturbed by the knock-backs.

■ EMPLOYMENT REGULATIONS

Work permits

Permanent residents can generally apply for any job open to Canadian citizens, though there may be restrictions on positions with high-level security access, such as senior government roles. Temporary workers normally require a work permit (unless they hold a working holiday permit or similar documentation). For details about permits and visa requirements, refer to p. 41 in Chapter 2 and visit the Citizenship and Immigration Canada website at www.cic.gc.ca.

Regulated occupations

Certain professions and trades in Canada are regulated, which means you can't practice without a specific licence or certificate. These professions are controlled by laws (usually provincial, but sometimes federal) that establish specific standards of practice and competence, and help ensure public health and safety. Around 20% of Canadians work in regulated professions, which include medicine and healthcare, veterinary science, law, financial accounting, engineering, and certain skilled trades. There is a push for additional trades to be regulated as well.

The Canadian Information Centre for International Credentials (CICIC) (416 962 9725; www.cicic.ca) is an invaluable resource for prospective workers. It provides extensive information on working (and studying) in Canada, and on how to go about having your international experience evaluated and recognised. Profiles on most trades and professions are available: these tell you whether or not the occupation is regulated, and include contact details for the relevant regulatory bodies and any applicable examination or evaluation organisations. You can search for your occupation at www.cicic.ca/en/prof.aspx?sortcode=2.19.21. Limited information on regulations for some of the major professions is given under *Permanent work* but for full details you should refer to CICIC and to the relevant provincial regulatory authority for your profession.

Mutual recognition agreements operate between provinces for many occupations, and internationally as well in very limited instances (engineering is one). The CICIC website provides more details. In certain trades, workers who have completed their apprenticeship or hold a provincial Certificate of Qualification (see p. 241) can write an Interprovincial Standards Examination and be awarded a Red Seal. This endorsement is recognised across Canada, and allows tradespeople to practice outside their own province without having to sit additional exams.

 Visit www.red-seal.ca or email redseal-sceaurouge@hrsdc-rhdsc.gc.ca for details of the Red Seal programme and the Interprovincial Standards Examination.

Skills and qualifications

Recognition of foreign qualifications

One of the biggest obstacles for foreign-trained workers in Canada is having their qualifications and experience recognised. For some professionals – particularly doctors and lawyers – meeting regulatory requirements can mean considerable financial costs and months or even years of additional study and supervised work. A number of government-operated programmes, organisations and information services are available to prospective immigrants to help them prepare for work. The Foreign Credentials Referral Service, part of Citizenship and Immigration Canada, is a central information source that can help head you in the right direction. For some occupations it's possible to have your skills and qualifications evaluated or assessed before you come to Canada; for others, you must wait until you arrive. The CICIC website's occupation profiles (see p. 236) can give you specific details. You can also look up your occupation in the National Occupational Classification (NOC), to see what qualifications are normally required.

> *i* Visit the Foreign Credentials Referral Service website at www.credentials. gc.ca, call them though Service Canada on 1 888 854 1805 (Canada only), or write to 365 Laurier Avenue West, Ottawa, Ontario K1A 1L1, Canada. The NOC can be accessed online through the HRSDC website (go to www5. hrsdc.gc.ca/NOC-CNP).

> ❝ I had a better type of work in my own country, in that there I could work in an office or in sales, but here I must do blue-collar work. The salary here is much better than in my country, though.
>
> **Dante Pizarro** ❞

Compulsory and voluntary trade certification

Certification is compulsory in some trades, which means you have to obtain a provincial or territorial Certificate of Qualification in order to practice that trade or be considered for a job. In other trades, certification is not legally required in order to practice, but it's often highly recommended – it indicates a high level of skill, and some employers or unions will require it even if provincial regulations don't. Designations vary between provinces, and each province has different training and certification programmes. You'll have to sit a written test, and you may have to complete an apprenticeship if you don't have sufficient experience.

> ❝ **The Maines had first-hand experience of the difficulties in transferring overseas qualifications to the Canadian workplace.**
>
> My wife trained as a registered nurse in the UK and has 30 years' experience, but she found her qualifications were not accepted here, and that she would have to sit an examination before being allowed to work. It seems very strange that even if a nurse has qualified in another part of Canada, he or she still has to sit the local exam before being allowed to work here – especially as there is such a shortage of nurses and other medical professionals in the province. ❞

> ℹ️ Contact the relevant provincial apprenticeship office to find out what you need to do to obtain endorsement – the Red Seal website (www.red-seal.ca) provides contact details for all apprenticeship offices.

TIP

■ Certification is compulsory in some trades, which means you have to obtain a provincial or territorial Certificate of Qualification in order to practice that trade or be considered for a job.

EXAMPLES OF COMPULSORY AND VOLUNTARY TRADES

Compulsory Trades	Voluntary Trades
■ Auto body repairer	■ Cook
■ Automotive service technician	■ Baker
■ Electrician	■ Bricklayer
■ Hairstylist	■ Millright
■ Motorcycle mechanic	■ Glazier
■ Refrigeration and air-conditioning mechanic	■ Electronics service technician
■ Crane operator	■ Painter and decorator
■ Plumber	■ Structural steel and plate fitter
■ Sheet metal worker	■ Machinist
■ Steam fitter	■ Tool and die maker

■ SHORT-TERM WORK

Toronto buildings under cloud, Ontario

This section outlines a few of the main short-term employment options. Working as a live-in caregiver for children, seniors or people with disabilities is another possibility, and can provide a direct route to permanent residence – this is discussed in detail on p. 46. If you're interested in coming to Canada under a working holiday or work exchange programme, refer to p. 62. p. 63 and p. 64 outline some of the work options for foreign students studying in Canada.

Teaching English or French as a second language

The Canadian government offers permanent residents free classes in English and French – see p. 71. Large numbers of immigrants and refugees from Eastern-European countries, Asia, and Africa mean there are many opportunities for ESL (English as a second language) teachers, either in public programmes or in the numerous private language schools. These private schools can be found in many parts of the country, but the bulk are in Toronto or BC. You'll generally need a university degree and some form of accreditation such as a TESL, TEFL, CELTA or TESOL certificate to be able to teach in English. The ESL in Canada website (www.eslincanada.com) provides useful – if editorialised and informally presented – information, and you can check out the websites of the organisations below. Go Teach (www.goteach.ca) is another helpful Canadian site, with course listings and an online ESL Job Centre. TESL Canada also maintains a job board, and provides links to provincial sites that have their own job boards. *Teaching English Abroad*, from Crimson Publishing (www.crimsonpublishing. co.uk), gives information on teaching English overseas and how to find English-teaching jobs. Many newspapers and job-search engines (both in your home country and in Canada) will list available positions, and you can try www.tesall.com, a worldwide job-trawling website for ESL or EFL (English as a foreign language) job hunters. The International Language Schools of Canada (ILSC) list available jobs within their schools at www.ilsc.ca/jobs.aspx. If you're fluent in French you may be interested in obtaining your CEFLE Certification (Certificat d'enseignement du français langue etrangère), so you can teach French as a second language. See the ILSC webpage at www.learnfrench. ca/cefle-preparation.aspx (in French only) for further details.

◼ Useful contacts

Teaching English as a Second Language in Canada (TESL Canada):
604 298 0312; admin@tesl.ca; www.tesl.ca
Teaching English as a Foreign Language in Canada (TEFL Canada):
www.teflcanada.ca
Teachers of English to Speakers of Other Languages, Inc. (TESOL):
1 703 336 0774 (USA); info@tesol.org; www.tesol.org
University of Combridge ESOL Examinations (for CELTA): www.cambridgesol.org
Language Studies Canada (LSC): 416 488 2200 (Toronto); toronto@isc-canada.com; www.isc-canada.com
International Language Schools of Canada (ILSC): 416 323 1770
(Toronto office); info@ilsc.ca; www.ilsc.ca

Hospitality and tourism

Tourism is big business in Canada. It requires endurance, patience, and people skills to be successful in this industry, but it offers a great chance to explore new regions and have fun without necessarily being tied to a long-term job. You can find work in the food and beverage service, retail, adventure touring or guiding, outdoor sports and recreation, administration, accommodation, or even on a cruise ship. Canada's snowy winters mean lots of winter sports, and a steady stream of (mostly) young, enthusiastic workers – particularly from Australia and New Zealand – make their way to the slopes each year to provide an array of services to tourists and visitors, from giving skiing lessons to pouring beers. Whistler in BC, Banff and Lake Louise in Alberta, and Quebec's Mont Tremblant are especially popular tourist destinations. The usual newspapers and online resources can be useful for finding tourism-related jobs, as can backpacker and travel magazines. Travel agencies in your home country can often give you helpful leads as well. See p. 63 for more on this area of work.

These websites are for hospitality job sites or large Canadian resorts, and provide some starting points:

- ◼ **www.cooljobscanada.com:** hospitality and retail job site
- ◼ **www.hcareers.ca:** hospitality job board listing positions across Canada at both management and non-management level

- **www.hospitalitycareers.ca:** part of the Canjobs.com network, focusing on hospitality jobs in all parts of Canada
- **www.hoteljobs.ca:** basic search engine that collates hotel and hospitality jobs around Canada
- **www.intrawest.com:** website for Intrawest, resort company based in Canada; click on *Employment* link for short-term and long-term job opportunities at various resorts, including ski resorts in the Rocky Mountains and Quebec
- **www.banffparklodge.com:** website for Banff Park Lodge, resort and conference centre in Banff, Alberta
- **www.whistlerblackcomb.com:** website for Whistler Blackcomb (an Intrawest resort); click on *Employment* for available jobs and dates of annual recruitment tours
- **www.extremejobs.ca:** job-search resource for travel, tourism, and adventure jobs across Canada
- **www.jobloft.com:** retail, hospitality, and food-service jobs, searchable by city or postcode
- **www.fairmontcareers.com:** international careers site for Fairmont Hotels and Resorts, which operates a number of properties in Canada. Allows searches for jobs at specific locations

Tourism is a key industry in BC, where the Whistler Mountain Gondola makes its glorious-viewed trek year round, come snow, sun or wildflowers

Temporary office work

If you have good computer and typing skills, and some administration or accounting experience, 'temping' is often the way to go. There are always companies looking for someone to fill in for a few days, weeks or months, or to work on a particular project. See *Temporary employment agencies* for more information. Your best bet is to sign up with a couple of good recruitment agencies that can contact you if suitable jobs come up. Temporary and contract positions are often listed on standard job-search sites as well.

Voluntary work

Canadians have a long tradition of voluntary work. Volunteering can be a rewarding way to meet people, make friends and get involved in Canadian society. Volunteer Canada (613 231 4371 or 1 800 670 0401; info@volunteer.ca; www.volunteer.ca) represents volunteer centres around the country and has a heap of information and resources on volunteering. The Charity Village website at www.charityvillage. com provides an excellent and extensive index to all

LENDING A HAND IN THE EVEN GREATER, WHITER NORTH

If you have the time and the relevant skills and experience, you can apply to volunteer with Frontiers Foundation. The foundation carries out a range of projects both in Canada and overseas, but their major volunteer programme is Operation Beaver. This programme's main focus is on helping to improve education and provide affordable housing in Aboriginal communities in Northern Canada, primarily in Nunavut, the Northwest Territories, and the Yukon. Construction projects under Operation Beaver require a three-month stay; volunteers in the education programme stay for 10 months. And if you can't devote that kind of time, help in the Toronto head office is always welcome. Visit www.frontiersfoundation.ca for full details. You can also phone the foundation on 416 690 3930, or send an email to Marco A. Guzman, Executive Director, at marcoguzman@frontiersfoundation.ca.

non-profit organisations in Canada, and lets you search for volunteering opportunities in particular geographical locations or areas of interest. You can also phone Charity Village on 905 460 9258 or 1 800 610 8134, or email help@charityvillage.com.

■ PERMANENT WORK

Tourism and hospitality

Much of the information on short-term work in this industry (p. 243) is also relevant to those looking for long-term or permanent work. The Canadian Tourism Human Resource Council (613 231 6949; www.cthrc.ca) is an excellent place to start, with lots of information on career options, training, certification, foreign workers and the labour market. It also maintains a job board, the Tourism Work Web (www.tourismworkweb.com). An associated website, Discover Tourism (www.discovertourism.ca), is another great resource, with relevant material for newcomers looking to work in the industry. Its Careers section outlines duties, experience and education requirements for numerous occupations, from casino dealer, to executive chef, to railroad conductor.

Administrative and executive

Administrative work – from assistant positions through to managers – is consistently advertised, and provided you have transferable skills, relevant experience, and the stipulated level of education, you should be able to find a job. If you're looking for an executive-level position in your field, check the recruitment agency websites given on p. 235 under Employment agencies – many of these offer executive placement services. You can also search the ACSESS website at www.acsess.org to find other agencies that focus on executive recruitment. The job-search resource Higher Bracket (1 866 636 9400; www.higherbracket.ca) lists high-level positions with six-figure salaries.

Financial services

According to major firms like KPMG, accountants (including foreign-trained accountants) will increasingly be needed as Canada's economy grows, which it is anticipated to begin doing from 2010. Accountants and financial auditors are regulated in most parts of Canada, but rules and requirements vary. The major accounting designations are Chartered Accountant (CA), Certified General Accountant (CGA), and Certified Management Accountant (CMA). Associations or institutions exist for each designation in each province, so contact the relevant provincial organisation to find out about licensing. You can get provincial details from the national associations: the Canadian Institute of Chartered Accountants (416 977 3222; www.cica.ca); the Certified General Accountants Association of Canada (604 669 3555 or 1 800 663 1529; www.cga-canada.org); and the Certified Management Accountants of Canada (905 949 4200 or 1 800 263 7622; www.cma-canada.org). Financial planners and managers aren't regulated (with the exception of financial planners in Quebec), though employers may require you to have certain licences or designations. Securities agents and traders are, and have to obtain certification from the Canadian Securities Institute (416 364 9130 or 1 866 866 2601; www.csi.ca).

 Licensing is handled by the securities commission in each province: see the Canadian Securities Administrators (CSA) website at www.csa-acvm.ca for links. You can also phone the CSA on 514 864 9510 or email csa-acvm-secretariat@acvm-csa.ca.

Information and communications technology

Information technology and computer science skills are always relevant. Recent reports have suggested almost 90,000 jobs for ICT professionals will open up in the next five years, though these numbers will likely be diluted somewhat until the current fiscal crunch has passed. The most sought-after people are computer, information systems, and e-commerce managers; information-systems, database, and business analysts; electrical, electronic, and software engineers; interactive media developers; web designers and developers; and computer programmes. Aside from engineers, ICT occupations aren't regulated – necessary qualifications are determined by employers. Wages are higher than average; unemployment is lower. Canada's professional association for ICT practitioners is the Canadian Information Processing Society (905 602 1370 or 1 877 275 2477; info@cips.ca; www.cips.ca); their website includes a job board. For the Quebec industry, contact the Fédération de l'informatique du Québec (514 840 1240; info@fiq.qc.ca; www.fiq.qc.ca).

The Information and Communications Technology Council (613 237 8551; info@ictc-ctic.ca; www.ictc-ctic.ca) provides industry information, career-building tools, and resources.

Skilled trades

There's a massive shortage of qualified skilled tradespeople working in Canada, which will only increase as the baby-boomer component of the workforce retires. Manufacturing, construction, transportation, and petroleum production industries are expected to be hit hardest, with a shortfall of over a million workers forecast for the near future. Many trade jobs pay very well, and there's lots of scope for prospective immigrants who have the skills Canada needs. Depending on your trade, certification may be compulsory or voluntary. Certification and licensing is regulated on a provincial basis, though it's possible to obtain a Red Seal endorsement for certain trades, which allows you to work in any province (see p. 57). General recruiters and job-search sites can help you find trade jobs.

 Canada Trade Jobs (604 685 5627; info@CanadaTradeJobs.com; www. canadatradejobs.com) recruits international tradespeople for Canadian companies, and helps foreign-trained workers to find employment.

WORKERS' COMPENSATION

If you are injured at work you can make a claim to the workers' compensation system in your province or territory, which may pay benefits while you are off work, assist with medical aid and rehabilitation, and help you return to work when you're well. The Association of Workers' Compensation Boards of Canada (online at www.awcbc.org) provides extensive information on benefits and regulations (which vary between provinces), as well as links to each province's compensation board or commission. Federal government employees fall under the jurisdiction of the Labour Program, and are covered by the Government Employees' Compensation Act. The webpage at www.hrsdc.gc.ca/en/labour/workers_compensation/index. shtml, on HRSDC's Labour website, provides full details. (A list of workers' compensation offices for federal government workers can be found at www.hrsdc.gc.ca/en/labour/contact_ us/workers.shtml).

Engineering

Engineering (whatever your specialisation) is a regulated profession in Canada, and to call yourself an engineer you must be licenced through the regulatory body in your province. Engineers Canada is the national engineering organisation (613 232 2474; info@engineerscanada.ca; evaluation@engineerscanada.ca for assessment information; www.engineerscanada.ca). (For Quebec, contact l'Ordre des ingénieurs du Québec at www.oiq.qc.ca instead.) Engineers Canada has mutual-recognition agreements with the United States, the UK, Ireland, Australia, New Zealand, South Africa, Hong Kong, Japan, and France, which make it easier for engineers trained in those countries to work in Canada (select *Mobility* on the Engineers Canada home page). The website provides links to provincial associations, and useful information on working as a foreign-trained engineer and having your qualifications assessed. Oversupply has been a factor in recent years (though demand for engineers in the energy and mining industries remained strong), so check out job opportunities to gauge demand.

 Roevin Engineering Recruitment (905 826 4155; www.roevin.ca), a subsidiary of Adecco, lists engineering, technical, and skilled trade positions. Technogénie Ressources (514 931 9880; www.technogenie.com) specialises in Quebec-based positions.

Mining

Canada's sizable oil and metals industries have meant plenty of opportunities for geologists, engineers, technicians, machinery operators, and mechanics, as well as

Canada's wealth of natural resources has created a surge of opportunities for workers over the past few years

for project managers, foremen, and administrative staff. Provided commodity prices bounce back in the next year or two, these opportunities will likely continue. The Mining Recruitment Group (604 696 2929; info@miningrecruitmentgroup.com; www.miningrecruitmentgroup.com) recruits specifically for Canadian mining companies, and you can find many more job openings listed on general recruitment sites such as those on p. 278. The Canada section of the Global InfoMine website is worth exploring as well: go to www.infomine.com/countries/canada.asp for a ton of information on the Canadian mining industry, as well as an extensive list of jobs. Natural Resources Canada provides considerable information on mining in Canada, and the webpage at http://mmsd1.mms.nrcan.gc.ca/mmsd/faqs/default_e.asp#3 has a helpful list of career and job-search links.

Teaching

As education is a provincial responsibility, prospective teachers from outside Canada need to contact the provincial regulatory body – usually the department of education – to find out how their qualifications translate. (See p. 185 for contact details.) Teachers in Ontario are registered through the Ontario College of Teachers (416 961 8800 or 1 888 534 2222; info@oct.ca; www.oct.ca); those in BC, through the British Columbia College of Teachers (604 731 8170 or 1 800 555 3684; www.bcct. ca). While teacher shortages were a concern – or an anticipated concern – a few years back, parts of the country are now oversupplied. However, there is a perennial shortage of qualified teachers for math, science, and technology subjects, as well as for French as a second language and special education. Teachers are also lacking in rural and northern areas, and in Aboriginal communities. The Education Canada Network's online job board (www.jobsearch.educationcanada.com) lets you search for teaching jobs across all levels of education. The Canadian Federation of Teachers (613 232 1505 or 1 866 283 1505; www.ctf-fce.ca) provides further information on teaching in Canada. Teacher exchange programmes may be another option – look up exchange organisations in your home country, or contact the Canadian Education Exchange Foundation (705 739 7596; www.ceef.ca) as a starting point.

Teaching at the college or university level isn't regulated, so it's generally up to the institution hiring you to decide what qualifications are appropriate. Job advertisements provide detailed descriptions of the necessary credentials and experience for particular positions. Post-graduate job sites include the Canadian Association of University Teachers job board (www.academicwork.ca), the *University Affairs* magazine job board (http://oraweb.aucc.ca/ua_e.html) and EduJobsCanada. com (www.edujobscanada.com).

Media and arts

Jobs in this industry (whether film, television, music, magazine or book publishing, radio, theatre or arts management) are often highly sought after, and you'll be competing with the local talent. That's not to say you won't have a good chance of finding work – some employers need people with regional or Canadian knowledge, but others will value the international skills and experience that an immigrant or foreign worker can bring to the role. Be prepared to search for a while, though, and use any contacts you have to find out about potential jobs and help you get a toe in the door. Working in a volunteer capacity at festivals or for an organisation in your

<aside>
FACT

■ There is a perennial shortage of qualified teachers for math, science and technology subjects, as well as for French as a second language and special education.
</aside>

> **Christina Chiam talks about the experience of job-hunting in the arts industry:**
>
> Being a 'foreigner' within a small arts community did make it difficult to find work initially. I didn't have the necessary contacts or 'foot in the door', and was applying for jobs without any Canadian experience. I was focused on one particular organisation but also applied for other positions that interested me. It took a small-world coincidence to get my application noticed, and thankfully an interview and job offer soon followed.

field of choice can give you invaluable Canadian experience, and increases your chances of being in the right place at the right time if opportunity knocks. Media-specific job sites include Media Job Search Canada at www.mediajobsearchcanada. com, and Jeff Gaulin's Journalism Job Board at www.jeffgaulin.com – this site lists a range of media and communications jobs and is free to search. Cultural Careers Council Ontario lists loads of arts, music, and theatre-related jobs at www. workinculture.ca – most are in Ontario, but you can often find positions in other provinces as well. Associations exist for many sectors of the industry, and include the Canadian Association of Journalists (613 526 8061; www.caj.ca) and the Editors' Association of Canada (416 975 1379 or 1866 226 3348; www.editors.ca).

Architecture

Architects are regulated in all parts of Canada. To be able to practice, foreign-trained architects must have their qualifications assessed by the Canadian Architectural Certification Board (CACB) and then be licenced by a provincial regulatory board – click *Links* on the home page of the CACB website (www.cacb.ca) for links to these. Internships and exams are usually required. You can also phone the CACB on 613 241 8399 or email them at info@cacb.ca. Both the CACB and the Royal Architectural Institute of Canada (RAIC) (613 241 3600; info@raic.org; www.raic.org) provide helpful advice for immigrants thinking of practising architecture in Canada. RAIC provides a job-search site through Workopolis at www.niche.workopolis. com/CareerSite/RAIC/careersite_e.htm, and provincial association websites post employment opportunities as well.

Medicine

Though Canada desperately needs more doctors, stringent regulations and transition requirements bar many foreign-trained physicians. (Snide comments about over-qualified taxi drivers are sometimes based on truth.) Most doctors with international qualifications have to undergo exams and additional training to practice in Canada, though some efforts are being made to improve the system. Ontario, for example, is considering an expedited system for doctors practising in countries with comparable healthcare systems. The Canadian Information Centre for International Medical Graduates (www.img-canada.ca) should be your first stop: it provides details of qualification, licensing and registration requirements, and includes links to the regulatory bodies in each province. Qualifying and evaluating exams are administered by the Medical Council of Canada (613 521 6012; MCC_Admin@mcc.ca; www.mcc.ca), and fees apply.

i The Canadian Medical Association (613 731 9331; www.cma.ca) publishes a range of print journals that advertise career opportunities, and also lists these online. Another source of medical and allied-health jobs is the Canadian section of job site Medhunters.com (www.medhunters.com/jobs/can.html).

Dentists have to undergo a similar process, passing an exam from the National Dental Examining Board of Canada (613 236 5912; director@ndeb.ca; www.ndeb.ca) and then applying to their provincial regulatory authority (see p. 177 for a web link to these). More information can be obtained from the Canadian Dental Association (see p. 177) and its Commission on Dental Accreditation of Canada (www.cda-adc.ca/en/cda/cdac). Optometrists should contact the regulatory board in their province – the Canadian Association of Optometrists provides a list of these at www.opto.ca/en/public/links.asp (beneath the list of associations). You may be required to sit an exam through Canadian Examiners in Optometry (905 642 1373; csao@ca.inter.net; www.ceo-eco.org). Optometrists from accredited North American institutions – those listed by the Accreditation Council of Optometric Education – won't need to undergo further assessment. (Lists are available on the American Optometric Association webpage at www.aoa.org/x5175.xml.)

With a current shortfall of around 2,500 each year, nurses are also in demand, but as with other foreign medical professionals, there are ethical restrictions on recruiting people from countries where their skills are needed. All nursing professions are regulated, and you may have to pass exams and meet other requirements. The Canadian Nurses Association provides more information on nursing in Canada, as well as links to the provincial regulatory bodies (613 237 2133 or 1 800 361 8404; info@cna-aiic.ca; www.cna-aiic.ca/cna).

Pharmacists can find information about pharmacy practice in Canada through the Canadian Pharmacists Association (613 523 7877 or 1 800 917 9489; info@pharmacists.ca; www.pharmacists.ca). The certification body is the Pharmacy Examining Board of Canada (416 979 2431; pebcinfo@pebc.ca; www.pebc.ca).

Law

Paralegals aren't regulated in Canada, except in Ontario, due to new legislation in 2007. Lawyers (and Quebec notaries), hardly surprisingly, are. As with doctors and other regulated professionals, foreign-trained lawyers must jump through various hoops to practice in Canada. The Federation of Law Societies of Canada (FLSC) (613 236 7272; info@flsc.ca; www.flsc.ca) is made up of the country's 14 provincial and territorial law societies (Quebec has two – one for notaries and one for lawyers who are members of the Quebec Bar). After having your legal credentials evaluated by the FLSC's National Committee on Accreditation, you need to apply for membership with a provincial law society. (In Quebec, you leave out the FLSC component and apply directly to whichever of the two regulatory bodies is relevant.) The FLSC website links to each provincial society, or you can find contact details on p. 57 of Chapter 2, under *Law societies*. Regulations for admission vary, but you normally have to pass exams and complete an articling programme and further study may be required. Working as a foreign legal consultant, where you practice your home country's law in Canada, is another option for some lawyers. Legal job-search sites and recruiters include www.legaljob.ca and ZSA Recruitment (613 232 8828; www. zsa.ca). Law society sites also post jobs, and the Canadian Bar Association (613 237 2925 or 1 800 267 8860; www.cba.org) provides recruitment and job-search services through The Counsel Network – select *Practice Tools* on the home page, then *Legal Careers*.

Public service

Government jobs offer good pay, good benefits, and high job security, but can be difficult to get and are subject to the bureaucracy of government employment that exists in any country. Knowledge of French is an asset, and bilingualism is required for some positions. Though permanent residents are eligible to apply, it's sometimes easier said than done. The Public Service Employment Act stipulates that preference for federal government jobs be given to Canadian citizens, and there may be restrictions on positions with high-level security access. In addition, the Employment Equity Act specifies hiring targets for four designated groups: Aboriginal peoples, women, visible minorities and people with disabilities. If you don't belong to one of these groups, this may also affect your chances of success.

 See www.jobs-emplois.gc.ca for federal government jobs, or contact the relevant provincial government (see p. 364) for opportunities at the provincial level.

◼ ASPECTS OF EMPLOYMENT

Salaries

The median annual salary for a full-time worker in Canada came in at $41,401 based on 2006 census figures. Around 6.5% of workers earn above the $100,000 mark. Teachers and professors have a median wage of $58,850; for mechanics the mid-point is around $45,950; and for senior managers it's just over $80,000. According to the Conference Board of Canada, there's currently an income gap of US$6,400 between Canada and the USA, meaning Canadians have less purchasing power to play with. At the highest levels of the corporate structure, Canadian executives still get paid a fraction of their American counterparts' salary, though this says more about the profitability and attitude of US companies than about the exploitation of Canada's CEOs (many still receive horrifyingly more than the average wage). Astronomically high salaries are uncommon in Canada, however, and you won't necessarily be able to enter the Canadian workforce at the salary level you've attained in your home country. You may need to take a lower-level job and work your way up, or switch jobs once you've accrued some Canadian experience. The census also recorded discrepancies between the salaries earned by immigrants and those of Canadian-born workers. In 2005, recent immigrant men earned just $0.63

AVERAGE WEEKLY EARNINGS	
Canada	$793
Newfoundland and Labrador	$745
Prince Edward Island	$653
Nova Scotia	$689
New Brunswick	$731
Quebec	$732
Ontario	$826
Manitoba	$727
Saskatchewan	$760
Alberta	$872
British Columbia	$787
Yukon Territory	$901
Northwest Territories	$1,048
Nunavut	$982

TIP

 You won't necessarily be able to enter the Canadian workforce at the salary level you've attained in your home country.

for each $1 earned by Canadian-born men. The rate for women was even lower, at $0.56. Figures improve substantially for established immigrants, but in terms of median wage they rarely achieve parity with their Canadian-born peers.

i You can find out salary information for different occupations by using the Working in Canada Tool at www.goingtocanada.gc.ca (see p. 177), or going directly to Service Canada's Labour Market Information website (which the Working in Canada Tool draws on) at www.labourmarketinformation.ca.

A minimum wage is set in each province and territory. This varies across the country, but currently ranges from $7.75 to $10.00 for adult workers (see p. 177 for more information). Incremental increases over the next few years are planned by some provinces. In Ontario and Quebec, 'tipped' staff – waiters and bartenders – are paid less, with the understanding that they'll earn gratuities.

Benefits and perks

Salaries are usually paid fortnightly, by cheque or direct deposit. Many companies have a plan in which employees receive an end-of-year bonus (traditionally known as the 'Christmas bonus'). In some cases this is based on business profits and distributed equally, but more and more companies have performance-based bonuses. For executives or high-level managers, this can drastically increase annual earnings. Income tax must be paid on all bonuses (though you may be able to circumvent this by having your employer deposit your bonus directly into your personal RRSP); similarly, taxes are payable on benefits such as company cars. Senior staff may receive other perks such as enhanced medical and dental insurance, pension schemes, and health-club memberships. Workers who travel frequently on business can often keep their frequent-flier mileage for their own use.

> **Dante Pizarro talks about the experience of finding work as an immigrant in Montreal:**
>
> There are many different types of jobs out there, some much better than others, and some employers do try to take advantage when they see you are an immigrant. The first job I got was in a clothing factory, doing simple work like packaging the clothes. The pay was really bad because it paid by piecework: $0.05 for wrapping each item in plastic, $0.10 for cutting and putting on a sticker, etc. It didn't end up being a high hourly wage. I left this job and started working in a pizzeria, making pizzas, cleaning, and sometimes washing the dishes. It was also hard work and low pay. They didn't even pay minimum wage, and we had to pay for any food we ate in the restaurant. Finally, I found a good job with a good company that has many benefits.

Employment regulations and working hours

Laws relating to employment conditions are the responsibility of the provincial ministries of labour, and vary between provinces. In addition to provincial labour codes there is also a Canada Labour Code, which regulates employment in federal sectors such as banks, railways and postal operations.

Each province defines its own standard and maximum working hours (some don't set specific limits), as well as the number of hours per week after which overtime must be paid. Though exceptions apply in various circumstances, this is 40 hours for federal government employees and in all provinces except Alberta, Ontario, and New Brunswick, where it's 44, and Nova Scotia and PEI, where it's 48. Standard overtime is one-and-a-half times the regular wage (Newfoundland and Labrador, New Brunswick and – for certain occupations – Nova Scotia, are only required to pay one-and-a-half times the minimum wage). If you earn a salary, overtime isn't always compensated; this is particularly true at the lower-management level. You might be offered time in lieu, or extra time off at the end of a particularly busy period, but in many companies you're simply expected to put in as many hours as the job requires.

In practice, most people work a five-day week of between 37 and 40 hours. An office workday often runs from 8am or 9am to 5pm, with an hour's (unpaid) break for lunch, but some companies are less formal than this. Short morning and afternoon breaks might also be given, though labour laws generally only stipulate one 30-minute break every five hours. Some companies offer family- and lifestyle-friendly 'summer hours' over the summer months, where you either work reduced hours, or begin early each day and then leave early on Fridays.

Vacations and public holidays

The largest sacrifice for many people who move to Canada is the decrease in vacation time. Unlike the four or more weeks that are usual in Europe, Australia, and

> **Steven Maine, vice president in charge of research at his company, finds Canada's limited vacation time difficult on workers:**
>
> From my experience, I think the working environment is generally quite hard, and I have tried hard to make things better for the people who work for me. The lack of holidays and the long working hours are very stressful. Most people only get two or three weeks' annual leave, and Nova Scotia has the fewest public holidays in Canada.

the UK, most workers are entitled to just two weeks' paid vacation plus between five and 10 statutory public holidays (depending on the province). (Public holidays are listed under *Public holidays and events*, p. 299.) Some employers do include extra vacation days over Christmas. Annual vacation increases with the number of years you spend at the company, but don't expect month-long holidays. During vacation you'll either be paid your usual salary, or an amount equivalent to 4% of your gross annual wages. If you leave a company before you've taken your accrued vacation, they must pay you the amount of vacation pay owing. If you work at your regular job on a public holiday, you're normally entitled to either a paid day off or around two-and-a-half times your regular pay (though variations and exclusions apply). Depending on your occupation and province, you may have to work on holidays if your employer asks you to.

Trade unions

Federal and provincial labour laws in Canada give employees the right (guaranteed by the Canadian Charter of Rights and Freedoms) to organise or join a union to represent their working rights. If a group of workers proposes to form a union, and a majority of employees vote in favour, the workplace becomes unionised. Some workplaces operate under a 'closed-shop' system in which joining (and paying fees to) the active union is a prerequisite for being hired. In 'open-shop' workplaces, employees don't have to belong to the union (though you may still be required to pay membership fees and dues, as you're considered to benefit from the union's representation even if you choose not to join). Over four million Canadians – almost 30% of the labour force – are unionised, more than double the US figure. The public sector is among the most unionised groups, with 71% of workers belonging to a union. Education, healthcare, utilities, and transportation industries are also union heavy. Unionisation rates are highest in Newfoundland and Labrador and Quebec, and lowest in Alberta. The average full-time wage for unionised workers is currently $24.79 per hour (versus $20.22 for non-union workers). There are 175 national, 39 international, and about 600 directly chartered or unaffiliated local unions in Canada. Through their union, most members are affiliated with particular labour congress organisations.

TIP

■ Over four million Canadians – almost 30% of the labour force – are unionised, more than double the US figure.

■ Major unions (10 largest, by membership)

Canadian Union of Public Employees: 613 237 1590; cupemail@cupe.ca or courrier@scfp.ca; www.cupe.ca (548,880 members)

National Union of Public and General Employees: 613 228 9800;
national@nupge.ca; www.nupge.ca (340,000 members)
**United Steel, Paper and Forestry, Rubber, Manufacturing, Energy, Allied
Industrial, and Service Workers International Union:** 416 487 1571;
info@usw.ca; www.usw.ca (280,000 members)
**National Automobile, Aerospace, Transportation, and General Workers Union
of Canada (CAW Canada):** 416 497 4110; cawtreas@caw.ca;
www.caw.ca (265,000 members)
United Food and Commercial Workers Canada: 416 675 1104;
ufcw@ufcw.ca; www.ufcw.ca (245,330 members)
Canadian Teachers' Federation: 613 232 1505 or 1 866 283 1505;
info@ctf-fce.ca; www.ctf-fce.ca (219,000 members)
Public Service Alliance of Canada: 613 560 4200 or 1 888 604 7722;
org-synd@psac.com; www.psac.com (166,960 members)
Ontario Teachers' Federation: 416 966 3424 or 1 800 268 7061;
www.otffeo.on.ca (155,000 members)
Communications, Energy and Paperworkers Union of Canada: 613 230 5200;
info@cep.ca; www.cep.ca (150,100 members)
Canadian Federation of Nurses: 613 526 4661 or 1 800 321 9821;
cfnu@nursesunions.ca; www.nursesunions.ca (135,000 members)

◼ Labour congresses

Canadian Labour Congress (CLC): 613 521 3400;
communications@clc-ctc.ca; www.canadianlabour.ca
Confédération des syndicats nationaux (CSN): 514 598 2121; www.csn.qc.ca
Centrale des syndicats du Québec (CSQ): 514 356 8888; www.csq.qc.net
Centrale des syndicats démocratiques (CSD): 418 529 2956;
info@csd.qc.ca; www.csd.qc.ca
Confederation of Canadian Unions: 416 736 5109; ccucsc@ca.inter.net;
http://pages.ca.inter.net/~ccu/

Employment contracts

Employment contracts aren't obligatory in Canada, but they're usually desirable.
They help protect employers against wrongful dismissal lawsuits, but they also give
you greater security as an employee, particularly if you're fired from a term-based
contract and need to file for damages, or if you're dismissed without due cause. For
temporary foreign workers, an employment contract is generally required before
your potential employer can apply for a Labour Market Opinion on your behalf.
Contracts provide a detailed written description of the position; the terms and
conditions of work, and those relating to termination (which have to be in line with
the labour laws of the province); and what benefits apply. (Your job may not entitle
you to benefits, particularly if you're hired in a casual position or as a contractor,
but as public health insurance is available to permanent residents, a lack of benefits
in Canada is less disastrous than in the United States.) Employers often specify a
probationary period of employment (three months is common) during which you
can generally be dismissed more easily – sometimes with little or no notice, though
employee rights are improving in this respect. Depending on the provincial laws,
you may have to be given a chance to prove your abilities if your performance

isn't initially considered satisfactory. This 'trial' period wouldn't necessarily be appropriate for senior-level staff, or employees who've been persuaded to close their own business or move from a secure position elsewhere in order to take the job (and if it is applied, such staff would have a better chance of successfully suing for damages if unfairly dismissed).

A clear warning must be given if your performance is unsatisfactory, and you can't be dismissed without being given a chance to improve. Length of notice for termination normally ranges from one to eight weeks, increasing with the duration of employment (though some executives negotiate far longer terms). Employees need to give 'reasonable notice' when resigning, which is commonly two weeks unless you have a contract stating otherwise. If you're able to give more warning, employers generally appreciate having the extra time to replace you. (Be wary of giving too much additional notice if you're quitting in less-than-ideal circumstances, though; your employer may not want you to work for the full period, and may not be willing to pay you for it either.)

Women in work

Women make up about 47% of the Canadian workforce. Equality of pay and equal access to jobs are guaranteed by federal law in Canada, though this has not yet been specifically legislated in all provinces, and considerable inequities still exist. Part-time jobs are twice as likely to be filled by women, and among full-time workers, women make just $0.70 for each dollar earned by men. Women continue to dominate in traditionally female occupations such as nursing, teaching, and administrative work. Sexual-discrimination lawsuits and increased legislation have woken employers up to issues of pay equality, promotions, and sexual harassment. It's illegal for an employer to make hiring decisions based on your sex or marital status, or on assumptions about whether or not you'll have children and leave the workforce. Parental leave is guaranteed in all provinces (see p. 194).

Organisations for working women can provide valuable contacts and support. The Canadian Federation of Business and Professional Women's Clubs, known as BPW Canada, is an advocate of women's working conditions and operates clubs around the country. Visit www.bpwcanada.com or email bpw@bpwcanada.com to find out about clubs in your area. Status of Women Canada (613 995 7835; www.swc-cfc.gc.ca) is a federal-government-run organisation and another useful

FACT

■ Equality of pay and equal access to jobs are guaranteed by federal law in Canada, though this has not yet been specifically legislated in all provinces, and considerable inequities still exist.

FACT

■ Part-time jobs are twice as likely to be filled by women, and among full-time workers, women make just $0.70 for each dollar earned by men.

SHARING THE LOAD

i

The majority of Canadian couple families are dual-income earners. Often one partner will work part-time, particularly when they have children. There's been a vast expansion in the part-time job market, with almost one-fifth of Canadians now employed in part-time positions (which usually provide fewer benefits). Part-time arrangements are common in the consumer sector, especially for retail and food services.

resource, with informative publications and regular news updates on the position of women in Canada. The Canadian edition of *Smart Women Finish Rich* (David Bach, Doubleday Canada, 2003) can provide useful advice on managing your finances and increasing personal wealth.

■ WORKING CULTURE AND ETIQUETTE

Business culture

Canadian work practices vary considerably between companies and industries, but as a rule, punctuality, reliability, and working hard are very important. Provided your employer meets the minimum legislated requirements, policies on breaks can vary. Retail and hospitality staff might get a break every two hours, or every four or five; business offices often just break at lunchtime, and may pause unofficially for a morning or afternoon cup of tea. Excessive socialising outside of breaks is usually frowned on, though it depends on the company culture (and 'excessive' is a subjective term). Some companies are happier for employees to work to an informal structure, as long as the work gets done, while others are distinctly stuffy and controlled. It's best to avoid making (or taking) extensive personal phone calls at work, or to spend too much company time surfing the internet for your own purposes or playing on Facebook – again, these matters are subjective and you'll need to use your judgement. (Some people prefer to send their personal emails from a non-work email address, for privacy and security reasons.)

Teamwork and a commitment to the company's aims are valued highly, and if you seem to avoid work, or insist on leaving the second your shift ends regardless of what remains to be done, you'll damage your chances of promotion. You need to be willing to pitch in to get the job done when necessary, even if this means donating a little unpaid overtime now and then. There's a fine balance to be maintained, though – if you're overly agreeable about taking on extra work you may set a precedent, and find yourself being exploited for it. Canadian offices are generally social and friendly, and managers and executives make themselves relatively accessible. Your boss is still your boss, but Canadians value initiative, and most

> **Christina Chiam found that in the arts industry, many of the characteristics and challenges of the workplace are universal:**
>
> My experience with the Toronto International Film Festival Group has shown me that the work environment in Canadian not-for-profit arts organisations is similar to that in Australia. Both countries face the same issues of limited and competitive government funding, the need for private and corporate support to enable organisations to sustain themselves, and a passionate but under-resourced workforce. So while the end product may vary, the work environment and challenges remain the same.

managers are open to new ideas and suggestions from less senior employees. Even in more casual offices, however, it's important to behave professionally and observe whatever hierarchical rules are in place. There are normally acceptable practices and processes to follow in any workplace – whether these are assumed, or spelled out in a 200-page employee handbook – and contravening them can be problematic. It's never wise, for example, to go above your immediate boss's head with a complaint (unless it's about them and you don't have a choice); this is bad form, and a sure-fire way to create ill will. Discussing salaries with your colleagues is strongly discouraged as well, as tempting as it may be – not only would your employer prefer you not to know if there's a pay discrepancy between you and any other workers, but the knowledge can badly affect morale and job satisfaction.

Business style

As with workplace culture, workplace style varies hugely. Corporate agencies may enforce a formal, suit-and-tie approach, while some other offices might let their employees come to work in flip-flops and shorts. People working in trades, health services or retail often have to wear uniforms or specified clothing. Always dress professionally for your first day in a new job, even if you know the company dress code is relatively casual. From that point on, take your cue from your co-workers; if their style is a little staid, dressing flamboyantly could liven things up, or it could frighten away your potential lunch buddies. (Choose your own adventure.) Most offices follow a smart-casual or business-casual style. Business meetings with clients or outsiders tend to be more formal and professional than internal meetings, and the dress code for these normally steps up a notch as well.

Working relationships

Some people become firm friends with their co-workers; others get along well in the context of the job, but don't normally socialise outside the workplace. You may end up working with someone who's open to making new friends, or someone who prefers to keep their non-work life private. A casual but professional approach is a good rule of thumb, unless you're in a highly corporate environment. Griping about other employees can create tension and end up reflecting badly on you, so it's best to keep things polite and friendly unless someone clearly oversteps the line and you need to speak out (in which case you should take your concerns to your immediate manager). People tend to gravitate toward those who have interests and values they can relate to, and if your company is divided into departments you'll find the employees in each area often stick together – working with particular people all day creates familiarity and a certain level of comfort. In retail or hospitality industries, employees often socialise after work (or congregate at work – though 'clustering' is actively discouraged in some retail stores), if only to share their woes about difficult customers or their sadistic boss. Some companies have an optional social club or committee that organises pub nights, staff parties, and outings to films or sporting events; others have the occasional after-work staff gathering; some never meet up outside work at all, unless it's enforced. Whatever type of workplace you find yourself in, being sociable and reasonably open will make your experience there much more enjoyable than hiding in your cubicle and avoiding interaction.

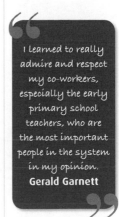

I learned to really admire and respect my co-workers, especially the early primary school teachers, who are the most important people in the system in my opinion.
Gerald Garnett

Attitudes to women

The balance of male and female employees varies between workplaces and between industries. The culture of your workplace may be dominated by either (or by neither), or by the attitudes of your manager and other senior staff. Most offices and other workplaces are strongly supportive of women, though the occasional traditionalist boss (almost certainly male, and usually of a certain age) lurks in the shadows of these enlightened times. The best approach is to know your rights without being overly defensive about them – being polite but firm will gain you more respect than aggression, though you should never allow anyone to subjugate you. Women are required (and expect) to be treated equally in the workplace, but discrimination and harassment, including sexual harassment, do still occur. Neither is acceptable, and your employer is responsible for investigating and dealing with any problems that arise. If you feel that you have been – or are being – discriminated against or harassed in a Canadian workplace, you need to tell your employer immediately. If your employer is the one causing the concern, or the problem is not being appropriately addressed, you can contact the Canadian Human Rights Commission or your provincial or territorial human rights agency.

 Contact the Canadian Human Rights Commission on 613 995 1151 or 1 888 214 1090, or go to www.chrc-ccdp.ca. To find links to provincial and territorial agencies, click on Links (under Resources on the home page).

▮ INDUSTRY OVERVIEW

This section is intended to provide a brief overview of some of the major industry areas relevant to the Canadian economy. Facts and figures change rapidly and the global financial crisis of 2008 has created considerable uncertainty in terms of the short-term outlook, so you're strongly advised to carry out more extensive research if you're looking to work in one of these areas. The online Industry Canada guide to business information by sector is at www.strategis.ic.gc.ca. You can also explore import and export trade data by product or industry on the searchable webpage at www.ic.gc.ca/epic/site/tdo-dcd.nsf/en/Home.

Automotive

Canada's automotive industry employs almost half a million people and produces 2.5 million passenger cars and trucks each year, as well as motor vehicle parts. Previously the largest single contributor to the Canadian economy, the industry has declined in recent years; 2007 actually saw it drop into trade deficit, despite exports of over $77,300 million. The demise in 1999 of the Canadian–US Auto Pact – which ensured that for every car sold in Canada, one would be produced in Canada – marked the start of a downward turn. Canada's major motor vehicle assembly plants are all in Ontario, and plant closures, most recently announced for Windsor and Oshawa, have become a familiar topic as Asian-based automotive manufacturers increase their share of the North-American market, and as demand from the US declines. In 1999 Canada had the fifth largest auto industry in the world; today it sits in ninth place. However, the country is still regarded as a leader in vehicle assembly, and places significant importance on automotive technology, research and development.

All car companies in Canada are foreign, but there is a significant, Canadian-owned auto parts industry, including Magna International – which has grown from a small tool-and-die shop in the 1950s into a major international supplier – and Quebec's Bombardier Inc., which manufactures rail vehicles and aircraft for companies around the world. Automotive companies in Canada include the North American 'big three' – Ford, General Motors, and Chrysler – as well as Toyota, Honda, CAMI Automotive (which makes Suzuki vehicles), Mazda, Mercedes Benz, Subaru, Volvo, Volkswagen, and BMW.

Banking and finance

Since becoming deregulated in the late 1980s, Canada has been an exciting place to work in financial services. The finance sector employs more than 750,000 Canadians and is becoming ever-more electronic, with online banking now extremely common and debit-card facilities provided (or expected to be provided) in every store. The Bank of Canada is a public institution that issues currency and controls the money supply (and thus, indirectly, the interest rates). The commercial banking sector includes chartered banks, credit unions, and groups specialising in mortgage or business loans. There are 20 domestic chartered banks and dozens more foreign banks and foreign-bank branches operating in Canada. About 4,000 trust companies, mortgage companies and credit unions also exist in Canada and are regulated by the government. Details of Canada's major commercial banks are included in the Banking section of *Daily Life,* p. 73–78.

Canada's major stock exchange is the Toronto Stock Exchange (TSX), which traded a record-breaking $1.7m worth of shares in 2007. The TSX is operated by the newly named TMX Group (previously TSX Group), which recently brought the Montreal Exchange – Canada's financial derivatives exchange – under its umbrella. It also operates TSX Venture Exchange, formed in the last decade due through the merging of the Vancouver, Alberta, and Winnipeg Stock Exchanges.

 Full details of TMX Group exchanges and companies can be found online at www.tsx.com (416 947 4670 or 1 888 873 8392; info@tsx.com).

Communications, science, and technology

In 1901, the future Nobel Prize-winning Italian Guglielmo Marconi received the world's first transatlantic wireless message from a base in St John's, Newfoundland. Since then, Canada has gone on to become a world leader in communications technology, including software, digital and media entertainment, biometrics, and wireless, security, radio, microwave, and satellite technologies. Two of the industry giants, Nortel Networks and Corel, had financial struggles at the beginning of this decade (Nortel's continue today), resulting in severe job losses and causing a drop-off in high-technology exports. However, with 589,000 jobs, and 32,000 companies grouped in regional clusters throughout the country, Canada's ICT industry remains globally significant. More than one-third of private-sector industrial research and development (R&D) goes into the industry – around $5.2 billion annually. Other major R&D fields include aerospace, astrophysics, molecular sciences, and ocean engineering, while emerging fields such as nanotechnology, photonics, and environmental and sustainable development technologies are also receiving focused attention. The Canadian government has set a goal of placing Canada in the top five for international R&D performance by 2010. The National Research Council of Canada (www.nrc.ca) fosters regional, cluster-based technological and economic innovation, with over 20 research institutions and programmes across the country.

Major telecommunications and technology firms include Research in Motion, Novadaq Technologies, BCE Inc, Micromem Technologies Inc, Cognos, Aeromechanical Services Ltd, IBM Canada, CGI Group, ATI Technologies, Ericsson Canada, CAE Inc, Ballard Celestica Inc, Alcatel Canada, Power Systems, Bell Canada, ATI Technologies, and X-Wave.

Mining and nuclear energy

When oil prices spiked with the 1991 Gulf War, new life was breathed into Canada's petrochemical industry. It became one of the most profitable sectors of the economy, particularly in Alberta, and jobs leaped 25% in just five years. Saskatchewan is also oil rich, and Newfoundland has grown significantly in off-shore oil and gas. Canada exports natural gas, crude petroleum and other energy products to the USA, Asia, and elsewhere. The oil crisis of the 1970s led to a boom in exploration and development

Canada is a significant consumer and exporter of electricity, produced from a range of resources including coal, natural gas, uranium and falling water (hydro)

of Canadian oil deposits, which Alberta in particular profited from – the province's oilsands give Canada the second-largest oil reserves of any nation worldwide, after Saudi Arabia. The rise in natural gas prices in the late 1990s meant similar advances for Canada's natural gas industry. Supply has been plentiful in BC and again in Alberta (which supplies around 80% of Canada's natural gas), though some reports suggest it's getting harder to find sufficient supplies to meet North American demand. Gas is conveyed via pipeline both south of the border and eastward to Ontario. Demand, prices, and exports for metals and minerals – having increased dramatically – plunged in late 2008, though a rebound is expected. In lucrative times, mining pays one of the highest average wages of any industry, at over $1,400 a week. Ontario, BC, Quebec, Saskatchewan, and Newfoundland and Labrador have especially rich metal and mineral resources. Canada produces the balance of the global supply of potash (34%, followed by Russia at 17.7%) and uranium (25%, followed by Australia at 19.2%). In line with the international Treaty on the Non-Proliferation of Nuclear Weapons, export of uranium for military purposes or weapons use is prohibited. Sixty minerals, including nickel, cobalt, magnesium, platinum, aluminium, cadmium, zinc, silver, and coal are found in abundance in Canada, and metals, ores and alloys account for about 11% of total exports. Diamond mining in northern regions is anticipated to become extremely profitable in the next few years as world demand outstrips supply. Based on 2006 figures, coal, metal, and mineral mining, and gas and oil extraction accounted for $39.6 billion of GDP, or 3.6%.

 Visit http://mmsd1.mms.nrcan.gc.ca/mmsd/minstatistics_e.asp for the latest statistics and information on minerals and mining, including salary and wage information.

Canada has a large nuclear programme; nuclear generating stations have supplied electricity to the country for more than 40 years. Based on their specific engineering and design, the reactors used are known as CANDU reactors (derived from *Canada, deuterium,* and *uranium*). Since 1960, CANDUs have been sold to South Korea, China, India, Pakistan, and other industrially developing countries around the world. The CANDU is designed to have a very high safety factor, with a double encasement barrier to prevent core damage in the event of a meltdown. Wear, tear and operating issues have plagued many of the older CANDUs in recent years, but the nuclear programme continues to develop and expand: the Generation 3+ Advanced CANDU Reactor (ACR-1000) is now entering the market. (If you're interested in the history and political complexity of CANDU sales, get hold of a copy of *The Politics of CANDU Exports*, Duane Bratt, University of Toronto Press, 2006.)

Canada has a combination of privately and provincially owned mining operations, including Hydro-Québec, Ontario Power Generation, Atomic Energy of Canada Limited, Inco, Falconbridge, Teck Cominco, Goldcorp, De Beers Canada, Petro-Canada, BP Amoco, Nova Chemicals, Shell Canada, Syncrude Canada, Imperial Oil, Dow Chemical Canada, Union Gas, and east-coast petroleum giant Irving.

Forestry, pulp, and paper

Around 18,000 Canadians are employed in the forestry sector, across a range of industries including forestry and logging services, paper, and pulp and wood products.

Canada's abundant forests, seen here from a floatplane in northern BC,
mean forestry has traditionally been a highly profitable industry

The major areas of employment are in Quebec, BC, and Ontario. On average, forestry work pays around $975 per week. Forestry's role in Canada's economy has been declining in recent years, particularly in relation to lumber and paper products, though exports of wood pulp and other wood products are currently holding their ground. Canada still exports more lumber, pulp, and newsprint than any other country, but increasing energy costs, the weak US housing market and global belt-tightening are having a significant impact. Disputes over duties on softwood lumber – most recently in the early 2000s – have also hurt exports to the US market, but a new Softwood Lumber Agreement has since been signed. The Natural Resources Canada website (www.nrcan-rncan.gc.ca) has current information on forestry and other natural-resource industries in Canada. Forestry, logging, and paper companies include Catalyst Paper Corporation, Cascades, Alberta-Pacific Forest Industries, Canfor Pulp, Tembec, and Tolko. Visit the Forest Products Association of Canada (www.fpac. ca) for a full list of their members.

Food products and agriculture

Canada's $86 billion agriculture and agri-foods industry includes farming, food manufacturing, beverage and tobacco production, and wholesale and retail sales. The food industry currently has the highest sales of any manufacturing industry in Canada, at around $74 billion or 12% of the total. Cereal and grain products like corn, wheat, and canola are leading the charge, with oils in demand for food and bio-diesel purposes, and the use of ethanol in gasoline growing throughout North America. Rising costs of food worldwide have also lifted commodity values. Canada's agricultural and fishing exports totalled $34.4 billion in 2007, of which $4.6 billion related to wheat. Along with industrial goods and energy commodities, agriculture comprised half of Canada's exports in that year. More liberal international trading terms, including trading agreements such as NAFTA, have increased Canada's global share in this sector. Organic farming is also increasing, with the organic sector aiming to have a 10% share of the Canadian retail market by 2010.

Employment in the industry currently stands at about 328,000. As is the case around the world, jobs have diminished as operations become increasingly mechanised and agriculture now accounts for less than 2% of the workforce. Almost 40% of Canadian farms grow field crops; other major farming industries are dairy, fruits and vegetables, poultry and eggs, and pigs. The greenhouse and nursery industry is also increasing significantly in terms of coverage. Most agricultural products in Canada are regulated by marketing boards that establish prices payable to farmers and producers. Some also set quotas on how much can be produced.

Many food-processing companies in Canada are offshoots of US firms, and the national breweries – Labatt, Molson, and Sleeman – are all now foreign-owned or foreign-controlled (though many regional and microbreweries are still resolutely Canadian). Major employers include Vincor Canada, Labatt, Molson, Cargill, McCain Foods, Maple Leaf Foods, George Weston, Nestlé Canada, Heinz, Kraft, and Unico.

Forage crops, which include baled hay, are essential both for export and for feeding Canadian livestock

 More information about the food and agriculture sector can be found at the Agriculture and Agri-food Canada website, www.agr.gc.ca.

Retailing

The retail industry employs around 1.8 million Canadians, pushing it just ahead of manufacturing to make it the country's largest employer. Shopping malls, chain stores, and big-box retailers dominate the Canadian retail scene. Malls and local shopping centres are common, and most people get their groceries from supermarket chain stores. The retailing market rebounded from the recession that followed the September 11 World Trade Center attacks in 2001, and low interest rates throughout 2002 and 2003 led to more consumer borrowing (and spending). Though overall in the last year retail sales increased, early 2008 saw flat results and consumers have been spending more cautiously since the middle of that year. The Hudson's Bay Company, known as the Bay, dominates the higher end of the department store market. Budget-oriented department stores like Zellers and Wal-Mart haven't yet

FACT

The food industry currently has the highest sales of any manufacturing industry in Canada, at around $74 billion or 12% of the total.

Large-scale retail and a convenient downtown locale draw the customers at Toronto's Eaton Centre

reached their saturation point, and continue to expand. Outlet stores and members-only warehouse stores (such as the incredibly popular Costco) continue to crop up in Canadian suburbs. Small stores still thrive in cities and small towns, however, with quality and service rewarded by customer loyalty. See *Other shopping*, on p. 164, for more on Canadian retail outlets.

◼ REGIONAL EMPLOYMENT GUIDE

The information in this section provides a brief overview of the major industries and current economic state in each area. Details of provincial business offices and chambers of commerce are also included. These offices publish brochures and journals – many available on request – and can be useful sources of information.

 The government-provided national online job bank allows you to search for employment opportunities by province, and can be accessed at www. jobbank.gc.ca.

Western Canada and the Prairies

British Columbia

Main cities: Vancouver, Victoria (provincial capital)

Regional newspapers:

▪ *Vancouver Sun*: 604 605 2000, 604 605 7381 or 1 800 663 2662; www.vancouversun.com

▪ *Victoria Times Colonist*: 250 380 5211; www.canada.com/victoriatimes colonist

British Columbia Chamber of Commerce: Suite 1201, 750 West Pender Street, Vancouver, BC, V6C 2T8; 604 683 0700; bccc@bcchamber.org; www.bcchamber.org

Provincial business office website: www.smallbusinessbc.ca

Industry and economy: despite some downturn in exports over the last year, particularly in the forestry industry, BC has one of Canada's more prosperous economies. In 2007 it led the country in residential construction investment, interprovincial migration (attracting almost 13,400 people from other provinces) and small business growth. Employment growth was also strong – second highest among the provinces – and 77,200 new jobs were created in the year preceding April 2008. BC is rich in forests, lakes, and mineral deposits, and forestry products, energy products, and industrial goods such as metals comprise its primary international exports. The bulldozers have been out in force as housing tracts and businesses grow – at the least in those areas not being contested under Aboriginal land claims – but a housing slowdown is expected over the next couple of years. After years of a left-wing NDP government, the Liberal Party was elected in 2001. (Though they share the same title, the BC provincial Liberal Party is a different entity to the federal Liberal Party – and leans much more heavily to the right.) Leader Gordon Campbell was quick to slash government jobs and corporate taxes, delighting the business community. BC's small and medium-sized businesses report above-average optimism about their future success though it's unlikely that all will come through 2008's financial squeeze unscathed, (according to Canadian Federation of Independent Business surveys). Small businesses (those with less than 50 employees) represent as much as 98% of all businesses in BC. The province receives more immigrants than any other save Ontario, and around half of all immigrants in investor, entrepreneur and self-employed categories choose to live here.

Main activities: forestry, mining, fishing, tourism, agriculture, manufacturing.

> **FACT**
>
> ▪ BC is rich in forests, lakes, and mineral deposits, and forestry products, energy products, and industrial goods such as metals comprise its primary international exports.

Alberta

Main cities: Calgary, Edmonton (provincial capital)

Regional newspapers:

▪ Calgary Herald: 403 235 7323 or 1 800 372 9219; www.calgaryherald.com

▪ Edmonton Sun: 780 468 0100; www.edmontonsun.com

Alberta Chambers of Commerce: 1808, 10025 – 102A Avenue, Edmonton, AB, T5J 272; 780 425 4180 or 1 800 272 8854; www.abchamber.ca

Provincial business office website: www.services.gov.ab.ca

Industry and economy: Alberta is considered the most business-friendly province in Canada (and also the most conservative in social terms). In recent years it's had one of the best job markets in the nation, and had received the most immigrants from other provinces (particularly Nova Scotia and Newfoundland) for over 10 years, until beaten by BC in 2007. Alberta produces 80% of Canada's natural gas and the lion's share of its petrochemicals, and Albertan oilsands make up the majority of Canadian oil reserves (which in turn comprise 15% of world reserves). Calgary underwent one of its periodic booms when oil prices spiked in 2004; exports to the USA increased and petrochemical companies become more enthusiastic than ever about Alberta's energy potential. With diminished commodity prices, as currently a game of wait and see as to the province's continuing success. Under popular right-wing Progressive Conservative Premier Ralph Klein Alberta cut taxes, doing away with the PST altogether. Ed Stelmach, Klein's successor, received a drubbing for his 'lacklustre' approach, but has survived a subsequent election and is moving forward with healthcare and climate change strategies. To counter the unpredictability of the oil market, Albertans have invested heavily in manufacturing and high-technology industries. Between 1997 and 2007, exports of goods and services more than doubled. Employment expanded by over 500,000 jobs in the same period. Almost two-thirds of Albertans live in one of the two major cities. The Rocky Mountains are a significant tourist attraction (and the monstrous West Edmonton Mall gets its share of visitors as well).

Main activities: cattle, field crops, energy products (oil, gas, coal and petrochemicals), forestry, manufacturing, high-technology research.

Saskatchewan

Main cities: Saskatoon, Regina (provincial capital)
Regional newspaper:
- Regina Leader-Post: 306 781 5211; www.leaderpost.com
- Saskatchewan Chamber of Commerce: 1630–1920 Broad Street, Regina, SK, S4P 3V2; 306 352 2671; www.saskchamber.com

Provincial business office website: www.ei.gov.sk.ca/Business-Development
Industry and economy: Saskatchewan is officially a prairie province, but its landscape includes a preponderance of ranch lands, parkland, and river valleys. Like much of the country, it's rich in natural resources. More than half the province is covered with forest, and along with Newfoundland and Labrador, it's Canada's top crude petroleum producer after Alberta. The commodity surge has overflowed from the neighbouring provinces to the west, causing recent, rapid change, and Saskatchewan – after years of a lagging economy and a declining population – is now on the rise. Exports increased by 13% in just a year, and the population has returned to the one million mark. Farmers are capitalising on the demand for canola and wheat, investors are investing substantially, and the renewed prosperity has boosted housing and auto sales and consumer spending. Tourism is also an important industry, employing around 55,000 people and providing a value to the economy of over $1.5 billion.

Main activities: minerals (potash, coal, uranium), oil and gas, agriculture, manufacturing, processing, technology, tourism.

Manitoba

Main city: Winnipeg
Regional newspaper:
- Winnipeg Free Press: 204 697 7000; www.winnipegfreepress.com
Manitoba Chambers of Commerce: 227 Portage Ave, Winnipeg, MB R3B 2A6; 204

FACT

More than half the province of Saskatchewan is covered with forest, and along with Newfoundland and Labrador, it's Canada's top crude petroleum producer after Alberta.

948 0100 or 1 877 444 5222; mbchamber@mbchamber.mb.ca; www.mbchamber.mb.ca

Provincial business office website: www.gov.mb.ca/ctt

Industry and economy: Manitoba has a diverse and growing economy based around farming, mining, electricity and gas, equipment manufacturing, transportation, and forestry. The beef market crashed in 2003 when a BSE-infected cow was discovered, and livestock producers have continued to suffer from high feed prices, and – in the case of hog farmers – restrictions on production. However, those same high crop prices meant high income from wheat, grain, and oilseeds, and the agri-food' industry brought Manitoba $3.3 billion in international exports over 2007 (as with many commodities, prices hovered lower in late 2008). Investment in information technology, health technology and apparel is actively encouraged to reduce reliance on natural resources. Financial services employ around 20,000 people, and manufacturing is gaining strength, particularly in relation to agricultural and construction machinery. Manitoba also supports the largest aerospace industry in Western Canada, and is a major transportation centre, providing railroad access to the north and to the United States. Media is big business in Manitoba – Winnipeg-based media giant CanWest now owns most of the newspapers in Canada, as well as Global Television, E! and numerous overseas media operations. Winnipeg, home to 60% of the province's residents, is a lively cultural centre.

Main activities: agriculture, minerals and metals, hydroelectricity, manufacturing, forestry.

Central Canada

Ontario

Main cities: Toronto (provincial capital), Ottawa

Regional Newspaper: Toronto Star: 416 367 4500 or 1 800 268 9213; www.thestar.com

Ontario Chamber of Commerce: 180 Dundas Street West, Suite 505, Toronto, ON M5G 1Z8; 416 482 5222; info@occ.on.ca; www.occ.on.ca

Provincial business office website: www.sbe.gov.on.ca

Industry and economy: with over 12 million residents, Ontario is Canada's most populous province and accounts for almost 40% of the country's GDP. Over $177 billion worth of merchandise was exported internationally in 2007. The right-wing Progressive Conservative party was routed by the Liberal Party, and leader Dalton McGuinty, in 2003. The pro-business climate remains, but McGuinty reversed some of the cuts to education and social services that characterised the Tory era. Manufacturing in Ontario – particularly of cars, machinery, electronics, wood products, and food – accounts for almost 48% of the Canadian total. The province is the nation's ICT leader, with major ICT clusters in Ottawa, Waterloo, and the GTA. Niagara Falls – a key tourist attraction – is also a bountiful source of hydro-electricity. Ontario is ideally placed; southern Ontario's industrial centre is within a day's drive of nearly half the US consumer market. Ontario has historically been Canada's most powerful province (though the others grit their teeth at the notion), but it's heavily dependant on the export market. As 85% of exports go to the USA, the rising Canadian dollar and slumping US economy has been keenly felt, particularly in

FACT

Ontario has historically been Canada's most powerful province (though the others grit their teeth at the notion), but it's heavily dependant on the export market.

While other grain crops are more widely grown in the Prairies, field corn is the main contender in Ontario and Quebec: as much as 96% of the Canadian total is grown in these provinces

relation to housing construction and auto manufacturing. Though declining exports are anticipated over the next few years, opportunities – and the straightened global economy is punishing surplus - proud Ontario into a 2008–2009 deficit – there are potential for sales of machinery, equipment and auto parts to countries such as Mexico, China, Russia, and the Ukraine. Around 55% of immigrants to Canada settle in Ontario.

Main activities: financial services, manufacturing, automotive, technology, agriculture, food processing, technology, life sciences, plastics and chemicals, call centres, tourism.

Quebec

Main cities: Montreal, Quebec City (provincial capital)

Regional newspapers:

■ *The Gazette* (Montreal): 514 987 2222; www.montrealgazette.com

■ *Le Journal de Montréal*: 514 521 4545; www.journaldemontreal.com

■ *La Presse*: 514 285 7272; www.cyberpresse.ca

Chambre de Commerce du Québec: 17, rue Saint-Louis, Québec, QC, G1R 3Y8 (418 692 3853; info@ccquebec.ca; www.ccquebec.ca

Provincial business office website: www.entreprises.gouv.qc.ca

Industry and economy: Quebec has a strong international reputation for research and high technology, is Canada's primary producer of hydroelectricity, and supplies around 7% of the world's aluminium. Natural resources such as minerals, metals and timber contribute significantly to the province's diverse economy, and manufacturing is vital, representing 20% of GDP. The service sector contributes as much as 70%. Quebec, like Ontario, is dependent on US trade, and weak US market – compounded by the strong Canadian dollar of pre-fiscal-crisis times – has caused damage to manufacturing and forestry. Aeronautical manufacturing is one of the province's specialities, however, and exports of helicopters, large passenger aircrafts, and parts are expected to increase to meet global demand. Pulp exports are also forecast to grow, but production of newsprint and paper is falling as newspapers and other media (particularly in the United States) move online. ICT has boomed in recent years (though exports to the US are also feeling the pinch) and tourism has increased. Both major cities are Meccas for art and culture lovers, and Quebec City's 400th anniversary (celebrated throughout 2008) has been internationally promoted. The province's many ski resorts are also a major tourist attraction. Premier Jean Charest and the Quebec Liberal Party lead the provincial government, and Charest's support for federalism (as opposed to separatism – see p. 330) has kept the economy relatively stable.

Main activities: manufacturing, aerospace, mining, forestry, agriculture, ICT, hydroelectricity, transportation, tourism.

Atlantic Canada

Newfoundland and Labrador, Nova Scotia, New Brunswick, Prince Edward Island

Respective capital cities: St John's, Halifax, Fredericton (though Moncton and Saint John – not to be confused with St John's – are larger), Charlottetown

Regional newspapers:

- *St. John's Telegram*: 709 364 6300; www.thetelegram.com
- *Halifax Chronicle-Herald*: 902 426 2811; www.thechronicleherald.ca
- *New Brunswick Telegraph Journal*: 506 633 5599; www.telegraphjournal.com
- *The Guardian* (Charlottetown): 902 629 6000; www.theguardian.pe.ca

Atlantic Provinces Chambers of Commerce: 236 St. George Street, Suite 110, Moncton, NB, E1C 1W1; 506 857 3980; www.apcc.ca

Provincial business websites: www.gov.nl.ca/doingbusiness; www.novascotia business.com; www.newbrunswick.ca; www.cbsc.org/pe

Industry and economy: Newfoundland and Labrador's economy was hard hit by a moratorium on cod fishing in 1992, that led to an all-out ban (though strictly regulated fishing – mostly recreational – has been permitted again since mid-2008). The province's fortunes have been turning of late, with 9.1% growth in GDP posted in 2007 – a far greater proportion than any other province, and almost all thanks to mining and oil and gas extraction. Fishing is still a key part of the agri-food industry for the four provinces of eastern Canada, with lobster, sea scallops, snow crab, and cultivated mussels chief among the seafood products. PEI is also a major potato-producing region, exporting both fresh vegetables and frozen french fries. The USA is Atlantic Canada's primary trading partner, however, and its weakened dollar creates a potentially risky export situation. Energy products represent the greatest export value for the provinces, with Nova Scotia's Sable Island facility feeding natural-gas demand, Newfoundland and Labrador pumping out crude oil, and New Brunswick producing liquefied natural gas through a new Irving terminal (Irving being the

Opportunities in Saint John, New Brunswick

Saint John is on the verge of an economic boom that carries the opportunity to transform not only the community but the entire province. Current and proposed development projects project an economic gain of up to $44 billion – a significant opportunity for such a small province. Lessons from the experiences of other regions and advanced planning will serve to avoid many of the pitfalls inherent in a change of this magnitude. The vast majority of this development is slated to occur in Saint John, resulting in an economic outlook that is incredibly positive, and a desperate need to ensure that there are enough skilled workers available to fill employment positions currently and in the future.

There are four strategic growth sectors in the region: tourism, healthcare, ICT and energy. These offer a diverse range of employment opportunities that will allow you work on your terms.

Taking advantage of Saint John's unique natural beauty and history, the **tourism** sector is vibrant and growing. A recognised cruise ship destination, the city received 83 port calls in 2008, injecting over $19 billion into the local economy. The industry is shifting to include more action and experience-oriented tourism options, expanding employment opportunities beyond traditional hospitality roles to adventure-recreation and eco-tourism operators. Saint John's culinary sector is also growing and with expanding cultural diversity, options for professionals in this specialty are more varied than ever before.

Healthcare is important to our community and is one of Saint John's strategic growth sectors. The Saint John Regional Hospital – the region's primary center for acute care – is one of only two accredited tertiary trauma centers in Atlantic Canada. The facility houses a nucleus of expertise in cardiac surgery, cardiology services, neurosciences, paediatric and Adult Oncology, and many other specialties. Saint John is also home to an integrated medical system with a large community healthcare centre located in the heart of the city, as well as outreach medical support. With the range of services and care provided in the region, your specialty is probably found here.

The province of New Brunswick is the recognised innovator of **Information and communication technologies** in Canada, and Saint John is home to many of the province's corporate head offices and small start-up firms. With exceptional business start-up support and incubator programmes available in the community, a number of entrepreneurs are keenly looking for people with a creative flair that can provide technical solutions to clients all over the world. The sector is growing and is continually on the hunt for talented and skilled professionals – a recent study by the local ICT association projects that over 76% of new employment in the province will be located in Saint John.

Provided by expert contributor

petroleum giant that dominates the province). Manufacturing of motor vehicles, parts and transportation equipment – particularly for the Aerospace industry – plays a respectable role in the export economy, and forestry also figures. Though forestry exports declined in New Brunswick in 2007, Nova Scotia actually saw strong growth in this industry.

Main activities: fishing, agriculture, oil and gas, metals, minerals, tourism, manufacturing.

Three bright boats on Grand Manan Island, New Brunswick, undergo preparations for another season's fishing

Northern Canada

Yukon, Northwest Territories, Nunavut

Respective capital cities: Whitehorse, Yellowknife, Iqaluit

Regional newspapers:

- *Whitehorse Daily Star*: 867 668 2002; www.whitehorsestar.com
- *Yellowknifer*: 867 873 4031; www.nnsl.com
- *Nunatsiaq News*: 867 979 5357; www.nunatsiaq.com

Whitehorse Chamber of Commerce: Suite 101–302 Steele Street, Whitehorse, YK Y1A 2C5; 867 667 7545; www.whitehorsechamber.com

NWT Chamber of Commerce: 3rd floor 4921–49th Street (NWT Commerce Place), Yellowknife, NT X1A 3S5; 867 920 9505; admin@nwtchamber.com; www.nwtchamber.com

Iqaluit Chamber of Commerce: PO Box 1107, Iqaluit, NU X0A 0H0; 867 979 4999; board@icoc.nu.ca; www.icoc.nu.ca

Provincial business websites: www.canadabusiness.ca/yukon; www.gov.nt.ca/agendas/business; www.canadabusiness.ca/nunavut

Industry and economy: industry in Canada's three territories is largely defined by mining. Diamond, gold, and copper mining have caused the economy in these

A loaded truck makes its way across the horizon at the Diavik Diamond Mine in the Northwest Territories

regions to surge, with both Nunavut and the Northwest Territories experiencing phenomenal economic growth of around 13% in 2007. These two territories are home to all of Canada's four diamond mines. The Yukon, which capitalises on gold and copper mining, also experienced solid growth, though at a more sedate 4%. Other industries include construction – particularly in relation to mining – and tourism, which has increased the relevance (and size) of the service industry. Forestry also has some relevance in the Yukon, while Inuit art plays an important part in Nunavut's economy and culture. The value of the arts and crafts industry in Nunavut is estimated at around $20m per year. Traditional hunting, trapping, and fur and subsistence harvesting are valued at up to $50m, and form an essential part of the livelihood of the Aboriginal peoples in many regions.

Main activities: mining (diamond, gold, copper), oil and gas, forestry, art, tourism, hunting and harvesting.

◤ DIRECTORY OF MAJOR EMPLOYERS

This directory lists a handful of the main employers in some of Canada's major industries. Industry Canada maintains a searchable database, Canadian Company Capabilities, at www.ic.gc.ca/epic/site/ccc-rec.nsf/en/home. While the aim of the database is to allow companies to find suitable suppliers, it's also a useful tool for finding out what businesses are available in different industry areas. The database contains around 60,000 Canadian businesses and can be searched by name or by category.

Accounting and finance

Ernst & Young: 416 864 1234 (Canadian head office); www.ey.com/global/content.nsf/Canada/Home
KPMG LLP: 613 212 5764 (Ottawa office); www.kpmg.ca
Deloitte & Touche LLP: 416 874 3874 or 416 874 3830 (national offices); www.deloitte.com
PriceWaterhouseCoopers: 416 863 1133 (Canadian head office); www.pwc.com/ca
CIBC Wood Gundy: 1 800 563 3193; www.woodgundy.com
Manulife Financial: 416 926 3000; www.manulife.ca
Fidelity Investments Canada: 1 800 263 4077; www.fidelity.ca

Agriculture and forestry

BC Public Service: 250 387 0518; www.employment.gov.bc.ca
Pioneer Hi-Bred Ltd: 519 352 6350 or 1 800 265 9435; www.pioneer.com/Canada
Canfor Pulp Ltd Partnership: 604 661 5241; www.canforpulp.com
Kruger Inc.: 514 737 1131; www.kruger.com
Cargill Ltd: 204 947 0141; www.cargill.ca

Pioneer Grain Company, Ltd: 306 751 7700; www.pioneergrain.ca
Canadian Wheat Board: 204 983 0239; www.cwb.ca

Banking

TD Bank Financial Group (TD Canada Trust): 1 866 222 3456 or 1 800 222 34561 (international); www.tdcanadatrust.com
BMO Bank of Montreal: 416 286-9992 or 1 877 225 5266; www.bmo.com
Canadian Western Bank: 780 423 8888; www.cwbank.com
RBC Royal Bank: 506 864 2275 (international collect) or 1 800 769 2511; www.royalbank.com
Scotiabank: 416 701 7200 or 1 800 472 6842; www.scotiabank.com
CIBC: 1 800 465 2422, 1 800 872 24221 (toll free from select countries) or 902 420 2422; www.cibc.com

Communications and public relations

Hill And Knowlton Canada: 416 413 4622; www.hillandknowlton.ca
MacLaren McCann Canada Inc: 416 594 6000; www.maclaren.com
Thomson Reuters: 416 360 8700; http://careers.thomsonreuters.com
Fleishman-Hillard Canada: 416 214 0701; www.fleishman.ca
National Public Relations: 514 843 2343; www.national.ca
Environics Communications: 416 920 9000; www.environicspr.com
PHD Canada: 416 922 0217; www.phdca.com

Energy

Atomic Energy of Canada Limited (AECL): 905 823 9040 or 1 866 513 2325; www.aecl.ca
BC Hydro and Power Authority: 604 224 9376 or 1 800 224 9376; www.bchydro.com
EnCana Corp: 403 645 2000; www.encana.com
Suncor Energy: 403 269 8100 or 1 866 786 2671; www.suncor.com
Petro-Canada: 647 837 2471 or 1 800 668 0220; www.petro-canada.ca
Shell Canada Ltd: 403 691 3111 or 1 800 661 1600; www.shell.ca
BP Canada Energy: 403 233 1313; www.bp.com

Food and beverage production

Campbell Company of Canada: 416 251 1131 or 1 800 410 7687; www.campbellsoup.ca
George Weston Ltd: 416 922 2500; www.weston.ca
Maple Leaf Foods Inc.: 1 800 268 3708; www.mapleleaf.com
McCain Foods Ltd: 506 392 5541; www.mccain.com
Molson Canada: www.molson.com
Vincor International Inc.: 905 564 6900 or 1 800 265 9463; www.vincorinternational.com
Parmalat Canada: 1 800 563 1515; www.parmalat.ca

Hospitality and tourism

Fairmont Hotels and Resorts: 416 874 2600; www.fairmont.com
Four Seasons Hotels and Resorts: 416 449 1750; www.fourseasons.com
Intrawest: 604 669 9777; www.intrawest.com
Sandman Hotels, Inns and Suites: 604 730 6600; www.sandmanhotels.com
G.A.P Adventures: 416 260 0999 or 1 800 708 7761; www.gapadventures.com
Pacrim Hospitality Services: 902 404 7474; www.pacrimhospitality.com

Information and communications technology (ICT)

Bell Aliant: www.bell.aliant.ca
Corel Corporation: 613 728 8200; www.corel.com
CGI: 514 841 3200; www.cgi.ca
Research in Motion: 519 888 7465; www.rim.net
Nortel Networks: 905 863 7000 or 1 800 466 7835; www.nortel.com
Celestica: 416 448 5800 or 1 888 899 9998; www.celestica.com
EDS Canada: 416 814 4500 or 1 800 814 9038; www.eds.com/Canada
GE Canada: 905 858 5100; www.ge.com/ca
Primus Telecommunications Canada Inc.: 416 236 3636; www.primus.ca
Microsoft Canada: 1 877 568 2495; www.microsoft.com/canada

Insurance

Medavie Blue Cross: 1 800 355 9133 (Ontario office); www.medavie.bluecross.ca
Belair Direct: 613 228 6400 or 1 888 280 9111 (Ottawa branch); www.belairdirect.com
Chubb Insurance Company: 416 863 0550; www.chubbinsurance.ca
AXA Canada Inc.: 514 282 1914 (head office); www.axa.ca
The Canada Life Assurance Company: 416 597 6981 or 1 888 252 1847 (head office); www.canadalife.com
State Farm: 905 750 4717 or 1 866 910 6222 (careers); www.statefarm.com
Manulife Financial: 416 926 3000; www.manulife.ca

Law

Borden Ladner Gervais: 416 367 6000; www.blgcanada.com
Gowling Lafleur Henderson: 416 862 7525; www.gowlings.com
McCarthy Tétrault: 416 362 1812; www.mccarthy.ca
Fasken Martineau: 416 366 8381 or 1 800 268 8424; www.fasken.com
Fraser Milner Casgrain: 416 863 4511; www.fmc-law.com
Blakes: 416 863 2400; www.blakes.com

Manufacturing

Bombardier Inc.: 514 335 9511; www.bombardier.com
Toyota Motor Manufacturing Canada Inc.: 519 653 1111; www.toyota.ca/tmmc

Magna International Inc.: 905 726 2462; www.magna.com
Wescast Industries Inc.: 519 750 0000; www.wescast.com
Raydan Manufacturing Inc.: 780 955 2859 or 1 888 472 9326;
www.raydanmfg.com

Mining and metals

Barrick Gold Corporation: 416 861 9911; www.barrick.com
Wardrop Engineering Inc.: 403 514 6908 or 1 877 987 3211; www.wardrop.com
Vale Inco: 416 361 7511; www.inco.com
Hatch: 905 855 7600; www.hatch.ca
US Steel Canada: 905 528 2511 or 1 800 263 9305; www.stelco.com

Pharmaceuticals

Nycomed Canada Inc.: 905 469 9333 or 1 888 367 3331; www.altanapharma.ca
AstraZeneca: 905 277 7111 or 1 800 565 5877; www.astrazeneca.ca
Bioniche Life Sciences Inc: 613 966 8058 or 1 800 265 5464; www.bioniche.com
Cangene: www.cangene.com
Apotex Inc.: 1 800 268 4623; www.apotex.com/ca

Retail

HBC (The Bay, Zellers, Home Outfitters, Fields): 1 866 746 7422; www.hbc.com
Canadian Tire Corp. Ltd: 1 800 387 8803 (Customer Relations);
careers@cantire.com; www.canadiantire.ca
Sears Canada Inc.: 416 362 1711; www.sears.ca
Winners Merchants International LP: 905 405 8000; www.winners.ca

Transportation

Air Canada: 514 422 5000; www.aircanada.ca
WestJet: 1 888 293 7853; www.westjet.com
Air Transat: 514 636 3630 or 1 877 872 6728; www.airtransat.com
Greyhound Canada: www.greyhound.ca
VIA Rail Canada Inc.: 514 871 6000; www.viarail.ca

■ STARTING A BUSINESS

How to start a business in Canada

Canadian immigration policy encourages foreign entrepreneurs to begin businesses in Canada. Canadian citizens and landed immigrants alike have access to a variety of government incentives, loans, grants, and counsellors, and with a resilient economy and ever-increasing access to US and Mexican markets, Canada offers great opportunities for skilled entrepreneurs. The rate of failure is high, however, and management skills, market research, and a viable service or product are crucial to success. The high level of government assistance available to new businesses can be accompanied by an equally high level of bureaucracy. If you intend to make use of government programmes, be aware that you'll normally be subject to some kind of review process, and you may have to maintain bookkeeping in line with government requirements. High taxation is also a factor for Canadian business owners, and hiring an experienced tax accountant is recommended.

People who are admitted to Canada under the Business Immigration Program (as entrepreneurs, investors or self-employed immigrants) will already have business experience in their own country. If you're in the entrepreneur category you'll be expected to establish your company relatively quickly; requirements for investors and self-employed business people differ – see p. 53 for details. However, working for someone else is usually the best way to gain experience and knowledge about the Canadian market and business environment. It's often easier to arrange financing, choose a location and create a successful business if you've worked in Canada first.

A local business opens its doors to customers

Procedures involved in starting a new business

As a prospective business owner you have the option of buying an established business, acquiring a franchise or starting a company entirely from scratch. The advantages of taking over an existing business or franchise are tempting: less bureaucracy, a tested market, and an established product or service. However, the purchase price of an established business is often prohibitively high, and companies may not be as financially viable as they appear. Many purchasers find it difficult or impossible to recoup their investment. For information about purchasing a business see *Franchising*, p. 286.

Preparation from scratch

Exhaustive research is crucial before you start taking steps towards setting up a business in Canada. One of the most valuable resources is the data published by Statistics Canada (www.statcan.ca). Studies are frequently updated and cover virtually all areas of Canadian demographics. Most information is available online and at public libraries. While their website takes a little navigating, it provides a phenomenal amount of material. You can also contact them by phone, email or mail (see details under *Useful contacts*, below). Statistics Canada has hundreds of publications that are available free (and many more that can be purchased) including the convenient and annually updated *Market Research Handbook* ($134), a collection of statistics seemingly tailor-made for prospective entrepreneurs. Other market information can be obtained from provincial business offices, publications, chambers of commerce, and business associations.

Preparation needs to go further than just finding a market for your product or service. Living in Canada, working with Canadians, and joining professional associations or service clubs can equip you with invaluable knowledge, contacts, and allies. The Business Development Bank of Canada (www.bdc.ca) offers a wealth of information and resources on starting a business, including small-business seminars and a range of business tools such as do-it-yourself business plans.

WEBSITES FOR BUSINESS PLANNING

- Canada Business: Services for entrepreneurs – www.canadabusiness.ca. Invaluable government site that functions as an access point for business owners and entrepreneurs looking to start out. Provincial sites can be accessed through the national site. Provides information on government services and programmes, an interactive business planner and links to provincial and covers financing, taxes, human resources, importing and exporting, research and statistics, government tenders, innovation, regulations, and more. (Can also be contacted by phone on 1 888 576 4444, or in person – see website for details.)
- Business Start-Up Assistant – www.bsa.canadabusiness.ca. Provided by Canada Business (above), this is another essential site, with step-by-step information, articles, and research on starting a business in each Canadian province.
- Industry Canada – www.strategis.ic.gc.ca. Useful information and links relating to starting or investing in a business, including current investment climate and opportunities, small business advice, business information by sector; company information, financing, development, and regulations.
- Paperwork Burden Reduction Initiative – www.reducingpaperburden.gc.ca. Federal government site that lets business owners know about efforts to reduce paperwork and red tape involved with government regulation compliance.
- Canada Small Business Financing Program – www.ic.gc.ca/epic/site/csbfp-pfpec.nsf/en/home. Maintained by Industry Canada, this site provides information on eligibility for loans, interest rates and how to apply, plus links to research materials, lenders, and more.

Provincial business offices and chambers of commerce are listed by province in the *Regional Employment Guide,* beginning on p. 266. You can also access Canada Business's provincial websites through the national site (see boxed text for details), spend some time exploring online business resources (ditto), and check the *Useful contacts* on p. 54 for business immigrants for a couple of additional sources.

◼ Useful contacts

Canadian Chamber of Commerce: 613 238 4000; info@chamber.ca;
www.chamber.ca
Retail Council of Canada: 416 922 6678 or 1 888 373 8245; www.retailcouncil.org
Canadian Association of Family Enterprise (CAFE): 1 866 849 0099;
office@cafecanada.ca; www.cafecanada.ca
Canadian Federation of Independent Business: 613 235 2373
(Ottawa office); cfib@cfib.ca; www.cfib.ca
Statistics Canada: 613 951 8116 or 1 800 263 1136; infostats@statcan.ca;
www.statcan.ca (mail can be directed to 100 Tunney's Pasture Driveway,
Ottawa, ON, K1A 0T6)
Business Development Bank of Canada: 613 995 0234 (Ottawa office) or
1 877 232 2269; www.bdc.ca

TIP

◼ The Business Development Bank of Canada (www.bdc.ca, see Useful contacts below) offers a wealth of information and resources on starting a business, including small-business seminars and a range of business tools.

Accountants

Though specific regulations for accountancy practice vary between provinces, in most cases accountants have to be a member of one of Canada's three major professional accounting associations. Depending on which of these he or she belongs to, an accountant is designated as a Chartered Accountant (CA), Certified General Accountant (CGA) or Certified Management Accountant (CMA). These professions are governed by provincial statutes, and members have to have passed relevant exams. You can contact the associations for assistance in finding a qualified accountant – see *Finance and banking*, p. 275, for contact details – or look under *Accountancy* in your local Yellow Pages (or online at www.yellowpages.ca). Major accountancy firms in Canada such as PriceWaterhouseCoopers, Deloitte & Touche and KPMG can provide advice and relevant publications to business people (details are listed under Accounting and finance, p. 275).

Choosing a location

Virtually every lifestyle, culture, and community – from rural to large city – can be found in Canada, and the decision on where to settle is normally based on personal preference and the type of business you plan to run. Different provinces have different employment and industry needs and different 'in-demand' fields, and many offer programmes for business people through the Provincial Nominee Program (see p. 54 for further details on this). Some provinces may be more particular than others about the types of businesses they'll encourage, and you should really only consider establishing a business in Quebec if you're prepared to operate in French. Statistics Canada publishes a vast amount of demographic information that can help you analyse prospective areas. The official government or immigration websites for each province and territory include information about the business environment and lifestyle opportunities in that part of the country:

◼ **Alberta:** www.albertacanada.com
◼ **British Columbia:** www.welcomebc.ca

- **Manitoba:** www.gov.mb.ca
- **New Brunswick:** www.gnb.ca/immigration
- **Newfoundland and Labrador:** www.hrle.gov.nl.ca/hrle/immigration
- **Nova Scotia:** www.novascotiaimmigration.com
- **Northwest Territories:** www.gov.nt.ca
- **Nunavut:** www.gov.nu.ca
- **Ontario:** www.ontarioimmigration.ca
- **Prince Edward Island:** www.gov.pe.ca/immigration
- **Quebec:** www.immigration-quebec.gouv.qc.ca
- **Saskatchewan:** www.immigrationsask.gov.sk.ca
- **Yukon Territory:** www.immigration.gov.yk.ca

TIP

Statistics Canada publishes a vast amount of demographic information that can help you analyse prospective areas.

Raising finances

When raising finances for a new business, it's a good idea to consult both government and commercial sources. Explore the websites on p. 362 to make sure you consider all the available options. Most commercial banks are cautious about lending money, but if you have a sound business background, a good idea and a clearly thought-out concept, you should eventually be able to obtain a loan to start your company, and a line of credit to help you run things on a day-to-day level. Make sure you look carefully at the conditions of any loan you're considering – collateral and repayment terms can be just as important as interest rates. The federal government operates the Canada Small Business Financing (CSBF) programme – listed in the text box on p. 280 – which is designed to help you get a bank loan of up to $250,000 by guaranteeing 85% of the amount. You choose which bank or financial institution you wish to apply to, and the loan, if granted, must be used towards fixed assets such as company premises and equipment.

 Details of the Canada Small Business Financing programme, including how to apply, are available at www.ic.gc.ca/epic/site/csbfp-pfpec.nsf/en/home. You can also phone 613 954 5540 or send an email via the website.

Many provinces and regional areas offer business incentives as well, such as interest-free, forgivable or guaranteed loans (see *Regional business offices and incentives* for further details). The Small Business Funding Centre (1 800 658 9792; www.grants-loans.org) and The Business Guide to Government Programs (754 8433 or 1 877 754 843; email info@businessguide.net; www.businessguide.net) are fee-based, independent operations aimed at helping entrepreneurs to obtain appropriate government financing for their business purposes, through loans or grants. The annual *Canadian Subsidy Directory* (Canadian Business Publications: 1 866 322 3376; www.mgpublishing.net) lists over 3,200 grants, loans, and programmes available to businesses and individuals. A CD-ROM or PDF of the directory is available for $69.95; the print version (with free CD-ROM) is $149.95. A separate edition, *Annuaire des subventions au Québec*, provides information for Quebec.

Regional business offices and incentives

Provincial chambers of commerce and small business offices provide information, guides, and research material for potential business owners, as well as information on provincial assistance and incentive programmes for small businesses. (Their contact details can be found in the Regional Employment Guide on p. 266.) Personal assistance and advisory services are generally available as well, either by phone or through face-to-face meetings. These organisations can also give you more information about which types of businesses are needed in a particular province, and which are already over represented. The range of finance and assistance options varies between provinces and is quite extensive. The Business Start-Up Assistant (www.bsa.canadabusiness.ca) provides a list of some – select Finance from the home page, then choose your province. A link to Industry Canada's Sources of Financing webpage, which allows you to search for either private-sector or government assistance, is provided here as well. Community business development programmes also exist in many areas, with the aim of supporting economic development on a local level by helping to create businesses and jobs in rural or smaller urban regions. These include Community Futures Programs in Ontario, Quebec, and Western Canada, and Community Business Development Corporations (CBDC) in the Atlantic Provinces (you can explore the CBDC website at www.cbdc.ca). Details and links to all programmes can be found on the Canada Business website under *Government Programs and Services* – select either *Starting a Business* or *Financing* to bring up the listing.

Business structures

There are four main business structures in Canada, though a number of variations and additional structures also exist. Fiscal or legal advisers can help you decide which form is right for you:

- **Sole proprietorship:** In a sole proprietorship, the business is registered in your own name, and business and personal income are considered to be one and the same. You indicate company profits and expenses on your personal tax return. Sole proprietorships are subject to relatively few formalities and are easily arranged. If business thrives, you can choose to re-register as an incorporated company. The major disadvantage of sole proprietorship is that you're personally liable for any debts incured by your business. Also, as you're essentially self-employed, you're not eligible for unemployment benefits if your business fails. In most provinces you need to register your business if you run it under any business name other than your own full name.

- **Partnership:** In a partnership, you and one or more other people operate a business together. Again, your share of profits and business costs are included on your personal tax return, and you and your partners are liable for any debts. If the business fails you won't be eligible for unemployment benefits, but it's possible to incorporate your company if it becomes very successful. Business partnerships can exist without a written contract, but it's always advisable to have a lawyer draw up the terms of the agreement to protect the parties involved.

- **Corporation:** This is the most formal business structure, and the most popular option in Canada. As a separate legal entity it gives business owners – the shareholders – freedom from personal liability, but it is heavily regulated and requires considerable record keeping and its own business tax return. There are various types of corporations, and businesses can be incorporated federally or provincially. Incorporated companies often have access to more government incentive programmes, and banks and other financiers may be more likely to finance start-up loans.

- **Cooperative:** This is a type of corporation that aims to fulfil the common needs of a group of owners, and is not primarily driven by profit. It functions on a democratic, one-person-one-vote basis, regardless of the amount of capital each member invests (though individual liability is limited to this amount), and can be consumer, producer or worker based, depending on the needs of the members. Co-ops are normally community-oriented ventures and have an ethos of social responsibility.

You can find out more about each type of business structure from Canada Business (see p. 362 for website and contact details). The Invest in Canada website (www.investincanada.gc.ca) also provides information, in its *Establish a business* section.

◼ Useful business publications

Canadian Small Business Kit for Dummies, Margaret Kerr and JoAnn Kurtz, John Wiley & Sons, 2007

A café in Moose Jaw, Saskatchewan makes the most of its town's distinct name in its signage, and offers customers traditional fare. Opening a café is a promising business venture in Canada – even better if you manage to sell your native food.

The Canadian Small Business Survival Guide, Benj Gallander, Dundurn Group, 2002
The Complete Canadian Small Business Guide (Third Edition), Douglas Gray and Diana Gray, Mcgraw-Hill, 2000
How to Start a Small Business in Canada, Tariq Nadeem, Self-Help Publishers, 2004
Starting a Successful Business in Canada, International Self-Counsel Press, 2004

◼ IDEAS FOR BUSINESSES

As any good entrepreneur knows, location, local demographics, and current trends determine what types of businesses or services will be successful. Canada Business (www.canadabusiness.gc.ca) provides a series of detailed online guides to starting common types of businesses, such as alternative healthcare services, hair and beauty salons, childcare centres, bed-and-breakfasts, restaurants and convenience stores. The guides include detailed industry overviews and outline the relevant regulations and licensing requirements. The Canadian Franchise Association sells a relevant range of publications through its online bookstore at www.cfa.ca including guides for specific business fields. Self-Counsel Press publishes a huge range of business books, including a 'Buy to Run' series tailor-made for those just starting out – go to www.self-counsel.com/ca and browse under *Business Books*, or phone 604 986 3366 or 1 800 663 3007.

JUST TO GET YOU STARTED...

Options for small businesses are just about endless. Here are a few fields that look promising right now:

- **Financial Services:** With deregulation of the financial industry, this field has opened up opportunities for financial service providers. The growing aging population means that many people are turning to advisors to plan and invest for their retirement. If you have knowledge of international and Canadian markets you may be able to find a market as an independent advisor, or proprietor of a small consulting business.

- **Restaurants:** Canadians eat out often, and while most major cities have numerous and varied restaurants, smaller cities and towns often welcome a new place to eat that either fills a gap or expands the culinary horizon. Chinese and Indian restaurants are relatively widespread now, but many ethnic foods – including traditional English fare – are under-represented on the local level.

- **Information and communication technology (ICT):** Canada is a major player in the international telecommunications, technology and computer market. New businesses could concentrate on providing services, web design and merchandise to companies as they continue to update and computerise their infrastructure, or on technological or programming innovations.

Franchising

Franchising is quite popular in Canada, with new chains expanding and old chains changing owners fairly regularly. Purchasing a franchise can be an attractive option for recent immigrants, as the company will already have an established structure, customer base, reputation, and support staff. If you can get your hands on a Tim Hortons store, for example, you'll have a steady stream of customers from day one. Franchising can involve buying the right to distribute a product, but more often it's based on purchasing a business that sells pre-set products or services, such as a fast food restaurant, weight-loss clinic or travel agency. Many pro-franchise sources promote franchises as having much lower failure rates than independent businesses, though other reports dispute the size of the gap. While your franchise may not fail, it won't always prove lucrative either: high start-up fees and the cost of overheads, equipment, training, and advertising need to be considered and allowed for. As a franchisee you'll also have to turn over a percentage of sales to the franchiser on an ongoing basis, as royalties. The Business Startup Assistant provides guides on franchising and links to other useful sources – go to www.bsa.canadabusiness.ca, then select *Franchising* from the list of topics. The Canadian Franchise Association (CFA) (416 695 2896 or 1 800 665 4232; www.cfa.ca) is another useful and detailed resource. The *CFA Information Kit* is available through their online bookstore. Websites listing Canadian franchise opportunities include Occasion Franchise.ca at www.canada.occasionfranchise.ca (you can also phone 1 819 840 8017 or email contact@occasionfranchise.com), and BeTheBoss.ca at www.betheboss.ca. The publications listed at the end of this section may also be helpful.

 Thoroughly research the background and legitimacy of any franchise operation you're considering buying into before committing yourself. You can check the company's record with the Better Business Bureau (http://bbb.org).

Importers and exporters

The Canadian government's export website (www.exportsource.ca), operated by Team Canada Inc (TCI) provides practical information, services, workshops, and step-by-step guides to help Canadian businesses export their goods and services internationally. TCI can also be contacted by phone through Canada Business on 1 888 576 4444 (Canada only). The equivalent services for importers are available at www.importsource.ca or by calling 1888 811 1119. Email queries for each can be sent through their respective websites. Export Development Canada (see below) offers assistance to small and medium-sized businesses in managing and financing international export and trade.

▪ Useful export and import contacts

Export Development Canada: 613 598 2500 or 1 866 283 2957; www.edc.ca
Canadian Manufacturers and Exporters: 613 238 8888; www.cme-mec.ca
Canadian Association of Importers and Exporters: 416 595 5333; info@iecanada.com; www.importers.ca
Canada Europa (Mission of Canada to the European Union): +322 741 06060 (Brussels); breu@international.gc.ca; www.dfait-maeci.gc.ca/canadaeuropa/EU/embassy2-en.asp
Australian Trade Commission: 416 323 3909; www.australiantrade.ca

▪ Useful franchise, export, and import publications

Be Your Own Boss: *The Insider's Guide to Buying a Small Business or Franchise in Canada*, Douglas Gray and Norman Friend, McGraw-Hill, 2002
Buying a Franchise in Canada: *Understanding and Negotiating Your Franchise Agreement*, Tony Wilson, Self-Counsel Press, 2004
Exporting From Canada, Gerhard W. Kautz, Self-Counsel Press, 2002
Building an Import/Export Business (Fourth Edition), Kenneth D. Weiss, John Wiley & Sons, 2007

▌ RUNNING A BUSINESS

Employing staff

Employment regulations are governed by provincial laws and can vary by industry. Anti-discrimination and employment equity laws can affect even a small business, and employers need to be highly aware of the threat that sexual harassment or wrongful dismissal lawsuits can pose. Unemployment rates are lower in some industries than in others, but in most cases, if you're offering decent working conditions and wages, you should have a good range of qualified and talented candidates to choose from. Canada Business (www.canadabusiness.ca) has detailed information for potential employers (select *Human Resources* on the home page), and HRSDC provides a range of useful services and guidelines at www.hrsdc.gc.ca/en/gateways/individuals/audiences/ee.shtml.

Trade unions

As mentioned earlier in this chapter, unionised workplaces in Canada may operate on either a closed-shop or an open-shop basis. Canada isn't generally riven with strikes or labour disputes, though they do of course occur. In 2007, Newfoundland and Labrador, Saskatchewan, and BC lost the most work hours to labour disputes or strikes (they're also among the most heavily unionised provinces).

Finding employees

While the Canadian government is on a permanent recruitment drive for skilled workers, particularly in certain fields, there are still plenty of well-trained people looking for work, or keeping an eye out for a more rewarding job. The unemployment rate is lowest in Alberta, the other Prairie provinces and BC, and highest in Newfoundland and Labrador. Ontario and Quebec have the greatest concentration of highly educated graduates, though equally skilled and capable workers can be found across the country. Canada has a high number of part-time workers, including many high school and college students who work around their school hours or take holiday jobs during the long summer break. Many employers take advantage (sometimes literally) of the inexpensive and flexible labour force that students represent.

Employee training

Employee training can be compulsory in certain jobs where occupational health and safety is an issue; for example, where workers are required to operate machinery or handle hazardous materials. Even if you're not required by law to provide training, it's essential for the proper running of your business, and for the performance and well-being of your staff. Many employers choose to subsidise or pay for training courses (or even degree programmes) for their employees. This tends to result not only in better-trained staff, but also in greater employee satisfaction and loyalty. Happy employees who feel their skills and experience are being developed, recognised and valued are far less likely to look elsewhere for work.

FACT

▌ Ontario and Quebec have the greatest concentration of highly educated graduates, though equally skilled and capable workers can be found across the country.

Minimum wage

Standard minimum wages currently range from $7.75 in PEI and New Brunswick to $8.00 in BC and $10.00 in Nunavut. A few provinces allow employers to pay less than this in specific situations (such as for staff who receive tips, or employees just starting out in the workforce), but aside from this it's illegal to pay less than minimum wage, even when your employees are in training. Some occupations also have minimum weekly or monthly wages. HRSDC provides details of these on their Database of Minimum Wages website, http://srv116.services.gc.ca/wid-dimt/mwa. Other than this there are no set salaries for private businesses, though you'll need to be guided by market rates for particular roles and industries.

Social security contributions

Employers and employees each contribute to the social security system. For the Employment Insurance programme, you must pay 1.4 times the amount that your employees contribute. Employer premiums have come down steadily from $4.13 per $100 of insurable earnings in 1996 to the current rate of $2.42, payable up to a maximum of $995.44. Employers are required to match their employees' Canada or Quebec Pension Plan contributions, which are based on 4.95% of eligible salary. More details are included under Social Services, p. 230. The Canada Revenue Agency (CRA) can send you an Employer's Kit containing the forms and information you'll need to ensure you're making the correct deductions from your payroll, or you can visit the website at www.cra-arc.gc.ca/tax/business/menu-e.html and select *Payroll* to access online and downloadable guides and forms.

Paid holidays and vacations

Statutory holidays and vacation pay are discussed in the *Aspects of employment* section on p. 252.

Taxation

Corporate taxes have been dropping for a decade and are projected to keep doing so. Corporations are liable for both federal and provincial income taxes, each of which can be charged at either a higher or a lower level depending on the type of corporation and its income for the year. The higher federal corporate income tax rate is 19.5%, but with full provincial taxes included you could pay as much as 31% to 35.5%. (This is a reduction from over 40% in 2002.) Canadian-controlled, private corporations may be eligible to claim a federal small-business deduction, which brings the federal tax rate down to as little as 11%, or 13%–16.5% if the lowest provincial taxes are added. Most provinces offer a range of business tax credits as well. Alberta and Quebec collect their provincial corporation tax independently of CRA. For information on Alberta's corporate taxes, phone 780 427 3035 or see the Ministry of Finance and Enterprise website at www.finance.alberta.ca (select Taxes and Rebates from the homepage). For Quebec, visit www.revenu.gouv.qc.ca/eng/entreprise/impot, or call 514 864 6299 or 1 800 267 6299 (Montreal office). Canadian corporate tax laws are complex and changeable, and most companies find it beneficial to use the services of a tax accountant to prepare their business tax returns and attempt to minimise the total payment.

 The CRA provides details, guides and forms for corporate taxes; go to www.cra-arc.gc.ca/tx/bsnss/menu-eng.html and select Corporations. You can then select Provincial and territorial tax for province-specific material.

■ RETIREMENT

Canada may not seem an obvious retirement choice, given its often harsh climatic conditions, but it enjoys incredible popularity among British retirees in particular, who ranked it as the top retirement-abroad option worldwide in a recent study. Most people who retire to Canada do so because they have family there, or because they've worked in Canada long enough to feel settled in the country. Canada's social services and healthcare provide a higher standard of living than that offered in some countries, and if you're fortunate enough to be enjoying a stronger currency in your home country – like in the UK, for example – the lower Canadian dollar can make your pension cheque stretch that much further.

Residence and entry

Canada no longer has a separate immigration category for retirees. People who already have permanent residence can remain in Canada when they retire. If you're one of the majority who don't, your options are to visit Canada for up to six months at a time (if you don't require a visitor visa); apply as a Family Class immigrant (if you qualify); or apply under one of the independent immigration categories – either as a skilled worker or as a business immigrant. To be granted entry as an independent immigrant you have to meet the standard requirements set by Citizenship and Immigration Canada, which means you need to apply while you still qualify under the point system, and while you're either still working or can satisfy the minimum requirement for recent work experience. In practice, this normally means coming to Canada while you're still relatively young – you lose two 'age' points for every year over 49, so timing can be critical. Most retirees, then, either have children or grandchildren in Canada already, or will have been living in Canada long before their retirement. Refer to *Visas, work permits and citizenship* for details of the immigration procedures for family class and independent immigrants. Problems can arise if you're in poor health, as your application may be rejected if you have a medical condition that would place an unreasonable burden on the healthcare system.

Where to live

Moving overseas is a major step at any stage in life. For those going into retirement, it often demands additional energy and optimism. If holidays in Canada have left you with a love of a certain area, you'll need to consider what it would be like to live in that area year-round. Adequate financial resources are essential, and if you're thinking of retiring in Quebec, knowledge of French is an important factor.

Possible retirement areas

The snowbird phenomenon, which involves fleeing to Florida or other US cities to escape the cold of winter, is common among Canadian retirees. If you're planning on retiring in – or to – Canada, however, you need to assume you'll be there in all seasons, and choose where to live with that in mind. If you have relatives and friends already in the country, being close to them will likely be a major factor in your decision making. Canada offers an excitingly diverse range of landscapes and lifestyles, and the choice is very much personal. Each town and city has its contingent of retirees – some far larger than others – and different regions will appeal for different reasons. The arctic regions of northern Canada are probably too extreme an adventure for most (though if you're prepared to move halfway across the globe to retire, who knows?), but the rest of the country offers a myriad of options. Two areas are particularly popular with both Canadian and foreign retirees:

- **British Columbia:** The advantages of BC are obvious: mild winters, beautiful scenery, city living if you want it, and resort and coastal towns with a laid-back approach to life. Large retiree communities, fantastic recreational opportunities, and easy access to healthcare and social services make BC the first choice for many retirees, and Victoria, on Vancouver Island, has the highest percentage of seniors in the country. Unfortunately, BC's home prices reflect this demand – though decreasing – and are substantially higher than in the rest of Canada.

A sailboat meanders through the Gulf Islands: beautiful BC

■ **The Atlantic Provinces:** Newfoundland and Labrador, New Brunswick, PEI, and Nova Scotia offer a choice of small coastal towns and friendly cities. Winters are milder than in central Canada, though rain, fog and storms are common. These provinces offer a slower pace of life and a sense of community arguably unsurpassed elsewhere in Canada. A large proportion of residents are of British descent. Property is also less expensive here – average housing prices in the four provinces are among the cheapest in the country.

Hobbies and interests

Retirement is the ideal time to explore new interests or devote more time to old or neglected hobbies. Part-time work is also an option, and your local Service Canada Centre can provide assistance in upgrading skills and finding employment (visit www.servicecanada.gc.ca, or see p. 231 for local and international phone numbers). Volunteering is a great way to diversify your experiences and do something beneficial for your local community – see Voluntary work on p. 244 and Making friends on p. 303 for information on where to start. Many retirees and seniors join CARP, Canada's Association for the Fifty-Plus (416 363 8748; carp@50plus.com; www.carp.ca), a powerful lobbying and social organisation with chapters across the country. CARP members also receive various benefits, services and discounts, including reduced insurance rates.

 The CARP website is one of a family of 50plus websites – the main site, at www.50plus.com, has information, news and lifestyle content. Canadian Senior Years (www.senioryears.com) provides links to numerous retirement news groups and organisations.

Seniors receive reduced (and occasionally free) admission to most entertainment events and educational programmes, and pay less to use public transit, which is a great incentive to get out and about and enjoy a little cultural overload. (Note that the age of 'seniority' may be 60 or 65, depending on the organisation charging the fees.) Expatriate networks and forums can be a helpful source of advice and support for people intending to retire abroad – see p. 364 for some examples.

Pensions

Provided you've made at least one contribution to the Canada Pension Plan (or to the Quebec Pension Plan if you've worked in Quebec), you can apply for a Canadian retirement pension at the age of 65. Contributions are normally deducted from your pay cheque. You may qualify to receive your pension early – between the ages of 60 and 64 – if you're not working or are earning little income at that time, though this permanently affects the amount

TIP

■ Seniors receive reduced (and occasionally free) admission to most entertainment events and educational programmes, and pay less to use public transit, which is a great incentive to get out and about and enjoy a little cultural overload.

Canada's wilderness parks and stunning landscapes are a veritable playground for retirees (and an incentive for some to retire early)

you receive. The amount is highest if you wait until the age of 70 to start your pension, though you obviously won't receive it for as long. The current maximum monthly benefit under the CPP at age 65 is $884.58; however, most people won't have contributed enough each year, for enough years, to receive this amount. The national average payment is $481.46.

You don't need to have worked in Canada to be eligible for the Old Age Security pension (OAS), though you must have lived in the country for at least 10 years. To get the maximum amount, you need to have been resident for 40 years, or meet other very specific criteria. The maximum benefit payable is $505.83 per month; if you and your spouse have a combined income over $65,000 you'll lose some or all of this amount. Other possible benefits include the Guaranteed Income Supplement (GIS) – a current maximum of $638.46 monthly – for low-income seniors, and the Allowance (with a monthly maximum of $927.45) for those aged 60–64 whose partner is eligible for both OAS and GIS. An allowance for widowed spouses is also available, and many provinces provide income supplements to keep low-income seniors afloat. The webpage at www.hrsdc.gc.ca/en/isp/common/relatedsites.shtml#3 lists useful links. CPP and QPP benefits are taxable, and rates are updated annually to allow for inflation. OAS is also taxable, though GIS and the Allowance are not; rates for all three are updated four times a year.

 Current pension and benefit rates and further information can be found on the Service Canada website, www.servicecanada.gc.ca.

Finance

The federal government and most provinces provide tax credits to low-income seniors, such as property or sales tax credits, which you may be eligible for when you file your return. A Services for Seniors guide is available on the Seniors Canada website (www.seniors.gc.ca) and includes details of tax savings at the federal level. For information on provincial savings and credits, check the Canada Benefits website (www.canadabenefits.gc.ca) or contact the relevant provincial government. Service Canada provides relevant links to provincial government and seniors' websites at www.hrsdc.gc.ca/en/isp/common/relatedsites.shtml#3. For more on tax-related matters, see Taxation, p. 289. The Canadian edition of David Bach's book Start Late, Finish Rich: A No-fail Plan for Achieving Financial Freedom at Any Age (Doubleday Canada, 2007) provides advice (and consolation) for those who think they've left their financial planning a little too late in life.

Wills, death, and legal considerations

Information on Canadian wills, inheritance laws, and probate fees is outlined under Inheritance Laws and Wills, p. 293. People of any age who have any assets at all should have a will, but this becomes increasingly important as you reach retirement age, particularly if you're living abroad. It's also wise to let friends and relatives know your wishes about funeral and burial arrangements earlier rather than later, in case you suddenly become ill or pass away unexpectedly. Various processes have to be followed when someone dies in Canada, including contacting a physician or coroner

INTERNATIONAL BENEFITS

Canada has social security agreements with many countries. These may allow you to claim social security benefits such as pensions from either country or from both. They may also take into account contributions or periods of residence in your home country to help you qualify for CPP or OAS if you wouldn't otherwise be eligible. Agreements differ between countries, and are often complex. Service Canada's International Benefits webpage at www.servicecanada.gc.ca/en/isp/ibfa/intlben. shtml lets you search the list of applicable countries, read or download information sheets, and link to social security websites worldwide. For additional information, phone Service Canada's International Operations at 613 957 1954 or 1 800 454 8731. If you have company or private pension plans you'll need to find out well in advance whether these can be paid to you in Canada, or, if necessary, whether they can be transferred. If you're eligible for the UK State Pension you can receive payments in Canada, but once you start drawing your pension the level is 'frozen,' or no longer indexed for the cost of living (though you can continue to make contributions). This isn't the case for British expats in many other countries, including the United States, and has provoked long-term campaigning against the British government.

to certify the death, overseeing funeral or transfer arrangements, cancelling personal documents, cards, pensions and benefits, and submitting a final tax return.

 Service Canada outlines these steps at www.servicecanada.gc.ca/en/lifeevents/loss.shtml and provides contact details for provincial governments and funeral boards, which can give you more detailed information.

Unless you have an expatriate or travel insurance policy that covers repatriation, having your body shipped home for burial is very expensive. Most people make arrangements to be buried or cremated in Canada, and funeral homes offer both religious and non-denominational memorial services. You can take out an insurance policy to cover funeral costs, which provides peace of mind for you and your family members.

Healthcare for seniors

For many people, concerns about health, and the need to make use of the healthcare system, increase with age. Health Canada has a dedicated webpage for seniors at www.hc-sc.gc.ca/h1-vs/seniors-aines/indx-eng.php, which discusses some of the health issues relevant to older Canadians, and includes information on ways to keep healthy. The HealthCare System webpage, www.hc-sc.gc.ca/hcs-sss/index-eng.php, provides links to all aspects of the Canadian health system, including home and continuing care, hospital care, nursing policy, and palliative and end-of-life care. Seniors Canada (www.seniors.gc.ca) is also a great resource, with information on health and wellness, and links to care and housing facilities across Canada.

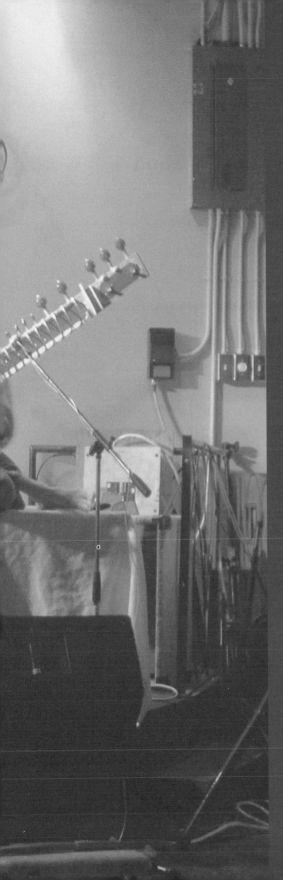

Time Off

■ INTRODUCTION

So, what do Canadians do when they've got a little spare time on their hands? When the workday is done, the week is over, the kids are off at grandma's (or bored and looking for something to do)? Long weekends see a mass exodus from the big cities, with hours of painful, crawling traffic that always seem worth it for that glimpse of dark pines against still, shiny water, or of snow-capped mountains looming up from the horizon. Even if you don't have the luxury of holiday time – if you've just got an hour or an afternoon to spare – there are plenty of ways to get busy, active, distracted or absorbed: films, galleries, and museums; dinner

CULTURAL CLASSICS, OR CLASSIC CULTURE?

Whether you're a tourist or a local, Canada promises a wealth of sights to see and things to do. Here are a few uniquely Canadian highlights, both on and off the beaten track.

- Admiring the Dali masterpieces at the Beaverbrook Art Gallery in Fredericton, New Brunswick
- Taking to the imaginary seas on the replica of sailing ship Nonsuch, at Winnipeg's Manitoba Museum, Manitoba
- Relaxing in hot springs by the sea in the remote Queen Charlotte Islands, BC
- Walking through the hoodoos by moonlight in Dinosaur Provincial Park, Alberta
- Eating lunch in an old-school diner in tiny Elbow, Saskatchewan
- Buying summer sausage from the Farmers' Markets in St Jacobs, Ontario
- Witnessing the Niagara Falls light show in winter, when sherbet colours light up the ice
- Taking in the view from the Pinnacle at Lake Lyster in the Eastern Townships, Quebec
- Chewing on dulse (edible seaweed) from a paper bag on Grand Manan Island
- Pondering the gravesites of the Titanic victims in Halifax, Nova Scotia
- Hiking through the mountains and meadows of Waterton National Park, Alberta
- Swimming in phosphorescence and forgetting time exists in the Gulf Islands, BC
- Eating a real Thanksgiving dinner with Canadian friends

with new friends; chamber music recitals at a local winery; team sports; or a sweaty workout at the local gym.

◼ PUBLIC HOLIDAYS AND EVENTS

Though Canadians don't get a lot of annual vacation time, they do enjoy a fair number of public holidays. Each province has legislation requiring that employees receive a specified number of paid statutory holidays every year, ranging from five to 10. The major national holidays are shown in the table overleaf, though not all of these are holidays in all provinces. Various additional holidays also apply at the provincial level. Most have a holiday on the first Monday in August; Alberta, Saskatchewan and Ontario take a mid-winter break for Family Day on the third Monday in February, as Manitoba concurrently celebrates Louis Riel Day; the Northwest Territories observe National Aboriginal Day on June 21; Quebec celebrates Quebec National Day (Saint-Jean-Baptiste) on June 24; Nunavut Day is July 9; Discovery Day in the Yukon is the third Monday in August; and Newfoundland and Labrador have numerous, predominantly British, extras.

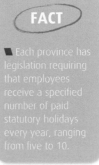

Halloween, 31 October, means dress-ups, trick-or-treating, pumpkin carving and ghoulishly decorated homes

PUBLIC HOLIDAYS		
New Year's Day	1 January	
Good Friday		
Easter Monday		Quebec holiday (instead of Good Friday)
Victoria Day	Monday preceding 21 May	Except New Brunswick, Newfoundland and Labrador, Nova Scotia, Prince Edward Island. 'Dollard Day' in Quebec
Canada Day	1 July	'Memorial Day' in Newfoundland and Labrador
Labour Day	First Monday in September	
Thanksgiving Day	Second Monday in October	Except New Brunswick, Newfoundland and Labrador, Nova Scotia, PEI
Remembrance Day	11 November	Alberta, BC, Saskatchewan, Northwest Territories, Nunavut, Yukon, federal employees
Christmas Day	25 December	
Boxing Day	26 December	Ontario, federal employees

Festivals and events

January

- Toronto's WinterCity Festival (416 395 0490; spevmktg@toronto.ca; www.toronto.ca/special_events/wintercity)
- Fête des Neiges de Montréal: outdoor winter festival (514 872 6120; www.fetedesneiges.com)

February

- Winterlude: three weekends of winter celebrations (613 239 5000 or 1 800 465 1867; www.canadascapital.gc.ca/winterlude)
- Yukon Quest, Whitehorse: 1,000-mile international sled-dog race from Yukon to Alaska (867 668 4711; questadmin@polarcom.com; www.yukonquest.com)

March

- Vancouver Playhouse International Wine Festival: premier wine event in Canada (604 872 6622; www.playhousewinefest.com)
- Vancouver Cherry Blossom Festival (info@vcbf.ca; www.vancouvercherryblossomfestival.com)

April

- Hot Docs Canadian International Documentary Festival, Toronto (416 637 5150; boxoffice@hotdocs.ca; www.hotdocs.ca)

May

- Doors Open Toronto: free access to architecturally significant buildings around the city (416 325 5000; doorsopenontario@ heritagetrust.on.ca; www.doorsopenontario.on.ca)
- Canadian Tulip Festival Ottawa: 18 days and 3,000,000 tulips (613 567 5757 or 1 800 668 8547; info@tulipfestival.ca; www.tulipfestival.ca)
- Vancouver International Marathon (604 872 2928; info@vanmarathon.bc.ca; www.bmovanmarathon.ca)
- Toronto Jewish Film Festival: 12 countries, 9 days, 86 films (416 324 8226; tjff@tjff.ca; www.tjff.com)

June

- Grand Prix du Canada, Montreal (514 350 0000; www.grandprix.ca)
- North by Northeast, Toronto: Music and Film Festival and Conference (416 863 6963; info@nxne.com; www.nxne.com)
- Bard on the Beach Shakespeare Festival Vancouver (604 739 0559 or 1 877 739 0559; www.bardonthebeach.org)
- Festival International de Jazz de Montréal (514 523 3378 or 1 888 515 0515; commentaires_jazz@equipespectra.ca; www.montrealjazzfest.com)

July

- Calgary Stampede (403 261 0101 or 1 800 661 1260; www.calgarystampede.com)
- Ottawa Bluesfest: largest blues festival in Canada (613 247 1188 or 1 866 258 3748; info@ottawabluesfest.ca; www.ottawabluesfest.ca)
- The Fringe: Toronto's Theatre Festival (416 966 1062 or 1 866 515 7799; fringe@fringetoronto.com; www.fringetoronto.com)
- Celebration of Light, Vancouver : pyro-musical fireworks competition over English Bay (604 642 6835; info@celebration-of-light.com; www.celebration-of-light.com)
- Just For Laughs Festival, Montreal and Toronto: (Montreal 514 845 2322 or 1888 244 3155, Toronto Ticketmaster 416 872 1111; www.hahaha.com)
- Beaches International Jazz Festival, Toronto (416 698 2152; infobeachesjazz@rogers.com; www.beachesjazz.com)

August

- Canadian National Exhibition Toronto (CNE): 18-day fair with agricultural shows, exhibits, rides, and games (416 393 6300; info@TheEx.com; www.theex.com)
- Pacific National Exhibition Toronto (PNE): (604 253 2311; info@pne.ca; www.pne.ca)

- Festival des Films du Monde, Montreal: Montreal's world film festival (514 848 3883; info@ffm-montreal.org; www.ffm-montreal.org)
- Canada's National Ukrainian Festival, Manitoba (204 622 4600; 1 877 474 2683; www.cnuf.ca)

September
- Toronto International Film Festival (TIFF), Toronto (416 968 3456 or 1 877 968 3456; tiffg@tiffg.ca; www.tiff08.ca)

October
- Halifax Pop Explosion: music, culture, media (902 482 8176; festival@halifaxpopexplosion.com; www.halifaxpopexplosion.com)
- Scotiabank Nuit Blanche, Toronto: free all-night celebration of contemporary art (scotiabanknuitblanche@toronto.ca; www.scotiabanknuitblanche.ca)
- Festival du Nouveau Cinéma, Montreal: new cinema and new media (514 282 0004 or hotline 514 844 2172; info@nouveaucinema.ca; www.nouveaucinema.ca)

November
- Banff Mountain Film Festival (403 762 6301 or 1 800 413 8368; box_office@banffcentre.ca; www.banffcentre.ca/mountainculture/festivals/2008)

December
- Christmas at Butchart Gardens, Victoria: light displays, ice skating and live entertainment (250 652 5256; email@butchartgardens.com; www.butchartgardens.com)

◼ SOCIALISING

Canadian society is an interesting mix of cultures and conventions, heavily influenced by the USA, the French and the British, and by generations of continuous, diverse immigration. Most Americans feel relatively at home among Canadians; travellers and immigrants from Canada's Commonwealth siblings tend to find common ground as well. Canadian spelling conventions are not the only British–American hybrid: many cultural, historical, and media references are also shared. Australians and Canadians often get along easily; they share a laconic, laid-back approach, and a big-wide-land understanding. Most Canadians value privacy and modesty, and they may be a little less gregarious and a little more reserved than their US neighbours, but they live up to their reputation for friendliness, particularly to newcomers. Aside from a sense of humour (and Canadians have an equal appreciation for European blackness, self-deprecating Australian dryness, and finely tuned English farce), a willingness to talk about sports, family, and politics will stand you in good stead. There aren't many topics of conversation Canadians shy away from. Political correctness, however, is ingrained in the Charter of Rights and Freedoms and in official employment policy, and it's unacceptable to make racist, sexist or discriminatory jokes or comments.

Hanging out at a bar with friends is a common social pastime

Making friends

Meeting locals

Canadians tend to have lots of casual acquaintances – usually a mixture of male and female – and a smaller collection of good friends. It's generally easy to find yourself in someone's outer circle; becoming close friends takes time, a little effort and a genuine connection. Many people make friends through their workplace, particularly if their workmates are of a similar age and have related interests. Being friendly and approachable, and taking part in work-organised social activities, is the best way to start. Even if your friendships don't extend too far beyond working hours, at least you'll have pleasant company at lunchtime or on your breaks. Neighbours can be warm and hospitable, particularly if you live in a family-based

> Through our New Zealand friends [in Calgary] and new work colleagues we met their Canadian friends, who welcomed us with open arms and wanted to help us get involved in Canadian life.
> **Andrea Crengle**

> Most of the people I meet in Canada are from my workplace, co-workers. I spend a lot of time at work so I know many of my co-workers who are immigrants like me. I also meet people through religious centres and community organisations.
> **Dante Pizarro**

> There is a constant need for volunteers in all the clubs and societies; we have to limit ourselves or we can be sucked into a whirlpool of commitments.
> **Gerald Garnett**

suburb or a smaller town – in busy city areas or large apartment buildings, people may be more inclined to keep to themselves. Don't expect all your neighbours to be instantly outgoing, though; they may feel just as awkward initiating conversation, or assume you're not interested in making friends. Say hi, let them know who you are, and think about inviting them over for a coffee or a summer-evening drink once you feel comfortable doing so.

Most cities have a range of social and service clubs that can be a great way to get to know people. Recreational sporting clubs (see p. 271) are one option, and allow you to burn off a few excess calories while honing your social skills. Other groups organise regular social activities. You could also take a short course in something you've always wanted to do (or never even considered), such as cake baking, massage therapy or photography. Learn how to kayak, knit or speak another language; or join a book club, writers' group or theatre group. Or consider volunteering, especially if you regularly have a few hours free each week. Contact your municipal council, or check out notice boards at your regional library or recreation centre to see whether local community organisations or festivals could use assistance. Charities such as the Salvation Army welcome help with everything from

TIP

■ Most cities have a range of social and service clubs that can be a great way to get to know people.

Christina Chiam settled into the Canadian social scene relatively quickly:

My social transition was helped by the fact that a good friend from Melbourne also lives in Toronto. She and her Canadian boyfriend gave me a roof over my head and introduced me to the social nuances and trends of Canadian culture. I've found the social scene to be fairly similar to what I'm used to – music gigs, dining out, socialising at bars or at people's homes. Canadians have a more pronounced love of everything outdoors – be it summer or winter, they'll find an excuse to get out of the city and into natural surrounds.

My experience with Canadians has been overwhelmingly positive. I find them friendly, easygoing, self deprecating and warm. I've been fortunate to work with young, like-minded people who are welcoming and thoughtful. I've met most of my friends through work, and some through mutual friends in Australia. I also met fellow travellers on a trip through Nova Scotia – given our similar experience living and working in a foreign country, we bonded quickly and easily.

office work to food programmes, and animal shelters are always in need of reliable volunteers. You may even want to work with one of the settlement organisations in your area to help other immigrants make the transition to life in Canada. (See p. 244 for more on volunteering.)

 Meetup, at www.meetup.com/cities/ca, is an online social network that facilitates real-life gatherings for classes, outings, seminars, drinks, and dinners.

Meeting singles

People meet potential partners (or potential flings) in many of the same ways they meet potential friends. Getting romantically involved with a co-worker – though not uncommon – is usually frowned on due to the risk of negative side effects (reduced productivity, nasty break-ups, sexual harassment allegations etc). Dating a subordinate (or your boss) is a particularly risky proposition. Once you start establishing friendships your social circle will widen, and opportunities for meeting other singles through friends will increase. Bar-hopping is one tried and true method (though more often than not it leads to casual encounters rather than long-term scenarios) and specific singles organisations are another way to go, whether it's for speed-dating, match-making, parties, dinners or online dating. Sport and social clubs like Single Horizons (www.singlehorizons.com) are also aimed at singles. However you go about it, getting out and being involved is the best way to up your chances.

> On that first visit I fell in love with a person and a place. My aunt worked in the Saanich library, and my future wife Mary was one of her assistants.
> **Gerald Garnett**

Meeting other expats

Many people find meeting or talking with other expats – especially those from their own home country – helpful in settling in to a new place. Various expat organisations operate in different parts of Canada, such as the Australian Canadian Association (www.yaca.ca) in Ontario, or the Royal Society of St George (www.stgeorgebc.ca) in BC. You can also join online expat forums, which can be a helpful source of informal advice and can lead to social meetings or outings with other forum members who live in your vicinity. Forums include www.expatforum.com, www.expatfocus.com, www.expatexchange.com and www.britishexpats.com. The Southern Cross Group (www.southern-cross-group.org) is a helpful resource for Australians abroad. Your home country's embassy or consulate in Canada may also list ex-pat events and information. For Brits, Europeans, and even Aussies, finding fellow ex-pats can often be as easy as ducking in to your local British-style pub for a pint (it's amazing how attuned your ear becomes to the sound of a familiar accent). While it's great to have friends who can empathise with your living-abroad experiences, be careful that you don't befriend expats to the total exclusion of 'local' Canadians – otherwise, you'll miss out on a huge part of the whole Canadian adventure.

 True Canada, a useful website run by a British expat, lists various discussion groups at www.truecanada.ca/?p=42.

> **For Steven Maine and his wife, the social adjustment wasn't always easy:**
>
> This is one of the things we found hardest to adapt to. We were used to mixing and having a fairly hectic social life. People are friendly on the surface, but seem reluctant to go further until they've known you for a long time. My wife, especially as she wasn't working, found this very difficult. We lived in the house for a year before our neighbours finally really spoke to us. Really the only people we know here are from my work, and members of the British Expats forum who have also moved to Nova Scotia. I honestly do think it is different in other parts of the province though, especially once you move away from the Halifax area.

Gay and lesbian Canada

Canada's Charter of Rights and Freedoms provides equal rights to gay and lesbian Canadians, and discrimination based on sexual orientation is illegal. Same-sex partners in common-law relationships now receive the same recognition and rights as opposite-sex common-law partners in terms of social insurance benefits, income tax, and other advantages and obligations. Same-sex marriage is legal in Canada, though it's taken many years of battling (including overcoming the Harper government's relatively recent attempt to reverse the decision) to get there. Small towns are small towns the world over, and attitudes and opportunities tend to be most expansive in Canada's larger cities (though many smaller cities are equally proud of their gay communities and events). Toronto, Montreal, and Vancouver are the biggest lifestyle and culture draw cards for gay, lesbian, bi, trans, and queer Canadians and travellers – all have gay pride celebrations, with Toronto hosting the country's largest each summer (see www.pridetoronto.com). You can find event listings and links at www.xtra.ca, www.gaycanada.com or www.gay.com, or check out www.outintoronto.com and the other Out in America websites, which include Alberta, Calgary, Halifax, Montreal, Nova Scotia, Ottawa, Quebec, and Regina. Street mags covering gay and lesbian entertainment and events include the print version of *Xtra!* (*Xtra! West* in Vancouver), or *Fugue*s in Montreal (www.fugues.com).

FACT

■ Same-sex marriage is legal in Canada, though it's taken many years of battling (including overcoming the Harper government's relatively recent attempt to reverse the decision) to get there.

■ SPORT AND FITNESS

In a land obsessed with hockey ('ice hockey' to non-Canadians), sport is a natural part of life. Opportunities abound, whether you're looking for extreme ventures, professional or amateur competition, or just something to keep you in shape from week to week. On the national level, sports include everything from archery to weightlifting, with an incredible range of options in between: athletics, bob-sledding, basketball, figure skating, golf, gymnastics, karate, softball, squash, table tennis, wakeboarding – if you can play it, chances are you'll be able to play it in Canada. The nationwide Canada Games are held every two years, alternating between summer and winter, and the Arctic Winter Games, for northern and Arctic athletes, occur in the interim years. Hosting duties pass between the provinces.

> The Sport Canada website at www.pch.gc.ca/progs/sc includes a full list of National Sport Organizations, and lots of other links and information.

Sports organisations also exist at provincial and municipal levels, and higher-level federations are responsible for international competitions. Canada participates in all major international games, including summer and winter Olympics and Paralympics (Vancouver will host the 2010 Winter Games), the Commonwealth Games, and the North American Indigenous Games. Not surprisingly, hockey and figure skating have traditionally been strong sports for Canadians. Specific government ministries look after sport and recreation in each province and territory, and you can find details of many organisations and programmes – both government and independent – on their websites. Sport Canada provides links to each ministry at www.pch.gc.ca/progs/sc/liens-links/prov-ter_e.cfm. There's a strong emphasis on health and fitness for children: the Government of Ontario, for example, has a range of kid-specific websites to encourage a more active lifestyle, such as Pause to Play (www.pausetoplay.ca) and Notgonnakillyou.ca (www.notgonnakillyou.ca). The federal government's newly introduced Children's Fitness Tax Credit, available to parents who enrol their kids in physical activity programmes, is also aimed at encouraging sports participation.

FACT

■ The federal government's newly introduced Children's Fitness Tax Credit, available to parents who enrol their kids in physical activity programmes, is aimed at encouraging sports participation.

Ice skaters make their way up the Ramsey Lake skate path in Sudbury, Ontario

Ice-skating and skiing are second nature for many Canadians, who've grown up accustomed to snow and frozen lakes – prepare to be shamed by four-year-old tots whizzing past as you tentatively negotiate the ice on skates for the first time! You can take ice-skating lessons if you prefer, though most people get the knack pretty quickly even without professional guidance. Snowboarding is popular on the ski slopes among locals and travellers alike, and a good snowfall means heading for the nearest decent hill with family or friends for tobogganing and sliding. In summer it's swimming, boating, and hiking. Kayaking and canoeing are a must if you live (or take vacations) lakeside, riverside or along the coast, and offer a fantastic way to explore Canada's stunning waterways – paddle serenely on still waters or plough through churning rapids, depending on your preferences and choice of location. Numerous local, national, and provincial parks offer walking trails for everything from Sunday strolling to strenuous climbs.

> Check out PlayDay (www.playday.com) for recreation and sporting ideas and links – horse-riding, white-water rafting, fishing, and skydiving are some of the activities they cover.

CanadianFitnessMatters.ca (www.canadianfitnessmatters.ca), a Canada Safety Council website, provides information on fitness safety standards and a directory for locating fitness facilities in your area, from fitness clubs to community recreation centres, to physiotherapists. (The comprehensive search options look more useful than they are, though – keep your search broad for the best results.) You can also phone the council on 613 739 1535 (ext. 230). Gyms and health centres are generally membership-based and charge monthly fees; these can range from around $40 to upwards of $100, and there are often minimum terms. Mega chains like GoodLife Fitness, Extreme Fitness, and Premier Fitness boast numerous (and conveniently located) clubs, but watch out for too-good-to-be-true introductory offers, locked-in annual contracts and inflated add-on fees for 'must-have' personal trainers – horror stories abound. If you're not interested in the hard sell, locally owned gyms, community centres or the nearest YMCA (416 967 9622; www.ymca.ca) are often a better bet. Many colleges and universities open their fitness centres to outsiders as well. Fitness chains that cater just to women include Curves (www.curvesinformation.com) and Contours Express (www.contoursexpress.ca).

Running and cycling are common activities, and aren't necessarily constrained to the warmer months. For the hardy and brave, bikes can be winterised, and it's not uncommon to see joggers, thermally clothed from head to toe, navigating snowy sidewalks in sub-zero temperatures. Many cities have sport and social clubs offering recreational leagues, tournaments, and outings for a range of sports – both indoor and outdoor, depending on the activity and the season. Soccer, hockey, basketball, volleyball, dodgeball, and bowling are common. Municipal councils have information on available programmes and leagues in the community, so a good place to start is your local council's website. You can also check the board at your local recreation centre, or ask friends or co-workers for suggestions; they may play in a team that's short a member or two, or know of other clubs in your area. Whether your idea of getting active is hardcore hiking, taking a yoga or Pilates class, practising tai-chi in a neighbourhood park, training for a triathlon or playing bocce with a beer in your spare hand, there'll be a time, a place and an opportunity to enjoy it in Canada.

TIP

If you're not interested in the hard sell from mega fitness chains, then locally owned gyms, community centres or the nearest YMCA are often a better bet.

> My wife is linked with a lot of horse riders, artists, a book and gossip club, and a gym. I work with an outdoor recreation club and do yoga.
> **Gerald Garnett**

Listings Canada, at www.listingsca.com, is a useful website: selecting your province or city, then the Sports/Recreation link, pulls up various listings for sports associations, clubs, festivals, and events.

THE LOVE OF THE GAME

There are three quintessentially Canadian offerings in the world sporting arena: the curious but highly competitive game of curling, and the country's two official national sports: lacrosse (summer) and hockey (winter). Lacrosse – fast-paced and adopted worldwide from England, to Singapore, to Sweden – developed in Canada from a spiritually significant game played by First Nations people. It's an iconic and proudly supported part of Canada's sporting tradition. But it is hockey that unites, divides, and ignites the passion of the people. Despite the USA's domination of the National Hockey League since joining in 1924 (there are now 24 US teams in the NHL, compared to just six from Canada), and the fact that the coveted Stanley Cup hasn't made it home for 15 years, Canadians remain deeply and patriotically attached to the game. The weekly Hockey Night in Canada is a television institution through the six-odd months of the regular season (despite CBC recently losing the rights to its anthem-like theme song), and the adrenalin-fuelled playoffs leading to the final series are broadcast nightly. Whether it's professional or amateur, a school comp, a game of shinny between friends or a couple of kids smacking a puck around on a frozen pond, hockey holds a pervasive and enduring appeal.

◾ ART, ENTERTAINMENT, AND CULTURE

Canada's culture and entertainment options are as varied as its landscape, from the roaring buzz of the Grands Prix in Montreal and Toronto (www.grandprix. ca; www.grandprixtoronto.com) to the inspiring eco consciousness of the Green Living Show (www.greenlivingonline.com). Maybe your idea of fun is trying out all 59 rides at the Canadian National Exhibition (www.theex.com), taking the kids along for some 3D IMAX drama (www.imax.com), or marvelling at time-and-space-defying sporting feats at the 2010 Vancouver Winter Olympic Games

Two soloists perform at the yearly Earth Day celebrations in Moncton, NB

(www.vancouver2010.com). Or perhaps you'd rather an evening of classical recitals, or an author event at Chapters/Indigo (www.chapters.indigo.ca) or your local independent bookstore. Whatever it is that rocks your cultural boat, you'll find something to suit your taste, your location and your budget.

Visual arts

Extensive collections of traditional and contemporary work by Canadian and international artists are held in museums across the country, and almost all international touring collections visit Canada. Montreal, Quebec City, Vancouver, Victoria, Edmonton, and Ottawa house some of the biggest and best collections; Toronto's AGO (Art Gallery of Ontario) has undergone massive renovations over the past year to become an undeniably world-class facility; and numerous hidden gems exist in smaller cities and towns, often overlooked by culture-munching, big-city-hopping tourists. Emily Carr, Tom Thomson, and the Group of Seven are among the best-known, most recognisable and most frequently touted Canadian painters, though a huge number of other artists – including sculptors, photographers, textile- and metalworkers, printmakers, and jewellers – exhibit both in the major art establishments and in small, locally-owned galleries throughout the country. Norval Morrisseau (who passed away in late 2007) is one of Canada's most highly regarded

First Nations artists, and Aboriginal art, particularly Inuit art, is a feature of many national and provincial collections.

 For more information on Canadian artists and collections, visit the Artists in Canada online directory at www.artistsincanada.com and the Virtual Museum Canada website at www.virtualmuseum.ca, where you can search for museums and galleries by city or province.

Dance and theatre

Canadians have a widespread and lively interest in the performing arts, and Toronto is the third-largest centre for performing arts in the world behind New York and London. Top-notch national companies coexist with countless professional and amateur groups, and all forms of traditional and experimental theatre, dance, and performance art can be found in Canada's urban centres. While professional dance in Canada has European roots, Afro-Caribbean, Indian, Korean, Ukrainian, and classical South Asian dance have influenced and diversified the scene. Top ballet companies are the National Ballet, Les Grands Ballets Canadiens de Montréal, the Royal Winnipeg Ballet, the Alberta Ballet, and Ballet British Columbia. The National Arts Centre (www.nac.ca) has regular programmes in dance, music, and both English and French theatre. Toronto theatre audiences have easy access to the renowned Stratford Shakespeare Festival (www.stratfordfestival.ca) and Niagara-On-The-Lake's Shaw Festival (www.shawfest.com), which run Shakespearean, classical, modern, and Shavian works between April and November each year. The world-famous performance troupe Cirque de Soleil (www.cirquedusoleil.com) is based in Montreal; Winnipeg presents outdoor shows on its Rainbow Stage; *Anne of Green Gables: The Musical* plays annually at the Charlottetown Festival; and the Atlantic Theatre Festival (www.atf.ns.ca) outside Halifax draws larger crowds every year. Aboriginal performance groups include Full Circle (www.fullcircleperformance.ca), which has musicians, actors, writers, and clowns who tour both at home and internationally, and which presents the six-day Talking Stick Festival each year.

Music

Names like Neil Young, The Guess Who, The Tragically Hip and the inevitable Céline Dion are typically associated with the Canadian music scene, but a multitude of other equally (if not more) worthy artists are a huge part of the current picture. Rumour has it the long, cold winters lead to a deepened creativity born of introspection. Whatever the reason, Canadians know how to do music, and do it well, from the phenomenal Arcade Fire to alt-rockers Sloan, Halifax's own gently tortured genius Joel Plaskett, fabulous Feist, pop-rock foursome Hedley, pure-voiced Sarah Harmer, Winnipeg's indie-rock icons The Weakerthans, the rollicking Sadies and a wealth of other home-grown talent. With a strong local music scene that's definitely not confined to the major cities, concerts, gigs, and festivals happen year round, and genres span everything from roots to hip hop, and punk rock to banjo-strumming bluegrass. For gigs in your area, check listings in local papers or alternative mags, or browse some of the websites listed on p. 363.

TIP

For gigs in your area, check listings in local papers or alternative mags, or browse some of the websites listed on p. 363.

Visit MapleMusic (www.maplemusic.com) for great information on Canadian artists and new releases, or MuchMusic (www.muchmusic.com) for music and entertainment news, updates, and gossip.

Classical music and opera

Fans of opera and chamber music will find their tastes catered to on both local and national levels. Almost all major cities have a professional symphony orchestra, and many have their own opera companies as well (visit Opera.ca at www.opera.ca for a list). Soprano Measha Brueggergosman and classical pianist Katherine Chi are among Canada's internationally renowned performers. The Ottawa-based National Arts Centre Orchestra has a mandate to commission original Canadian works, while the Symphony Orchestra of Canada – an ensemble of Toronto Symphony Orchestra, National Ballet of Canada and Canadian Opera Company (COC) members – ensures that half its repertoire at every concert is Canadian-composed. The COC is Canada's largest opera company, staging seven full productions and a free concert series of 100 shows each year. Tapestry (www.tapestrynewopera.com) produces and performs new contemporary opera works, and opera, classical, and jazz festivals are

Whether it's in a tiny bar or a concert hall, live music is a big part of Canadian entertainment culture

held throughout the country. Youth companies include the National Youth Orchestra of Canada and the Canadian Children's Opera Chorus.

Cinema

While the North American movie scene is still dominated by the USA, and US producers are inclined to see Canada as convenient and inexpensive location fodder (see Louis Leterrier's *The Incredible Hulk* for downtown Toronto dressed as New York), the Canadian film identity is original, strong, and growing steadily. Toronto, Montreal, Vancouver, Victoria, Ottawa, Halifax, and Banff have their own film festivals – the granddaddy of which is the Toronto International Film Festival (TIFF) – and feature full-length films, documentaries, animation, and shorts. The Oscar-winning National Film Board (NFB) is Canada's public film producer and distributor, and a rich heritage of local filmmaking is supported by grants from the Canada Council for the Arts and similar provincial organisations. David Cronenberg, Denys Arcand, Atom Egoyan, and actor-turned-director Sarah Polley are on the list of notables, while the current crop of young acting stars include Ellen Page, Seth Rogen, Ryan Reynolds, and Ryan Gosling. Canada has the usual inevitable range of garish multiplex cinema giants, but smaller chains and art-house or rep theatres provide that good old-fashioned movie-going experience – cheaper tickets, red velvet curtains, and all.

Fashion

Each spring and fall sees designers, buyers, the media, and an assortment of celebrity visitors head to Montreal, Toronto, and BC for their respective fashion weeks. The downtown Calgary Fashion Week is held annually, as is Montreal's public-oriented, outdoor Fashion and Design Festival (which also came to Toronto in 2007) with its designer labels, live music, and pervasive glamour. Where fashion week was once only for industry folk and the famous, many events are now accessible to the fashion-hungry masses as well (or at least to limited numbers of them). Trade exhibitions and events occur throughout the year and the country, and are open to the public on designated days.

 Check out BizTradeShows.com at www.biztradeshows.com/canada for upcoming shows (select by industry area to pull up the relevant listings). Canadian style magazine Flare (www.flare.com) lists fashion and beauty events, or see Minimidimaxi's online industry portal The Canadian Fashion Stage (www.minimidimaxi.com) for a directory of designers, manufacturers, and retailers.

Lida Baday, David Szeto, Ross Mayer, Arthur Mendonça, and Susan Harris are among current industry names, while Native-designed and influenced fashion is coming to the fore thanks to designers like Denise Brillon, Ronald Everett, and Dorothy Grant. To get your fashion fix, keep an eye out for sample and warehouse sales, peruse the boutiques of local designers, or head to an official apparel shrine such as Winnipeg's Costume Museum of Canada (www.costumemuseum.com), or the Bata Shoe Museum in Toronto (www.batashoemuseum.ca).

ACTIVITIES FOR CHILDREN

Sport

Keeping your kids busy and active in Canada isn't a difficult task. Organised and competitive sports options are provided through sports associations and leagues, and cover everything from soccer and baseball to gymnastics and figure skating. The National Sport Organizations for each sport provide links or contact details for their provincial offshoots, which in turn provide links or contact details for local leagues or associations, including those at junior and minor level.

> See the Sports Canada website at www.pch.gc.ca/progs/sc for the list of National Sport Organizations.

TIP

■ Community rec centres, your child's school or the local council are good places to get information on sports options for kids.

Family fun centres or indoor playgrounds can be great in the winter, with rock-climbing, play equipment, mini golf, and arcade games. Most communities have access to a community recreation centre, an indoor pool or a YMCA (or all of the above). The Children's Fitness Centres of Canada offers health and skill development through their gymnastics-based training programmes (see www.childrensfitnesscentres.com), and dance programmes are widely available, covering ballet, hip hop, tap, jazz, and creative dance. The Boys and Girls Clubs of Canada offer kids a range of sporting and non-sporting activities and programmes – visit www.bgccan.com for full details. Community rec centres, your child's school or the local council are good places to get information.

Art and entertainment

Many theatre, ballet, orchestral, and even opera companies offer performances and programmes aimed at children. Art galleries and museums frequently run craft and learning programmes and holiday activities for kids, and science centres, museums, and zoos are obvious destinations. Public libraries are heaven for bookworms, and they also tend to be central locations for community events and programmes that offer story-time readings, art-and-craft workshops, or events with authors or comedians. Municipal councils provide a range of activity programmes and events for kids, and are a great starting point for finding out about others. Movies are a perennial favourite, and most of Canada's major cities now have an IMAX cinema. There are also film festivals designed specifically for children, such as Sprockets (www.sprockets.ca) in Toronto, which holds year-round events as well as the major festival in April, or Flicks (www.flicksfilmfest.org) in Saskatchewan. For something with a little more live action, find out if a circus, fair or exhibition is in town, or head to one of the more kid-friendly historic sites, such as a fort or garrison with interactive displays and opportunities to play dress-up.

Outdoors

Getting outdoors can mean grabbing the tent, sunscreen, and some bug spray and heading to one of Canada's gorgeous parks, teaching the kids how to fish (or maybe they'll be teaching you), or playing catch in the playground down the street. Camps

School students dressed in period jackets watch the goings on at Fort Henry in Kingston, Ontario

and other activity programmes are available through the summer months while schools are closed, and in the winter, those long, cold weekends can often be spent playing in the snow – sliding, sledding, tobogganing, building snowmen or snow forts, or ice skating. Most towns and communities have access to at least one public skating rink. Berry picking, picnics or trips to the beach make for great whole-family outings in the milder months; smaller children will get a buzz out of visiting baby animals and seeing the workings of children's farms; and older kids and teens can wear themselves out with paintballing, skateboarding, snowboarding, mountain biking, rafting, trekking or any number of other outdoor pursuits.

About Canada

■ HISTORY OF CANADA

Exploration and colonisation

As is the nature of history, there are various seeds from which 'the true north strong and free' arguably grew. John Cabot's 1497 voyage of discovery to the North American continent, perhaps, when he landed at Nova Scotia or Newfoundland (the exact location was never confirmed). Or the east-coast travels of explorer Giovanni da Verrazzano in 1524, who dubbed the region New France (before coming to a horrific end some years later at the hands of cannibals in the Caribbean). Or, as most commonly suggested, Jacques Cartier's three voyages between 1534 and 1542, over the course of which he landed in the Gaspé, plunged the fleur-de-lys-bearing flag into the ground and formally claimed the land for the French king, took in the future sites of Quebec City and Montreal – then Aboriginal settlements known as Stadacona and Hochelaga – and attempted, with little success, to establish a colony. The next two centuries saw a series of French exploration and settlement attempts. In 1605, after a failed effort at Île Sainte-Croix the preceding year, Pierre du Gua de Monts and Samuel de Champlain founded a colony at Port Royal (now Annapolis Royal) on the continent's eastern coast. Thus began the first permanent, if initially unstable, European settlement in what we now know as Canada, and the development of Acadia – a region roughly comprising the present-day Maritime Provinces. Alliances were forged between the French settlers and Acadia's Aboriginal inhabitants, the Mi'kmaq and the Maliseet. In 1608, Champlain – considered the 'father' of New France, and later appointed governor – established a trading post at Cap Diamant, Quebec, to control and further expand the burgeoning fur trade. The famed Cardinal de Richelieu, under Louis XIII, emulated English and Dutch colonial policy in the 1620s by setting up a joint-stock company – the Company of New France, known as the Compagnie des cent-associés. Its 100 shareholders were charged with promoting Catholicism in New France (particularly, though particularly unsuccessfully, to the Aboriginal population), developing the lands and bringing out new settlers. The British briefly wrested Quebec from the French from 1629 to 1632, and in 1663, with economic progress and population expansion continuing to elude New France, and attacks from the disenchanted Aboriginal Iroquois intensifying, Louis XIV took control of the colony and made it a province of France.

Carved pole detail, Gwaii Haanas National Park Reserve, Haida Gwaii (Queen Charlotte Islands), BC

Conquest and control

Skirmishes between the French and the British were destined to continue. From 1670 the English-backed Hudson's Bay Company (HBC) was a major fur-trading and exploratory presence in the north-west regions of the land, and it clashed frequently with the French over trading rights. (After 1776, HBC's main competition would instead be the North West Company, formed by Montreal-based Scots.) New France expanded, but was compelled to relinquish the Hudson Bay regions, Newfoundland, and most of Acadia (Nova Scotia, as it was called in its British incarnation) to the British in 1713. Île Saint-Jean (now Prince Edward Island) and Île Royale (now Cape Breton Island) remained with France. Fearing an uprising, and angered by the Acadians' lack of enthusiasm in pledging loyalty to England, the British authorities began a devastating process of deportation in 1755, scattering the Acadian settlers down the Atlantic coast as far south as Georgia. Around three-quarters of the Acadian population was relocated, or perished in the process. In September 1759, during the Seven Years' War (1756–1763), the Marquis de Montcalm's French troops famously fell to the English soldiers of General James Wolfe, on Quebec's Plains of Abraham (you can visit the spot today in Battlefields Park, Quebec). Montreal was lost the following year. The French surrendered and the British takeover of New France, formalised through the 1763 Treaty of Paris (and referred to ever after as the Conquest, *la Conquête*), left them just two tiny islands off the coast of Newfoundland: St Pierre and Miquelon, which still belong to France today.

The Quebec Act, passed in 1774, replaced the first constitution for Britain's re-titled Province of Quebec. It was conciliatory towards the French Canadians, officially recognising their language, civil code, and freedom of religion as Catholics, and it enlarged the province's boundaries in all directions (including far into the current USA). The Act outraged the American colonies to the south and was one of the triggers of the American Revolution in 1775, which included an ultimately unsuccessful attack on Quebec. Defeat in Virginia in 1781 saw Britain acquiesce to the Americans, accepting US independence. Thousands of United Empire Loyalists fled north, settling in Nova Scotia – including the portion that became New Brunswick in response to Loyalist lobbying – and in Quebec. Many moved into the region that would eventually become Ontario. Demands by these Loyalists for British laws and legislative systems caused conflict with the Quebec Act, and resolution came in the form of the Constitutional Act of 1791. The province was divided in two: Upper Canada, which was primarily English speaking; and Lower Canada, on the lower section of the St Lawrence River, which was predominantly French. (The name 'Canada' developed from *kanata,* a Huron-Iroquois word meaning 'village' or 'settlement'. It was used by Jacques Cartier in the 1500s to refer to Stadacona – now Quebec City – and the surrounding regions.) The USA invaded Canada during the War of 1812 in a second attempt to conquer Britain's North American colonies. Their only true success, however, was in uniting the Canadians against them. While there was no formal winner, and the conquered land on either side was returned through the Treaty of Ghent, it was a cohesive force in binding together those of all backgrounds, cultures, and languages – at least for a while.

FACT

■ The name 'Canada' developed from *kanata,* a Huron-Iroquois word meaning 'village' or 'settlement'. It was used by Jacques Cartier in the 1500s to refer to Stadacona – now Quebec City – and the surrounding regions.

Canada – from province to dominion

The evolution towards true parliamentary democracy in Canada was ignited by the rebellions of 1837, which occurred in both Upper and Lower Canada. The Canadians wanted self-government, but the rebellions degenerated into violence and failed. Lord Durham, sent from Britain to investigate, recommended reuniting the two Canadas and instituting responsible government, allowing the people greater influence over government decisions. A major theme of Durham's report was the assimilation of the French Canadians, which he felt essential to peaceful coexistence. The Act of Union, implemented in 1841, brought the united Province of Canada into being. The British decision-makers loved the concept of anglicising the French (French was prohibited), hated that of responsible government (this was refused), and were more than happy to replace the previous two governments with one. Especially as both Canada East and Canada West (as they were now to be known), despite their considerably different population sizes, were given an equal number of seats in the new house of assembly – a further help to the English in subjugating the French. Outcry and reform prevailed, and in 1848 the French language was recognised once again, and responsible government was granted to Canada and Nova Scotia. By 1855 it was operating in all the existing provinces.

Political divisions and deadlock became an increasing problem for the Province of Canada, and a federation of Britain's North American colonies – or some of them, at least – seemed to offer a solution. Uneasiness about potential aggression from the USA was also a factor. Nova Scotia, New Brunswick, and PEI (an independent colony since 1769) had already been ruminating on a possible Maritime Union, and Canada asked to join the discussions. Three conferences followed, in Charlottetown, Quebec, and London (England), and on 1 July 1867, confederation was born under the British North American Act. The Province of Canada divided once more, and

Province House in Charlottetown, PEI, site of the Charlottetown Conference on confederation

Quebec (Canada East), Ontario (Canada West), Nova Scotia, and New Brunswick became the original four provinces of the new Dominion of Canada. The city of Ottawa, selected by Queen Victoria as the capital of the Province of Canada, was now capital of the Dominion.

Rupert's Land and the North-Western Territory, purchased from the Hudson's Bay Company in 1870, became the Northwest Territories. The then-diminutive Manitoba was created from this land, followed by the Yukon in 1898, and Alberta and Saskatchewan in 1905. BC and PEI entered the confederation in 1871 and 1873. Newfoundland contributed the last portion of Canadian land when it finally joined in 1949, and Nunavut – subdivided from the Northwest Territories as a result of land settlements between the Canadian government and the Inuit people – completed the current picture, becoming the country's third territory in 1999. See the Regional Guides, p. 347, for more on the history of Canada's provinces and territories.

THE EXPLOITATION OF EXPLORATION

The European explorers who first set foot on the Canadian shore didn't just arrive in an empty, uninhabited land. At the time European contact was made, around 300,000 Aboriginal people lived on the land. They – or their ancestors – had been there for over 4,000 years. While trade with the white men may have brought some advantages, contact with Europeans meant death and destruction for many Aboriginal groups. Infectious diseases such as smallpox and tuberculosis had a devastating impact: the Haida people along Canada's west coast were literally decimated as a result, and Haida Gwaii (the Queen Charlotte Islands), once a Haida stronghold, are now scattered with the remnants of deserted villages. Some Aboriginal groups altered their seasonal migrations and hunting patterns to meet the demands of traders. Others were slaughtered; traditional habitats and hunting grounds were encroached upon; modern weaponry virtually wiped out animal species, causing starvation. The Beothuk people of Newfoundland died out completely. From the 1830s, Aboriginal children were taken from their homes and placed in harsh, often abusive residential schools, with the aim of assimilation. Land-cession treaties created reserves for Aboriginal use, but these have been plagued by neglect, poverty, and unemployment. Today, an increased respect is given to Canada's Aboriginal peoples, and land-claim settlements aim to recognise their rights and relationship to the land.

■ GEOGRAPHICAL INFORMATION

Area and geography

The sheer vastness of Canada can be difficult to comprehend. At almost 10 million sq km, it spans six time zones, is bordered by three oceans, and represents 7% of the earth's surface. Canada is around 40 times the size of Great Britain, and second in area only to Russia. A breadth of 5,514 km means that a Newfoundlander is closer to the African continent than to his or her fellow Canadians in BC. Much of the land has never been permanently settled, with many sections of the Arctic tundra and islands remaining uninhabited. From east to west and up to the Arctic tree line, forest covers almost half the landscape. The Canadian Shield, a plateau of ancient rocks extending over the north from Manitoba to Quebec, is the major physiographic region of the country. The Cordillera regions of western Canada include the Richardson, Coast, and Rocky mountains, and extend throughout most of BC and the Yukon, and into parts of Alberta and the Northwest Territories. As well as mountains, BC boasts fertile valleys such as the Okanagan. Alberta's impressive mountain ranges – which include some of the best skiing locations in the country, such as the world-famous Banff – drop abruptly into flatlands, which continue through Saskatchewan and Manitoba. The plains of the three prairie provinces have an underrated beauty – less superficially striking than mountain or coast, they contain many lakes and Canada's

FACT

■ At almost 10 million sq km, Canada spans six time zones, is bordered by three oceans and represents 7% of the earth's surface.

Capturing the beauty of the Rockies – Canada's landscape is diverse

FACT

■ The Canadian Shield, a plateau of ancient rocks extending over the north from Manitoba to Quebec, is the major physiographic region of the country.

richest farmland, and offer phenomenal skies, breathtaking weather displays, and a patchwork of glowing colours. The Great Lakes/St Lawrence Lowlands of southern Ontario and southern Quebec are filled with forests and lakes, and the Appalachian mountain chain stretches east from the St Lawrence River to the New Brunswick coast. Islands dot all of Canada's coastal regions, to the east, the west, and the north.

Regional divisions

Canada is divided into 10 provinces and three territories. BC, with its mild weather, rugged, beautiful landscape and trendy west-coast culture, is the westernmost province; its capital is Victoria, but its largest city is Vancouver. Alberta, Saskatchewan, and Manitoba are often grouped together as the Prairies. These three provinces, with their stretches of wheat fields, grasslands, lakes, and mountains, cover an area greater than Mexico. Their capital cities are Edmonton, Regina, and Winnipeg, respectively. Ontario and Quebec, though substantially different in many ways, are recognised as 'Central Canada', based on the economic centrality of cities like Toronto and Montreal, their respective capitals. Ottawa, the capital city of Canada, is also located in Ontario. Half of all Canadians live in the southern regions of these two provinces, in the 5% of Canada that forms the Great Lakes–St. Lawrence Lowlands.

Newfoundland and Labrador, New Brunswick, Nova Scotia, and PEI border on the Atlantic Ocean and are collectively known as the Atlantic Provinces. The latter three, which joined the confederation of Canada long before Newfoundland and Labrador, are commonly referred to as the Maritimes. Their capitals, in order, are St John's, Fredericton, Halifax, and Charlottetown. These eastern provinces – particularly the Maritimes – are the smallest in Canada, and their friendly, relaxed style is often attributed to their size. The northern third of the country, which is predominantly Arctic, is divided into three territories: the Yukon, the Northwest Territories, and Nunavut, with Whitehorse, Yellowknife, and Iqaluit their capital cities.

FACT

■ Half of all Canadians live in the southern regions of Ontario and Quebec, in the 5% of Canada that forms the Great Lakes–St. Lawrence Lowlands.

Population

Given the enormity of the country, Canada's population of 33.3 million – just 0.5% of the world's residents – is surprisingly small. Between the 2001 and 2006 censuses, the population grew by 5.08%, the highest growth rate of all G8 countries and a noticeable increase from the 1996–2001 rate of under 4%. An aging population and a decreasing birth rate are responsible for the continuing drop in natural population increase, and immigration now accounts for approximately two-thirds of growth. Overall, Canada's population increases by one person every one minute, 36 seconds. Senior citizens comprise almost 14% of the population; the median age of Canadians is at an all-time high of 39.5, almost two years higher than in the last census. Aboriginal Canadians comprise almost 4% of the population, with approximately 698,000 First Nations people (40% of whom live on reserves), 389,800 Métis, and 50,500 Inuit.

Economic and climatic factors have resulted in an uneven distribution of people throughout the country. While the enormous amount of uninhabited land gives an overall density of just 3.5 people per sq km, more than four-fifths live in urban areas, and the larger cities average 245 people per sq km (Vancouver, and Westmount in Montreal, cram in over 5000 people per sq km). This varies significantly between provinces, however, with the Atlantic Provinces and the three territories having the highest proportions of non-urban dwellers. In 2006, 86% of Canadians were living in Ontario, Quebec, BC or Alberta. The three territories, despite their huge size, account for just 1% of the country's population. Around 90% of Canadians live within 160 km (100 miles) of the Canada–US border, with major centres being Toronto (5.1 million), Montreal (3.6 million), Vancouver (2.1 million), and Ottawa–Gatineau (1.1 million). Calgary and Edmonton are substantial cities as well, with each now supporting over 1 million residents. Population growth is generally slower – and in some cases is in decline – in rural areas, which tend to lose residents to nearby urban centres, or to job prospects in other provinces. Ontario, BC, and – particularly in recent years – Alberta are the favoured destinations of immigrants from within and outside Canada. Census results for Saskatchewan and Newfoundland and Labrador show repeated population declines – primarily due to interprovincial migration – though the fortunes of these two provinces, and their resident numbers, now seem to be turning around, thanks to the success of their natural resource industries (see p. 227).

Overall, 57.8% of Canadians claim English as their mother tongue and 66.7% speak it at home. Just over 22% of Canadians have French as their mother tongue (most are in Quebec), and one in five Canadians have a mother tongue other than English or French. Almost the same number – 6.19 million – are foreign born. The largest proportion of recent immigrants come from Asian and Middle Eastern countries, with recent European immigrants – particularly those from the UK and Romania – coming in second. Immigration from Central and South America and the Caribbean is rising gradually, making this the third-largest group of newcomers, followed by those from African countries. Canada's multiethnic population is usually referred to as a 'mosaic' – as distinct from the 'melting pot' of the United States – with highly visible minority groups maintaining their cultural and religious heritage. Over 52% of recent immigrants live in Ontario, with 17.5% going to Quebec, 16% to BC, and 9.3% to Alberta. Manitoba gains only 2.8% of newcomers, but its overall immigrant population is fourth largest, proportionately, in the country. Atlantic Canada's foreign-born population stands at 3.8%, though it has grown notably since the last census, and most immigrants to these provinces are UK or US born. Immigrant traffic to the three northern territories is low – around 1000 people between 2001 and 2006 – though the Yukon is starting to increase the

FACT

■ An aging population and a decreasing birth rate are responsible for the continuing drop in natural population increase, and immigration now accounts for approximately two-thirds of growth.

" Canada is a multicultural country with people from many different countries, different cultures and different races. The mix of cultures enriches the country and we can learn a lot from it.
Dante Pizarro

promotional push. Most immigrants to the territories hail from the Philippines, the UK, and the US. The vast majority of newcomers settle in Canada's large urban centres, and the vast majority of these – seven out of every 10 – choose Toronto, Montreal or Vancouver. For many, the presence of family or friends is the deciding factor, though job opportunities (Toronto), French language (Montreal), and climate (Vancouver) also play a part. Just 2.8% of newcomers, and 5.1% of all immigrants, live in rural areas. More details on population distribution, demographics and ethnicity are included under *A culture of diversity*, p. 8, *Immigration and the income gap*, p. 96, and in the neighbourhood and city guides from p. 100.

 Statistics Canada's Portrait of the Canadian Population in 2006 Census (also available as a PDF) and other analysis documents can be viewed online at www12.statcan.ca/english/census06/analysis.

Climate

AVERAGE TEMPERATURES (°C) FOR COLDEST AND WARMEST MONTHS						
City	Coldest month	Average max.	Average min.	Warmest month	Average max.	Average min.
Calgary, AB	January	-2.8	-15.1	July	22.9	9.4
Charlottetown, PE	January	-3.3	-12.6	July	23.2	13.8
Edmonton, AB	January	-7.3	-16.0	July	22.8	12.1
Fredericton, NB	January	-4.0	-15.5	July	25.6	13.0
Halifax, NS	January	-1.2	-10.7	July	23.6	13.5
Iqaluit, NU	February	-23.8	-32.2	July	11.6	3.7
Montreal, QC	January	-5.7	-14.7	July	26.2	15.6
Ottawa, ON	January	-6.1	-15.3	July	26.5	15.4
Quebec, QC	January	-7.9	-17.6	July	25.0	13.4
Regina, SK	January	-10.7	-21.6	July	25.7	11.8
St John's, NL	February	-1.5	-9.3	August	19.9	11.1
Toronto, ON	January	-2.1	-10.5	July	26.8	14.8
Vancouver, BC	January	6.1	0.5	August	21.9	13.4
Victoria, BC	January	6.9	0.7	August	22.0	10.8
Whitehorse, YT	January	-13.3	-22.0	July	20.5	7.7
Winnipeg, MB	January	-12.7	-22.8	July	25.8	13.3
Yellowknife, NT	January	-22.7	-30.9	July	21.1	12.4

A red-roofed cabin perches above a frozen, snowy lake near Manitoulin Island, Ontario

The image of Canada as a snow-bound land with year-round cold temperatures is pervasive but (thankfully) incorrect. In fact, parts of BC offer rainforests and mild winters, while most of southern Canada has summers far hotter than those common in Britain, and equally as warm as many summer days in Australia or other southern-hemisphere countries. Winter in the Prairies can be extremely cold, however, with temperatures plunging below −40°C on occasion (but more commonly dipping to minimums of between −15°C and −25°C) and snow on the ground for around 80–130 days each year. Snowfall is also heavy in the central region, especially in Quebec and northern Ontario, and Montreal and Ottawa often have very snowy winters. Toronto receives far less snow than these cities (though it can still be considerable – the almost record-breaking winter of 2007–2008 was a case in point, with 194cm over the season), and has a reputation for being somewhat alarmist when it comes to dealing with it. To be fair, in a city that size, even a light snowfall can trigger delays, accidents, and traffic chaos (see p. 196 for tips on driving in winter weather). Humidity in both summer and winter is a factor in Canada's largest city, and though winter temperatures may not be extreme, it tends to be a damp cold, with less sunshine to dry the air and lift the spirits. Alternate thaws and freezes are common as the weather swings between positive and negative temperatures. More northerly and inland regions experience a dry cold, where the climate, though often substantially colder, can actually be easier to bear. Winters are still long, but frequently bright and sunny, with blue skies over blinding white snow, and rays of sun hardy enough to emit real warmth. The lack of moisture can take you (and your skin) some time to adjust to, so moisture-rich hand wash, shower gel, and body lotion often become necessities. Rain is rare or nonexistent during the true winter in these regions, which include cities such as Calgary and Edmonton, whereas the east and west coasts – and even southern Ontario – can experience rain throughout. Vancouver and Victoria are especially rainy, and get little snow. Freezing rain and ice storms can occur across the country, and the worst are devastating, snapping power lines and poles, making driving impossible and generally creating chaos. The Maritime climate is wet and stormy, with a winter cloud-cover reminiscent of England or Scotland, while weather on the exposed island of Newfoundland is notorious: St John's is the wettest, windiest, cloudiest, foggiest, and snowiest city in Canada (and its residents are rightly proud of the fact).

TIP

The lack of moisture during winter can take you (and your skin) some time to adjust to, so moisture-rich hand wash, shower gel, and body lotion often become necessities.

 For more Canadian weather and climate information, visit Environment Canada at www.ec.gc.ca or The Weather Network at www.theweathernetwork.com.

> **Gerald Garnett talks about living with the weather in the mountainous Kootenay region of BC:**
>
> I think the European in me loves the definite division into four seasons. There is something so exhilarating about the return of the swallows and the flowering crocuses in the spring. I love all this water. There's over 3m of snow each year at our ski cabin. It's just magical touring around at 6,000 ft in the depths of winter. In the summer in the Kootenays a hot day is 80°F (26.5°C), with none of that open-oven-door wind of Australia, or hot nights sweating under a sheet.
>
> Yet the first winter our water pipes froze on Christmas morning. We had to run a black plastic hose from the creek through the snow and leave it running 24 hours a day for the next three months. If it froze, we would drag it inside and wind it around our kitchen, living room, and dining room until it coughed up buckets of little ice pellets.

IN THE DEEP MID-WINTER: EXPERIENCES FROM NORTHERN CLIMES

- You can definitely feel the difference between −10°C and −20°C. And between −20°C and −30°C. Anything below that defies description.
- When it's really cold, you can't make snowballs – there's no moisture, so the snow won't stick together.
- When it's that cold snow doesn't stick to your boots either. It's like walking through caster sugar (if you've ever tried that).
- There is no other sensation quite like that of your nose simultaneously running and freezing.
- The steam from your breath freezes into tiny icicles on your scarf/hood/any other item of clothing it comes into contact with.
- When it gets below about −15°C the air makes you cough and your nose goes tingly when you inhale.
- Water pipes freeze. And burst.
- Washing machines in unheated basements have been known to freeze, so you can't wash your clothes.
- Wet clothes in unheated basements (i.e. the clothes you couldn't finish washing in the frozen washing machine) freeze so hard they don't even feel damp anymore.
- Ice forms on the inside of car windscreens. Credit cards are really useful for scraping it off.
- When your fingers go numb even with gloves on, you can help them thaw by pulling them out of the glove fingers (but keeping them in the glove) and curling your hand up into a fist.
- Numb thighs feel very strange.
- People talk about how mild the day is when it gets anywhere near freezing point.
- No matter how 'safe' the ice is, almost every night there's something on the news about someone's foot/relative/snowmobile/truck going into a lake/pond/river.

■ POLITICS AND ECONOMY

Political structure

Canada's parliament consists of the Senate (Upper House) and the House of Commons (Lower House), with the Governor General representing the Queen. The Senate was originally intended to mirror the old-style British House of Lords, but given that Canada had no landed aristocracy, Senate members were appointed, rather than determined by hereditary entitlement. There are 105 seats in the Senate, and each province has a given number of Senators appointed by the Governor General on recommendation from the Prime Minister. Senators are appointed until the age of 75, at which point retirement becomes mandatory. The House of Commons is composed of members of Parliament who are elected by the voting public. Powerful provinces such as Ontario and Quebec have the lion's share of the House's 308 seats. For a bill to become law, both the Senate and the House of Commons must approve it. Either house can pass, amend, delay or defeat a bill. While the Senate can initiate bills (with the exception of bills proposing to spend public money or impose taxes), those relating to public policy are normally introduced in the House of Commons. The Senate's powers of veto are limited where constitutional amendments are proposed that affect both provincial and federal legislatures, though it may enforce a six-month waiting period before the relevant amendment can be re-approved by the provinces and the House of Commons.

The ruling government of Canada consists of a cabinet led by the Prime Minister. Most cabinet ministers head specific government ministries or departments, though assisting ministers, known as ministers of state, may also be part of the cabinet. Ministers are normally members of the House of Commons, and, on occasion, may be members of the Senate.

The constitutional structure of the 10 provincial governments parallels that of the federal government (though provincial Upper Houses were abolished by 1950). The legislative assembly in each province plays a similar role to the House of Commons, the provincial cabinet is led by a premier, and a lieutenant governor represents the Queen. Since 1867, provincial governments have grown in power and influence relative to the federal government – an unforeseen consequence of the division of powers set down in the Constitution Act, 1867. The responsibilities bestowed upon the provinces, such as health, social services, and education, have become important areas of public-sector control and administration. Canada's three territories are not constitutionally entrenched and have traditionally been federally administered, though all now have legislative assemblies and a premier. A commissioner in each territory plays a largely ceremonial role (similar to provincial lieutenant governors), representing the government of Canada.

Interior view of Canada's Parliament Buildings in Ottawa, Ontario

There are roughly 4,000 municipal governments in Canada: municipal or local governments derive all their authority from the provincial government, and have no formal association with the federal government. Southern Ontario and southern Quebec also have a county government system.

Canada's political structure evolved between 1867 and 1931, when the British parliament passed the Statute of Westminster, recognising Canada's shift from British colony to independence within the Commonwealth framework. In 1949, Canada's legal system also gained full independence when appeals to the Judicial Committee of the Privy Council at Westminster were abolished. Further constitutional change came with the proclamation of the Constitution Act, 1982. Two major constitutional innovations were entrenched: a formula for amending the Canadian constitution that didn't require the formal approval of the parliament at Westminster; and a Charter of Rights and Freedoms, which delimited the power of federal and provincial governments to pass legislation that, in the view of the courts, violated any of the rights or freedoms set out within the Charter. While Canada has always had judicial review, the advent of the Charter moved the Canadian political system away from the model of the British parliament and towards that of the United States.

Political parties

Between 1841 and 1867, leadership of United Canada (now Ontario and Quebec) swung between Conservative and reform governments, including the French–English coalition of reformers Louis-Hippolyte La Fontaine and Robert Baldwin, who twice led the united province. On confederation in 1867, the Dominion of Canada's first federal election was won by the Liberal Conservative party (generally known as the Conservative Party), headed by Sir John A. Macdonald. He served until 1873, then again from 1878 to 1891. In 1896, Sir Wilfred Laurier, as leader of the Liberal party, was elected, holding the position until 1911. This firmly established the pattern of Liberal and Conservative governments vying for power. The Conservative party returned to office from 1911 until the outbreak of the First World War, at which point a Union government – consisting of Conservatives, Liberals, independents, and one token labour member – was formed to implement conscription. (Unlike the United States, Canada entered both the First World War and the Second World War within a week of the initial declaration of aggression.) After the First World War, the Conservative party found great difficulty in getting and staying elected. The winning coalition originally struck by Macdonald had essentially been supplanted by the Liberal Party, which drew on the formula of a strong Quebec presence and a coalition of disparate factions of English-speaking Canada.

Between 1935 and 1957 the Liberals remained in office, guiding the country through the end of the Depression, the Second World War, and the post-war economic boom. In 1957, a Prairie lawyer named John Diefenbaker led the (newly titled) Progressive Conservatives to an upset victory, forming first a minority government, and then, in 1958, a majority government. Diefenbaker's nationalism was unappealing to French Canadians, as well as a constant source of irritation to the government south of the border. These two factors conspired to reduce him to a minority government in the election of 1962, with outright defeat following in 1963. The Liberals returned to power under Lester B. Pearson; Pierre Trudeau took over as Prime Minister in 1968 and held office (with one brief interruption) until 1984.

By that time the Progressive Conservatives had abandoned their former nationalistic outlook and elected Brian Mulroney, an English-speaking Quebecer, as their leader. In September 1984, Mulroney, with a sizable Quebec base and substantial support from Western Canada, was able to reforge a coalition and put together the largest parliamentary majority in Canadian history.

After a long and controversial reign, which included the passing of the Free Trade Agreement and two failed constitutional initiatives, Mulroney resigned as Prime Minister in February 1993. Kim Campbell was elected leader of the Progressive Conservative Party and was, by convention, immediately appointed Prime Minister (in the process becoming the first woman to take on the role). During the 1993 federal election campaign, forces combined to undermine the support bases that Mulroney had managed to re-establish. Lucien Bouchard, a former member of the Mulroney government, had formed the Bloc Québécois in 1990. Though the Bloc ran no candidates outside Quebec, they won 54 seats in Parliament. Furthermore, in Western Canada, the Reform Party, which had been created in 1987, took 52 seats. Its leader, Preston Manning of Alberta, capitalised on Western alienation from the federal system, perceived inequities in the distribution of powers, resentment of Quebec's demands and a desire for a more populous and less expensive system of government similar to that of the United States. Between these two new parties, 106 seats were captured. This robbed the Progressive Conservatives of their foundations, and the party suffered a humiliating fall from majority government status to the election of just two seats. A Liberal government took over under the leadership of Jean Chrétien; ironically, the separatist Bloc Québécois became the official opposition, or 'Her Majesty's Loyal Opposition'.

In 2000, the Reform Party tried to expand outside the West, changing its name to the Canadian Alliance. Meanwhile, the Progressive Conservatives, under the leadership of former Prime Minister Joe Clark, raised their public profile. The two right-leaning parties split the conservative vote in many ridings, contributing to the Liberal victory of November 2000. Chrétien resigned in December 2003, and Paul Martin, a one-time finance minister who made no secret of his desire for Chrétien to step down, won the party leadership with little competition. At that same time, members of the Canadian Alliance and the Progressive Conservatives voted to merge, forming the new Conservative Party of Canada. Led by Stephen Harper, the new party seemed poised to win enough seats for a minority or even a majority government in the national election of June 2004. They lost, and the Liberals, taking 135 of the 308 seats, formed a fragile minority government. Too fragile for long-term power, however: the Conservatives rallied and in January 2006 won their own minority government, with just 124 seats. The effort was repeated in October 2008, with 143 seats won. Harper's popularity is far from universal, and not helped by the cronyism observed with (and equally distrusted in) other recently vanquished world leaders such as US President George W. Bush and Australia's John Howard. However, the Liberals, under the frequently attacked leadership of francophone Quebecer Stéphane Dion, have been faring much worse in terms of public support, and preparations for the selection or a new party leader are currently underway.

FACT

■ The Liberals currently hold 76 seats, the Bloc Québécions 50, and New Democratic Party (NDP) 37, with two seats held by independents.

Montreal City Hall, Quebec, and the balcony from which French president Charles de Gaulle made his notorious speech

Quebec and separatism

In the early 1960s, la belle province awoke from what some historians have described as a pre-modern slumber, in which a powerful government and church officials worked in unison to regiment the beliefs and behaviour of the population as a whole. The conservative Union Nationale, led by Maurice Duplessis, faded following his death in 1959. A new provincial Liberal government, under the leadership of Jean Lesage, embarked on a programme of modernisation, secularisation, and liberalisation throughout the educational, economic, and governmental realms of the province. The Lesage years, 1960–1966, became known as the Quiet Revolution. This coincided with the rise of a new form of Quebec nationalism, which the Liberals coalesced under the slogan *Maîtres chez nous*! (masters of our own house). The principal political dynamic in Quebec then – as now – involved the protection and promotion of French language and culture. These concerns became more pressing as the distinctive Catholicism that distinguished the province from the largely Protestant continent no longer formed a barrier to external cultural influences. French president Charles de Gaulle outraged the Canadian government and much of the country when he visited Quebec in 1967 and famously declared '*Vive le Québec libre*' to a cheering crowd of Québécois in Montreal. The struggle turned bloody in 1970, when the terrorist group Front de libération du Québec (FLQ) kidnapped a member of the British consular service, James Cross, and later murdered Quebec's immigration, manpower, and labour minister, Pierre Laporte.

> **FACT**
>
> ▉ The principal political dynamic in Quebec then – as now – involved the protection and promotion of French language and culture.

The early 1970s saw Robert Bourassa's provincial Liberal government bring in legislation aimed at promoting French while also protecting non-francophone minority rights: it proclaimed French the official language of Quebec, and regulated the schools that children could attend and the languages to be used in business. These efforts were unable to stem the tide of sentiment in the province, and in 1976 the Parti Québécois (PQ) – dedicated to seceding Quebec from Canada – was elected into government, with René Lévesque as Premier. During its first four years in office, the PQ introduced Bill 101, Charte de la langue française, which prescribed strict and widespread use of French in Quebec and forbade the use of other languages (including English) on advertising or commercial signs. This, among other reasons, drove thousands of anglophone Quebecers out of the province forever.

In 1980, Lévesque held a referendum on the proposal to negotiate sovereignty-association, a state that would allow economic association with the rest of Canada, but political independence. A majority of francophone Québécois voted *oui*; however, when the votes of those who voted *non* were added to those of anglophone Quebec (which predominantly voted against the proposal), sovereignty-association was defeated 40–60. This was a watershed in Quebec's political history, though the failure didn't prevent the PQ from being re-elected in the 1981 election. In 1985, however, Robert Bourassa performed a great feat of political resurrection, returning as leader of the Liberal party and Premier of Quebec. Throughout his nine years in office, he became a master of bending with the political winds and navigating the narrow course between appeasing Quebec nationalist sentiment and cooperating constructively with the federal government.

The defeat of two constitutional initiatives designed to clarify Quebec's position within Canada – the Meech Lake Accord of 1990 and the Charlottetown Accord of 1992 – left federalist forces with fewer arguments in their arsenal and serious concerns about the long-term viability of Canada as it was then constituted. These concerns were borne out in the election of 1994, when the PQ, now led by Jacques Parizeau,

A NATION WITHIN A UNITED CANADA

In November 2006, Prime Minister Stephen Harper introduced a motion to recognise the Québécois as forming 'a nation within a united Canada.' Controversial though it was, the motion passed with 266 votes to 16. Its sense is sociological rather than legal, and the reference to 'the Québécois' as distinct from 'Quebec' has caused confusion and raised complex questions about exactly who, or what, the nation represents. The Québécois have long seen themselves as a nation, and traditionally celebrate Quebec National Day – more commonly called Saint-Jean-Baptiste, or just Saint-Jean – on 24 June each year. However, the recent move by the government of Canada is seen by many Canadians as a formal, and important, recognition of the Quebec people by Canada as a whole.

won 78 of 125 seats in the Quebec National Assembly. Though a British-educated anglophile, Parizeau was associated with the militant secessionist wing of the PQ.

Quebec's Aboriginal peoples, who belong to 11 groups including Inuit, Crees, and Mohawks, lay claim to much of the province's land. Their refusal to separate from Canada along with Quebec has been plainly stated, and their fight will likely win the support of the federal government and the international community as well as most of anglophone Canada. In 1998, Canada's Supreme Court ruled that Quebec cannot secede unilaterally; secession must therefore be negotiated with the federal government. Premier Bouchard (who took over from Parizeau after a second, agonisingly close referendum failure in 1995 – the vote coming in at 50.6 to 49.4 in favour of those opposed) resigned in 2000, when it became apparent that no referendum would be successful in the near future. Liberal Jean Charest was elected in 2003, a move seen as a rejection of the Parti Québécois and separatism; however, neither the Parti Québécois nor the federal Bloc Québécois have ruled out future votes on the separatist issue.

Economy

Canada's early economic policy, introduced by the Macdonald government in the 1880s, was to raise high tariff walls around imported goods in order to build up a manufacturing sector in Ontario and Quebec. Within that arrangement, the western and eastern regions of Canada supplied the centre with natural resources and agricultural products, and in turn bought manufactured goods. Canada underwent rapid industrialisation during World War I, and used the industrial capacity and skills developed during the war effort to start producing automobiles and other advanced technological products. The same process, at an accelerated pace, took place during the Second World War, after which the country's economy expanded rapidly. Much of this was due to the premium paid for the natural resources – such as pulp, paper, and minerals – that Canada exported throughout the world.

In the late 1960s, government growth was matched by rapid growth in economic production and activity. However, during the early 1970s the value of the exported natural resources, when adjusted for inflation, began to fall behind. Despite this reduction in wealth creation, the government continued to spend as if the economy were still growing at its previous rate. Universal healthcare and generous social services have not come cheaply. The federal government ran a deficit for nearly 30 years before then-finance minister Paul Martin and deputy minister Scott Clark balanced the budget in 1997–98. The government has been in surplus every year since (though global economic downturn may press it into a deficit for 2009–2010). While the NDP believes the surplus should be spent on social programmes and the Conservatives argue it should be returned to taxpayers, by convention it's used to pay down the national debt, which now stands at $467.3 billion.

In 1988, Canada signed the US–Canada Free Trade Agreement (FTA). This package of trading rules received considerable hostile attention from Canadian economic nationalists, and much journalistic and academic opinion was against it at the time. The FTA threw open the domestic market to competition, forcing Canadian companies and entire business sectors to restructure, to reinvest and to upgrade their technological and administrative strategies. Though a painful process, it ensured that Canadian goods would remain competitive on the world market. At the start of 1994, Canada, the USA and Mexico implemented the North American

FACT

▪ The federal government ran a deficit for nearly 30 years before then-finance minister Paul Martin and deputy minister Scott Clark balanced the budget in 1997–1998. The government has been in surplus every year since though global economic downturn may press it into a deficeit.

Free Trade Agreement (NAFTA). This further extended the principles of the FTA, and opened up the USA and Canada to competition from lower-labour-cost industrial areas in Mexico. It also increased Canada's appeal to foreign investors, and made it much easier for Canadian executives and scientists to work in the USA (though conditions for granting work permits can still be stringent).

In comparison to the USA, Mexico's significance as a Canadian trading partner seems minimal: according to trade data from Industry Canada it accounts for just 1.1% of Canadian exports (almost 80% head to the United States), and 4.2% of imports (US imports comprise 54.2% of Canada's total). Both imports and exports have risen steadily since the introduction of NAFTA, however – exports for 2007 were worth $4.95 billion – although the higher level of imports means Canada now runs a trade deficit with Mexico of around $12 billion. Canada runs a trade deficit with almost every country in the world except the USA, with which it runs a substantial surplus, and (on a more modest level) the UK; in 2007, Canada's imports from the States totalled $269.75 billion based on Statistics Canada figures; it exported $356.09 billion worth of merchandise. That merchandise trade surplus actually pushes Canada into a world trade surplus, despite a high degree of foreign ownership and dividend payments flowing out of the country. After the USA, Canada's largest export markets are the UK, China, and Japan. Exports to Europe have also been growing. In 2007, Canada's real GDP increased by 2.7%. Comprehensive figures for 2008 were not yet available at the time of press, but some decline seems inevitable.

FACT

■ After the USA, Canada's largest export markets are the UK, China, and Japan. Exports to Europe are also growing.

Canada's current economic climate is characterised by fluctuating commodity oil prices, an ailing manufacturing industry, and a dollar that has swung from US parity to a startling low (it's currently around US $0.84). While Canada is in an enviable position – relatively speaking – to weather the global financial storm, the weakened US market has also meant a weaker US demand for many products and services that have previously been among the most significant contributors to the Canadian economy. Canada has also been criticised for its lack of innovation, including the absence of a specific innovation policy to promote new discoveries and emerging, cutting-edge industries, and to capitalise on its economic benefits. In a mid-2008 report from the Conference Board of Canada, ranking the world's 17 wealthiest countries on a number of economic and social indicators, Canada placed just 15th for innovation (it placed second for education, and ninth overall). The government's commitment to research and development in science and technology is clear nonetheless: the National Research Council of Canada actively furthers innovation with an eye to both its economic and technological importance (as outlined on p. 261). Though natural resources play a substantial role in Canada's economic security and growth, the country is less dependent on these today than used to be the case. The number of people now employed in finance, insurance, scientific and technical services, for example, far outweighs those working in agriculture, forestry, fishing, mining, oil, and gas. Further details on the Canadian economy are included in Chapter 5, Working in Canada – see *A guide to the market* (p. 226), *Industry Overview* (p. 260) and the *Regional Employment Guide* (p. 266).

For the most recent economic indicators and a variety of statistics on Canada's economic position visit Canadian Economy Online, at www.canadianeconomy.gc.ca.

■ RELIGION

The canvas of religion in Canada is as broad, and as diversely painted, as the country's population. The vast majority of Canadians are either Roman Catholic (originating with the French colonists) or Protestant (originating with the British), though Protestant numbers – once substantially higher than Catholic – are falling as fewer young people affiliate themselves with the Anglican and United churches. According to the 2001 census (the most recent census to analyse religion), around 43% of the population is Roman Catholic, 29% is Protestant, and another 4% is Christian Orthodox or of another Christian faith. Jewish, Buddhist, Hindu, and Sikh religions each account for around 1% of Canadians, while 2% are Muslim. Around 100,000 people, or 0.3%, belong to other religions, and an increasing number – nearly five million people, or 16.5% – don't identify with any. The non-religious trend is most apparent in younger people, and is also notable among immigrants, particularly those from Hong Kong, Taiwan, and China.

These figures have shifted substantially as immigration alters Canada's ethnic and cultural make-up. Given the changes in the 10 years preceding the 2001 results – particularly the decline in Protestant numbers, and the rise in Islam, Hinduism, Sikhism, and Buddhism (all of which increased by between 84% and 129% over the period) – it seems reasonable to assume that by 2011, the time of the

A small roadside chapel between Vancouver and Flat Springs, BC

next census, the scene will have changed even more notably. There are marked differences between the provinces. Roman Catholics number highest in Quebec (83% of the province's population) and New Brunswick (54%), where Canada's largest French populations are. More than half of all Jewish Canadians and over 60% of Muslim Canadians live in Ontario, while half the country's Sikh population lives in BC. Newfoundland and Labrador has extraordinary levels of religious affiliation: though residents reporting 'no religion' have increased substantially, they still represent just 2.5% of the province's population. Proportions of non-affiliation are far higher in the Yukon (37%), BC (35%), and Alberta (23%). The Church of Jesus Christ of Latter-Day Saints is one of the top 10 denominations in Alberta, though it forms less than 2% of the total. Mennonites account for a similar proportion in Saskatchewan, and for 4.7% in Manitoba. Various Mennonite groups live in southern Ontario as well, though their numbers are small in comparison to other religions. Some, 'Old Order' Mennonites or Old Order Amish, are distinctive for their traditional dark clothing and for the horse-drawn buggies they drive. Canada promotes religious tolerance, and it's entrenched in the country's Charter of Rights and Freedoms, but this doesn't mean political and ideological clashes don't occur. A pre-election debate over equal funding for non-Catholic, faith-based schools in Ontario in 2007 was a case in point (and directly influenced the provincial election result).

Brightly coloured leaves light up a church doorway in Quebec

■ REGIONAL GUIDE

The following regional overviews aim to convey a little of the flavour and history of Canada's remarkably diverse provinces and territories. The population, area, and capital city of each is listed, as are other major cities, towns, villages, and even hamlets, where relevant. Many provinces also have rural or regional municipalities, which may be larger than some of the smaller urban centres, but these have not been included here.

Western Canada

British Columbia

Population: 4.11 million   **Area:** 944 735 sq km   **Capital city:** Victoria (pop. 330,088)

Other cities: Vancouver (pop. 2.12 million), Kelowna (pop. 162,276), Abbotsford (pop. 159,020), Kamloops (pop. 92,882), Nanaimo (pop. 92,882), Prince George (pop. 83,225), Chilliwack (pop. 80,892), Vernon (pop. 55418), Courtenay (pop. 49,214), Penticton (pop. 43,313)

'Western Canada' is a flexible term. It's sometimes used to refer to everything west of Ontario – a definition which encompasses the Prairies and may or may not include the Yukon and parts of the Northwest Territories. It's sometimes used to indicate BC and the regions surrounding the Rocky Mountains, including those of western Alberta. And it's sometimes used to mean beautiful BC alone. This long swath of land, which stretches up the entirety of Canada's west coast, is home to around 13% of Canada's population. Its obvious physical beauty and moderate climate draw immigrants from across Canada as well as from around the world,

> **Gerald Garnett, from Kaslo, BC, previously lived in the UK and Australia, and has an abiding love for his adopted country:**
>
> I especially love the feeling that it is only just emerged from the ice, so all the landscape has a new-minted quality. It doesn't have that soiled and smeared-by-human-footprints feel of Europe, where present life seems a ragged fringe of new growth on all that previous history. It doesn't have that bone-weariness in the old weathered soils of Australia, which have baked relentlessly in the sun for eternity. I love the flavour that the French-Canadians bring to this impossible country, although I hope it does not decay into ugly tribal nationalism. Only distance prevents us from seeing what a disparate bunch of people are supposed to be one culture. Just what are the Texas swagger of Alberta, the French musicians of the Gaspé, and the Newfoundlanders on their rock doing in one country? In BC I think it's a wonderful experiment in multi-nationalism, which the world itself has to undertake peacefully.

Alberta, the fast-track to a new life abroad

Alberta offers opportunities for everyone – a place where individuals and families can realise their dreams.

Why should you consider making Alberta your new home?

- Big blue skies, clean air, low crime and world-class recreation opportunities
- A fabulous lifestyle and lower cost of living than in the UK
- A booming economy with the lowest income tax rates in Canada
- One of the highest-ranked education systems in the world
- Excellent free public health care system
- Widespread career opportunities for skilled and semi-skilled workers

Alberta Immigrant Nominee Program (AINP)

In as little as six to 18 months, you, with the help of your employer, may apply to the AINP to accelerate your application for permanent residency through Citizenship and Immigration Canada. Your spouse and children may be included in your nomination.

There are several different ways to become nominated:

- Employer Stream
- Family Stream
- Self-Employed Farmer Stream

For information about the Alberta Immigrant Nominee program, visit: **www.AlbertaCanada.com/ainp**

For more information about the lifestyle and career opportunities Alberta has to offer, visit: **www.AlbertaCanada.com/immigration**

Misty forest view from Sleeping Beauty Mountain, Haida Gwaii (Queen Charlotte Islands), BC

and over 20 million visitors pass through each year. BC's development as a province was tied to the make-or-make-destitute field of gold prospecting, which sent out its fever-inducing call in 1858 on the discovery of gold along the Lower Fraser River. Europeans had been in the west coast regions in various forms since the 1770s, drawn by the fur trade – James Cook and his expedition are believed to have been the first to go ashore, landing at Vancouver Island. Key explorations in the BC interior had later been made by men such as Sir Alexander Mackenzie, Simon Fraser (for whom the Fraser River was named) and David Thomson of the North West Company. The Hudson's Bay Company had stretched its fingers out as far as the Island by 1849, where it had its headquarters and responsibility for a new colony at Victoria. But it wasn't until the gold rush that things began to gather speed: the colony of BC was established on the mainland, soon united with Victoria, and joined the confederation. Despite the fact that Europeans and the diseases they brought had severely diminished many Aboriginal communities, settlers in BC were still outnumbered by the First Nations people of the region in 1881. Today the opposite is true, and the Aboriginal population is just 5% of the provincial whole (though with almost 200,000 people identifying as Aboriginal, numbers are higher here than anywhere in Canada bar Ontario).

With major cities like Vancouver and Victoria, and large centres like Kelowna and Kamloops, BC has plenty of opportunities for urbanites. Yet its real appeal, and its main fame, comes in the form of hundreds of thousands of square kilometres of dense forest, craggy mountain ranges, and stunning river valleys (some of which are prime fruit- and wine-producing areas). Many towns – some just tiny hamlets – can be found throughout these regions, and for many they offer a rewarding, if remote, way of life. Remoteness is something all of Canada does well, and in BC you can travel a full day by ferry up the west coast, through a channel of seemingly endless mountains and trees, and see barely a sign of civilisation. Coniferous trees abound: western cedar, Sitka spruce, Douglas fir, lodgepole and ponderosa pine, balsam, hemlock, tamarack, and western larch. Mountains peak at well over 4,000m; unbelievably blue-green glacial rivers are as wonderful to watch as to raft down (the glaciers themselves, though melting drastically, are impressive as well); Vancouver Island and the beckoning Gulf Islands are worth some serious discovery time; and seven national parks – more than any other province – allow for days, weeks or months of breathtaking exploration.

> I left the gloom of England behind and bicycled and camped around the Gulf Islands. There can be few more beautiful places on earth and I was ecstatically happy.
> **Gerald Garnett**

FUR, FARMING, AND RETAIL THERAPY

The Hudson's Bay Company (HBC) first arrived in Canada in 1670, with fur-trading its main game. A joint-stock company overseen by governors and an operating committee, it was granted a monopoly over the Hudson Bay drainage system – all the lands that drained into the Hudson Bay. This huge territory in the north of the continent was named Rupert's Land, for the prince – a cousin of Charles II – who made the expedition possible. In 1821 a coalition was formed with rival fur-traders and explorers, the North West Company, under the HBC name. HBC had a directing role in the theatre of Prairie and northern Canadian history: not only were the provinces carved from the great parcel of land sold by the company to the Dominion of Canada in the late 1800s, but as part of the agreement, HBC was entitled to one-twentieth of the land's fertile regions. This comprised a substantial area, and with a flow of incoming settlers, HBC became a major real-estate player, pushing farmland sales across the west. Expansion into natural-resource development then diversified into non-fur-related retail and wholesale operations. Increasingly elaborate department stores opened in BC and the Prairies, and many – under the simplified moniker of The Bay – still operate today.

FACT

■ Mention of the Praires conjures up iconic images of flat, endless wheat fields, luminous skies, and picturesquely rolled bales of hay but it's not all farmland and wide horizons.

Prairies

Alberta

Population: 3.29 million	**Area:** 661 848 sq km	**Capital city:** Edmonton (pop. 1.03 million)

Other cities: Calgary (pop. 1.08 million), Lethbridge (pop. 95,196), Red Deer (pop. 82,772), Grande Prairie (pop. 71,868), Medicine Hat (pop. 68,822), Wood Buffalo (pop. 52,643)

Saskatchewan

Population: 968,157	**Area:** 651 036 sq km	**Capital city:** Regina (pop. 194,971)

Other cities: Saskatoon (pop. 233,923), Prince Albert (pop. 40,766), Moose Jaw (pop. 33,360), North Battleford (pop. 17,765), Yorkton (pop. 17,438), Swift Current (pop. 16,553)

Manitoba

Population: 1.15 million	**Area:** 647 797 sq km	**Capital city:** Winnipeg (pop. 694,668)

Other cities: Brandon (pop. 48,256), Portage la Prairie (pop. 20,494), Thompson (pop. 13,593), Steinbach (pop. 11,066), Selkirk (pop. 9,515), Winkler (pop. 9,106)

An abandoned truck sits under turbulent skies near Estuary, in south-western Saskatchewan

Mention of the Prairies conjures up iconic images of flat, endless wheat fields, luminous skies, and picturesquely rolled bales of hay. The three Prairie provinces – Alberta, Saskatchewan, and Manitoba – do offer some of Canada's most distinctive scenery, but it's not all farmland and wide horizons. Wetlands, lakes, snaking rivers, and even waterfalls break up an expanse of grasslands, parklands, and boreal forest. From the air, the varied waterways appear as iridescent jewels in a mosaic of greens, browns, and ochres. It's clichéd perhaps, but true – most notably in Manitoba, the 'land of 100,000 lakes.' Here, a true wealth of surface water – elongated lakes Winnipeg, Winnipegosis, and Manitoba the largest repositories – forms a startling 16% of the province's area. It's a solid few days' journey from Manitoban to Albertan border by car or train; faster of course, though less tactile, by air. The Trans Canada crosses the Prairies on its journey from sea to sea, passing through a number of major cities: Winnipeg and Brandon in Manitoba; Regina and Moose Jaw in Saskatchewan, with the larger Saskatoon on the Yellowhead Highway (the Trans Canada's northern fork) and Prince Albert further north; Calgary in Alberta, with Lethbridge to the south, Red Deer to the North, and Edmonton up on the Yellowhead. Some of these are covered in the City guides, p. 115. A diversity of national and provincial parks provide recreation and adventure, and get you off the beaten track. Manitoba's offerings range from Riding Mountain National Park – an escarpment-elevated expanse with hiking, camping, and panoramic views – to famed polar-bear haunt Wapusk National Park on the edge of Hudson Bay. In Saskatchewan, enjoy the quiet charms of lakeside Douglas Provincial Park, discover rare prairie plants and animals in Grasslands National Park, or climb the highest hills between the Rocky Mountains and Labrador in Cypress Hills Interprovincial Park – an undulating plateau of land stretching either side of the Saskatchewan–Alberta border, and the only interprovincial provincial park in Canada. Alberta is spoiled for choice, with fascinating dinosaur history (complete with fossils) and surreally beautiful Badlands formations at Dinosaur Provincial Park; a gorgeously varied intersection of praires, lakes, and mountains at Waterton Lakes National Park; and the dramatic beauty of its Rocky Mountain parks at Jasper and Banff. With its oil money, cattle, Christian fundamentalism, and rodeos, Alberta is the closest Canada gets to an 'American-style' west.

Rebellion, relocation, and immigration were major factors in the evolution of these provinces. Manitoba owes its existence to the acts of a rebel group (primarily Catholic, francophone Métis) led by spokesman Louis Riel. When the United States purchased Alaska in 1867, alarming Canada into land-purchase negotiations with the Hudson's Bay Company, the inhabitants of the Red River Colony – in the area occupied by Winnipeg today – became alarmed themselves. Realising their occupational rights were likely to be ignored in the land transfer, they fought, and their struggle resulted in a small area of land (much enlarged since) being designated the province of Manitoba. (Riel would ultimately hang for his role in a later battle, the Northwest Rebellion of 1885, in Saskatchewan.) In order to open up its new prairie regions for agricultural development and immigration, Canada then negotiated the Aboriginal populations off their land through a series of treaties, which effectively limited them to reserves – though First Nations people and Métis maintain a strong presence in Manitoba and Saskatchewan, which have the highest proportion of Aboriginal residents (at around 15% each) in Canada, after the three territories. Farming and urban growth spilled over into Saskatchewan and Alberta, and immigrants arrived from eastern Canada (particularly Ontario, but also Quebec), Iceland, Russia, the Ukraine, Holland, Germany, and Scandinavia. These new inhabitants brought a medley of languages and religions, and groups such as the Hutterites and Mennonites maintain an active presence today. Around 5.5 million people, of whom 505,000 are Aboriginal, now call the Prairies home.

Central Canada

Ontario		
Population: 12.16 million	**Area:** 1.08 million sq km	**Capital city:** Toronto (pop. 5.11 million)
Other cities: Ottawa (pop. 812,129), Hamilton (pop. 692,911), London (pop. 457,720), Kitchener (pop. 451,235), St Catherines–Niagara (pop. 390,317), Oshawa (pop. 330,594), Windsor (pop. 323,342), Barrie (pop. 177,061), Greater Sudbury (pop. 158,258), Kingston (pop. 152,358)		

Ontario is by far the most populous province in Canada, with around 39% of the total population and over 20% of the country's Aboriginal population. Almost as many people live in the Greater Toronto Area as in the entire expanse of the Prairies. Along with Quebec, Ontario also forms the industrial and economic heartland of the country, accounting for around 58% of Canada's GDP and over 55% of interprovincial exports. In terms of international exports, it leads by a mile: $177 billion worth of goods in 2007, followed by Alberta with $80.6 billion, Quebec with $67 billion and British

FACT

■ Manitoba's offerings range from Riding Mountain National Park – an escarpment-elevated expanse with hiking, camping, and panoramic views – to famed polar-bear haunt Wapusk National Park on the edge of Hudson Bay.

"

It was very interesting to learn of the First Nations people and their history, and to realise that their past and ongoing issues are very similar to those of the New Zealand indigenous people, the Maori.

Andrea Crengle

"

The importance of networking

Setting up in Canada

If you are considering going to Canada from the UK to set up a business or to start working for an employer in Canada, wouldn't it be helpful to talk to those who have already gone and successfully tried to do the same? Wouldn't you welcome some expert advice on the pitfalls and cultural and commercial differences between the UK and Canada? Wouldn't you welcome some introductions in advance of boarding the plane in the UK, and in Canada once you arrive? Once in Canada and set up wouldn't you benefit from trade referrals, including transatlantic trade referrals, and on-going professional advice from like-minded businessmen and women?

Advice before you go

Having an overview of the business opportunities to you in Canada across the country in the different provinces and territories, cities and towns and rural areas, could make the difference to you in terms of success or failure. Before setting off and incurring the expense of site visits, you need to have introductions and contacts that can save you precious time and money from a reliable organisation. There are many business networking organisations in the UK and Canada, but few offer a unique Canadian-British perspective, having a wide range of organisational and personal contacts.

Getting the right start

Whatever your sector of specialisation, the Canada-UK Chamber of Commerce based in London can offer you advice and contacts that can make a significant difference to you when making that transatlantic move. Its member companies and contacts include leading Canadian and British businesses, UK Government departments, Canadian Federal and Provincial department representatives in the UK and Canada, foreign direct investment representatives and many others. Membership benefits include attending events in the UK, advertising and brand awareness opportunities, notification of events and trade fairs in Canada and the UK, receipt of and the chance to contribute to our Chamber newsletter, directory of members, corporate lists of British companies in Canada and Canadian companies in the UK, FAQ Sheets, members discounts, business advice from other member experts including on starting a business in Canada, legal and tax advice and sector specialists.

Canada-UK Chamber of Commerce
www.canada-uk.org
info@canada-uk.org
+4420 7258 6578

Provided by expert contributor

Columbia with $31 billion. The full impact of the US and global recession remains to be seen. Ontario (or its government, at least) is proud of its size and power, and of playing host to Canada's capital city, Ottawa – though Ottawa-Gatineau, the official capital region, is actually shared with Quebec. And while the recent downturn in manufacturing has put something of a dent in both Ontario's pride and its economy, the province isn't planning to let go of its status in a hurry. Including Toronto – the city that most Canadians love to hate – and the capital region, Ontario has six of the 12 largest urban centres in Canada: among them are Hamilton – a growing city with almost 700,000 residents, Kitchener, London, the St Catherines–Niagara region, Oshawa, and Windsor (though auto-plant closures in these last two areas may have an impact on population). Barrie, Kingston, the nickel-belt boomtown of Sudbury, Guelph, Brantford, Thunder Bay, and Peterborough all have populations of well over 100,000.

Like Quebec, much of Ontario is covered by the rocky plateau, forests, and waterways of the Canadian Shield – such a distinctive element of the Canadian landscape that musical-comedy trio The Arrogant Worms even wrote a song ('Rocks and Trees') about it. (They also wrote one called 'Ontario Sucks,' but that's another story, and arguably untrue.) Ontario-based artist Tom Thomson and the famed Group of Seven painted Canada's natural environment exhaustively and extraordinarily in the first few decades of the last century – the McMichael Canadian Art Collection, on the outskirts of Toronto, is a permanent salute to the group, and the place where

Pretty Elora Gorge reflects the golden hues of fall in southern Ontario

many of them are buried. Ontario is bordered by Hudson Bay along its northern edge, and Lake Superior, Georgian Bay, and Lake Ontario – part of the Great Lakes system – to the south. Almost a sixth of the province's area is water, and water-based recreation and vacations are a big part of life for Ontarians. A vast and stunning array of national and provincial parks, beaches, rivers, and lakes beckon to those with an appreciation of the outdoors and even the smallest spirit of adventure. Algonquin Provincial Park, 7,630 sq km of wilderness, offers camping, fishing, and days (if not weeks) of canoeing; the Bruce Peninsula and Georgian Bay provide phenomenal hiking and paddling opportunities; and Manitoulin Island, the largest freshwater island in the world, is perfect for a day trip or an extended vacation, with beaches, boating, trekking, and climbing on the northern extension of the Niagara Escarpment, and the romantically pretty Bridal Veil Falls. Whether you live in, or just visit, Ontario, a trip to Niagara Falls – just 90 minutes from Toronto – is a must. Prepare to get wet, especially if you take a ride on the *Maid of the Mist*. If it's winter, prepare to be cold, though the incredible iced-over landscape and lack of tourists make a visit at this time of year worthwhile. Despite the remarkable tackiness of the surrounding town, the beauty and power of the Falls themselves – the sheer volume of rushing, gushing water, and the evidence of nature doing its unstoppable work – make it a highlight.

Quebec		
Population: 7.55 million	**Area:** 1.54 million sq km	**Capital city:** Quebec City (pop. 715,515)
Other cities: Montreal (pop. 3.64 million), Sherbrooke (pop. 186,952), Saguenay (pop. 151,643), Trois-Rivières (pop. 141,529), Saint-Jean-sur-Richelieu (pop. 87,492), Drummondville (pop. 78,108), Granby (pop. 68,352), Shawinigan (pop. 56,434)		

Quebec plunges into winter in a way that makes you feel you've stepped back in time. As you drive through tiny hillside towns on rough-patched country roads, children, huddled into their hoods, struggle home from school through drifts of snow. Black horses, stark like cut-outs against the cold white fields, toss their heads and trot restlessly. This monochrome landscape with its shades of white and grey, and pastel sunset tints, is by no means confined to Quebec – it's one of the joys (and one of the sometime tribulations) of winter in many parts of Canada. Perhaps it's the vivid colours of this province's other seasons that make it seem so apparent here: the lush greens of spring, the bold opacity of summer, and the subtleties and sharp, strong hues of fall. Quebec is probably the most romanticised of the provinces, and with good reason – the farmlands are enviably pretty, the cobbled streets of the capital or of Old Montreal are a photographer's dream, and small villages, complete with chapels or steepled churches, nestle into rural and bayside settings in a very European way. It's not all like this, of course; Quebec has its share of industrial areas, suburban sprawls, and socioeconomic concerns. And like most romantics, beneath its graciousness and charm – sometimes not all that far beneath – is a steel-like core: a steady resolve and a strong sense of what really does amount to national (as in *Québécois*) pride. After all, a history of conquest and suppression is not easy to forget, and provincial motto, *je me souviens* ('I remember') attests to this. Refusal to forget sometimes blurs into a refusal to forgive, however, a point illustrated recently by complaints from some Quebec sovereignists that Paul McCartney's free concert, part of the celebrations for Quebec City's 400th anniversary, was inappropriate given

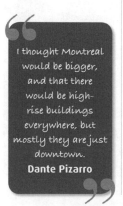

I thought Montreal would be bigger, and that there would be high-rise buildings everywhere, but mostly they are just downtown.

Dante Pizarro

Streetlight reflections in Quebec City, Quebec

his British roots and the history of British conquest. (McCartney's response? In true Beatlesque form, 'it's time to smoke the pipes of peace.')

Among Canada's provinces and territories, Quebec comes in second in terms of total area, behind only Nunavut. It stretches up into the Arctic north, wrapping around the eastern side of Hudson Bay, and down to where the waters of the St Lawrence River widen before filtering into the Atlantic Ocean. Quebec draws a big tourist crowd, particularly to its two largest cities, and has options galore for art, culture, and history buffs. Copiously covered by the lake-speckled, forested expanses of the Canadian Shield, with the fertile St Lawrence Lowlands and sections of the Appalachian Mountains to the south, the province offers endless outdoor opportunities as well. Soak in the agricultural ambience of the apple orchards and farms on Ile d'Orléans, just outside Quebec City; board a ferry in Montreal for a two-day cruise to the Magdalen Islands, with their extraordinary scenery and sculptural red sandstone cliffs; hike through the forests of the Laurentian Mountains (or ski the slopes in the winter); camp on the Gaspé Peninsula; or meander alongside the St Lawrence River, stopping at towns like Baie-Saint-Paul, beautiful Saint-Irénée or Tadoussac along the way. While the French language dominates throughout the province, as a visitor you can get by without it reasonably well in Montreal, and even in Quebec City. Outside of these regions life is much more straightforward if you have some French-speaking ability, though anglophone communities do exist, especially in areas such as the Eastern Townships (settled by British Loyalists from the USA following the American Revolution), the Gaspé, and the Ottawa Valley.

TIP

While the French language dominates throughout the province, as a visitor you can get by without it reasonably well in Montreal, and even in Quebec City. Outside of these regions life is much more straightforward if you have some French-speaking ability.

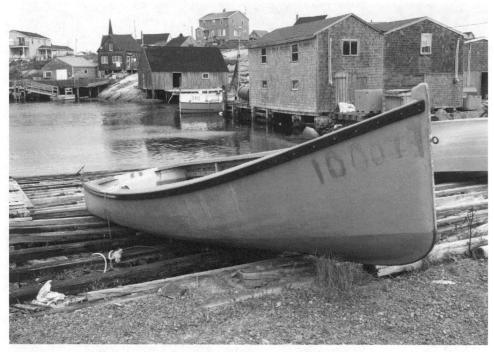

The famously picturesque Peggy's Cove in Nova Scotia lives up to its reputation

Atlantic Canada

Newfoundland and Labrador

Population: 505,469   **Area:** 405,212 sq km   **Capital city:** St John's (pop. 181,113)

Other cities: Corner Brook (pop. 26,623), Mount Pearl (pop. 24,671), Conception Bay South (pop. 21,966), Grand Falls–Windsor (pop. 13,558), Paradise (pop. 12,584), Bay Roberts (pop. 10,507), Happy Valley–Goose Bay (pop. 7,572), Labrador City (pop. 7,240)

Nova Scotia

Population: 913,462   **Area:** 55,284 sq km   **Capital city:** Halifax (pop. 372,858)

Other cities: Cape Breton (pop. 105,928), Truro (pop. 45,077), New Glasgow (pop. 36,288), Kentville (pop. 25,969), Lunenburg (pop. 25,164)

New Brunswick

Population: 729,997   **Area:** 72,908 sq km   **Capital city:** Fredericton (pop. 85,688)

Other cities: Moncton (pop. 126,424), Saint John (pop. 122,389), Bathurst (pop. 31,424), Miramichi (pop. 24,737), Edmundston (pop. 21,442)

Prince Edward Island

Population: 135,851   **Area:** 5,660 sq km   **Capital city:** Charlottetown (pop. 58,625)

Other cities: Summerside (pop. 16,153), Stratford (pop. 7,083), Cornwall (pop. 4,677)

FACT

Among Canada's provinces and territories, Quebec comes in second in terms of total area, behind only Nunavut.

These four provinces, cupped around the country's eastern perimeter, make up just 7% of the total population. Collectively and individually, they are a distinct – and a distinctly beautiful – part of Canada: PEI, the baby of all the provinces, with its wide beaches and rolling sand dunes, endless fields, deep red soil, and inextricable association with Anne of Green Gables. Nova Scotia, with the liveliness of Halifax, photogenic and fascinating history in Annapolis Royal and Lunenburg, and gorgeous views along Cape Breton Island's looping Cabot Trail. New Brunswick, with the northern shore of the remarkable Bay of Fundy (Nova Scotia has the facing shore), rugged Grand Manan Island and the Fundy Isles, colourful heritage in Saint John and international art exhibits in Fredericton. For many people, there's something almost mystical about the Island of Newfoundland, which, along with Labrador, its mainland counterpart, is far and away the largest of the Atlantic Provinces. Perhaps it's the fog. Or the relative remoteness. Or the fact that Newfoundlanders tend to speak differently, with an inflection and an extensive vocabulary of slang and riddles that has evolved over the last 400 years. Or maybe it's the ridiculously picturesque villages nestled along the coast, the icebergs that glide by each spring and summer, or the truly awe-inspiring geography of Gros Morne National Park. Labrador's share of the province is often overlooked, despite being substantially larger than the Island: much of it is tundra, barren and rocky, with forested regions in the southern interior and the imposing Torngat Mountains in the north. Its harsh, Arctic-like climate is described by Environment Canada's Atlantic Climate Centre as 'somewhere between inhospitable and invigorating'. Most settlements perch along the Atlantic coast or on Lake Melville (really a 250km-long inlet), though Labrador City and its sister town of Wabush are located inland. With a combined population under 10,000, they form Labrador's largest urban centre. Labrador's name was only officially incorporated into the province's title in 2001. Aside from Labrador, the winter climate in this eastern zone is generally more temperate than in much of the country (the west coast and parts of southern Ontario are exceptions). Some residents do find the winters overly long and wet, particularly in the coastal regions, but for most, this is more than made up for by the proximity to so much natural beauty. Between them the Atlantic provinces have seven national parks, covering a spectacular range of coastal and mountain landscapes.

Since 2001, the population of the Atlantic provinces has grown, though that of Newfoundland and Labrador dropped by about 7,500. The highly resource-dependent province was badly hurt by the cessation of cod fishing (see page 271), but its fortunes now seem to be looking up, with population increases recorded in the past year. New Brunswick, with many residents of French or Acadian origin, is home to Canada's largest francophone population outside Québec. People of English, Irish, and Scottish descent heavily populate all four provinces, and these accents – in combination with the Canadian – are often still discernible. Though Aboriginal residents are relatively few, ranging from a little over 1% of the PEI population to around 5% in Newfoundland and Labrador, numbers have increased substantially in recent years.

> Winter is not too bad here, but we don't get as much snow as other parts of Canada and it doesn't get so cold – down to around -25°C at the coldest from December to March.
> **Steven Maine**

FACT

Between them the Atlantic provinces have seven National Parks, covering a spectacular range of coastal and mountain landscapes.

Dictionary of Terms
Saint John, New Brunswick,

Saint Johner (sənt dʒɒnə) *n*
A resident of Saint John – typical
sense of humour, and a tendency

Explore (ɪk'splɔːr) *vb*
To experience and discover
– an activity with unending
potential in Saint John.

Supportive (sə'pɔːtɪv) *adj*
One of the most common
characteristics of Saint John
residents – the desire to
encourage, help, and assist.

Life on Your Terms (laɪf ɒn jɔː tɜːmz) *n*
The ability to live a life of your choosing

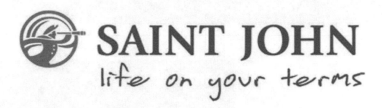

SAINT JOHN
life on your terms

Canada

characteristics include a friendly, welcoming attitude, an excellent
to demand a high quality of life.

Enriching (ɪnˈrɪtʃɪŋ) *adj*
Driven by the immense cultural capital of the community, something that nurtures, fulfills and makes life more meaningful.

Prosperity (prɒˈspɛrɪtɪ) *n*
A successful, flourishing or thriving condition common to the residents of the Saint John Community.

based on your priorities, without compromise.

Saint John

The New Brunswick city of Saint John is perched on the north shore of the Bay of Fundy at the mouth of the St John River. It is the oldest incorporated city in Canada, and is the largest city in New Brunswick, despite Moncton having a larger Census Metropolitan Area. The city is surrounded by two mountain ranges – the St Croix Highlands and the Caledonia Highlands – which run along the Bay of Fundy. There are numerous freshwater lakes, and three rivers systems and acres of national park.

Saint John experiences an even mix of all four seasons. Its climate is tempered by the Bay of Fundy, and so the area tends to experience fewer extreme temperature swings than other Canadian communities. Winters can be very snowy with an average temperature of -4°C. Springs are colourful due to the large variety of local flora and fauna (gardeners must beware of raiding rabbits and deer, even in the city centre). Summers bring early-morning fog to the coastal areas providing relief from the heat, and the sun's rays to the river communities, with an average temperature of 22°C. Autumn is arguably the most beautiful time of year in Saint John, when the last summer heat still clings and the trees turn a riot of fall colours.

Supported by four major growth sectors, the local economy has been transformed from a reliance on manufacturing and commodities to a healthy mix of professional, skilled trades, service and cultural-based employment. The growth sectors – information and communications technology, healthcare, energy and advanced manufacturing, and tourism – and complimentary entertainment and retail industries result in a sustainable local economy that is successfully weathering the economic uncertainty being felt elsewhere across the country.

Provided by expert contributor

COD, CLASHES, AND CONFEDERATION

The roots of each of the Atlantic provinces stretch back to the beginnings of Canada's European history, and Newfoundland's story is particularly dramatic: Viking settlement at L'Anse aux Meadows; Portuguese, Spanish, and British explorers; seas heaving with cod; clashes between the British and French; piracy; and violent domination by England's West Country Merchants. Settlements and some semblance of law eventually gained purchase on the Island, and with strong growth and responsible government by the mid 1800s, the colony decided against joining the Dominion of Canada. However, economic and government collapse following World War I and the Great Depression forced Newfoundland to return to British rule, until it could get back on its feet. By the end of World War II it had, and the population then voted – by a narrow margin – to enter Confederation.

Northern Canada

The Yukon		
Population: 30,372 **Area:** 482,443 sq km		**Capital city:** Whitehorse (pop. 22,902)
Other cities: Dawson (pop. 1,327), Watson Lake (pop. 846), Haines Junction (pop. 589)		
Northwest Territories		
Population: 41,464 **Area:** 1.35 million sq km		**Capital city:** Yellowknife (pop. 18,700)
Other cities: Hay River (pop. 3,648), Inuvik (pop. 3,484), Fort Smith (pop. 2,364)		
Nunavut		
Population: 29,474 **Area:** 2.09 million sq km		**Capital city:** Iqaluit (pop. 6,184)
Other cities: Rankin Inlet (2,358), Arviat (pop. 2,060), Baker Lake (pop. 1,728), Igloolike (pop. 1, 538), Cambridge Bay (pop. 1,477)		

Canada's three territories haven't traditionally been strong immigration destinations, though the Yukon government actively promotes immigration in an effort to change that trend, and operates a Provincial Nominee Program. Overall, immigrants account for 10% of residents in the Yukon, 6.9% in the Northwest Territories and 1.6% in

Russet plants sprawl across the rocky tundra in the Northwest Territories

Nunavut. In the five years leading up to 2006, the number of immigrants moving to each province was 385, 600 and 55, respectively. Winters in the territories are extremely cold, and the average summer high in Iqaluit, the capital of Nunavut, only just reaches into double figures. Despite their northern location, the capital cities of the Yukon and the Northwest Territories – Whitehorse and Yellowknife – actually have quite temperate summers, though nights are often chilly. A combination of mountains and plateaus, this massive expanse of northern land forms an extraordinary landscape. Much of the land is Arctic or Subarctic tundra, and in the northern regions of the Northwest Territories and Nunavut, ice covers the islands and seas for much (if not all) of the year. Between the three territories there are 11 national parks. These include Kluane National Park and Reserve and the northern section of Wood Buffalo National Park, and feature some of the most remote and striking environments in Canada. Many Inuit and First Nations groups, themselves descended from earlier Aboriginal peoples, inhabited the territories before Europeans first ventured into the area. There are two major Aboriginal cultures: the Dene, First Nations peoples who live in the subarctic regions of the land; and the Inuit, who live on the mainland and islands in the arctic zone. Within these larger groups are many other cultural groups, and a range of language dialects. The Métis are also a significant part of the Aboriginal population in the territories, forming around 11% of the Aboriginal population in the Yukon, and about 17% of that in the Northwest Territories. Nunavut's Aboriginal population is almost entirely Inuit.

The Northwest Territories was formed from the land sold to Canada in 1870 by the Hudson's Bay Company (see History of Canada, p. 318, and Fur, Farming and retail therapy, p. 341). Its borders were redefined a number of times: shrinking as other provinces were created or enlarged; swelling with Britain's transfer of the Arctic islands to Canada in 1880; and finally reducing to its present size, when Nunavut became a territory in its own right in 1999. Nunavut was created as part of a land settlement agreement between the Inuit and the federal government, and is divided into three land designations: some land is remains crown-owned, but the Inuit retain hunting, fishing and management rights; and the remainder is freehold, with either surface or subsurface rights. Like BC, the Yukon had established various settlements following European explorations and fur-trading quests, but it was the discovery of gold that fast-tracked the province's development. Prospectors had made their way north of the BC border, and in 1896 three men – the colourfully named George Washington Carmack, Skookum Jim, and Tagish Charley – struck gold on an offshoot of the Klondike River. The rush began. The city of Dawson sprang up in response, becoming the Yukon's first capital in 1898, the same year the territory became a separate entity and joined the Dominion of Canada. The 2,300 km Alaska Highway, built during the Second World War, brought an influx of newcomers and passed directly through the transportation hub of Whitehorse. Whitehorse took over as capital in 1953. These years represented a major shift in population, with the Yukon's Aboriginal population being outnumbered for the first time. Aboriginal Canadians now comprise around one quarter of the total population. In the Northwest Territories they represent just over half; and in Nunavut as much as 85% of the population is Aboriginal. The vast majority of people in Northern Canada live in the capital cities, which are also the major urban centres. The remainder live in smaller towns, or in communities that are often quite remote.

> **Gerald Garnett finds himself somewhat torn between promoting the Canada he loves, and keeping it a quiet secret:**
>
> There's a children's game called 'Sardines', where you go and hide, and everyone else has to find you. Gradually your hiding place becomes more and more squashed as you are discovered and people press in beside you. I feel that I have found the most beautiful hiding spot in the whole world. When asked to give advice to other people thinking of coming to live and work in Canada, I am tempted to say that I heard Chile was nice, or perhaps New Zealand or Tasmania.

Appendices

■ METRIC CONVERSIONS

The metric measurement system became legal in Canada in 1871, but it wasn't formalised – and didn't replace the British imperial system – until it became mandatory in the early 1970s. Imperial measurements haven't entirely disappeared: trade with the USA (which never converted) has maintained some degree of awareness, though certain US industries use metric conventions; fruit and vegetables tend to be priced by both the pound and the kilogram (though always sold by the kilogram); cookbooks often use both systems; and many Canadians – particularly those of older generations – are familiar with at least some imperial units. But the Metric System is now the one Canadians live by: decimals are used instead of fractions; and distances and speeds are expressed in kilometres, weights in grams and kilograms, liquids in litres and millilitres, and temperatures in degrees Celsius.

CONVERSION CHART

LENGTH (NB 10 mm = 1 cm, 100 cm = 1 metre)

cm	1	2	3	5	10	20	25	50	75	100
inches	0.4	0.8	1.2	2	4	8	10	20	30	39
inches	1	2	3	4	5	6	9	12		
cm	2.5	5	7.5	10	12.5	15.2	23	30		

WEIGHT (NB 14lb = 1 stone, 2,240 lb = 1 ton, 1,000 kg = 1 metric tonne)

kg	1	2	3	5	10	25	50	100	1000	
lbβ	2.2	4.4	6.6	11	22	55	110	220	2204	
lbβ	1	2	3	5	10	14	44	100	2246	
kg	0.45	0.9	1.4	2.3	4.5	6.4	20	45	1016	

DISTANCE

km	1	5	10	20	30	40	50	100	150	200
mile	0.6	3.1	6.2	12	19	25	31	62	93	124
mile	1	5	10	20	30	40	50	75	100	150
km	1.6	8	16	32	48	64	80	120	161	241

VOLUME

1 litre = 0.2 UK gallons	1 UK gallon = 4.5 litres
1 litre = 0.26 US gallons	1 US gallon = 3.8 litres

TEMPERATURE

Celsius	10	15	20	25	30	35	40
Fahrenheit	50	59	68	77	86	95	104

CLOTHING

Canada (and USA)	6	8	10	12	14	18	
UK	8	10	12	14	16	18	2
Europe	36	38	40	42	44	46	4

■ USEFUL BOOKS AND FILMS

Culture and Canadian

Brown, C, *Louis Riel: A Comic-Strip Biography* (Drawn & Quarterly: 2006)
Chesters, G, *Culture Wise Canada: The Essential Guide to Culture, Customs & Business Etiquette* (Survival Books Ltd: 2008)
Colburn, K, *So, You Want to Be Canadian* (Raincoast Books: 2004)
Ferguson, W and Ferguson, I, *How to Be a Canadian: Even If You Already Are One* (D & M Publishers Inc., 2007)
Hayes, D, *Canada: An Illustrated History* (Greystone Books: 2008)
McKinley, M, *Putting a Roof on Winter: Hockey's Rise from Sport to Spectacle* (Greystone Books: 2002)
MacLead, DP, *Northern Armaseddon: The Battle of the Plains of Abrahams* (D&M Publishers Inc, 2008)
Vaillant, J, *The Golden Spruce: A True Story of Myth, Madness, and Greed* (Knopf Canada: 2006)

Guidebooks and travelogues

Eyewitness Travel Guides Canada (Dorling Kindersley Ltd: 2008)
Ferguson, W, *Beauty Tips From Moose Jaw: Travels In Search Of Canada* (Knopf Canada: 2005)
Fischer, G and Hudson, N, *Unforgettable Canada: 100 Destinations* (Boston Mills Press: 2007)
Kerasote, T, *Out There: In the Wild in a Wired Age* (Motorbooks International: 2004)
Kreuzer, TL, *How to Move to Canada: A Primer for Americans* (St Martin's Press: 2006)
Lonely Planet Canada (Lonely Planet Publications, 10th edition: 2008)
Paterson, RM, *Far Pastures* (TouchWood Editions: 2005)

Food and drink

Duncan, D, *Canadians at Table: Food, Fellowship, and Folklore: A Culinary History of Canada* (Dundurn Group: 2006)
Hardy, A, *Where to Eat in Canada* (Oberon Press: 2008)
Murray, RA, *Taste Of Canada: A Culinary Journey* (Whitecap Books: 2008)
Penfold, S, *The Donut: A Canadian History* (University of Toronto Press: 2008)
Sneath, AW, *Brewed in Canada: The Untold Story of Canada's 300-Year-Old Brewing Industry* (Dundurn Group: 2001)
Stewart, A, *Anita Stewart's Canada: The Food, the Recipes, the Stories* (HarperCollins Canada: 2008)

Fiction

Atwood, M, *Moral Disorder* (McClelland & Stewart: 2009)
Lare, P, *Red Dos, Red Dos* (McClelland & Stewart: 2008)
Montgomery, LM, *Anne of Green Gables* (McClelland & Stewart: 2008)
Munro, A, *Alice Munro's Best: Selected Stories* (McClelland & Stewart: 2008)
Ondaatje, M, *In the Skin of a Lion* (Knopf Canada: 1996)
Toews, M, *A Complicated Kindness* (Knopf Canada: 2008)

Films

Away From Her (2006)
Bon Cop, Bad Cop (2006)
Goin' Down the Road (1970)
Highway 61 (1991)
Léolo (1992)
My Winnipeg (2007)
Project Grizzly (1996)
The Apprenticeship of Duddy Kravitz (1974)
The Decline of the American Empire (1986)
The Sweet Hereafter (1997)

◣ USEFUL WEBSITES

Immigration

Citizenship and Immigration Canada: www.cic.gc.ca
Ministère de l'Immigration et des Communautés culturelles
(Immigration-Québec): www.immigration-quebec.gouv.qc.ca/en
Human Resources and Social Development Canada: www.hrsdc.gc.ca
Canada Border Services Agency: www.cbsa-asfc.gc.ca
Going to Canada: www.goingtocanada.gc.ca

Settling in

Service Canada: www.servicecanada.gc.ca
Yellow Pages: www.yellowpages.ca
Canadian Real Estate Association: www.crea.ca
Canada Mortgage and Housing Corporation: www.cmhc.gc.ca
Insurance Brokers Association of Canada: www.ibac.ca

Business and work

Business Immigrant Program (Provincial and territorial partners):
www.cic.gc.ca/english/immigrate/business/investors/provinces.asp
Canada Business – Services for Entrepreneurs: www.cbsc.org
Industry Canada: www.ic.gc.ca

Business Development Bank of Canada: www.bdc.ca
Workopolis: www.workopolis.com
Monster.ca: www.monster.ca
Service Canada Job Bank: www.jobbank.gc.ca
Canadian Chamber of Commerce: www.chamber.ca
Association of Canadian Search, Employment and Staffing Services:
www.acsess.org
Association of Workers' Compensation Boards of Canada: www.awcbc.org
Better Business Bureau: www.bbb.org

Shopping

Hudson's Bay Company (The Bay, Zellers, Home Outfitters): www.hbc.com
Sears: www.sears.ca
Roots: www.roots.com
Future Shop: www.futureshop.ca
Staples: www.staples.ca
Chapters/Indigo: www.chapters.indigo.ca

News

CBC News: www.cbc.ca/news
The Canadian Press: www.thecanadianpress.com
Macleans: www.macleans.ca
The Globe and Mail: www.theglobeandmail.com
National Post: www.nationalpost.com
Canadian Newspaper Association: www.cna-acj.ca
Metro: www.metronews.ca

Entertainment

Canada Events: www.canadaevents.ca
Where: www.where.ca
Xtra.ca: www.xtra.ca
Maple Music: www.maplemusic.com
Exclaim.ca: www.exclaim.ca
TVGuide.ca: www.tvguide.ca
Sport Canada: www.pch.gc.ca/progs/sc

Travel

Air Canada: www.aircanada.com
West Jet: www.westjet.com
Greyhound Canada: www.greyhound.ca
VIA Rail: www.viarail.ca
Canadian Urban Transit Association: www.cutaactu.ca
Canadian Automobile Association: www.caa.ca

Expats

www.expatforum.com
www.expatfocus.com
www.expatexchange.com
www.britishexpats.com
Southern Cross Group: www.southern-cross-group.org
Australian Canadian Association: www.yaca.ca
Royal Society of St George: www.stgeorgebc.ca

Government websites

Foreign Affairs and International Trade Canada: www.international.gc.ca
Canadian Human Rights Commission: www.chrc-ccdp.ca
Canada Revenue Agency: www.cra.gc.ca
Revenu Québec: www.revenu.gouv.qc.ca
Health Canada: www.hc-sc.gc.ca
Study in Canada: www.livelearnandsucceed.gc.ca
Public Safety Canada: www.publicsafety.gc.ca

■ GOVERNMENT CONTACTS

Most provincial and territorial governments provide regional service centres at various locations throughout their jurisdiction for in-person queries and services. Visit the website addresses provided below for addresses and additional contact information.

Federal government

Government of Canada: 1 800 622 6232 within Canada (for details on how to phone the Government of Canada from international locations go to www.canada.gc.ca and select *Contact us* on the home page); fax 613 941 1827; sitecanadasite@canada.gc.ca; www.canada.gc.ca

Provincial and territorial governments

Government of Alberta: 780 427 2711 outside Alberta (to call toll-free within Alberta phone 310 000 before number); www.alberta.ca
Government of British Columbia: 250 387 6121 (Victoria), 604 660 2421 (Vancouver) or 1 800 663 7867 (within BC); EnquiryBC@gov.bc.ca; www.gov.bc.ca
Government of Manitoba: 204 945 3744 or 1 866 626 4862; mgi@gov.mb.caj; www.gov.mb.ca
Government of New Brunswick: 506 453 2240; www.gnb.ca
Government of Newfoundland and Labrador: info@gov.nl.ca; www.gov.nf.ca (no general information number available – visit website for specific department contacts)
Government of Nova Scotia: 902 424 5200 or 1 800 670 4357; askus@gov.ns.ca; www.gov.ns.ca
Government of Nunavut: 1 888 252 9869; www.gov.nu.ca

Government of Ontario: 416 326 1234 or 1 800 267 8097; www.gov.on.ca

Government of Prince Edward Island: 902 368 4000; island@gov.pe.ca; www.gov.pe.ca

Government of Quebec: 418 644 4545 (Quebec City), 514 644 4545 (Montreal) or 1 877 644 4545 (within Quebec); www.gouv.qc.ca

Government of Saskatchewan: www.gov.sk.ca (no general information number available – visit website for specific department contacts)

Government of the Northwest Territories: 867 873 7500; www.gov.nt.ca

Government of Yukon: 867 667 5811 or 867 667 5812 (toll free within Yukon 1 800 661 0408); information@gov.yk.ca; www.gov.yk.ca

◼ EMBASSIES AND CONSULATES

Canadian offices overseas

For a complete list of Canadian embassies, consulates, high commissions, and trade offices around the world, visit the Foreign Affairs and International Trade Canada website at www.international.gc.ca and select *Canadian Offices Abroad.*

Canadian High Commission in London (United Kingdom): Canada House, Trafalgar Square, London, SW1Y 5BJ, United Kingdom; 020 7258 6600; fax 020 7258 6533; ldn.consular@international.gc.ca (consular) or ldn.passport@international.gc.ca (passports); www.london.gc.ca. For visa and immigration enquiries contact Macdonald House, 38 Grosvenor Street, London, W1K 4AA, United Kingdom; fax 020 7258 6506; www.canada.org.uk

Canadian Embassy in Dublin (Ireland): 7–8 Wilton Terrace, Dublin 2, Ireland; 353 1 234 4000; fax 353 1 234 4001; dublin@international.gc.ca; www.dublin.gc.ca

Canadian Embassy in Washington (United States): 501 Pennsylvania Avenue NW, Washington, DC 20001, United States; 202 682 1740; fax 202 682 7726; www.washington.gc.ca

Canadian High Commission in Canberra (Australia): Commonwealth Avenue, Canberra, ACT 2600, Australia; 61 2 6270 4000; fax 61 2 6270 4081; cnbra@international.gc.ca; www.australia.gc.ca

Canadian High Commission in Wellington (New Zealand): Level 11, 125 The Terrace, Wellington, New Zealand; 64 4 473 9577 (toll free in Auckland 09 309 8516); fax 64 4 471 2082; wlgtn@international.gc.ca; www.newzealand.gc.ca

Canadian High Commission in South Africa: 1103 Arcadia Street (corner Arcadia and Hilda Streets), Hatfield, Pretoria, South Africa; 27 12 422 3000 (visa and immigration 27 12 422 3090); fax 27 12 422 3052 (visa and immigration 27 12 422 3053); pret@international.gc.ca (visa and immigration pretoria-im-enquiry@international.gc.ca); www.southafrica.gc.ca

Canadian Embassy in France: 35, avenue Montaigne, 75008 Paris, France; 33 1 44 43 29 00 (visa and immigration 33 1 44 43 29 16); fax 33 1 44 43 29 99 (no visa or immigration enquiries); www.france.gc.ca

Embassy of Canada in Berlin (Germany): Leipziger Platz 17, 10117 Berlin, Germany; 49 30 20312 0 (visa and immigration automated service 49 30 20 31 24 47); fax 49 30 20312 121 (visa and immigration 49 30 20312 134); www.germany.gc.ca (see website for email contacts)

Embassy of Canada in Spain: Núñez de Balboa, 35, 28001 Madrid, Spain; 34 914 233 250; fax 34 914 233 251; mdrid@international.gc.ca; www.spain.gc.ca

Foreign offices in Canada

To find contact details for foreign embassies or representatives in Canada that are not listed here, visit Foreign Affairs and International Trade Canada's Diplomatic Gateway to Canada website at w01.international.gc.ca/protocol. This site provides a search engine that enables you to find full contact details for diplomatic missions, consular offices and other international offices in Canada.

British High Commission in Canada: 80 Elgin Street, Ottawa, ON K1P 5K7; 613 237 1530 (after-hours emergency 613 239 4288); fax 613 237 7980; www.ukincanada.fco.gov.uk

Embassy of Ireland in Canada: Suite 1105 (11th Floor), 130 Albert Street, Ottawa, ON K1P 5G4; 613 233 6281 (after-hours emergency 613 233 6281 for Ottawa office or 353 0 1 408 2000 for Dublin office); fax 613 233 5835; www.embassyofireland.ca

The Embassy of the United States of America: 490 Sussex Drive, Ottawa, ON K1N 1G8 (mail to PO Box 866, Station B, Ottawa, ON K1P 5T1); 613 688 5335; fax 613 688 3082; http://ottawa.usembassy.gov

Australian High Commission in Canada: Suite 710 (7th Floor), 50 O'Connor Street, Ottawa, ON K1P 6L2; 613 236 0841 (after-hours emergency 1800 364 9180 within Canada or 61 2 6261 3305 for Canberra office); fax 613 236 4376; www.ahc-ottawa.org

New Zealand High Commission in Ottawa: 99 Bank Street, Suite 727, Ottawa, ON K1P 6G3; 613 238 5991; fax 613 238 5707; info@nzhcottawa.org; www.nzembassy.com/canada

South African High Commission in Canada: 15 Sussex Drive, Ottawa, ON K1M 1M8; 613 744 0330; fax 613 741 1639; rsafrica@southafrica-canada.ca (consular and administrative) or admin@southafrica-canada.ca; www.southafrica-canada.ca

Embassy of France: 42 Sussex Drive, Ottawa, ON K1M 2C9; 613 789 1795; fax 613 562 3735; www.ambafrance-ca.org (for consular services, contact the French Consulate in Montreal, Quebec, Toronto, Vancouver or Moncton)

Embassy of the Federal Republic of Germany: 1 Waverley Street, Ottawa, ON K2P 0T8; 613 232 1101 (24 hours 613 227 9481); fax 613 594 9330; germanembassyottawa@on.aibn.com; www.ottawa.diplo.de

Embassy of Spain in Ottawa: 74 Stanley Avenue, Ottawa, ON K1M 1P4; 613 747 2252, 613 747 7293, 613 747 1143 or 613 747 6181; fax 613 744 1224; emb.ottawa@mae.es; www.mae.es/Embajadas/Ottawa/en/Home

■ INDEX

Essential Phone Numbers

Emergency services

Fire service, police, ambulance	911 (or dial 0 for operator)
Poison control centres	dial 911 for nearest centre

Health

Provincial telehealth – nurse on call (service not available in all provinces and territories)

Alberta	1866 408 5465
British Columbia	1866 215 4700
Manitoba	1888 315 9257
New Brunswick	1800 244 8353
Northwest Territories	1888 255 1010
Ontario	1866 797 0000
Quebec	514 488 9163
Saskatchewan	1877 800 0002

Phone information

Directory assistance	411
Operator	0
International access code (if calling from Canada)	011
Country code	+1

Travel

Toronto Pearson International Airport

Administration	416 776 3000
Travel inquiries	1866 207 1690
Vancouver International Airport	604 207 7077
Montreal Pierre Elliott Trudeau International Airport	1800 465 1213
Citizenship and Immigration Canada	1888 242 2100

Canada Border Services Agency

English	1800 461 9999
French	1800 959 2036
Transport Canada	613 990 2309

Other information

Service Canada	1800 622 6232
Crime Stoppers	1800 222 8477
Kids Help Line	1800 668 6868

Embassies

United Kingdom

Ottawa	613 237 1530
Toronto	416 593 1290
Vancouver	604 683 4421
Montreal	514 866 5863

Ireland

Ottawa	613 233 6281
Toronto	416 366 9300
Vancouver	604 683 9233
Montreal	514 848 7389

United States

Ottawa	613 238 5335 or 613 688 5335 (24h)
Toronto	416 595 1700 or 416 201 4100 (24h)
Vancouver	604 685 4311
Montreal	514 398 9695 or 514 981 5059 (24h)

Australia

Ottawa	613 236 0841
Toronto	416 323 1155
Vancouver	604 684 1177

New Zealand

Ottawa	613 238 5991 (x221 24h)
Toronto	416 947 9696
Vancouver	604 684 7388

South Africa

Ottawa	613 744 0330 (24h)
Toronto	416 944 8825
Vancouver	604 688 1301

France

Ottawa	613 789 1795 (24h)
Toronto	416 847 1900
Vancouver	604 681 4345
Montreal	514 878 4385 or 514 878 6221
Quebec	418 266 2500

Germany

Ottawa	613 232 1101 or 613 227 9481 (24h)
Toronto	416 925 2813 or 416 953 3817 (till 10.00pm)
Vancouver	604 684 8377 or 604 218 1390 (24h)
Montreal	514 931 2277